WHY PAMPER LIFE'S COM.

SMYTHE LIBRARY

Stamp this label with the date for return.
Contact the Librarian if you wish to renew this book.

= 7 JUL 2013		

MANCHESTER
1824

Manchester University Press

MUSIC AND SOCIETY

Series editors Peter J. Martin and Tia DeNora

Music and Society aims to bridge the gap between music scholarship and the human sciences. A deliberately eclectic series, its authors are nevertheless united by the contention that music is a social product, social resource, and social practice. As such it is not autonomous but is created and performed by real people in particular times and places; in doing so they reveal much about themselves and their societies.

In contrast to the established academic discourse, *Music and Society* is concerned with all forms of music, and seeks to encourage the scholarly analysis of both 'popular' styles and those which have for too long been marginalised by that discourse – folk and ethnic traditions, music by and for women, jazz, rock, rap, reggae, muzak and so on. These sounds are vital ingredients in the contemporary cultural mix, and their neglect by serious scholars itself tells us much about the social and cultural stratification of our society.

The time is right to take a fresh look at music and its effects, as today's music resonates with the consequences of cultural globalisation and the transformations wrought by new electronic media, and as past styles are reinvented in the light of present concerns. There is, too, a tremendous upsurge of interest in cultural analysis. *Music and Society* does not promote a particular school of thought, but aims to provide a forum for debate; in doing so, the titles in the series bring music back into the heart of socio-cultural analysis.

The land without music: music, culture and society in twentieth-century Britain
Andrew Blake

Music and the sociological gaze: art worlds and cultural production
Peter J. Martin

Sounds and society: themes in the sociology of music
Peter J. Martin

Popular music on screen: from the Hollywood musical to music video
John Mundy

Popular music in England 1840–1914: a social history (2nd edition)
Dave Russell

The English musical renaissance, 1840–1940: constructing a national music (2nd edition)
Robert Stradling and Meirion Hughes

Time and memory in reggae music: the politics of hope
Sarah Daynes

WHY PAMPER LIFE'S COMPLEXITIES?

Essays on The Smiths

edited by

Sean Campbell and Colin Coulter

Manchester University Press

Manchester and New York

distributed in the United States exclusively by Palgrave Macmillan

Published by Manchester University Press
Oxford Road, Manchester M13 9NR, UK
and Room 400, 175 Fifth Avenue, New York, NY 10010, USA
www.manchesteruniversitypress.co.uk

Distributed in the United States exclusively by
Palgrave Macmillan, 175 Fifth Avenue, New York,
NY 10010, USA

Distributed in Canada exclusively by
UBC Press, University of British Columbia, 2029 West Mall,
Vancouver, BC, Canada V6T 1Z2

British Library Cataloguing-in-Publication Data
A catalogue record for this book is available from the British Library

Library of Congress Cataloging-in-Publication Data applied for

ISBN   978 0 7190 7840 8 hardback

ISBN   978 0 7190 7841 5 paperback

First published 2010

Typeset
by Servis Filmsetting Ltd, Stockport, Cheshire
Printed in Great Britain
by TJ International Ltd, Padstow

Contents

Notes on contributors

Joseph Brooker teaches modern literature at Birkbeck College, University of London. He is the author of *Joyce's Critics* (University of Wisconsin Press, 2004), *Flann O'Brien* (Northcote House Publishers, 2005) and *Literature of the 1980s: After the Watershed* (Edinburgh University Press, 2010).

Fergus Campbell is Reader in Social and Cultural History at Newcastle University. He is the author of *Land and Revolution: Nationalist Politics in the West of Ireland, 1891–1921* (Oxford University Press, 2005) and *The Irish Establishment, 1879–1914* (Oxford University Press, 2009).

Sean Campbell is Senior Lecturer in the Department of English and Media at Anglia Ruskin in Cambridge. He is the author of '*Irish Blood, English Heart*': *Second-Generation Irish Musicians in England* (Cork University Press, 2010), and is co-author (with Gerry Smyth) of *Beautiful Day: Forty Years of Irish Rock* (Atrium Press, 2005).

Kieran Cashell is Coordinator of Research, School of Art and Design, Limerick Institute of Technology and author of *Aftershock: The Ethics of Contemporary Transgressive Art* (IB Tauris, 2009) and 'More Relevance than Spotlight and Applause: Billy Bragg in the British Folk Tradition' in I. Peddie (ed.), *Popular Music and Human Rights, Volume I, British and American Music* (Ashgate, 2010).

Colin Coulter teaches Sociology in the National University of Ireland, Maynooth. He is the author of *Contemporary Northern Irish Society: An Introduction* (Pluto, 1999) and the co-editor of *The End of Irish History?: Critical Reflections on the Celtic Tiger* (Manchester University Press, 2003) and *Northern Ireland After the Troubles: A Society in Transition* (Manchester University Press, 2008).

Eoin Devereux is Senior Lecturer in Sociology at the University of Limerick, Ireland. He is the author of *Understanding The Media, Second Edition* (Sage, 2007) and *Media Studies Key Issues and Debates* (Sage, 2007).

Jonathan Hiam is Assistant Professor of Music at the University of Hawaii at Manoa. He is currently writing a book about music at Black Mountain College.

Kari Kallioniemi is researcher in Cultural History at the University of Turku, Finland. He is the author of *Put the Needle on the Record and Think of England: Notions of Englishness in the Post-War History of British Pop Music* (University of Turku, 1998).

Karl Maton is Senior Lecturer in Sociology at the University of Sydney. He is the co-editor of *Social Realism, Knowledge and the Sociology of Education* (2010, Continuum) and *Disciplinarity* (2011, Continuum). His book, *Knowledge and Knowers: Towards a Realist Sociology of Education* is being published by Routledge.

Cecília Mello is FAPESP Postdoctoral Fellow in the Film Department, University of São Paulo. She is co-editor (with Lúcia Nagib) of *Realism and the Audiovisual Media* (Palgrave Macmillan, 2009).

Julian Stringer is Associate Professor in the Department of Culture, Film and Media at the University of Nottingham. He is author of *Blazing Passions: Contemporary Hong Kong Cinema* (London: Wallflower, 2007) and *Wong Kar-Wai's 'In the Mood for Love'* (Hong Kong University Press, 2008).

Sheila Whiteley is Professor Emeritus at the University of Salford, Greater Manchester. She is author of *The Space Between the Notes: Rock and the Counter Culture* (Routledge: 1992); *Women and Popular Music: Popular Music and Gender* (Routledge: 2000); *Too Much Too Young: Popular Music, Age and Identity* (Routledge: 2005), and is editor of *Sexing the Groove: Popular Music and Gender* (Routledge: 1996) and *Christmas, Ideology and Popular Culture* (Edinburgh University Press, 2008).

Nabeel Zuberi is Senior Lecturer in the Department of Film, Television and Media Studies at the University of Auckland, Aotearoa/New Zealand. He is the author of *Sounds English: Transnational Popular Music* (Urbana and Chicago: University of Illinois Press, 2001) and the co-editor of two volumes on *Media Studies in Aotearoa/New Zealand* (Auckland: Pearson, 2004 and 2010).

ACKNOWLEDGEMENTS

The editors would like to thank those whose support and encouragement were indispensable in bringing the book to completion. In particular, we wish to express our gratitude to Barney Hoskyns, Johnny Marr, Joe Moss, Jon Savage, Stephen Wright, John Harris, Simon Goddard, the Department of English and Media at Anglia Ruskin in Cambridge, the organisers of the Helsinki seminar on The Smiths and especially Jan Liesaho, Eirú Ward, Gavin Macarthur, Angela Nagle, Darragh Farrell, Nuala Doherty, Fiona Dunne, Martin Hargreaves, and Greg Thorpe and Tony Mason at MUP.

1

'WHY PAMPER LIFE'S COMPLEXITIES?':
AN INTRODUCTION TO THE BOOK

Sean Campbell and Colin Coulter

There are certain moments when the winds of popular cultural appraisal shift with a pace and in a direction that few could have anticipated. The radical re-evaluation of The Smiths that has occurred in recent years marks an especially striking case in point. It might seem odd to recall now, but there was a time not so long ago when the cultural stock of the band was at a low. Amid the ascent and ubiquity of dance music in the early 1990s, The Smiths – who had disbanded acrimoniously in 1987 – appeared to have become deeply unfashionable. The literate, melodic songs of Morrissey and Marr appeared to be viewed in many quarters as embarrassing relics of a previous, ostensibly more baleful age.[1] The subsequent flowering of Britpop might reasonably have been expected to have revived the reputation of The Smiths. After all, many of the bands associated with the period were quick to acknowledge their debt to the Manchester quartet. Nonetheless, the resurgence of British guitar-based music in the mid-1990s served little to alter the location of The Smiths on the margins of popular cultural memory. The fragile introspection that defined many of the compositions that Morrissey and Marr wrote together was clearly out of step with the 'laddish' ethos of the time. Moreover, the resolutely independent[2] disposition of The Smiths stood in stark contrast to the brash commercialism that marked Britpop at its peak. As 'Country House' and 'Roll With It' whipped up a feeding frenzy among the record buying public, it was hard to hear 'Hand In Glove' as other than the sound of the spectre at the feast.[3]

As the 1990s drew to a close, therefore, The Smiths appeared to exist solely on the fringes of the popular imagination and had come increasingly to be rendered through a sequence of well-worn pejoratives such as 'miserable' and 'depressing'.[4] The scorn that was quite often heaped upon the band was typically embodied in a caricature of the early stage persona of their vocalist. As the millennium turned, it appeared that The Smiths had come to be remembered only dimly as that strange band with the eccentric singer – the one with the quiff and the flowers and the hearing aid.

Even devotees of The Smiths seemed unable to avoid pandering to some of the more disabling perceptions of the band that existed in the public mind. In the summer of 1999, the high-profile comedian Harry Hill made an appearance on a popular British television programme in which members of the public and, occasionally, celebrities assume for the night the voice and persona of a famous singer of their choice. The contestants who appear on *Stars in Their Eyes* invariably select to perform familiar hits by fairly uncontroversial figures in popular music. The particular persona that Hill elected to adopt for the evening, in contrast, had the potential to be distinctly contentious. The comedian chose to mark his status as a fan of The Smiths by offering a rendition of the band's breakthrough single. As Hill disappeared offstage to get into character, the show's cloyingly anodyne host Matthew Kelly sought to frame the performance to come by informing the audience that they were about to hear a song by a band that had made 'miserable fashionable'. The screens then parted to reveal Hill dressed up as an early version of Morrissey and prepared for a hearty rendition of 'This Charming Man'. The song selected for the programme had the potential of course to be deeply transgressive. It is not that often that you get to hear a tale of rustic homoerotic desire rendered quite so lustily in front of a teatime family audience.[5] The subversive potential of the song was inevitably defused, however, by the context and style of its rendition. The radical intent of the lyrics simply dissipated in the face of the performance of a tiresomely familiar cultural caricature. The sight of Hill with his prosthetic quiff and flailing gladioli clearly met with the approval of the studio audience. As the final bars of 'This Charming Man' faded out, the performance was greeted with the kind of rapturous applause that people in attendance at light entertainment shows reserve for moments when they have had their prejudices confirmed with the minimum of discomfort.[6]

The fading reputation of The Smiths during the 1990s might, therefore, be attributed to the actions of fans and critics alike. It should also be acknowledged, however, that the band were at times the architects of their own misfortune. During their brief period together, The Smiths had no consistent or adequate management. The chaos that inevitably ensued was instrumental of course in the untimely demise of the band and would also spark a sequence of events that would land the four erstwhile friends and colleagues in court a decade later. In December 1996, the former drummer Mike Joyce successfully sued Morrissey and Marr for recording royalties that he claimed were owed to him. The acrimonious proceedings – in which Judge Weeks famously castigated Morrissey as 'devious, truculent and unreliable' – appeared to have done irreparable damage not only to relations between the former members of The Smiths but also to the very reputation of the band itself.[7] The dispute became the major lens through which accounts of the band would, for a while, be filtered.[8] Perhaps the most notable aspect of the court case was not, however, the verdict but rather the absence of any real popular interest in the proceedings. There are today a great many people willing to part with large sums of cash for the privilege of seeing The Smiths together in the same room.[9] Back in 1996, however, only one fan was sufficiently interested to take the opportunity to see free of charge the compelling spectacle of the four former band-mates facing one another across an open court.[10]

As the 1990s came to a close, then, the standing of The Smiths appeared to be at an all-time low. Even some of the most ardent supporters of the band seemed to find it difficult to imagine a time when The Smiths would be afforded the attention and respect that their work evidently deserved. Articles penned during this period by the band's admirers often had a distinctly valedictory tone.[11] Within a few short years, however, the course of popular cultural memory would begin to turn in ways that few could have anticipated.

The return of the repressed

The advent of the twenty-first century has signalled a remarkable reversal in the fortunes of The Smiths. The resurgence of guitar-based music, heralded by bands like The Strokes and The Libertines, has ensured that the Manchester group is now deeply fashionable – even more so perhaps than in their 1980s heyday. Since about the beginning of the 2000s, it has become commonplace for successful young bands to identify The Smiths as a major influence on their work.[12] Much of this praise has come from expected sources, not least 'alternative' rock acts like Arcade Fire, who frequently covered 'Still Ill' on their 2007 tour. In addition, though, the very dance scene that seemed to have rendered The Smiths obsolete has also played a part in their rehabilitation. In 2007, the in-vogue producer Mark Ronson recorded a dance floor 're-version' of the band's 1987 track 'Stop Me If You Think You've Heard This One Before', which reached number two in the UK charts – the highest ever chart position for a Smiths song. Two years later, a synth-pop rendition of 'This Charming Man' by the female singer V.V. Brown underlined The Smiths' resonance. By 2010, mainstream pop stars such as Lady Gaga would heap praise on the group in interviews.

The increasing influence of The Smiths has stretched of course well beyond the parameters of popular music. The songs that the band recorded have, for instance, provided the inspiration for work in the fields of contemporary dance, video art and literature.[13] In addition, the lyrics that Morrissey crafted back in the mid-1980s have gradually percolated into wider popular discourse. In this context, it is remarkable how frequently phrases from The Smiths' songbook appear in print and on air. There is a marked tendency for journalists and authors to adapt or rework one of the band's distinctive song titles, for instance, even when commenting on matters that have nothing whatsoever to do with popular music. Thus, a 2009 article on the British politician William Hague was entitled 'William, It Was Really Nothing', while a review of Monty Python star Michael Palin's diary was called 'This Charming Man's Charmed Life'.[14] Perhaps the most bizarre illustration of this trend appeared in a BBC natural history programme that follows the fortunes of various species struggling to emerge from the hardships of winter. The 2009 instalment of *Springwatch* entailed the engaging spectacle of presenter Chris Packham striving to cram as many, usually utterly gratuitous, Smiths song titles as possible into his commentary. This peculiar quest made for compulsive and hilarious viewing and by the final episode of the series a presumably largely unsuspecting viewing audience had been treated to no fewer than thirty references to The Smiths.[15]

There are of course countless other instances of the practice of citing Morrissey and Marr song titles that exist outside the unlikely setting of natural history programmes.[16] A couple of further examples will perhaps help to illustrate the more specifically *literary* influence that The Smiths' songs have come to exert. In the summer of 2006, the superbly fractious online political commentary *spiked* featured an article concerned with the terrorist attacks on London the previous year. The essay by Neil Davenport offered the distinctly questionable interpretation that the 7/7 suicide bombers were not driven by political zeal but rather by the kind of adolescent petulance that he discerns as the natural idiom of popular music. In a doomed attempt to square the circle of his own twisted logic, the author selected a resonant title to frame the piece: 'Heaven Knows I'm an Islamist Now'.[17] The appearance of a reworked Smiths song title on the libertarian space marked out by *spiked* does not of course come as a complete surprise. It would, after all, be expected that at least some of the playful iconoclasts that produce the weekly blog have more than a passing acquaintance with 1980s indie. What is rather more remarkable is that the lyrics of The Smiths have gradually moved beyond the exclusive and marginal spaces defined by the hipster vernacular of the lapsed left and have begun to appear in the realm of other, rather less fashionable but infinitely more popular, literary forms.

The spring of 2008 saw the latest publication by the hugely popular Irish novelist Marian Keyes. While Keyes ordinarily deals in a romantic genre often sniffily dismissed as 'chick lit', this latest slice of fiction sees her delve into the rather darker territory of domestic violence. The novel is also noteworthy because of its resonant and deliberate choice of title.[18] As we write, in 2009, *This Charming Man* sits aloft the bestseller lists on both sides of the Irish Sea. It is hard to know whether many of Keyes' readers are familiar with The Smiths' song of the same name but this is perhaps immaterial in any case. The very existence of a romantic bestseller entitled *This Charming Man* arguably attests to the sheer breadth of the cultural influence of the band. Over time, the songs of The Smiths have slipped their moorings and gradually begun to appear in the most unlikely of places. Even people who may not be aware of the band are repeatedly introduced to phrases that first appeared in Morrissey's lyrics. The title of one of the romantic blockbuster novels of 2008 and 2009 suggests then that the work of The Smiths has over time left an indelible inscription on the deep tissue of popular culture.

Perhaps the most striking affirmation of the revival of The Smiths, however, was that offered by the music weekly that was the major champion of the band in their heyday. In the spring of 2002, the *New Musical Express* (*NME*) scoured their own back issues in a bid to establish the most influential recording artists of the previous fifty years. While most observers presumed that The Beatles would emerge triumphant from the survey of the magazine's cover stories, features and letters, it was in fact another Northern English four-piece that was duly anointed.[19] In naming The Smiths as the most important band of all time, the *NME* confirmed the group's changing fortunes since the late 1990s.

The unanticipated anointment of The Smiths by the *NME* might be considered emblematic of a growing and much wider recognition of the achievements of the band in the post-2000 period. Throughout the opening decade of this century, there has been a slew of special issues of music magazines dealing with the legacy of The Smiths, as well as a series of books by journalists devoted to the band.[20] The changing view has also been reflected among the general public. A *VH1* poll conducted in 2006 saw 'How Soon Is Now?' chosen as the second-best rock lyric of all time. In the same year, The Smiths' singer finished as runner up in the BBC's survey of Britain's best-loved Living Icons.[21] This ongoing appraisal was echoed in the world of academia. A conference dealing with The Smiths was held in Manchester in 2005, drawing 200 delegates as well as a great deal of interest from the national and international media.[22] Moreover, in 2007, the prowess of Johnny Marr as both a musician and a commentator was acknowledged when he was appointed to the position of Visiting Professor at the University of Salford.[23]

The last few years have, therefore, witnessed a swift rehabilitation that has seen The Smiths inducted into the pantheon of 'great' bands. While the ongoing resurgence of interest in the band might be broadly considered a welcome development, it should not, however, cloud our powers of critical judgement. There are certain aspects of the logic and effects of The Smiths' canonisation that are somewhat troubling and that should, therefore, be examined and contested.

The more disparaging views of The Smiths that were cited above had their origins not only in the vagaries of aesthetic judgement but also in a very specific set of political agendas. The popular construction of the band as a collection of fey eccentrics often served to conceal their critical edge.

Although it is often overlooked, The Smiths represented one of the most radical political voices of a deeply polarised era. The subversive aspects of the band often centred upon the outlandish pronouncements of their singer. In his lyrics and in interviews, Morrissey would issue bile at an entire gallery of villains – the monarchy, the Thatcher regime, the record companies, the meat industry and so forth. The radicalism of The Smiths, however, stretched far beyond the specific establishment objects of their vocalist's ire and into a realm that was more specifically aesthetic. Many of the songs that the band wrote invite the listener beyond the constraints of the everyday, and in so doing issue a reminder that – to pilfer a resonant phrase from the present – another world is possible.

In view of the radical politics and aesthetics of The Smiths, the frame in which they were until recently placed begins to make rather more sense. The songs of Morrissey and Marr undermined the mores and practices at the very heart of the prevailing social order – the work ethic, the cult of the consumer, the imperatives of inherited privilege, the instrumentalism of the culture industries and so on. The critique of bourgeois society tendered by The Smiths was always, therefore, likely to provoke the wrath of the political and cultural establishment.[24] If, at first, the wish to marginalise The Smiths entailed out-right denunciation it would later centre upon more scornful derision. This was perhaps an entirely predictable development. It is often laughter rather than anger that transpires to be the most effective instrument of power.[25] The ridicule that was directed at the group might be seen, then, as a form of backhanded compliment. The artless mockery to which The Smiths were often subjected offered compelling evidence that elements of the political and cultural establishment took the band very seriously indeed.

While the judgement of those who dismissed The Smiths might well be considered questionable, it was at least consistent with their own political dis-position. The band's body of work was an affront to the values and interests of the establishment and the vehemence that they drew was in a sense, therefore, entirely appropriate. Those who denounced The Smiths, in other words, at least denounced them for what were – according to their own lights – the right reasons. It might well be the case, however, that the recent reappraisal of the band turns this particular sequence completely the other way round.

The process of canonisation that operates within popular culture and which has recently recast the reputation of The Smiths is of course far from new. The propensity towards creating a canon of pop cultural artefacts was noted in embryonic form by Adorno as long ago as the 1930s.[26] And the prac-tice of identifying the artists and albums deemed worthy of the accolade of 'greatness' has been an irrepressible habit of music journalists since the 1960s at least.[27] While the process of canonisation may not be particularly new, then, it might be argued that its scope and pace have altered considerably in recent times. In order to understand the significance, and possibly the purpose, of these changes, we need to locate them in the context of the wider social transformations of which they are a telling part.

The work of pop in the age of digital reproduction

In the writings of Fredric Jameson, the principal characteristic of what is often defined as 'postmodernism' – but which he more accurately designates as 'late capitalism' – is the intrusion of the form and logic of the commodity into realms of our lives that had previously been essentially untouched.[28] This relentless process of commodification occurs, Jameson insists, not merely across space but across time as well. One of the hallmarks of the era of late capitalism is the plunder of the often very grave substance of the real lives of the past in order to cater for the idle amusement of the often surreal lives of the present. Historical figures, events and styles are extracted from their original context only to reappear in the guise of the pastiche[29] – a blank stylistic parody that has no satirical intent or purpose. According to Jameson, the increasingly ubiquitous practice of running different historical moments and styles through one another has calamitous consequences for our sense of who we are and where we come from. The harnessing of the past principally as a resource for the production of the commodity serves, he suggests, to erode the crucial sense of historical time and development. The inevitable outcome is that of a widespread historical amnesia that is both symptom and cause of the abiding 'depthlessness' of late capitalist society.[30]

The dystopian prognosis that we find in the work of Jameson assumes a particular resonance when we turn to consider the manner in which historical memory is organised in the sphere of contemporary popular music. In the last generation, there has been a marked and rapid increase of interest in recalling and restoring those artists and works that are considered to be genuinely 'classic'[31] – a process that the arch English satirist Luke Haines has snidely dismissed as the inauguration of 'heritage rock'.[32] The growing preoccupation with the historical development of popular music assumes a variety of guises: the constant reissue of 'remastered' albums, the proliferation of books and television programmes concerned with 'classic' recordings,[33] and the success of monthly publications such as *Mojo* and *Uncut* that have the rock canon on heavy rotation. It should be acknowledged that there are a number of advantages that arise out of the increasing preoccupation of the popular music industry with aspects of its own past. Allied to the advances in digital technology and the advent of websites comprising user-generated content, this backward glance enables, for instance, those with sufficient interest to access information, recordings and footage that were until very recently unavailable. While the orientation of the contemporary music industry toward the past has in principle the potential to nurture a greater and more critical historical understanding, its effect in practice has, arguably, more often been precisely the opposite.

The process of canonisation within the field of popular music rests upon distinctive notions of originality and, in particular, 'authenticity'.[34] Those albums that are widely held to be worthy of the status of 'classics' are invariably depicted as the pioneering recordings of singular talents. While the drive to curate certain musical texts hinges upon the conviction of their uniqueness, the impact of the actual process itself is, ironically, to erode this essential quality. As the canon expands both its contemporary scope and its historical reach, certain works begin to lose their association perhaps with a particular time and place. The specificity of particular albums threatens to unravel as they are conjoined in a sequence of equivalence that is their shared status as 'classic' recordings. Hence it is that *Horses* becomes a sibling of *Astral Weeks*, which in turn begins to bear something of a resemblance to *Nevermind*.

The essential point here is that while the manner in which historical memory has come to be organised within popular music promises to enable us to remember, it actually seeks to persuade us to forget. The potential dangers of this particular version of cultural amnesia become readily apparent when we turn to consider the ongoing reappraisal of The Smiths. An adequate recollection of the band demands an acknowledgement of their own particular and complex brand of political radicalism. There were of course few figures in popular music as outspoken in their views as Morrissey during the dangerous and doleful age of Thatcherism. The close – if admittedly complex – association between The Smiths and the causes of socialism and republicanism might appear to make the band unlikely candidates for canonisation by a music business that is, after all, notoriously conservative. It should be remembered though that the current reappraisal of the group is a distinctly selective and sanitised one. The particular version of The Smiths that has recently come into widespread circulation is one that dislocates the band from their historical context and seeks to dispel their political charge. In the heady carnival of late capitalism, The Smiths are intended to function as a free-floating and generic signifier of some hazy, bygone age. The consumer is expected to associate the band with jangly guitars and amusing metaphors but under no circumstances with seditious political intent. Those fantasies of regicide are to be repressed. Thatcher is to be allowed to live long and pass peacefully in her sleep.

The good people laugh

The apparent success of this revision of The Smiths is illustrated most vividly in the recent and very public declarations of devotion to the band of someone who might not previously have dared to do so. In 2005, the relatively unknown figure of David Cameron assumed the leadership of a Conservative Party pummelled by three successive electoral defeats. Eager to shake off the distinctly fusty image of the Tories, Cameron has been at pains to underline his credentials as a fan of popular music. The band that the Conservative leader has most frequently expressed his enthusiasm for is, quite incredibly, The Smiths. When invited on the long-running BBC radio programme *Desert Island Discs*, Cameron selected 'This Charming Man' as one of his indispensable recordings.[35] This interest has been underlined by the Conservative leader's well-publicised visits to Salford Lads Club, the principal place of homage for fans of The Smiths.[36] On one such occasion, Cameron returned surreptitiously to avoid a repeat of previous protests against his presence by local Labour activists, and recreated Stephen Wright's famous photograph of the group outside the building that graces the gatefold sleeve of *The Queen is Dead*.[37] Meanwhile, in 2008, Cameron chose to mark a brief visit to the United Kingdom by Barack Obama with a gift of some of his favourite albums. Among the CDs selected for the future US President were some recordings by The Smiths.[38]

At first glance, the very public praise that David Cameron has heaped upon The Smiths simply beggars belief. Indeed, it is difficult to think of a more inappropriate musical passion that could be harboured by a leader of the Conservative Party. The songs of The Smiths conjure up a vision of the social world starkly at odds with the one inaugurated when the Tories were previously in power – a point underlined by the protests that greeted Cameron's visits to Salford. In his lyrics and in his interviews, Morrissey sought to champion the marginalised and to heap scorn on the kind of inherited privilege enjoyed precisely by an old Etonian[39] like David Cameron. And more importantly, of course, The Smiths' frontman made no secret of his murderous desire towards the most infamous of modern Conservative leaders, Margaret Thatcher. After calling for her assassination in an interview, Morrissey expressed his disappointment when an attempt on Thatcher's life – at the Conservative Party Conference in 1984 – left the Iron Lady unscathed.[40] In an effort to underline the point, The Smiths, whose work has been described as a 'blues against Thatcher',[41] decided to call their third album *Margaret on the Guillotine*.[42] Pressure from their record company would, however, force the band to rename the record *The Queen Is Dead*, an alternative title that would generate its own controversies and draw the ire of outraged Tory MPs.[43] In effect, then, the current incumbent of the Tory leadership has spent the last few years volunteering his adoration of a band whose singer was wont to demand the public execution of his most illustrious predecessor. It really is a most bizarre turn of events. It is something akin, for instance, to finding out after all these years that the redoubtable Sir James Anderton – who was the notoriously prejudiced and draconian Chief Constable of Greater Manchester during The Smiths' career – likes nothing better of an evening than to recline in a favourite armchair and unwind to the sound of 'Cop Killer' on repeat play.

The musical tastes of the current Conservative leader begin to appear rather less peculiar, however, when we return to consider the particular and increasingly hegemonic version of popular cultural recollection that we sketched above. While The Smiths have returned to public prominence and widespread acclaim in recent years, the specific version of the band that has come into circulation is a rather distorted and pallid one. The culture industries are keen to repackage the group solely as purveyors of idiosyncratic but nonetheless 'classic' indie rock. The more explicitly political elements that inform the work of The Smiths are nudged into the background or at times airbrushed out of the picture altogether. A new generation of consumers are invited either to overlook the radicalism of the band or to enjoy it as yet another expression of their renowned 'eccentricity'.[44]

In view of these attempts to housetrain The Smiths, the recent appearance of fans of the band in the most unlikely of places begins to make a little more sense. The version of the group that has gained currency of late is sufficiently sanitised to enable their songs to be enjoyed by those who might ordinarily be repelled by their politics. Even the most prominent Conservative in the United Kingdom is, remarkably, both willing and 'entitled' to be a Smiths fan. The logic and effect of the current canonisation of The Smiths is to defuse the radicalism of the band through their inauguration into the pantheon of the venerable in which only issues of musical performance are considered relevant. Once the critical political edge of the group is softened, even an establishment figure like David Cameron can feel entitled to, and comfortable with, public declarations of devotion to them. On those relatively rare occasions when the leader of Her Majesty's Government is prompted to reflect upon the incendiary nature of Morrissey's lyrics and pronouncements, he does not appear to find them unduly troubling or threatening. On the contrary in fact, those seditious calls for the bloody end of the principal establishment figures in the land are deemed – with a rather telling adjective – to be merely 'amusing'.[45]

Talk about precious things

The amusement with which the Conservative leader (dis)regards the radical politics of The Smiths offers perhaps the most telling intimation of the problems associated with the way in which the band has been recalled into popular memory in recent times. The version of the group that has been repackaged of late is sanitised and bloodless, and often passes only a spectral resemblance to the one remembered by those fortunate enough to catch the quartet first time around. We would suggest, therefore, that there is a pressing need for a more informed and faithful account of what The Smiths meant and indeed continue to mean more than two decades after their demise. The essays that are collected between the covers of *Why Pamper Life's Complexities?* are intended to provide such an account. While the collection has been driven and informed by a range of concerns, there are two that suggest themselves as especially important.

Firstly, the appearance of the book reflects a conviction that The Smiths represent a very particular band and that there is a need to recognise them accordingly. Those in the pay of the music business routinely strive of course to place The Smiths within the continuum of the agreed classics of rock. But such claims of equivalence ultimately prove to have little merit. As the late BBC DJ John Peel was wont to observe, the band's boldly innovative songs had few obvious reference points, and seemed 'to have not been influenced by anything that preceded them'.[46] The Smiths are, in other words, one of those aberrations that appear every generation or so to reinvent the idiom of popular music. The essays collected in the book set out to establish that which makes the group so very singular, to explain why it is that, more than two decades after Morrissey and Marr went their separate ways, their songs retain the power to intrigue so many people.

It will be readily apparent then that this is a text whose contributors make little attempt to disguise their passion for, or pleasure in, their subject matter. In the strangely desiccated world of academia, however, such candour tends invariably to be rather frowned upon. The insistence upon the pursuit of 'objectivity' makes a great deal of sense of course in relation to the examination of many aspects of the social world. Whether it has quite the same value in the study of popular culture, however, remains open to question. In his important text *Performing Rites*, Simon Frith suggests that any adequate academic analysis of popular music must acknowledge the very particular nature of its cultural form and appeal. According to Frith, pop songs have a 'unique emotional intensity' that needs to inform the ways in which we think, talk and write about them.[47] The realm of popular music is one, he insists, that cannot be understood without making aesthetic judgements and distinctions. Every seasoned fan of pop already knows this to be the case. Anyone who has enjoyed the singular pleasure of debating their favourite bands and albums is only too aware that engaging with popular music is a profoundly 'adjectival experience'.[48]

While aesthetic judgement may well represent an indispensable element of the study of popular music, academics working in the area have often shied away from making these kinds of distinctions. Such aversion owes a great deal to certain conventions of scholarship. The anxiety for popular music studies to be 'taken seriously' as an academic sub-discipline has often dissuaded writers from saying what they really like and what they do not.[49] This squeamishness prompts Frith to map out an alternative path for pop-music studies. In future, he insists, those who write about popular song need to be more willing to engage in normative evaluations and distinctions. This openness towards aesthetic judgement will enable the study of popular music to cease being an 'oddly bloodless affair' and allow those who practise it to acknowledge the emotional charge that drew many of them to the form in the first place.[50]

The substance and spirit of this particular book are informed in part by the injunctions that are delivered in the pages of *Performing Rites*. While the essays that follow cast a critical eye over The Smiths, they also seek to underline that which explains the enduring appeal of the band. The accounts that we provide represent in part a counterpoint to some of the popular misconceptions that have survived the recent return to favour of the band. Many readers will doubtless be familiar with the recurrent taunts that The Smiths are 'miserable' and 'depressing'. The origins of these judgements are not of course difficult to discern. The band's penchant for introspection and melancholy was always likely to draw accusations of 'miserablism'. It would, however, be hard to come up with a more inappropriate designation for the band. While The Smiths explored some of the darker recesses of the human condition, they did so in a manner that was invariably uplifting and at times jubilant.[51] Indeed, the joyous quality of their songs offers credence to Adorno's claim that 'thought achieves happiness in the expression of unhappiness'.[52] Any sense of The Smiths as 'miserable' was also allayed by the mood of their concerts. As Johnny Marr has observed, the group's live shows were typically boisterous events at which the atmosphere was often reminiscent of that of a football match.[53] The work of The Smiths deserves rather more, therefore, than the hackneyed tag of 'miserablism' that critics have often levelled at the band.

A second, and not entirely unrelated, consideration that informs the text is a concern to shift the focus of how The Smiths are often regarded. In more specific terms, a number of the chapters seek to underline an aspect of the band that is often conveniently overlooked, namely their profoundly radical disposition. While The Smiths may well have been the funniest band in the history of popular music, they were also deadly serious. The songs that bear their name are, inevitably, the product of a very specific time and place. There can be few chronicles of the Thatcher years as compelling as that scripted in Morrissey's caustic lyrics. While the oblique and invariably odd view of the world that we encounter in The Smiths' songs was very much of its time, it also has an enduring resonance. Their work, therefore, supplies not only an invaluable guide to the recent past but also considerable insight into the present moment. The essays that follow will endeavour to capture both of these compelling attributes of the band.

All heady books

In the two decades since The Smiths broke up, there has been a good deal written about the band by critics and biographers alike. The recent rejuvenation of interest in the band has prompted a new wave of publications that have inevitably varied in quality. The purpose and promise of this particular text is to add to the existing literature devoted to The Smiths in at least two specific ways. First, the approach adopted by the contributors to *Why Pamper Life's Complexities?* is rather different from others who have recently turned their attention to the band. While the accounts that journalists have offered of The Smiths have often proved very valuable, they have tended at times to be narrowly descriptive. The essays that follow do not set out to systematically tell the tale of how the band met, recorded the songs and fell apart. This particular narrative has already been recounted on a great many occasions and in exhaustive detail. Those readers who are unfamiliar with the story would be usefully directed towards Johnny Rogan's substantial biography *Morrissey and Marr: The Severed Alliance*.[54] And anyone keen to find out how The Smiths' songs were conceived and recorded would be well advised to consult Simon Goddard's comprehensive and illuminating tome *The Smiths: Songs That Saved Your Life*.[55] The rationale for this particular text is to shift the focus away from the narrative and towards the ultimately more rewarding realm of the analytical. The essays that are gathered here bring together academics from a range of disciplines to take a more finely grained look at what The Smiths meant and indeed continue to mean after all these years. It is hoped that the breadth of the book will offer a comprehensive introduction to The Smiths for those not particularly familiar with their work, and that its depth will provide new insights for those who feel they know the band inside out.

Second, *Why Pamper Life's Complexities?* seeks to offer a rather wider frame of analysis than is typically adopted in accounts of the nature and significance of The Smiths. Most considerations of the band have tended to focus more or less exclusively on their singer and certain aspects of his subjectivity. In the relatively few academic essays that address The Smiths, the emphasis has tended to fall upon the uncertain and ambiguous nature of Morrissey's sexuality.[56] This is of course a fascinating and entirely legitimate subject and indeed a number of the essays that follow touch upon it. The collection also seeks, however, to look beyond Morrissey and his vexed sexual persona. While the abiding preoccupation with the singer is entirely understandable, it has tended unfortunately to conceal the contribution of the other members of the band. In particular, the cult of Morrissey has served to obscure the fact that without Johnny Marr The Smiths would not and indeed could not have existed.

Notwithstanding the fact that Marr brought The Smiths together, he was the group's sole composer and arranger and also acted, at crucial times, as both producer and manager.[57] (It's worth noting, in this regard, Morrissey's description of The Smiths as 'Johnny's venture'.[58]) Marr's melodies, textures and guitar work not only shaped The Smiths' soundscape but also set the mood for Morrissey's singing (a point that the latter is keen to acknowledge).[59] Moreover, at a time when popular music was, as Allan Moore notes, 'flowing not with guitars, but with synthesizers',[60] Marr remodelled the guitar as a tool of rock innovation, via unusual tunings, inventive overdubs and unashamed eclecticism, drawing on folk ('Back To The Old House') and funk ('Barbarism Begins At Home'), as well as jazz ('Heaven Knows I'm Miserable Now'), and high-life ('Ask') styles. Despite such diversity, Marr's work had a distinctive (and declamatory) character, albeit one that served the band's songs more than the guitar itself, hence the player's eschewal of the conventional solo, a trait that underscored The Smiths' critique of (rock) machismo.[61]

Some of the essays that appear in the text attempt to redress the frequent imbalance in accounts of the band by shifting the focus away from the lyrics and towards the music in order to stress the critical role played by Marr. The essays that feature in *Why Pamper Life's Complexities?* address The Smiths from a range of perspectives and through a series of lenses. In particular, the authors attempt to examine the work of the band from the vantage points afforded by issues such as nationality, subjectivity and social class. In redirecting the focus in this way, it is hoped that the book will offer a much broader and, perhaps, more critical understanding of the nature and importance of the band.

Dancing about architecture

The very notion of academics being engaged in the study of popular music tends of course to draw a great deal of hostility from a range of sources. The idea that music is something that can or should be analysed is invariably met with the resistance of those who create it. Compositions that are in fact the product of a great deal of expertise and effort are typically depicted by popular musicians themselves as the outcome simply of ineffable moments of intuition.[62] The contention that we should not 'read too much' into popular music tends to be especially strong among journalists.[63] As the media's response to the 2005 Smiths conference made clear,[64] those who write for the music press are often deeply resentful of academics straying into what they consider to be their domain by right. The endeavour to arrive at a scholarly understanding of what popular music means is routinely despised as a form of self-indulgent folly. The irony of those who make a living from writing and talking about pop striving to prevent others from doing likewise often seems to be somewhat lost on most music journalists.

The injunction against 'taking things too seriously' is also of course one that actually appears in the songs of The Smiths themselves. Among the various threads that run through Morrissey's lyrics is a coveting of the intuitive and the sensual. When we listen to The Smiths we are often incited to stop thinking so much and to begin actually living, to 'ignore all the codes of the day' and let our 'juvenile impulses sway'. The recurrent chiding of the reserved and the cerebral that we encounter in the songs informed the choice of title for this book. This is of course drawn from 'This Charming Man', and forms one half of a memorable couplet: 'Why pamper life's complexities / When the leather runs smooth on the passenger seat?'[65] The enquiry issued in these lines returns to one of the binaries and dilemmas that often feature in Morrissey's lyrics. The oblique narrative that provides the focus for the song centres upon a male figure stranded by a puncture while out for a cycle in the countryside. The unscheduled arrival in his car of the 'charming man' of the title offers both the possible safety of a lift home and the potential danger of what might most obviously be rendered as a homoerotic encounter on a 'hillside desolate'. The dilemma of the male lead is both stated and resolved in the couplet noted above. Who in their right mind would allow their anxieties and sensitivities to prevent the possibility of some spontaneous, sensual pleasure, even if it is to be only that offered by the lush interior of an upmarket vehicle?

The couplet at the heart of 'This Charming Man' sets up then a familiar binary between the intellectual and the sensual, between the mind and the body. On this particular occasion, the dilemma is, apparently, resolved by Morrissey in the favour of impetuous desire. In light of this, it will hopefully be apparent that the choice of title for the book represents a mild but intentional rebuke to ourselves. In choosing to call the text *Why Pamper Life's Complexities?*, we have sought to acknowledge that there is a substantial danger that intellectual analysis of popular music can obscure and even eliminate its appreciation on a more intuitive, emotional level. The title of the book offers a gentle reminder, in other words, that the close analysis of something as fragile, and ultimately ineffable, as a pop song holds various perils, not the least of which is the possibility of losing sight of that which drew you to it in the first place.

It should be remembered, however, that the work of The Smiths is defined by a profound and recurrent ambivalence.[66] For every sentiment that is expressed in any given song, there is almost always the precise opposite to be found elsewhere. While the words that Morrissey set to Marr's music certainly seek to encourage thoughtless spontaneity, they also strive to nurture thoughtful introspection. Among the many achievements of the band was – as the essays in this collection will seek to illustrate – the rendering of a whole sequence of intellectual concerns and dilemmas through the medium of the pop song. Indeed, the novelist Will Self goes so far as to suggest that the early song 'Still Ill' represents nothing less than the last couple of centuries of western philosophical thought compressed into three rapturous minutes.[67] The songbook of The Smiths offers a rare reminder of the facility of popular music to incite and inform. Those playful, thoughtful and provocative compositions that the band committed to record represent not only an invitation to look more closely but an absolute instruction to do so. Why pamper life's complexities? We hope that the essays that follow will offer ample justification for doing so.

Notes

1 For an academic rendition of this view, see J. Gilbert and E. Pearson, *Discographies: Dance Music, Culture and the Politics of Sound* (London: Routledge, 1999).

2 The impeccable 'indie' credentials of The Smiths were of course compromised when the band chose to leave Rough Trade and move to EMI. The contract signed with the major label would not be honoured due to the subsequent demise of the group.

3 For an account of Britpop, see J. Harris, *The Last Party: Britpop, Blair and the Demise of English Rock* (London: Fourth Estate, 2003). It is perhaps also worth mentioning that events in Morrissey's solo career, not least his infamous performance at Finsbury Park in 1992, played a part in how The Smiths were retrospectively viewed in this period. For an account of the Finsbury Park show, see N. Zuberi, *Sounds English: Transnational Popular Music* (Urbana and Chicago: University of Illinois Press, 2001), pp. 17–18.

4 D. Sheppard, 'Interview with Johnny Marr', *Q/Mojo: The Smiths & Morrissey Special Edition* (May 2004), p. 23.

5 For a discussion of the desires and aversions that inform many of Morrissey's lyrics, see M. Simpson, *Saint Morrissey* (London: SAF, 2004), especially pp. 98–112. For a detailed account of the derivation and various incarnations of 'This Charming Man', see S. Goddard, *The Smiths: Songs That Saved Your Life* (London: Reynolds & Hearn, 2004, second edition), pp. 49–55.

6 The performance can be viewed at www.youtube.com/watch?v=8ozllRKzebE (accessed on 15 January 2010).

7 Simpson, *Saint Morrissey*, pp. 161–2; P. Reid, *Morrissey* (Bath: Absolute Press, 2004), p. 74.

8 See, for example, *Young Guns Go For It: The Smiths* (BBC2, 22 January 1999).

9 In 2007, The Smiths were offered $75 million for a re-union tour. See www.billboard.com/bbcom/news/article_display.jsp?vnu_content_id=1003630174 (accessed on 15 January 2010).

10 J. Dee, 'I'm Not Sorry', in *Q/Mojo: The Smiths & Morrissey Special Edition*, p. 112.

11 See, for instance, M. Simpson, 'The Man Who Murdered Pop', *Guardian*, 'Friday Review' section, 5 November 1999, pp. 14–15.

12 For examples of post-2000 'indie' bands citing The Smiths as an influence, see D. Simpson, 'In From the Cold', *Guardian*, 'Friday Review' section, 7 July 2000, p. 15; A. Needham, 'Comrades! Friends! Music Lovers! Meet Your New Leaders', *NME*, 27 March 2004, p. 22; P. Whaite, 'This Charming Man: An Interview with Pete Doherty', *Socialist Review* (April 2004), p. 24; C. Rudebeck, 'Some Bands are Bigger than others. . .', *Independent*, 2 April 2005, pp. 20–1.

13 See M. Sawyer, 'Total Mozzer', *Observer*, 'Review' section, 19 June 2005, p. 6; E. Schambelan, 'Phil Collins', *Artforum* (May 2006), pp. 287–8; P. Wild (ed.), *Paint A Vulgar Picture: Fiction Inspired by The Smiths* (London: Serpent's Tail, 2009); D. Coupland, *Girlfriend In A Coma* (London: Flamingo, 1998); W. Russell, *The Wrong Boy* (London: Doubleday, 2000).

14 D. Jones, 'William, It Was Really Nothing', *GQ*, September 2009, pp. 35–7; C. Boucher, 'This Charming Man's Charmed Life', *Observer*, 20 September 2009, p. 21.

15 A compilation of Packham's references is available at: www.youtube.com/watch?v=FT9hGAlt890 (accessed 14 January 2010).

16 See, for example, Gabby Logan, 'Boy with the Thorn in his Side', *The Times*, 'The Game' section, 5 April 2004, p. 4; Gabriele Marcotti, 'How Soon is Now, Arsène?', *The Times*, 'Champions League Handbook', 11 September 2004, p. 13; Ariel Leve, 'This Charming Man', *Sunday Times*, 'Magazine' section, 7 January 2007, p. 12; Anne Ashworth, 'Heaven Knows Estate Agents are Miserable Now', *The Times*, 'Bricks and Mortar' section, 12 October 2007, p. 2; Ruth Gledhill, 'Heaven Knows Why We Are All Miserable Now, say the Christian MPs', *The Times*, 12 May 2008, p. 8.

17 N. Davenport, 'Heaven Knows I'm an Islamist Now', *spiked*, 7 July 2006. Available at www.spiked-online.com/index.php?/site/article/940 (accessed 15 January 2010).

18 In a short piece carried in the *Guardian*, Keyes mentions successfully approaching Morrissey for permission to use the title. See Anonymous, 'The Week in Books', *Guardian*, 28 February 2009, p. 5.

19 See *NME*, 20 April 2002.

20 For examples of the 'special issues' and cover features on The Smiths that have appeared in the post-2000 period, see *Mojo* (April 2001; March 2008), *NME* (7 June 2003; 10 June 2006), *Record Collector* (June 2003; June 2005), *Q/Mojo: The Smiths & Morrissey Special Edition* (May 2004), *Uncut* (January 2006; March 2007), *Q/Mojo Classic: Morrissey and Manchester* (March 2006), *Hot Press* (14 November 2007). For examples of books published on The Smiths (and The Smiths/Morrissey) in this period, see Goddard, *The Smiths*; Simpson, *Saint Morrissey*; Reid, *Morrissey*; R. Carman, *Johnny Marr: The Smiths & The Art of Gun-Slinging* (London: Independent Music Press, 2006); J. Rogan, *Morrissey: The*

Albums (London: Calidore, 2006); P. Slattery, *The Smiths: The Early Years* (London: Omnibus Press/Vision On, 2007); P. Gatenby, *Panic on the Streets: The Smiths and Morrissey Location Guide* (London: Reynolds & Hearn, 2007); P.A. Woods (ed.), *Morrissey in Conversation: The Essential Interviews* (London: Plexus, 2007); Len Brown, *Meetings with Morrissey* (London: Omnibus Press, 2008); G. Hopps, *Morrissey: The Pageant of His Bleeding Heart* (New York: Continuum, 2009); S. Goddard, *Mozipedia: The Encyclopaedia of Morrissey and The Smiths* (London: Ebury Press, 2009).

21 See D. Bhat, 'Top Pop Lyric is from U2', *The Times*, 17 April 2006, p. 13; K. Spencer, J. Carpenter and K. Bohdanowicz, 'Morrissey's Green Streak', *Daily Express*, 19 December 2006, p. 11.

22 See, for example, S. O'Neill, 'Academics of the World Unite for a Gig with the Smiths', *The Times*, 29 March 2005, p. 9; C. Moran, 'So tell me, what was that all about?', *The Times*, 29 March 2005, p. 9; C. Rudebeck, 'Some Bands are Bigger than others. . .', *Independent*, 2 April 2005, pp. 20–1; *Daily Star*, 29 March 2005, p. 17; *Daily Mirror*, 29 March 2005, p. 3; *The Sun*, 29 March 2005, p. 7; Eddie Smack, 'Hatful of Homework', *NME*, 23 April 2005, p. 29;, S. Goddard, 'Oxbridge Here We Come', *Uncut*, June 2005, p. 28; G. Dent, 'Meeting is Murder', *Guardian*, 'Guide' section, 23 April 2005, pp. 4–6; É. Fraga, 'The Smiths polemiza como tema acadêmico', *Folha de São Paulo*, 8 April 2005; K. Gomes, 'Académicos debatem os Smiths numa universidade de Manchester', *Público*, 8 April 2005, p. 48. See also *Channel 4 News*, 9 April 2005.

23 See P. MacInnes, 'Guitar Legend Marr Moves To Academia', *Guardian*, 19 October 2007, p. 5.

24 There were from the outset, for instance, numerous attacks on The Smiths in the right-wing press. See, for example, Anonymous, '"Ban Child-Sex Pop Song" Plea to Beeb', *The Sun*, 5 September 1983, p. 26; M. Dunn and N. Ferrari, 'Smiths' "Sick" Royal Disc Rapped', *The Sun*, 16 June 1986, p. 13.

25 F. Nietzsche, *Thus Spoke Zarathustra* (London: Penguin, 1961 [1885]), p. 324.

26 T.W. Adorno, 'On the Fetish Character in Music and the Regression of Listening' [1938], in Adorno, *The Culture Industry: Selected Essays on Mass Culture*, ed. J.M. Bernstein (London: Routledge, 1991), pp. 26–52.

27 A.V. Karja, 'A Prescribed Alternative Mainstream: Popular Music and Canon Formation', *Popular Music*, Vol. 25, No. 1 (2006), pp. 3–20.

28 F. Jameson, *Postmodernism, Or, The Cultural Logic of Late Capitalism* (London: Verso, 1991).

29 Ibid., pp. 16–25.

30 Ibid., p. 6.

31 R. v Appen and A. Doehring, 'Nevermind The Beatles, Here's Exile 61 and Nico: "The Top 100 Records of All Time" – A Canon of Pop and Rock Albums From a Sociological and an Aesthetic Perspective', *Popular Music*, Vol. 25, No. 1 (2006), pp. 21–39.

32 The track 'Heritage Rock' appears on Luke Haines' 2006 album *Off My Rocker at the Art School Bop* (Degenerate Records).

33 See, for example, Continuum's *33 1/3* series, and the BBC's *Classic Albums* series. We are aware, of course, that this book might be viewed as a part of this same trend.

34 For an account of 'authenticity' in rock culture, see K. Keightley, 'Reconsidering Rock', in S. Frith, W. Straw and J. Street (eds), *The Cambridge Companion to Pop and Rock* (Cambridge: Cambridge University Press, 2001), pp. 131–9.

35 *Desert Island Discs* (BBC Radio 4, 28 May 2006). See also J. Harris, 'Hands Off Our Music!', *Guardian*, 'G2' Section, 18 March 2008, p. 5.

36 For a typically astute account of the significance and meaning of Salford Lads Club in the presentation and recollection of The Smiths, see Zuberi, *Sounds English*, pp. 35–6.

37 M. Woolf, 'Heaven Knows I'm Triumphant Now', *The Sunday Times*, 23 March 2008, p. 3.

38 R. Woods, 'He Came. He Saw. He, er, Left', *The Sunday Times*, 27 July 2008, p. 3.

39 Eton College is generally regarded as the most prestigious fee-paying school in the United Kingdom. A nursery for the British political establishment, the school boasts no fewer than nineteen Prime Ministers among its 'old boys'. In 2009, the annual basic fee for attending Eton stood at £28,000 (source: www.etoncollege.com). The median annual wage of full-time employees in the UK in the same year was £23,700 (source:www.statistics.gov.uk/cci/nugget.asp?id=285).

40 See J. Henke, 'Oscar! Oscar! Great Britain Goes Wilde for the "Fourth-Gender" Smiths', *Rolling Stone*, 7 June 1984, p. 45; I. Pye, 'A Hard Day's Misery', *Melody Maker*, 3 November 1984, p. 31.

41 *Record Collector* (June 2003), p. 3.

42 G. Brown, 'Laughter in Paradise!', *Sounds*, 14 June 1986, p. 16.

43 See Dunn and Ferrari, 'Smiths' "Sick" Royal Disc Rapped', p. 13.

44 This sanitising feature is, of course, partly facilitated by the increasing use of download technology, which has a de-contextualising effect on music's reception.

45 Harris, 'Hands Off Our Music!', p. 7.

46 See Peel's comments on the *South Bank Show* (ITV, 18 October 1987). See also M. Heatley, *John Peel: A Life in Music* (London: Michael O'Mara, 2004), p. 131.

47 S. Frith, *Performing Rites: Evaluating Popular Music* (Oxford: Oxford University Press, 1996), p. 273.

48 Ibid., p. 263.

49 On the iniquity of 'objectivity', see also G. Marcus, *Double Trouble: Bill Clinton and Elvis Presley in a Land of No Alternatives* (London: Faber and Faber, 2000), p. 109.

50 Frith, *Performing Rites*, p. 11.

51 See, for example, Rudebeck, 'Some Bands are Bigger Than Others . . .', pp. 20–1;

The Importance of Being Morrissey (Channel 4, 8 June 2003); N. Kent, 'Dreamer in the Real World', *The Face* (May 1985), p. 67; *South Bank Show*.

52 Adorno, *The Culture Industry*, p. 175.

53 *I Love 1984* (BBC2, 17 February 2001).

54 J. Rogan, *Morrissey and Marr: The Severed Alliance* (London: Omnibus Press, 1992).

55 Goddard, *The Smiths*.

56 See, for instance, S. Reynolds and J. Press, *The Sex Revolts: Gender, Rebellion and Rock 'n' Roll* (Cambridge, MA: Harvard University Press, 2005); S. Hawkins, *Settling The Pop Score: Pop Texts and Identity Politics* (Aldershot: Ashgate, 2002), pp. 66–103; N. Hubbs, 'Music of the "Fourth Gender": Morrissey and the Sexual Politics of Melodic Contour', in T. Foster, C. Siegel and E.E. Berry (eds), *Bodies of Writing, Bodies in Performance* (New York: New York University Press, 1996), pp. 266–96.

57 For an account of the complex convergence of these roles, see J. Harris, 'Trouble at Mill', *Mojo* (April 2001), pp. 60–1.

58 J. Robb, *The North Will Rise Again: Manchester Music City 1976–1996* (London: Aurum, 2009), p. 195.

59 See S. Goddard, 'Crowning Glory', *Uncut* (January 2006), p. 52; *Dave Fanning*, RTÉ 2FM, 8 November 2002. Marr typically developed musical ideas on guitar, which were subsequently passed (via audio cassette) on to Morrissey, who would then conceive of song lyrics and vocal melodies. See Harris, 'Trouble at Mill', pp. 58–9; *Top Ten Guitar Heroes* (Channel 4, 24 March 2001); M. Roach, *The Right to Imagination & Madness: An Essential Collection of Candid Interviews with Top UK Alternative Songwriters* (London: Independent Music Press, 1994), p. 322.

60 A.F. Moore, *Rock: The Primary Text. Developing a Musicology of Rock* (Buckingham: Open University Press, 1993), p. 133.

61 A. Mueller, 'Johnny Marr', *Melody Maker*, 30 September 1989, p. 8. For an account of machismo in rock, see S. Frith and A. McRobbie, 'Rock and Sexuality', *Screen Education*, No. 29 (Winter 1978/79), pp. 5–8.

62 M. Bannister, '"Loaded": Indie Guitar Rock, Canonism, White Masculinities', *Popular Music*, Vol. 25, No. 1 (2006), pp. 77–96, p. 86.

63 As Jon Savage has observed, a 'fear of being thought too serious' is among the 'tedious tropes that bedevil much music writing'. See J. Savage, 'Vinyl Ventures', *Guardian*, 'Review' section, 2 August 2008, p. 6.

64 See Fergus Campbell, '"When we're in your scholarly room, who will swallow whom?": Media Representations of a Conference on The Smiths', University of Helsinki, 14 May 2005.

65 There are numerous versions of 'This Charming Man'. In some renditions, the lyric involves the singular 'complexity'. The version referred to here with the plural 'complexities' is the one that featured in a BBC session for the John Peel Radio

Show in September 1983 and subsequently appeared on the 1984 compilation *Hatful of Hollow*.

66 For an account of ambivalence in The Smiths, see Sean Campbell's chapter in this volume.

67 W. Self, 'The King of Bedsit Angst Grows Up', in P.A. Woods (ed.), *Morrissey in Conversation: The Essential Interviews* (London: Plexus, 2007), p. 165.

2

'HAS THE WORLD CHANGED OR HAVE I CHANGED?': THE SMITHS AND THE CHALLENGE OF THATCHERISM

Joseph Brooker

Welcome me, if you will,
as the ambassador for a hatred
who knows its cause
(Frank O'Hara, 'For James Dean')[1]

What's frightened you? Have you been reading the newspapers?
(Shelagh Delaney, *A Taste of Honey*)[2]

The Smiths' recording career roughly corresponded to Margaret Thatcher's second term in office. 'Hand In Glove' was released a month before 1983's general election; *Strangeways, Here We Come* appeared four months into Thatcher's third term. Such facts can be suggestive, but they do not necessarily signify substantial connections. In an important sense, The Smiths' career had little to do with contemporary political events. When Johnny Marr remembers the band he talks most intensely not of society at large but of 'the feeling of being in the studio at half-two in the morning when two chords suddenly crash into each other'.[3] What were The Smiths trying to achieve? Musical greatness, a living, fame and adulation, to be sure. But, more than most artists, they also sought political confrontation and significance. 'Times *are* desperate', Morrissey announced in 1984.[4] What he meant by that, and what he tried to do about it, are this chapter's quarry.

The Thatcher syndrome

The 1980s in Britain were politically dominated by Thatcher's three Conservative administrations, elected in 1979, 1983 and 1987. Thatcher was unusually driven and controversial – a 'conviction politician' determined to change the fabric of Britain. Arguably, she succeeded. The Britain whose governance she reluctantly surrendered in November 1990 was very different from the one she inherited from Labour's Jim Callaghan in May 1979. Some of the changes were beyond her control – a function of global trends, for instance. Others were unwelcome to her. But, to an unusual degree, much of what had happened was driven by her and her political allies. Over the preceding ten years, Johnny Marr remarked in May 1987, British social attitudes had 'changed *remarkably*'.[5]

Thatcher headed the British wing of a transatlantic political tendency, the New Right. It corresponded conveniently to the American administrations of Ronald Reagan, from 1980 to 1988, and his successor, George Bush Sr. In both countries, the New Right aimed to overturn the perceived gains of progressive and left-wing movements, most notably those associated with the 1960s. Thatcherism became associated with a more specific goal: the dissolution of the post-war consensus in which both Labour and Conservative parties had agreed to manage a welfare state, and to use the state to increase social and economic equality. The declared aim now was to shrink state spending and increase the influence of private companies and entrepreneurial individuals.

Thatcherism commenced with economic recession. Industry was hard-hit, unemployment high, and the government unpopular. It has become axiomatic that what saved Conservative electoral fortunes was the Falklands War in the early summer of 1982, in which military force recaptured a small set of islands in the south Atlantic which had been claimed by an Argentinian dictator. Thatcher's second term saw the popular entrenchment of policies we now think of as 'Thatcherism'. Property prices, debt and credit rose considerably. Through the decade, the top rate of income tax was drastically reduced, openly benefiting society's richest members. Meanwhile, in 1984–85, Thatcher saw off her strongest domestic challenge, a year-long strike by the National Union of Mineworkers in protest at the closure of pits. This episode emblematised her successful confrontation with organised labour. It also crystallised the renewed perception of a regional divide, in which the older industries that had dominated the north were run down while wealth clustered in south-east England. The perception was not without foundation. Between December 1979 and September 1986, Ian Jack reported, 'ninety-four per cent of *all* jobs lost ... were north of a line drawn between the Wash and the Bristol Channel'.[6] By Thatcher's third term, Britain showed signs of transformation, and her political programme seemed triumphant. On the election's eve, Marr called the country a 'Conservative dream'.[7] By the time Thatcher's triumphalism and isolation had led to her downfall, The Smiths were long sundered, and *Bona Drag* in the charts.

The overview sketched above already announces many themes central to this enquiry. Unemployment and poverty, disproportionately affecting the north; the consumer boom, new wealth and rising inequality; a government that was internally confrontational and outwardly jingoistic. 'I follow her career', Morrissey commented. 'Obviously, I find the entire Thatcher syndrome very stressful and evil and all those other words'.[8] The 'Thatcher syndrome' was certainly not his only idea of the political foe. In the 1987 *South Bank Show* on The Smiths, for instance, Morrissey describes the demolition of areas of Manchester in the late 1960s as a political strike against working-class people. That was not the work of the New Right. Likewise, it would be a mistake to see all of the misery catalogued in his songs as a result of Thatcherism. Many of those scenes and moods had germinated since before punk. But Thatcherism was the image of power that coincided with the start of Morrissey's pop career. Arguably, indeed, their careers peaked simultaneously. There was a certain grim fortune in this. Thatcherism gave Morrissey a target, a vision of political dominance that was peculiarly, even grotesquely clear. The enemy was easily named. A Wilson or Callaghan would not have provided such ready fare. Yet Thatcherism also belied this apparent clarity. It was an image of conservative hegemony: entrenched power about which little could be done. But it was also vexingly new and transformative. We shall return to this ambiguity. But let us recall first what Morrissey and Marr emphasised: the New Right's authoritarianism and traditionalism.

Clean and orderly

As early as January 1979, Stuart Hall identified 'the key themes of the radical right' as 'law and order, the need for social discipline and authority in the face of a conspiracy by the enemies of the state, the onset of social anarchy, the "enemy within"'.[9] The value and importance of family, law, discipline, morality and nation were reiterated, with a strong accompanying sense of their peril. These are standard right-wing refrains. But they were played with peculiar gusto. Single-parent families were regarded with suspicion. The 'promotion' of homosexuality in schools was banned. Progressive education was attacked, and more regimented schooling recommended. The traditional Tory grip on law and order was strengthened. The police were viewed as politically partisan by those they confronted, not least the miners. The themes of law and order overlapped with those of nation and flag. As David Edgar put it, 'zapping the enemy without on the beach-heads of the South Atlantic was an effective and timely corollary to confronting the "enemy within" on the streets of London, Toxteth and Moss Side'.[10]

The authoritarian side of Thatcherism was conveniently exemplified in the persona of the Prime Minister herself. She was happy to appear unbending, determined to the point of rigidity. Her best-remembered soundbites played up to this role. The effects of the persona were overdetermined by gender. As the first female Prime Minister, Thatcher emphasised her strength to a degree that might have seemed eccentric in a male politician, but for a woman in her position was more a necessary ideological compensation. She also projected herself as a provincial housewife for whom the country's budget was to be managed like a household's. As Hall showed, such projections helped her to capture the ground of ideological 'common sense'. The 'spendthrift state' could not dispense 'wealth the nation has not earned'. The enemy of ordinary people was 'the "welfare scrounger", living off society, never doing a day's work (here, the Protestant Ethic makes a late return)'.[11]

A notable cultural corollary of Thatcherism's traditionalist and authoritarian dimension was the increased prominence of national heritage. The government quickly produced two Heritage Acts and fostered an interest in what Patrick Wright called 'the historicized image of an instinctively conservative establishment'.[12] Cultural historians have argued that the popularity of period drama in the era, notably the series of Merchant–Ivory films, belongs to the same mood of English museology. But, in the particular context in question, a different engagement with the past is especially crucial. This is the denigration of the 1960s, and a corresponding revaluation of the 1950s. 'We are reaping what was sown in the sixties', Thatcher proclaimed: 'The fashionable theories and permissive clap-trap set the scene for a society in which the old virtues of discipline and self-restraint were denigrated'.[13] As the American critic Michael Ventura perceived, '[v]irtually every aspect of the New Right's program, both social and political, attempts to turn back what happened to us in the sixties'.[14] In a 1988 interview with the *Daily Mail*, Thatcher decried 'Sixties culture':

> Permissiveness, selfish and uncaring, proliferated under the guise of the new sexual freedom. Aggressive verbal hostility, presented as a refreshing lack of subservience, replaced courtesy and good manners. Instant gratification became the philosophy of the young and the youth cultists. Speculation replaced dogged hard work.

The 1950s, by contrast, Thatcher remembered as 'clean and orderly'.[15] Whatever the reality, part of the New Right's self-image was of returning society to that state, undoing the upheavals that had created the present undisciplined mess.

Doorstep rebellion

Thus conceived, Thatcherism offered a clear target to an oppositional youth culture. Insofar as the 1960s were at stake, the cultural politics of that decade might be scratchily replayed – which is one way of reading The Smiths' early deployment of flowers. Authority and interdiction provoked rebellion. Sober traditionalism needed the sting of satire. The Smiths' place in this confrontation was clear enough. 'The entire history of Margaret Thatcher', Morrissey announced in mid-1984, 'is one of violence and oppression and horror. I think that we must *not* lie back and cry about it'.[16]

Some of their most explicitly oppositional gestures were benefit concerts which demonstrated their affiliation to a cause. In June 1984, just before the confrontation between police and striking miners reached its height at Orgreave, they played the Jobs for a Change festival organized by the Greater London Council. Ken Livingstone's imaginative leadership of the GLC had made it one of the left's few concrete resources of hope at the time, as Stuart Hall noted.[17] 'This must be what socialism is', Billy Bragg thought that day.[18] The following year, Bragg and Paul Weller launched Red Wedge, their programme of youth activism affiliated to the Labour Party. The initiative's main contribution was live concerts. Johnny Marr and Andy Rourke played alongside Bragg, who had already toured with The Smiths in the USA. The Smiths themselves made one, impromptu contribution, in January 1986. Marr remembers it as 'one of the best things we ever did', though he seems prouder of the band's solidarity with him than of its political significance.[19]

The Smiths' more memorable interventions, though, were verbal: public statements and song lyrics. As John Harris reminds us, these stances were not struck in isolation. They were taken to exemplify the attitudes of what he terms a particular 'counterculture' of opposition to Thatcherism.[20] Like its 1960s precursor, this was largely formed of the young and centred around popular music: notably the network of independent bands, record companies and shops. The scene was typified by students, but was not exclusively middle-class. Many, of course, did not take Morrissey at his own valuation. But his anti-establishment and anti-consumerist opinions were consensual for this community, not least in its house journal, the *New Musical Express*.

Pronouncements were peculiarly crucial to The Smiths' career. Even such *auteurs* as Lennon and Dylan had not been so deliberately grandiloquent. Morrissey's outpouring of opinions testified to their long damming hitherto. Like Jarvis Cocker after him, he had spent years preparing to be a pop star, and arrived with ideas and images fully formed. As his statements became more explicitly political around 1985, the media's keenness to give him space cast him as a kind of anti-establishment sage. If Thatcher and Norman Tebbit provided one rhetorical account of Britain, he offered another, sometimes a critique of that official view. Inflammatory assertions were tempered with bathos and punchlines: the model was more Oscar Wilde than Arthur Scargill. He could even match one summative slogan ('There Is No Alternative', 'On Your Bike') with another ('Meat Is Murder', 'The Queen Is Dead'). Of course, Morrissey was marginal to the discursive contests of the day, and his contributions altered no politician's course. Thatcherism had more prominent, accredited opponents: Neil Kinnock, Ken Livingstone, Edward Heath. Even within pop, Morrissey might be resented for producing so much inflammatory eloquence, without rooting it in the activist work-rate of some of his contemporaries. But his ability and eagerness to pronounce on the state of the nation gave him an unusual role. This was already announced in the opening gambit of 'Still Ill': 'I decree today. . .'. What the song decrees, and decries, is the unfairness of British society; Morrissey demands welfare on hair-raisingly unrealistic terms. The Smiths' swansong would begin with one last echo of this messianic role: 'A Rush And A Push And The Land Is Ours', an assertion so immoderate that it could only be ironic.

Morrissey touched most notes on the scale of progressive issues. Some of these – vegetarianism, feminism – were only tangentially linked to Thatcherism itself, but signalled a broader allegiance to the left. Even nuclear war was fleetingly invoked ('Ask', 'Shoplifters'). Racial injustice might seem a notable omission, although it should be remembered that the band did play an anti-apartheid benefit. But the bugbear that Morrissey made his own was the monarchy. In some ways, this was a diversion from Thatcher. But it could lead back to her. The theme announced on *The Queen Is Dead* had been prefigured in 'Nowhere Fast', whose analysis of the monarch – 'the poor and the needy are selfish and greedy on her terms' – was expanded in several interviews. His 1985 diatribe to Simon Garfield is archetypal:

> It's fairy story nonsense . . . the very idea of their existence in these days when people are dying daily because they don't have enough money to operate one radiator in the house, to me is immoral. As far as I can see, money spent on royalty is money burnt. I've never met anyone who supports royalty, and believe me I've searched. Okay, so there's some deaf and elderly pensioner in Hartlepool who has pictures of Prince Edward pinned on the toilet seat, but I know streams of people who can't wait to get rid of them. It's a false devotion anyway. I think it's fascist and very, very cruel. To me there's something dramatically ugly about a person who can wear a dress for £6,000 when at the same time there are people who can't afford to eat.[21]

A certain rhetorical arsenal is recurrently at work in statements like this. Some phrases have a febrile eloquence: 'dying daily', 'dramatically ugly' (the latter phrase, which makes aesthetic into moral censure, is in keeping with Morrissey's earlier celebration of the words 'charming' and 'handsome'). He spontaneously generates imaginary scenes and characters – the Hartlepool pensioner, and the teen conjured by Morrissey's tirade against Band Aid:

> The whole implication was to save these people in Ethiopia, but who were they asking to save them? Some 13-year-old girl in Wigan! People like Thatcher and the royals could solve the Ethiopian problem within ten seconds. But Band Aid shied away from saying that – for heaven's sake, it was almost directly aimed at unemployed people.[22]

The rhetorical recourse to the north is insistent. The references to Wigan, Hartlepool and so on imply a kind of allegiance to this territory – a tic echoed twenty years on when he told Paul Morley that his youthful aspiration was to a 'comfortable life. And I don't mean Alderley Edge'.[23] The names are also delivered tongue-in-cheek. The bathos of self-conscious northernness is close to that of Alan Bennett and Victoria Wood. Even 'money spent on royalty is money burnt' sounds like a piece of *Coronation Street*-corner wisdom, an inflammatory upgrade of the sayings lovingly catalogued by Richard Hoggart. In a word, there is a strong flavour of camp to the pronouncements. This enables, rather than undercuts, their extremity. Morrissey's statements in this vein consistently describe both wealth and poverty as obscene. They are extravagantly egalitarian, and effectively leftist. 'Thatcher and the royals' is a significant yoking. He is keener to fill the dock with the powerful than to draw fine distinctions between them.

The rejection of Band Aid is particularly telling. Even intellectuals like Dick Hebdige and Stuart Hall were cautiously optimistic about that campaign.[24] Morrissey refuses to join the consensus, insisting on its effacement of class relations. There is certainly an element of overgrown teen wilfulness to the refusal. But there is also a substantial political point. His stance is reminiscent of what Mike Marqusee has observed in the early Bob Dylan. Dylan, Marqusee shows, was not content with liberal sentiments. In songs like 'Only A Pawn In Their Game', 'Masters Of War' and 'With God On Our Side', he displaced them with structural critique. More scandalously, he refused serene hope for vindictive anger. Spite took on political significance. Joan Baez refused to sing the verse in which Dylan doggedly follows the war-profiteer's 'casket' to his grave, and stands over it 'Til I'm sure that you're dead'.[25] The trail from that grave leads down through pop time, to the grave of Margaret Thatcher over which Elvis Costello yearned to stand in 'Tramp The Dirt Down' (1989). Morrissey had already essayed this sub-genre, a year earlier. The title *Margaret On The Guillotine* had originally been slated for *The Queen Is Dead* – a bracing thought, as though *Sgt Pepper*'s working title had been *Bring Me The Head Of Mr Wilson*. Again the elision is striking: one matriarchal leader is substituted for another. The phrase was salvaged to conclude Morrissey's first solo LP. Unlike Costello, Morrissey does not bother exploring Thatcher's policies and their effects at any length. His death sentence is all the more outrageous for its lazy refusal to examine the charge sheet. Predictably, he was unrepentant. Asked if he'd really like to see Thatcher dead, he replied:

> 'Instantly.'
> In a cruel, bloody sort of way?
> 'Yes.'

Would you carry out the execution?
'I have got the uniform, ready.'[26]

He had long hankered after such violent reprisal. 'She's only one person, and she can be destroyed. It's the only remedy for the country at the moment', warns a 1984 interview.[27] The sorrow of the Brighton Bomb, he maintained, was that Thatcher had escaped unscathed.[28] Such talk may be deemed petulant and irresponsible. Morrissey himself, while insisting on his song's seriousness, admitted that it had an air of 'doorstep rebellion, and stamping of feet'.[29] But he had already formulated an extensive, if irregular, critique of politics, rather than personality.

The show is over

Several of Morrissey's songs brought their own soap-boxes. Some were direct, practising the finger-pointing that he would physically demonstrate on the *South Bank Show*: 'Meat Is Murder', 'The Headmaster Ritual'. 'Shoplifters of the World Unite', like 'A Rush And A Push. . .', parodied the messianic role itself. But the greatest was the most dense and ambiguous. 'The Queen Is Dead', Morrissey admitted, was 'certainly a kind of general observation on the state of the nation'.[30] It was among the band's longest tracks, the resounding keynote of their masterpiece, and Morrissey's most extensively detailed lyric. Marr's contribution was the most explosive music the band ever played. It actualised his idea of the MC5, a band whose political zeal made The Stones or The Who seem like dilettantes. In a sense, the track brings to a climax the polemical tendency we have been observing. England's 'cheerless marshes' are decried; the monarchy is rudely caricatured; the opening verse dreams of violence against the monarch. Nine years earlier, the Sex Pistols' 'God Save The Queen' had been perhaps the most politically controversial hit record in the UK since rock'n'roll began. The Smiths' song clearly aims to succeed it: even the Pistols' dismissal of 'England's dreaming' is picked up. The Pistols' lyric has its nuances,[31] but much of it, like its Jubilee title, boils down to heavy irony. Morrissey's lyric is also mischievous – but fantastical rather than sarcastic. Its satirical fantasies are followed by the crazy narrative of breaking into Buckingham Palace. The elements of absurdity and fabulation are important. They already rescue the track from threadbare agit-pop or arid anger. As Alexis Petridis observes, they grant it a provisional quality akin to Morrissey's interviews. But what, through or beyond the laughter, does the song say?

Petridis reckons it a fantasy of regicide.[32] But whereas 'Margaret On The Guillotine' luridly ends with the fall of the blade, this song does not describe that action. Like the palace intruder who supposedly inspired the song, all the protagonist apparently does is talk to the monarch.[33] Perhaps this is enough to tell him that the monarchy is finished. It is at this point that Morrissey keens of 'all those lies about England and its dreaming'[34] and we next find him on the move again:

> Passed the pub that saps your body
> And the church who'll snatch your money
> The Queen is dead, boys
> And it's so lonely on a limb

This final verse sketches national life in the most brutally materialistic terms. The point may be that the death of the Queen is what reduces the nation to this condition. The values of transcendence, unity and continuity that she is supposed to embody are absent.

Morrissey surely does not view the Queen that way. Twenty years later, he insists: 'The monarchy is a memory. It doesn't exist any more, and quite rightly so . . . [The Queen is] horrified because she can see the whole ship slip away, like the Titanic under the waves. . .. Everybody knows the show is over'.[35] Here is the same structure of thought, decreeing the monarchy's extinction as an idea even as it persists in material fact. The mood is of disdain, not sorrow. Marr asserted that the Queen made for a 'ridiculous' national politics; monarchism he considered 'naïve'.[36] It is not even as though Elizabeth II can be separated from a hitherto glorious institution. The verse fancifully tracing the singer's own royal lineage makes monarchical genealogy sound suspect. Yet if – physically or ideologically – the Queen is dead, the song does not sound like a celebration of the fact. Perhaps the closest analogy for Morrissey's perception is Nietzsche's 'God is dead': the point being that we have not yet learned to live with this knowledge. What comes next is crucially at stake. For it is not just an old world of hierarchy that threatens Morrissey. 'We're moving rapidly into a sphere that nobody wants to go into', he had declared in 1984. 'Progress doesn't seem to be in any degree pleasant. Everything modern is quite foul'.[37] At the heart of the song is a pivotal, repeated line: 'Oh, has the world changed or have I changed?' It is a strange question for a revolutionary. If anything is worse than England's decayed traditions, it is England's new decade.

The leading edge

Morrissey's occasional alignment of Thatcher and Elizabeth was telling. For the only time in British history, the nation's two senior political figures were women. *The Queen Is Dead*'s interest in matriarchal power perhaps reflects this. This concern is manifested in the desperate appeal of 'I Know It's Over', as well as the dysfunctional motherhood envisaged on the title track. Morrissey's aggressive relation to Thatcher herself gains another dimension if considered as a stand-off between a 'masculine' woman and an effeminate man: the Iron

Lady and the Prophet of the Fourth Gender.[38] (The heavy use of the word 'Queen' picks up on this last ambiguity; the phrase 'The Queen Is Dead' itself had its origins in sexual unorthodoxy, not English republicanism.[39])

Politically, though, the alignment of PM and Queen had a limit. Not only did the Queen find Thatcher personally more awkward to deal with than any of her male predecessors; more substantively, she was actually said to disapprove of Thatcherite policy. In 1986 a senior palace source – allegedly the Queen's press secretary, Michael Shea – told the *Sunday Times* that the Queen found Thatcher's premiership 'uncaring, confrontational and socially divisive', citing the miners' strike as an instance. Thatcher herself sighed to a confidant that the Queen was 'the kind of woman who could vote SDP'.[40] The two women emblematised different brands of conservatism. When the Queen was alleged to have expressed dissatisfaction at Thatcher's 'abandonment of the nation-sustaining post-war consensus in British politics', she was associated with an older 'One Nation' Conservatism, which kept up a residual rearguard action against New Right radicalism.[41]

Thatcher, of course, was a monarchist. But she was impatient with the culture of Buckingham Palace, as she was with that of other establishment institutions such as the BBC or the Church of England. Her power was not hereditary but fiercely won. Her roots were among provincial Methodists. She might, like the Queen, have seemed an immovable object, devoted to rank and tradition. But she was simultaneously reconstructing British society. Thatcherism crucially meant not just tradition, but modernisation. These complexities contribute to the ambivalence of 'The Queen Is Dead'. The song alternately attacks the old order and mourns it; iconoclasm against one opponent might collude with an even worse foe.

Among other things, Thatcherism was a particular way of managing the transition from production to consumption – from Britain's old manufacturing base of cars and ships, to an economy of services and transactions. The government promoted a new commercial dispensation. The promotion of share options in newly privatised industries was highly significant. The ideological aim – 'popular capitalism' – was to remake common sense around entrepreneurial individualism. Concomitantly, the financial sector claimed a new prominence in popular culture and public imagery. Peter York would put it hyperbolically: 'The City had taken hold of our minds: City buildings (now thrusting, futuristic) lurked in the backgrounds of car promotions, insurance commercials, *moderne* electric cooker ads – symbolizing wealth, power, *tomorrow*'.[42] Enterprise Zones were created to encourage new industrial growth. The flagship was London's Docklands. By the close of the 1980s, this previously run-down peninsula was becoming a new landscape, a Manhattan-on-Thames.

The culture of consumption transformed the rest of Britain too. The cultural historian Frank Mort cautiously relays the pronouncements of the advertisers and retailers of the time: that 'the leading edge of economic processes . . . had moved away from manufacturing and towards the sites of exchange', and that 'the new consumption was driven by the appearance of intensified forms of individualism'.[43] The rise of the style press, starting with *The Face* in 1980, was symbiotic with this analysis. The high street altered, even when it was not being relocated to a shopping mall. New businesses became iconic and almost omnipresent: *Our Price, Virgin, Sock Shop, The Body Shop*.[44] Peter York sees George Davies' clothes chain *Next* as emblematic in diffusing a new commercial aestheticism: 'Next brought the Design-educated London Look *everywhere*'.[45] York's descriptions are knowingly euphoric. But he records a real transformation, in accordance with new retail models and conventions of design.

Design, consumption, money – preferably plastic: this is a different facet of the dominant culture from those we scanned earlier. Its other major connotation was America. The USA seemed already the apotheosis of consumer culture. The Thatcher–Reagan alliance confirmed the connection at another level.

Just say no

This culture did not catch The Smiths napping. Their hostility to it made for a peculiar, implicit politics, distinct from the agit-pop mode we considered above. Simon Reynolds saw this most clearly. The rock rebellion of The Stones, The Who and The Jam, he proposed, 'was based in some kind of activism or at least action, an optimism about the potential of collective or individual agency. But The Smiths' rebellion was always more like resistance through withdrawal, through subsiding into enervation'.[46] To explain The Smiths' position, Reynolds limned the culture as follows.

Pop in the 1980s had become dominated by funk, soul and dance: music of black origin, but now lucratively taken up by white artists too. Such music bore several related associations. It was slick, glossy, 'over-produced'. It sounded American, even when performed by British artists. It was highly sexualised; its vocal tones and rhythms connoted carnality. The body, Reynolds argued, was no longer the credible site of transgression it had seemed in 1960s counter-culture. It was thoroughly absorbed into a new system of eroticised consumption, and even into a craze for fitness and athleticism. Contemporary culture, he averred, '*insists* on enjoyment, incites us to develop our capacity for pleasure'. America represented 'the supreme incarnation of the modern, of the coming health-and-efficiency culture . . . In pop terms we're talking about MTV and videos, stadiums and nightclubs and wine bars, growing links between Hollywood and rock and between advertising and rock'. The local result was 'a Thatcherite vision of classless, "popular capitalism", of a Britain that would be more like America. Those modern figures – the yuppie, the soul boy, the B-boy – are all infatuated with the American vision of the future'.[47]

In almost every respect, The Smiths could be seen to invert this vision. Even small gestures like their initial reluctance to make music videos were emblematic. So was the larger gesture of Morrissey's life. To borrow a sentence from Lorrie Moore: 'In the land of perversities he had maintained the perversity of refusal'.[48] Little could be more radically removed from the carnal marketplace than the declaration of celibacy. Vegetarianism was another kind of anti-carnality, a virtuous refusal of flesh. Drugs and alcoholic excess were disdained. It is a nice detail that what provokes Morrissey's worry about social change in 'The Queen Is Dead' is 'some nine-year-old tough who peddles drugs: I swear to God, I swear, I never even knew what drugs were!' The child of Thatcherism is a compound of ills, suggesting deadbeat delinquency, but also making money from hedonism. Morrissey heightened his own abstinent persona in response. 'That old thing of Morrissey going to bed early, that was true, really', recalls Geoff Travis.[49] In a 1986 interview, Morrissey speaks of having been reading at home: 'I haven't seen anybody or haven't been out of the house in five days. The doorbell hasn't rung, either'.[50] Of course, this regime did not extend to the rest of the band – though when Marr asked Andy Rourke to join he stressed the need to be 'totally clean', as 'part of our manifesto'.[51] Even leaving aside Rourke's heroin addiction and the excesses of The Smiths' 1986 US tour, it is clear that much of the music was recorded on dazed late nights of alcohol and cannabis.[52] But this was not the significant image of the band at the time.[53]

This aspect of Morrissey's programme might be gathered in a word: puritanism. It extends into more perverse areas. If sex was countered with chastity, rude health was met with illness. 'These Things Take Time', 'What Difference Does It Make?' and 'Still Ill' all repeat this trope. The early songs also centre on another refusal, which exemplifies the idiosyncrasy of this mode of dissidence. 'No I've never had a job, because I've never wanted one'; 'I was looking for a job and then I found a job / And heaven knows I'm miserable now'; 'And if you must go to work tomorrow / Well, if I were you I wouldn't bother': the hostility to work, in Reynolds' analysis, matched the refusal of modern leisure. Actually, the two refusals are in some tension. The rejection of 'southern' hedonism would seem to imply solidarity with a 'northern' proletarian spirit. But Morrissey goes out of his way not to endorse the value of work itself – this at a time of mass unemployment, de-industrialisation and finally, concurrent with the release of all three songs quoted above, the 'Great Strike for Jobs'. 'Jobs reduce people to absolute stupidity', he declared in 1983; 'There's something so positive about unemployment'.[54] Clearly, the rejection of work is not a Thatcherite mockery of the industrial past. On the contrary, for many it was a rallying cry not to work for her new England, which was becoming 'simply taking and not giving'. But it cannot be marshalled under the banner of labour either. The contemporary puritan blithely jettisons one of the great historic elements of Puritanism – the work ethic – in the name of neither capital nor labour but of his own wilfulness.

Sex, drugs, health, work: in an extravagantly sustained gesture, The Smiths seemed to reject them all. It is as though Morrissey was a hunger-striker, refusing all sustenance until the arrival of the 'better world', the 'next world' of love, peace and harmony. In the present world, happiness itself was tainted. Hence the endless conjuring of malcontents ('Unloveable', 'The Boy With The Thorn In His Side') whose pleasures were furtive and perverse (haunting cemeteries, 'spending warm summer days indoors'). More orthodox recreations were suspect, and sometimes denounced. The miserable club in 'How Soon Is Now?' reaps the whirlwind in 'Panic'. That brief single carries much of The Smiths' strangeness. Compared to other songs, it is an incendiary provocation. Its national panorama seemed to extend the fantasia of 'The Queen Is Dead', released a month earlier. But it is notoriously a song at war with the present, appalled by the state of pop. It evades sheer killjoy status by its own contribution to the musical battle: its implicit status as the record the DJ *ought* to play. As Reynolds shrewdly saw, the goal of The Smiths and their indie kin was not anti-pop but perfect pop; not the rejection of happiness but the pursuit of a higher happiness, indecipherable as such to the outsider, the world that wouldn't listen.[55]

Ambitious outsiders

The puritanical, celibate malingerer was a strange counter-cultural hero – though actually a conveniently easy one for youth to emulate, compared with The Rolling Stones. The reactionary establishment would receive his broadsides; the England of wine bars and share options would be affronted by his whole persona, which could stand for virtues that were being hastily forgotten. But there is surely a significant irony here. To stand so thoroughly counter to Thatcher, did Morrissey not have to resemble her? The account so far suggests a chess game between the two, in which old and new ideological elements are advanced and blocked. The reactionary (authoritarianism, the monarchy) is met with the progressive (irreverence, republicanism); the modern (Americanisation, hedonism) is countered with the residual (England, puritanism). That puts a complex, ongoing encounter very schematically. But it can be put still more simply: the *radical conservatism* sweeping Britain coincides with the band's *conservative radicalism*.

The stand-off seems curiously intimate. One reason for this, perhaps, can be found in Raphael Samuel's account:

> Morrissey's traditionalism allowed him to act as an innovator ... while yet sounding as though he were a voice from the past ... The watchwords may have been conservative, but they were used for subversive ends, to destabilize established authority; to mobilize resentment against the status quo; to give historical precedent to what was essentially a new turn. He could thus appear simultaneously as a fierce iconoclast and a dedicated restorationist, an avatar of the future, pointing the way forward, and a voice from the past, calling on the British people to return to its traditional ways.[56]

The pronouns, of course, have been changed: this is really a description of Thatcher. The resemblance can surely flatter neither. But the parallels tempt. Both drew on their backgrounds in England's regions to articulate their creeds. Both arrived in the centre of public attention with a messianic sense of purpose, determined to scourge established institutions. Both were provincial puritans, possessed of a zeal and self-belief that could reach absurd heights and inspire fanaticism in others. Their clarity of purpose and image lent themselves to caricature, which was one sign of their success. Both were defining figures of the 1980s, who by the turn of the century had diminished in the eyes of all but a hard core of supporters – yet who had left an often unacknowledged influence everywhere.

The analysis is worryingly plausible. But it underestimates a major difference of temperament. Thatcher is notoriously, almost inhumanly devoid of humour. Morrissey is among the wittiest stars pop has produced. While at different times his pronouncements have been strident, passionate or melancholic, they have most consistently been dry, wry, skewed by an ironic spirit that cannot take them entirely seriously. That difference is telling. Thatcher was politically iconoclastic; but, culturally and personally, she was deeply orthodox and unimaginative. That orthodoxy informs her view of the past, which in turn animated her politics. Morrissey's own relation to history was more productively perverse.

What tradition means

Thatcherism, we have seen, offers a Scylla and Charybdis of cultural tendencies: tradition and modernisation. Andrew Gibson reminds us that the route between Scylla and Charybdis involves not sailing straight down the middle, but cleaving more closely to the former than the latter.[57] Morrissey, indeed, does not balance his position between past and present. Such moderation is alien to his spirit. He fearfully recoils from Thatcher's Britain, and seeks refuge in the past. The move surely risks falling into conservatism. But his peculiar negotiation with the past produces something stranger. How?

Morrissey's fascination with the past might seem to involve a vaguely

defined 'Englishness'. Thus conceived, it seems a short hop to Tory lamenta-
tion. But his sense of history was more compelling than that. It was specific
and eclectic: a strange patching together of images and phrases, akin to
(and embodied in) his scrapbook compilation of The Smiths' record sleeves.
Fundamental, of course, was the idea of a vanishing north. The pictures of
Viv Nicholson and Pat Phoenix; the Salford photo-shoots; the references to
kitchen-sink dramas and Angry Young Men; the lyrical settings of the old
grey school, iron bridge, funfair, disused railway line: the catalogue is easily
generated. It all suggests an affection for this milieu, heavily dependent on its
residual, already archaic character.

The position is already complex. It is deeply retrospective, but avoids
simple conservatism – in three ways. For one thing, what is cherished is not
what Patrick Wright christened the 'deep England' of heritage – largely rural,
southern and picturesque. It is urban, northern and, by conventional standards, ugly. If anything, it is the fortresses of Labourism, not the palaces of the
establishment, that are revered. Meanwhile, nostalgia is undercut. The past is
memorialised, but with an insistence on its real hardships. Notoriously, the
world of the songs is often unhappy: squalid and impoverished ('Miserable
Lie', 'Jeane'), or violent (*Meat is Murder*). 'Them was rotten days', the run-off
slogan of *The Queen Is Dead*, is hardly nostalgic.[58] It warns against misplaced
sentimentality. Morrissey's stance is thus consciously ambivalent, open about
its own faultlines. In 1986, he explained it almost programmatically: 'I'm torn
between the ties of my roots, which are very binding, and a hatred, because
I've spent so many unhappy years here'.[59]

But that scratched slogan points to a third feature: the layered intertextuality of Morrissey's heritage. It is quoted from the film of *Saturday Night and
Sunday Morning*: recontextualised from an adaptation of a representation.
The source itself is complex. Alan Sillitoe's novel is not simply a portrait of
a lost north. It is a controversial depiction of social change. The hero Arthur
Seaton is a rebel against established mores. He scorns his job, performing
it only to fund his hedonism. The community depicted in the novel is ultimately gravitating towards the 'ugly new houses' of the estate, and the new
technology of television. The text thus prefigures the turbulence and anger
of the 1980s as much as it offers a stable past to return to. In a different
way, this is also true of the most important source of all. Shelagh Delaney
made it on to more Smiths sleeves than (almost) anyone else,[60] and no text
exerted more influence on Morrissey's writing than *A Taste of Honey*. The
play falls in with the themes above. Its picture of Salford makes *Coronation
Street* seem genteel. The first stage direction specifies 'a comfortless flat'.
Helen sarcastically points out that 'there's a lovely view of the gasworks, we
share a bathroom with the community and this wallpaper's contemporary'.
The 'ghastly district' offers 'Tenements, cemetery, slaughterhouse'. The river,

naturally, is 'the colour of lead'.[61] The 1950s, it appears, are not clean and orderly, but dirty and chaotic.

That implicit assertion is important. Insofar as Delaney informs most of Morrissey's early work, it is insistent. But the play's interest goes beyond this. It stages deeply unorthodox lives. The details bear recalling. Helen is a mother who looks 'a sort of well-preserved sixty' and behaves like a wilful teen, and spontaneously marries a one-eyed alcoholic car salesman. And she is the voice of relative conservatism. Her daughter Jo has a Smithsian flightiness, but also a kind of wisdom beyond her years. To that extent the generations are inverted. Jo dallies with a black sailor, a male nurse with 'beautiful brown eyes and gorgeous curly hair'. Just to undercut the exoticism, he announces that his ancestors are from Cardiff, not Africa. Unmarried, she becomes pregnant. She is not always happy to play the radiant expectant mother, declaring 'I hate babies'. At the news of an imminent mixed-race child, Helen is shocked. The nurse will not be, says Jo: 'she's black too'. Jo is set to be a single mother. She has previously been cohabiting in a kind of surrogate marriage with a (tacitly, uncertainly) gay art student whom she considers 'just like a big sister' and would 'make someone a wonderful wife'. 'I can't stand people who laugh at other people', he protests.[62]

Thus described, it sounds like a play from the 1980s; perhaps a spin-off from *Brookside*,[63] with at least a cameo from Morrissey. But what it actually represented, when refunctioned by him, was more radical than that. It was a discovery of perversity, deviance and strangeness in the 1950s. For the New Right, the counter-culture had destroyed British norms. In this context, the message of *A Taste of Honey* was: *we have never been normal*. Rather than pit a contemporary deviance against an old normativity, Morrissey had found normativity absent from the beginning. Tracing his descent from 'some old queen or other' is an analogous gesture. So is his celebration of Oscar Wilde. But that would bear a chapter of its own, as would Morrissey's other icons. What is worth emphasising about them here is their incongruity. Wilde, Warhol, Dean, Capote, Presley: some have their own connections (not least, in several cases, their sexuality). But their principal connection to Delaney and Pat Phoenix is simply . . . Morrissey. One might imagine that his northern favourites were simply natural extensions of his own upbringing. What the other icons help to emphasise is the bold creativity of his canon. It was flagrantly, in Raymond Williams' phrase, a selective tradition.[64] Familiarity has made it too easy to forget that. The incongruity is even stronger if we factor in Marr's music, and find Elizabeth Smart and Roger McGuinn, Victoria Wood and Keith Richards, suddenly inhabiting the same imaginative world. The Smiths' cultural portfolio can be granted its own political values, which themselves protested against Thatcherism: a defence of the beleaguered north; a celebration of sexual dissidence. But this recasting of history is most inspiring in its sheer eccentricity. Morrissey's primary concern was not to craft a systematic critique of modern Conservatism. But his private obsessions had a way of becoming public, broadcast as unsettling cultural signals.

Life is very long

Reynolds repeatedly compared The Smiths to The Rolling Stones, inverted for 'contracted and beleaguered times'.[65] But their relation to what Harris terms the 1980s 'counterculture' also recalls Dylan's to that of the 1960s, or even James Joyce's oblique contribution to the Irish revolution. They could be downright agitational, naming names and fantasising violence. But they were ultimately fellow travellers rather than footsoldiers. A considerable ego would not be swallowed by political imperatives. Instead it issued in a richness beyond the reach of its contemporaries, but vitally formed by the political conditions they were addressing. When the era's more straightforward representatives had dwindled to the status of amiable curiosities, what once appeared eccentric would be reckoned among the truest guides to its time.

In 1986, Morrissey was asked what he hoped for The Smiths' records. 'It would be very nice', he admitted, 'if, in 20 years' time, people referred to them as, not a turning point in their lives, but a song that reminds them of a certain period. Whether it be good or bad, I don't mind'.[66] He probably meant 'period' in personal, private terms. The Smiths have been cherished, let alone referred to, in that capacity. But one reason they have endured, far better than he here dared hope, is their engagement with the period in its wider, public sense. At an intimidating time, they were strangely fearless, and fearlessly strange. And the courage they promoted was salutary in its unorthodoxy: it takes guts to be gentle and kind.

Notes

1 F. O'Hara, *Selected Poems*, ed. D. Allen (Harmondsworth: Penguin, 1994), p. 96.

2 S. Delaney, *A Taste of Honey* (London: Methuen, 1982), p. 71.

3 Johnny Marr interview in Q: *The Smiths and Morrissey Special Edition* (May 2004), p. 23.

4 I. Pye, 'A Hard Day's Misery', *Melody Maker*, 3 November 1984, p. 31.

5 Johnny Marr interview, May 1987, on *The Smiths: The Interview*, CD (Music Collection International, 1998), c.03:00.

6 I. Jack, *Before the Oil Ran Out: Britain in the Brutal Years* (London: Vintage, 1997, revised edition), p. xv.

7 Marr, *The Smiths: The Interview*, c.03:00.

8 Quoted in S. Lowe, 'England Made Me', Q: *The Smiths and Morrissey Special Edition*, p. 99.

9   S. Hall, 'The Great Moving Right Show', *Marxism Today* (January 1979), p. 16.

10 D. Edgar, 'Bitter Harvest', in J. Curran (ed.), *Future of the Left* (Cambridge: Polity Press and New Socialist, 1984), pp. 39–40.

11 S. Hall, The *Hard Road to Renewal: Thatcherism and the Crisis of the Left* (London: Verso, 1988), pp. 144–5.

12 P. Wright, *On Living in an Old Country: The National Past in Contemporary Britain* (London: Verso, 1985), p. 47.

13 Quoted in Edgar, 'Bitter Harvest', p. 51.

14 M. Ventura, 'The *Big Chill* Factor', in H. Kureishi and J. Savage (eds), *The Faber Book of Pop* (London: Faber, 1995), p. 607.

15 Quoted in A. Sinfield, *Literature, Politics and Culture in Postwar Britain* (Oxford: Blackwell, 1989), p. 296.

16 J. Henke, 'Oscar! Oscar! Great Britain goes Wilde for the "fourth-gender" Smiths', *Rolling Stone*, 7 June 1984, p. 45.

17 See Hall, *Hard Road*, p. 237.

18 A. Collins, *Billy Bragg: Still Suitable for Miners* (London: Virgin, 2002, second edition), p. 162.

19 S. Goddard, *The Smiths: Songs That Saved Your Life* (London: Reynolds & Hearn, 2004, revised and expanded edition), p. 190.

20 See J. Harris, *The Last Party: Britpop, Blair and the Demise of English Rock* (London: Fourth Estate, 2003), pp. 3–10.

21 S. Garfield, 'This Charming Man', in Kureishi and Savage (eds), *Faber Book of Pop*, pp. 599–600.

22 Ibid., p. 600.

23 P. Morley, 'The Last Temptation of Morrissey', *Uncut* (May 2006), p. 60.

24 See Hall, *Hard Road*, pp. 251–8, and D. Hebdige, *Hiding in the Light: On Images and Things* (London: Routledge / Comedia, 1988), pp. 216–23.

25 See M. Marqusee, *Chimes of Freedom: The Politics of Bob Dylan's Art* (New York: The New Press, 2003), pp. 69–72.

26 S. Reynolds, *Blissed Out: The Raptures of Rock* (London: Serpent's Tail, 1990), p. 19.

27 *Q: The Smiths and Morrissey Special Edition*, p. 122.

28 Quoted in Pye, 'A Hard Day's Misery', p. 31. The bomb in question was detonated by the Irish Republican Army at the hotel where Margaret Thatcher and senior Conservatives were staying during their party conference in October 1984.

29 Reynolds, *Blissed Out*, p. 19.

30 J. Black, 'Recording *The Queen Is Dead*', *Q: The Smiths and Morrissey Special Edition*, p. 48.

31 For the lyric and a celebration of it, see J. Savage, *England's Dreaming: Sex Pistols and Punk Rock* (London: Faber and Faber, 1991), pp. 348, 351–8.

32 A. Petridis, 'The Regina Monologues', *Q: The Smiths and Morrissey Special Edition*, p. 50.

33 In this, the protagonist echoes his apparent real-world inspiration. When Michael

Fagan broke into Buckingham Palace in July 1982 and found his way to the Queen's bedroom, he did no more than talk to the monarch. Margaret Thatcher pronounced herself 'shocked and upset', elaborating: 'Every woman in this country was upset because we all thought, oh lord, what would happen to me?' (J. Campbell, *Margaret Thatcher, Volume Two: The Iron Lady* (London: Jonathan Cape, 2003), p. 161).

34 Morrissey's vocal is distorted on this line, leaving its content somewhat ambiguous. But Simon Reynolds heard the line this way in the 1980s: see his *Melody Maker* booklet on The Smiths, 23 September 1989.

35 Morley, 'Last Temptation', p. 66.

36 Marr, *The Smiths: The Interview*, c.48:00.

37 Henke, 'Oscar! Oscar!', p. 45.

38 That was the epithet Morrissey had claimed in 1984, according to *Rolling Stone*: see Henke, 'Oscar! Oscar!', and J. Rogan, *Morrissey and Marr: The Severed Alliance* (London: Omnibus, 1992), pp. 198–9. Another essay might begin from the gender contrast signalled here. Meanwhile see S. Reynolds and J. Press, *The Sex Revolts: Gender, Rebellion and Rock'n'Roll* (London: Serpent's Tail, 1995), pp. 48–9.

39 Morrissey drew it from Hubert Selby's *Last Exit to Brooklyn*: see Goddard, *The Smiths*, p. 177.

40 The Social Democratic Party (SDP) was founded in 1981 by senior political figures disaffected with the leftward turn of the Labour Party. The party was intended to work a middle way between the perceived extremes of Labour and the Tories. This aversion to radicalism ensured that in the 1980s the term 'SDP' became a sort of shorthand for a genteel political centrism. Although the party topped opinion polls for a while, they proved unable to fuflfil their ambition to 'break the mould' of British politics and by 1988 had merged with the Liberal Party to form the Liberal Democrats. See B. Pimlott, 'Two Queens: Thatcherism and the Monarchy', in S. Pugliese (ed.), *The Political Legacy of Margaret Thatcher* (London: Politico's, 2003), pp. 312–22; for the SDP quotation, Campbell, *Iron Lady*, p. 467. The *Sunday Times'* supposed scoop about the Queen's distaste for Thatcher ran in July 1986, a month after the belated release of *The Queen Is Dead*: the point is not that Morrissey drew on these particular revelations, but that a perception of the personal and political tensions between the two women persisted through Thatcher's tenure.

41 Pimlott, 'Two Queens', p. 319.

42 P. York and C. Jennings, *Peter York's Eighties* (London: BBC, 1995), p. 108.

43 F. Mort, *Cultures of Consumption: Masculinities and Social Space in Late Twentieth-Century Britain* (London: Routledge, 1996), pp. 3–4.

44 John Campbell notes that many successful entrepreneurs, like Richard Branson and Anita Roddick, were 'children of the 1960s and 1970s' who had turned their counter-cultural enthusiasms into Lawson-era fortunes: see *Iron Lady*, p. 245, and chapter 6, *passim*, on the 'popular capitalism' of the age.

45 York and Jennings, *Eighties*, p. 62.

46 Reynolds, *Blissed Out*, p. 19.

47 S. Reynolds, 'Against Health and Efficiency: Independent Music in the 1980s', in A. McRobbie (ed.), *Zoot Suits and Second-Hand Dresses* (Basingstoke: Macmillan, 1989), pp. 245, 252–3.

48 L. Moore, *Like Life* (New York: Plume, 1988), p. 20.

49 Black, 'Recording *The Queen Is Dead*', *Q: The Smiths and Morrissey Special Edition*, p. 47.

50 M. Aston, 'The Lost Interview', *Q: The Smiths and Morrissey Special Edition*, p. 53. This interview was conducted in November 1986.

51 Marr, *The Smiths: The Interview*, c.34:00.

52 See for instance Goddard, *The Smiths*, pp. 108, 227.

53 Stephen Duffy, once of Duran Duran, would retrospectively reflect on his former band's identification with Thatcherism in the public mind: 'Duran Duran were decadent in public, and had decadence twinned with the Thatcher era. I'm sure Johnny Marr was just as decadent but nobody wrote about him.' Quoted in S. Malins, *Duran Duran: Notorious – The Unauthorised Biography* (London: Sevenoaks, 2005), p. 95.

54 Goddard, *The Smiths*, p. 77.

55 Reynolds, 'Against Health and Efficiency', p. 248.

56 R. Samuel, *Island Stories: Unravelling Britain – Theatres of Memory, Volume II* (London: Verso, 1998), p. 343.

57 A. Gibson, *Joyce's Revenge: History, Politics and Aesthetics in 'Ulysses'* (Oxford: Oxford University Press, 2002), pp. 64–5.

58 The slogan was shown as a piece of graffiti during the 1970s episode of Andrew Marr's *History of Modern Britain* in early summer 2007. A subsequent episode on the Thatcher revolution used 'How Soon Is Now?' as the soundtrack to its portrayal of the attendant social division and conflict: a fairly typical tactic in post-millennial televisual retrospectives of the 1980s, but a clear enough signal of the meaning that The Smiths had by now acquired in cultural history.

59 Quoted in Lowe, 'England Made Me', p. 97.

60 Except for Viv Nicholson, who appeared on three – but apart from the sleeve of 'Heaven Knows I'm Miserable Now', Nicholson's other two appearances were special cases: the German (and UK promotional) release of 'Barbarism Begins At Home', and a withdrawn CD single of 'The Headmaster Ritual'. Delaney's own appearances – 'Girlfriend In A Coma', *Louder Than Bombs* – were belated; by the time they were released in 1987, Morrissey's affection for her was rather old news.

61 Delaney, *A Taste of Honey*, pp. 7, 17, 54.

62 Ibid., pp. 29, 27, 25, 55, 86, 55, 48. The film's plot veered away somewhat from the play's.

63 When the independent British television station Channel 4 was launched in 1982, *Brookside* was one of its flagship programmes. While ostensibly a fairly

conventional soap opera, the Liverpool-based show differed from its contemporaries with its adoption of the local vernacular and its treatment of themes that were often deemed controversial in their day. As a consequence, *Brookside* might be placed in the social realist tradition of the kitchen sink dramas so beloved of Morrissey. The final episode of the show was aired in 2003.

64 R. Williams, *The Long Revolution* (London: Chatto & Windus, 1961), pp. 66–9.

65 Reynolds, *Blissed Out*, p. 29.

66 Aston, 'The Lost Interview', p. 55.

3

'Irish blood, English heart': Ambivalence, unease and The Smiths

Sean Campbell

The dominant forms of popular music in most contemporary societies have emerged, notes Simon Frith, 'at the social margins – among the poor, the migrant, the rootless'.[1] This has certainly been the case in Britain, where, as one high-profile music magazine put it, 'a potent shebeen of home-grown music' has been ensured only by 'a multi-ethnic mix' in which 'the immigrant Irish have proved most crucial'.[2] The vital role played by second-generation Irish musicians in English popular music is evinced through figures such as John Lydon, Kevin Rowland, Boy George, Noel and Liam Gallagher and The Smiths. Most writing on these figures has, however, shown scant concern for this issue, with critics stressing the musicians' English nationality, whilst making little or no reference to their (second-generation) Irish ethnicity.[3]

In this context, The Smiths have been seen as an archetype of Englishness in rock. Michael Bracewell, for instance, views The Smiths as 'organically English', deeming Morrissey the 'pop cultural embodiment' of 'English sensibility.'[4] Mark Sinker, meanwhile, has claimed that The Smiths 'sang for or of England ... with a music that could only come from the urban heart of England'.[5] In a similar vein, the *New Musical Express* (*NME*) observed, in the band's oeuvre, 'avowedly Anglo-Saxon' qualities, arguing that they aspired to a 'myth of English purity'.[6]

Such readings did not go unnoticed by The Smiths themselves. 'It was always odd', explained Morrissey of The Smiths' reception, 'when I was described as being "extremely English" because other people would tell me that I looked Irish, I sounded Irish and had other tell-tale signs.'[7] It is certainly true that observers would occasionally note, in Morrissey's voice, an 'Anglo-Irish ancestry', and detect a 'slightly Irish manner', and the singer and Johnny Marr would invoke their Irish ethnicity in interviews and through other performative acts, not least wearing Claddagh rings (a popular symbol of Irish ethnicity) in press photographs, and inscribing the word 'Eire' in the run-off groove of vinyl LPs.[8] Such gestures were underlined by the band's extensive

Irish concert tours, which took in not only the established circuit of venues in Dublin, Cork, Limerick and Galway (itself quite unusual for major acts of the period, who typically only visited the capital city), but also smaller towns such as Waterford, Dundalk and Letterkenny.[9] The band's Irish shows often began with a performance of 'Please, Please, Please, Let Me Get What I Want' (1984), a track that was originally called 'The Irish Waltz', and which critics felt was redolent of an 'Irish folk song', with its 'emphatically Irish air'.[10] Meanwhile, Morrissey would alter certain song lyrics, such as the opening lines of 'Still Ill' (1984), to sing '*Ireland* is mine', instead of the customary 'England'.[11]

The group would, though, eschew Irish sounds and styles in their eclectic venture into 'independent' rock (which drew on pop and funk as well as folk and country music).[12] Moreover, their work would often evoke an expressly English milieu, via the citation of local places in song words, interviews and record sleeves (as well as the regional accent of much of Morrissey's singing).[13] The band's Irish provenance was, then, less pronounced than that of their second-generation Irish contemporaries such as Shane MacGowan of The Pogues (whose post-punk reconfiguration of Irish folk music articulated a peculiarly London-Irish experience) or Kevin Rowland of Dexys Midnight Runners (who sought to fuse Irish music with soul).[14] In stark contrast to such exteriorised conceptions of ethnicity, The Smiths would arguably dramatise (in oblique and abstracted ways) certain second-generation sentiments, not least via the trope of ambivalence in their address to both origins and 'home'. With such issues in mind, this chapter explores The Smiths as a form of second-generation Irish music-making, viewing their work as an 'Irish-English' musical 'route'.[15]

Accounts of the second-generation Irish in England detail the ambivalence that this generation has felt towards both the host culture and the ethnic 'home'. Rather than assuming a clear-cut stance on either side of an Irish/English binary, then, many second-generation people have expressed degrees of 'in-between-ness' or uncertainty.[16] Several Irish-English creative figures have also situated themselves in this way. The London-Irish playwright Martin McDonagh, for instance, has explained that he 'always felt somewhere kind of in-between [Irish and English]'.

> I felt half-and-half and neither, which is good … I'm happy having a foot in both camps. I'm not into any kind of definition, any kind of -ism, politically, socially, religiously, all that stuff. It's not that I don't think about those things, but I've come to a place where the ambiguities are more interesting than choosing a strict path and following it.[17]

Significantly, both Morrissey and Marr have expressed similar views[18] and – with this in mind – it's striking that the work of The Smiths, rather than seeking to resolve ambivalence through asserting an excessive ethnicity (in the manner of, say, The Pogues), or striving to pass as native (which Morrissey briefly did in his solo career)[19] offered instead an evocation of this ambivalence itself, with the group invoking a marked uncertainty towards issues of origins and 'home'.

My account of The Smiths is not based, then, on the assumption that an essential Irishness somehow underpins their work. Certain Irish critics have set out to detect, in The Smiths' work, quintessentially Irish qualities. John Waters, for example, has argued that the band's 'dark introspection, tragic narcissism, ironic world-view and swirling tunefulness fashioned a profound, existential connection with those of us born [in mid-twentieth-century Ireland], a connection which it is impossible to explain in other than mystical terms'.[20] The tacit intention of such critics is to upend the taken-for-granted view that The Smiths were archetypically English with the suggestion that they were, in fact, quintessentially Irish. Such perspectives are, of course, born of essentialist views of national/ethnic identity, a standpoint I hope to dispute by viewing The Smiths as an expressly *second-generation* venture that eschewed the constrictions of both Irish essentialism and English assimilation, and pointed to an often intricate accommodation of Anglo-Irish issues (marked by in-between-ness). Before I present my analysis, however, it is first of all necessary to outline the particular socio-cultural context from which the group emerged.

A (pre) history of The Smiths

Morrissey's parents left Dublin for Manchester in the 1950s, where the singer was raised amongst a large extended Irish family all living on the same street.[21] Morrissey recalls that he 'grew up in a strong Irish community', explaining: 'We were quite happy to ghettoise ourselves as the Irish community in Manchester'. The Irish aspects of this milieu 'steeped', as Morrissey puts it, 'into everything [he] knew growing up'. 'I was very aware of being Irish', he explains, stressing: 'we were quite separate from the . . . kids around us – we were different to them'.[22] This awareness of Irish ethnicity was accentuated by family trips to Ireland (which Morrissey found 'immensely attractive'), as well as by his subjection to anti-Irish prejudice, not least being addressed as 'Paddy' at a time when it served as a 'malevolent slur'.[23] In this context, it was perhaps unsurprising that Morrissey felt a distinct sense of un-belonging in 1970s Manchester: 'with so much Irishness around us', he says, he 'never really felt' Mancunian.[24] As a consequence, the experience of growing up second-generation Irish was, for Morrissey, 'confusing'.[25]

The parents of Marr (born Maher) hailed from Athy, Co. Kildare, and settled – during the early 1960s – amongst a large extended Irish family in Manchester.[26] Marr recalls that he was raised in a 'young Irish community', and was 'surrounded', in his early years, 'by Irish culture', noting that 'it does rub off'.[27] If this dimension of Marr's upbringing was augmented by visits to Ireland, it was also maintained by his experience of anti-Irish prejudice, with the teenager becoming 'accustomed to being branded an "Irish pig" at school and on the terraced streets of his native Ardwick'.[28] 'I had to put up with an awful lot of snide remarks and false media reports about the Irish in England', he recalls, explaining: 'I certainly did feel very different from the rest of my friends'.[29] In common with his future collaborator, then, Marr felt somewhat at odds with the 'host' milieu: 'growing up in an Irish family in Manchester . . . you did feel at a bit of a remove'.[30] In this context, the guitarist would come to view his second-generation Irish peer group as a 'floating generation', suggesting a sort of in-between-ness (a theme that he would later address in his post-Smiths solo work).[31]

Andy Rourke, who attended the same Catholic school as Marr, was raised by an Irish-descended father (whose family came from Cork), after his English mother had left the family home. As Rourke explains: 'we were quite a traditional Irish Catholic family rather than an English one.'[32] Mike Joyce, meanwhile, grew up with a father from Shrule, Co. Galway and a mother from Co. Kildare. He recalls visits to Ireland with his family, as well as the 'solidarity' of the community in which he was raised.[33]

The band's collective Irish upbringing was, for Marr, a major point of group commonality,[34] and played a crucial part, notes Simon Goddard, in The Smiths' intra-group 'chemistry'.[35] 'We had an absolute affinity because of our Irishness', suggests Mike Joyce, who saw this as so intrinsic to the group's dynamic that it did not require expression. 'It was just *there*', the drummer recalls, 'We didn't need to express that'.[36] As Marr explains, however, this second-generation Irish context would serve to inform, in various ways, the band's work and persona.[37]

Songs of ambivalence and unease

As noted above, studies of the second-generation Irish in England have laid stress on the ambivalence that has marked the everyday lives of this generation, highlighting 'the ambivalent status' that 'places them at the meeting point of two cultural, social and political worlds', and explaining that a major source of this condition is 'the job of assimilating conflicting demands on their allegiances to both English and Irish cultures'.[38] This issue of ambivalence has also been evoked in second-generation Irish creative work. In an account of Irish-English literary texts, Arrowsmith notes that ambivalence and uncertainty – as well as instability, indeterminacy and confusion – have imbued this body of work. Indeed, the trope that is most prevalent in second-generation Irish literary expression is what Arrowsmith calls 'the sheer confusion of identity', with a 'disorientating and contradictory relationship to any sense of identity' effecting the 'figuration of . . . confused identity through the indeterminacy or absence of "home"'.[39]

This theme has also been observed in The Smiths. Savage, for instance, suggests that an 'ambivalence towards their roots' is evident in The Smiths, discerning, in their oeuvre, 'an aspirant will to succeed, to move on up and out, to go further than their parents were allowed to go, allied to a fierce pride and anger about their background'.[40] Similarly, Rogan has observed, in The Smiths, 'a peculiar sense of longing . . . which betrayed the ambivalence of first generation immigrant sons caught between present and past'.[41] Such comments provide a useful point of departure from which to assess The Smiths' work, as their address to 'home' and origins was marked by such uncertainty.

The early track 'Back to the Old House' (1983) is illuminating in this regard. This sparingly arranged slow-tempo lament features a plaintive first-person speaker who repeatedly asserts, in the opening section, that he would 'rather not go / back to the old house', before referring, in the high-register bridge, to the 'too many bad memories there'.[42] This refusal of 'home' sits at odds, however, with the song's musical setting: a 'folksy' acoustic guitar arpeggio more commonly linked with a craving for home (or what Moore calls the 'backward glance').[43] The quietly contrapuntal dynamic that emerges between the song words and their musical context is, however, somewhat assuaged in the song's closing verse, when Morrissey emits a notable volte-face, revealing a previously undisclosed longing for 'home': 'I would *love* to go / back to the old house', he sings, 'but I never will'. And if this lyrical gesture – with its acknowledgement of the futility of such yearning – connotes ambivalence rather than closure, this is underlined by Marr's coda, which revisits the track's opening segment, but only to conclude on a (major 7th) chord that conjures melancholy. Moreover, as the song fades out, the guitar player gently hammers on the note (D from C♯) that would at least offer harmonic (in the absence of thematic) closure, in a teasing musical gesture that simply lingers unresolved.

The contrary impulses that were evinced in this formative track would re-emerge elsewhere in The Smiths' canon, not least in songs that deal with journeying and relocation – themes that are, of course, at the hub of migrancy. And while the second-generation Irish are not strictly speaking migrants in the sense that they have not physically moved from one place to another, the 'psychological journey of migration', as Bobby Gilmore has explained with regard to the Irish in England, 'is far longer than the geographical one', and does not simply end with the migrating generation.[44] What this ongoing condition of migrancy has entailed for the second generation, then, is as Gray explains, a certain 'state of being "in-between' – not least 'between here and there' – as well as 'the experience of living in [one] place' with strong 'memories of somewhere else'.[45]

This sense of spatial in-between-ness is evoked in songs such as 'Is It Really So Strange?' (1987), which offers a first-person account of a ceaseless geographical journey between an intended destination and an original point of departure. The opening lines of each verse thus signal the direction in which the subject is heading. As the song unfolds, however, the locales of 'here' and 'there' become conflated, until the speaker (who is openly 'confused') repudiates, in the final bars, the possibility of returning to any home-like place (stressing that he can 'never, never go back home again'). The only stable conclusion that the song's subject is able to reach on this confusing journey, then, is the fact that 'home' is a place that cannot be restored.

If the seriousness of this coda is allayed by the song's upbeat tone (engendered by the singer's jovial asides and Marr's jaunty guitar-slides), it is more strikingly assuaged by the track's closure on (what is known as) its 'home triad' – the 'chord on the key-note of a song' – in this case a ringing 'open' major in E.[46] As Whiteley points out, such chords have 'strong connotations of home-centredness',[47] and thus render the song's refusal of 'home' – in the final verse – somewhat incongruous.

A similar impasse emerges in 'London' (1987). In this song, Marr's repetitious guitar riff (on a single, low-register note) works, with Joyce's percussive shuffle, to conjure the train journey narrated by Morrissey's speaker.[48] The anxious uncertainty of the song's home-leaving addressee is invoked in the repeated lyrical hook ('Do you think you've made / the right decision this time?') which signals the conclusion of each of the verses as well as the lyric's finale. This theme of indecision is augmented, moreover, by Morrissey's repeated groans (and the guitar's staccato stuttering). However, it is also counterpoised by the exhilaration of the band's fast pace (conjuring the thrills of 'going away'), an aspect underscored by the singer's emphasis on the 'jealousy in the eyes' of the 'ones who had to stay behind' – a 'grieving' family unit whose cloying domesticity is matched by the compressed and flattened tenor of Marr's unusually 'dry' guitar.

The tension invoked by the song's contrary impulses in the end effects only indeterminacy, though, as the track concludes with a ceaseless (and frustratingly circular) cycle of minor chords that refuses (in the absence of any semantic closure) to offer harmonic resolution. The song in this way is unable to reconcile its own contradictory urges, and is consequently left to fade out. Thus, if 'the musical scale . . . with its intervals, progressions and modulations' is capable, as Gerry Smyth claims, 'of creating impressions of home [and] travel',[49] then songs such as 'London' evince an aversion to the key which serves as their 'home', rendering the speaker's journey always unfinished or incomplete. The ambivalence that imbues such songs – which convey a sense of living between different spaces, with no satisfactory conclusion – suggests that there was, for The Smiths' protagonist, simply no *place* like home.

This ambivalence was, moreover, an aspect of The Smiths' oeuvre about which Marr was highly conscious. He confirms the songs' sense of ambivalence, and suggests that this was born, at least for him, of certain aspects of his early migrant milieu, which he feels has informed his musical character.[50] In this context, Marr points to the mixture of vibrancy and melancholia that marked the musical culture in which he was raised, and notes a dynamic tension that he felt between, on the one hand, an excitement about being in England and the sense of adventure that this entailed whilst, on the other, feeling a certain yearning for an (absent) Ireland that was evoked in innumerable ways in his early migrant milieu.[51] Thus, while he was taught by his parents to be 'very pro-Manchester' and to 'appreciate the opportunities we were being given in Manchester', he was at the same time immersed in Irish culture, not least via the iconography of his parents' home, which was decorated with harps, shamrocks and Irish flags, as well as other 'strong Irish Catholic symbols'.[52] Marr's investment in Manchester was offset, then, by an 'appreciation of Irish culture, music and iconography',[53] which left him with (what he calls a 'schizophrenia',[54] a term that has been used by second-generation Irish people to denote ambivalence or duality.[55] Marr suggests that this was a quality that he shared with Morrissey. Referring to the sense of excitement that, he says, informed The Smiths' work, Marr explains that,

> balanced with this [excitement] was this sensibility that has always been tuned to melancholia – which wasn't that difficult because me and Morrissey had that disposition in us. It was a strange thing: we were ecstatic about what was happening to us and we had the melancholy.[56]

Reflecting on this point, Marr suggests that this was 'an Irish thing', 'a weird schizophrenic disposition' (by which he appears to mean ambivalence), noting that: 'the two of us were harnessing that melancholy and putting it into our music'.[57]

Notwithstanding such comments, it is clear that the songs that have been addressed thus far have invoked the theme of ambivalence in fairly abstract ways, evading any specific Irish context in which this might be staged. However, as Arrowsmith has explained, engagements with Irishness in second-generation creative work often bear the traces of other discourses (such as region and class), and thus if some of The Smiths' songs cited above are ostensibly concerned with, say, the absence of a former physical home, or travel between a north–south English divide, the sentiments engaged in such songs can nevertheless serve as an index of the band's broader stance on issues of origins and 'home' (whether in terms of Irishness or, for instance, Northernness).[58] Moreover, at key points in The Smiths' career, Morrissey made it clear that his lyrical ideas had been shaped by the marginality he had experienced as a second-generation Irish youth.[59] The opening lines of 'Never Had No One Ever' ('When you walk without ease / On these / streets where you were raised') are striking in this regard.[60]

Prompted by the kit's awkward preface (and curiously languid pace), Morrissey's vocal displays 'the kind of "blue" or "dirty" notes' that he otherwise 'studiously avoids'.[61] If this connotes anxiety, the lyrical theme of unease is compounded by Marr's cyclical sequence of minor seventh chords, set in taut 12/8 time.[62] The guitarist recalls that this music was composed whilst reflecting on his migrant Irish milieu,[63] and Morrissey's words emerged, the singer has said, from a certain second-generation experience. 'It was the frustration I felt at the age of 20', he explained, 'when I still didn't feel easy walking around the streets on which I'd been born, where all my family had lived – they're originally from Ireland but had been here since the Fifties.' Expounding on this point, the singer confessed: 'It was a constant confusion to me why I never really felt "This is my patch. This is my home. I know these people. I can do what I like, because this is mine." It never was. I could never walk easily.'[64]

Morrissey's framing of his song lyrics in terms of this particular experience corresponds with remarks made by other Irish-English creative figures, such as Brian Keaney, a second-generation writer who was raised in England at the same time as the singer. Keaney explained in 1985 – the year in which The Smiths composed 'Never Had No One Ever' – that his semi-autobiographical short stories were born of a wish to address 'what it feels like to be growing up slightly at odds with your surroundings . . . as a boy I felt not entirely *at ease* with either my Irish parents or my English companions. I think this is something that a lot of children of immigrants feel.'[65]

This theme of unease – a crucial trope, for Eamonn Hughes, of Irish cultural expression in England – arguably imbued The Smiths' work, and perhaps explains, to some degree, the view of the group as 'miserabilist'.[66] Alongside the band's exploration of unease, though, was an ongoing impulse in their oeuvre to mock the very notion of origins, hence the speaker's reference – in 'Stretch Out And Wait' (1985) – to the 'Eskimo blood' in his veins, or the protagonist's discovery, in 'The Queen Is Dead' (1986), that he's the '18th pale descendant' of 'some old queen or other'.[67] This irreverent engagement with ancestry surfaced elsewhere as an obfuscation of personal provenance, hence the narrator's famous pronouncement, at the start of 'How Soon Is Now?' (1984), that he is the 'son' and the 'heir' of 'nothing in particular'.[68] Such gestures certainly resonated with the singer's public comments at this time. During a 1985 interview, for instance, Morrissey dealt with questions about his 'Celtic blood' with conspicuous reticence (and not a little humour). 'No, no, no', he avowed, 'I've got no blood anymore', concluding: 'no blood . . . all drained'.[69]

Such pronouncements were perhaps symptomatic of what Hubbs calls the singer's 'complex and elusive subjectivity'.[70] As Hubbs explains, Morrissey's persona, in this regard, bore a striking resemblance to that of Oscar Wilde,[71] a figure with whom the singer had identified since his adolescence. He had first been introduced to Wilde by his Dublin-born mother ('She instilled Oscar Wilde into me', he later explained), and the Irish writer would go on to suffuse The Smiths' oeuvre, via references in interviews, song lyrics, photographs, video clips and run-off groove inscriptions.[72]

The singer's most noted homage to Wilde – in The Smiths' song 'Cemetry [sic] Gates' (1986)[73] – perhaps provides a clue to his position on Irish/English affairs. In the first verse of the song, the speaker makes overt his affiliation with the author: 'Keats and Yeats are on your side', he relates to an addressee, 'While Wilde is on mine'. This gesture is repeated, moreover, in the closing moments of the song, when Morrissey's speaker concludes: 'Keats and Yeats are on your side / *but you lose* / because Wilde is on mine', instancing a closure underscored by Marr's return, in the coda, to the song's buoyant intro. In this song, then, the singer eschews authors associated with England (Keats) and Ireland (Yeats), and affiliates himself instead with a figure (Wilde) who has occupied ambiguous terrain between these national frames.[74] (And if Wilde's sexuality also played a part in this identification, then Morrissey's view of his own orientation as 'in the middle somewhere, straddling', might serve to parallel his stance on Irish-English affairs.[75])

Such sentiments were underlined by the band's public comments on social boundaries. Thus, while Morrissey informed journalists of the group's Irish provenance, he at the same time made clear his desire 'to produce music that transcends boundaries', asserting that 'the main blemish' on English life was 'the absolute segregation which seems to appear on every level, with every-thing and everybody'.[76] These are striking remarks from someone raised in an immigrant enclave, for rather than announcing ethnic difference, or express-ing an assimilative wish, such signals conveyed a rejection of the notion of boundaries *per se*.

In this respect, The Smiths' address to 'outsiderness' went beyond the tropes of ambivalence and unease, pointing to a more enabling conception of marginality. As John McLeod has explained, many immigrant-descended figures have elected to make 'a virtue from necessity' by asserting that 'the displaced position' associated with migration 'is an entirely valuable one', with the marginalised figure being in a conceivably 'better position than others to realise that all systems of knowledge, all views of the world, are never totalising, whole or pure, but incomplete, muddled and hybrid'. Thus, while the experience of displacement 'may well evoke the pain' and 'loss' of 'not being firmly rooted in a secure place', it can also provide 'a world of immense possibility with the realisation that new knowledges and ways of seeing can be constructed'.[77]

This migrant perspective has also been pursued by many second-generation Irish musicians, such as Cait O'Riordan (of The Pogues), who suggests that it is 'a privilege to be an immigrant's kid in a colonial nation' because the experience affords what she calls 'an outsider perspective' that 'makes you look at *both* sides'.[78] In a similar vein, The Smiths would lay claim to the benefits of this marginalised view. 'When you're detached and sealed off', Morrissey explained, 'you have a very clear view of what's going on. You can stand back and you can look and you can assess.'[79] Irish-descended writers such as Hilary Mantel, meanwhile, have explained that their migrant upbringings enabled them to 'realise that there was this thing called "Englishness", but it wasn't necessarily what you possessed. It was located somewhere else.'[80] With such viewpoints in mind, it's worth noting that The Smiths – who didn't hold back from making statements on Irish issues ('I certainly don't think that in England there's any desire, politically, to make life any easier in Belfast', claimed Morrissey[81]) – put aside the politics of Irish particularity for an attack on hegemonic Englishness. This attack was primarily staged, as Joseph Brooker notes in his chapter in this volume, through the band's critique of the British Prime Minister and the royal family.

'England's dreaming'

In the immediate aftermath of Thatcher's accession to power, the rock critic Bill Graham observed that a certain second-generation Irish musician, John Lydon – whom he viewed as 'an outsider' formed by an Irish upbringing – would act against this 'proprietoress [sic] of "English" culture': '*he won't be one of Margaret's pupils*', noted Graham, in a remark that would serve as an apposite index of Morrissey.[82] In interviews, the latter would describe Thatcher's reign as 'one of violence ... oppression and horror', demanding that people 'must *not* lie back and cry about it', before – in effect – calling for her assassination: 'I just pray that there is a Sirhan Sirhan somewhere. It's the only remedy for this country at the moment.'[83] Clearly such remarks were overblown, and one probably ought, as Hubbs suggests, to exercise a certain scepticism when considering the singer's comments (with their 'obvious myth- and money-making potential'[84]). However, it is doubtful that even the most desperate of record-company publicists would have endorsed Morrissey's remarks when an actual attempt was made on Thatcher's life by the IRA at Brighton's Grand Hotel in October 1984. In the immediate aftermath of this bomb attack, which 'came within an ace' of killing the Prime Minister,[85] and took the lives of five people (whilst injuring thirty more),[86] there was widespread shock and anger, as well as public claims – from

Establishment figures – that those responsible were 'as guilty as Guy Fawkes' and should be 'hanged for high treason'.[87]

In this fraught atmosphere, blame for the bomb was quickly (and erroneously) apportioned to second-generation Irish people, with the British press claiming that the bombers were 'English-born volunteers, second and third generations from Irish families living here' whose *apparent Englishness . . .* could have allowed them to visit the Grand Hotel in Brighton, where they planted the bomb, over the year'.[88]

Despite the fact that the attack had been linked to the second-generation Irish, Morrissey was quick to issue his own public response, praising the IRA for being 'accurate in selecting their targets', whilst stressing his 'sorrow' that Thatcher had 'escaped unscathed'.[89] Against the pervasive sense of shock and condemnation, then, Morrissey was 'relatively happy' about the attack.[90] Such comments – which caused serious offence to many British music fans, and were condemned in the Manchester press[91] – were an unlikely publicity scheme for the group at the time, as they were about to perform a series of shows in Northern Ireland. The band's anxiousness about the trip increased when they were handed a copy of the Irish Republican newspaper *An Phoblacht* by an IRA-affiliated individual in Manchester.[92] The paper, whose pages were usually taken up with 'war news', praised Morrissey for his Brighton bomb comments (which it reprinted in full), and laid stress on The Smiths' Irish provenance: 'with names like that who could doubt their antecedents?' The newssheet – not known for its interest in rock – also praised The Smiths' 'anti-establishment' ethos and concern for the 'dispossessed', before offering a ringing endorsement: The Smiths, proclaimed *An Phoblacht*, were 'very good indeed'.[93]

When the band arrived in Northern Ireland, then, they were 'worried', their tour manager explained, 'about more extreme attitudes' because they had – in his words – 'affiliated themselves with the IRA'.[94] Such was the apprehension on the tour that the group had to re-arrange certain plans due to a perceived paramilitary 'threat'. Consequently, when the tour concluded at Belfast's Ulster Hall, there was a degree of 'tension in the air' because of the 'concern with security'.[95]

Despite such difficulties, though, The Smiths continued their assault on Thatcher, naming their third album *Margaret On The Guillotine*, a title they were forced to withdraw before the record's release.[96] And while the grounds for this decision are unclear, one of the group's associates has explained that when a song titled 'Margaret On The Guillotine' was included on Morrissey's first solo album, the question of the vocalist's 'clandestine affiliation with a radical terrorist organisation [presumably the IRA] was raised with the Manchester police', resulting in a Special Branch interview with the singer at his home.[97] In any case, the band would simply switch targets, re-naming the record *The Queen Is Dead*, a title that, for Morrissey, was a 'very obvious reference' to '*drowning* the monarchy'.[98] The song lyrics for 'The Queen Is Dead' were, however, shaped by more broad concerns than simple anti-royalism, hence Goddard's description of the track as 'a howl of near-Swiftian disgust at Thatcher's decaying Britain', offering 'a rejection of England itself'.[99] Considering this point in the light of Laing's suggestion that 'the political effects of a musical utterance are first and foremost a factor within the particular politics and balance of forces *within* music',[100] allows us to track the performance – in the song's opening section – of a satirical attack on Englishness.

The track begins with a sampled extract of 'Take Me Back To Dear Old Blighty', a jingoistic British Services tune, invoking the troops' desire for home (for which 'Blighty' had emerged as a term during British rule in India). The archaic mood of the piece – heightened by the haughty inflection of the sampled singer (Dame Cicely Courtneidge, who had sung for the troops in World War Two)[101] – is abruptly disturbed when Marr's unsettling guitar feedback (and incongruous 'wah-wah' effect) converge with Joyce's speedily struck drums and ominously 'swelling' cymbal. In this respect, the song acts as an instance of 'codeswitching',[102] in this case between patriotic English music hall ('Blighty') and radical US proto-punk (Marr's intro self-consciously evoked the MC5).[103] Mark Slobin refers – in a discussion of migrant music in post-war America – to 'a clear-cut example of sharp, stark codeswitching' that acts as an interesting analogy for 'The Queen Is Dead'. Describing a 'Jewish-American comedy number of the late 1940s' that 'begins with . . . a perfectly standard recitation of Longfellow's hoary all-American poem "The Midnight Ride of Paul Revere"', Slobin explains that the 'diction and dialect' are 'standard, slightly pompous American English'. 'Suddenly', however, 'the nationalistic reverie is broken by a brief silence' and – what Slobin calls – 'a highly dramatic codeswitch', in this case evidenced by 'a band playing an Eastern European Jewish dance tune'.[104]

While the above-mentioned Smiths song does not shift to an ethnic idiom in the manner outlined by Slobin, the song's parodic re-working of a British Forces tune emits an implicit critique of Englishness that has been seen, by certain critics, as the point in The Smiths' oeuvre where 'the group's Irish rebel roots show through most defiantly'.[105] The song was certainly viewed, in its initial reception, as an attack on hegemonic Englishness, provoking, as Slee explains, 'a flourish of quasi-nationalistic consternation', with audiences 'heckling the placard [that bore the song's title] with which Morrissey opened the live shows', and tabloid newspapers complaining that the group had 'showered abuse at the royals' in this allegedly 'sick' song.[106] Meanwhile, British MPs denounced the song as 'utterly sick' and 'offensive', and asked the Home Secretary to 'crack down' accordingly.[107] The band also faced attacks (from far-right groups) at certain live shows, at least one of which was terminated when the group were assailed with maliciously thrown objects during their performance of this track.[108] 'I saw Morrissey walking off and he had blood all over him', explained Marr. 'I was pretty scared; I finished the song and got off.'[109]

Such episodes recall the attacks faced by another second-generation Irish musician – The Sex Pistols' vocalist John Lydon – in response to his 'God Save The Queen' (1977) song lyrics.[110] The hostility of such reactions was somewhat misplaced, however, as these tracks could scarcely be viewed as sectarian expressions of anti-English sentiment. As Lydon has claimed: 'You don't write "God Save the Queen" because you hate the English race, you write it because you love them and you're fed up with them being mis-treated.'[111] Similarly, Morrissey has explained: 'There are very few aspects of Englishness I actually *hate*', maintaining instead that he 'see[s] the narrow-ness, and love[s] to sing about it'.[112] What such pronouncements point to is a lineage of second-generation Irish music-makers that has offered, most notably, an assault on Englishness from a marginal standpoint, over any forthright expression of Irish difference. Such critiques of Englishness were, moreover, rendered more persuasive by the eschewal – in the case of The Smiths – of Irish sounds and styles, a point that I will explore in the chapter's conclusion.

Conclusion: elusive outsiders

The dissident gesture that was staged by The Smiths was arguably less easy to classify (in the sense of 'control' or 'contain') than that of their second-generation Irish contemporaries such as Shane MacGowan. If the latter had – like Morrissey – expressed overt approval of an IRA bomb, it would almost certainly have been dismissed as a stereotypical 'mad Paddy' response. Indeed, it's interesting to note, in this regard, that MacGowan was keen to dissociate The Pogues from IRA actions, which he condemned as 'stupid' and 'revolting'.[113]

In marked contrast to Morrissey, then, MacGowan was often reluctant to comment on Anglo-Irish tensions. From the latter's point of view, there was a worrying conflation, amongst the British press and public, of Irishness and the IRA. 'They think that because you do "Paddy on the Railways", that you're an active service unit!', MacGowan maintained.[114] Also during this period, another second-generation Irish musician, Kevin Rowland, started to sense that his engagement with Irish issues on the Dexys Midnight Runners' album *Don't Stand Me Down* (1985) had been 'too much of a statement', prompting the singer's withdrawal of certain lyrics to offset any inference of empathy with the IRA.[115] In such a fraught context, The Smiths' evasion of an overtly Irish subject position enabled them to attack hegemonic Englishness (via

Thatcherism, the monarchy, and military jingles) without being dismissed as 'plastic Paddies'.[116]

As Savage has explained, popular music typically operates 'not by specifics or slogans, but by hints and inferences loose enough for the imagination to leap in and resonate'. The audience's 'tolerance of divergence' (with regard to social difference) thus 'only goes so far', and 'usually evaporates when things get a bit real', as evidenced by certain gay musicians (such as the 1980s synth group Soft Cell), who, for Savage, 'paid the price of flaunting their divergence'.[117] Similar points have been made about Irish-descended musicians, some of whom encountered, as Rolston explains, 'negative consequences' when they 'broke from the herd'.[118] Most strikingly, The Pogues' song 'Birmingham Six' (1988) – an address to the mistreatment of Irish migrants in Britain's judicial system – was proscribed by a government ban.[119] Prior to this, Paul McCartney had faced a similar ban – as well as public criticism – for the single he released after 'Bloody Sunday': 'Give Ireland Back To The Irish' (1972), whilst John Lennon met such a negative response for his Irish-themed songs 'Sunday Bloody Sunday' and 'Luck Of The Irish' (1972), that a planned single of the latter was withdrawn.[120]

The Smiths' eschewal of such overt Irish signalling perhaps enabled them, then, to enact certain forms of dissent at which more openly Irish figures would have baulked. Thus, Morrissey's father – who turned up at a Smiths concert in Dublin shortly after the singer's pronouncements on the IRA bomb – registered his 'shock' at his son's comments, before adding, tellingly: 'He says things I wouldn't dare say'.[121] If the 'apparent Englishness' of the assumed Brighton bombers had enabled them to access Thatcher's hotel residence, then The Smiths' evasion of an Irish subject position afforded them a useful platform for their 'outsider' views.

The work of The Smiths in this way might be read as a second-generation Irish musical 'route'. As theorists of diaspora, such as Avtar Brah, have argued, post-war migrant settlements – whether 'African-Caribbean, Irish, Asian [or] Jewish' – have re-shaped England's cultural fabric, with these (and other) migrations interweaving 'with the entity constructed as "Englishness"', and 'thoroughly re-inscribing it in the process'.[122] Thus, if migrant Irish forms have (like those of other migrant groups) reconfigured England's cultural fabric, then the work of The Smiths (alongside that of Lydon, MacGowan and Rowland) might be seen as a second-generation Irish thread in English popular music. With this in mind, Savage has explained that little in English pop has been able to 'match the wit and gleeful, lacerating revenge of the Sex Pistols' "God Save The Queen", Dexys Midnight Runners' "Dance Stance" [and] the Smiths' "The Queen Is Dead"'.[123]

Rather than dismissing the Irishness of The Smiths on the basis of their absence of 'traditional' sounds – or seeking to square their work with essentialist conceptions of ethnic song – what Savage's point illuminates is a mode of second-generation music-making that has eschewed both Irish essentialism and English assimilation. In this context, Morrissey explains that he had 'the best of both places [Dublin and Manchester] and the best of both countries [Ireland and England]'. 'I'm "one of us" on both sides', he suggests.[124] Meanwhile, Marr has explained: 'I don't consider myself either [Irish or English] . . . I hate nationalism of any kind. I feel absolutely nothing when I see the Union Jack, except repulsion . . . and I don't feel Irish either'. 'I'm Mancunian-Irish', he resolves.[125] Recognition of this in-between-ness allows us to more adequately grasp the 'route' pursued by The Smiths, illuminating the intricacies of their address to the often complex dialectic between 'where you're at' and 'where you're from'.[126]

Notes

1 S. Frith, 'Music and Identity', in S. Hall and P. du Gay (eds), *Questions of Cultural Identity* (London: Sage, 1996), p. 122.

2 S. Maconie et al., 'The 100 Greatest British Albums Ever!', *Q* (June 2000), pp. 83–4.

3 For a discussion of this point, see S. Campbell, '"Race of Angels": The Critical Reception of Second-Generation Irish Musicians', *Irish Studies Review*, Vol. 6, No. 2 (1998), pp. 165–74.

4 M. Bracewell, *England is Mine: Pop Life in Albion from Wilde to Goldie* (London: Harper Collins, 1997), pp. 219, 223.

5 M. Sinker, 'Look Back in Anguish', *NME*, 2 January 1988, p. 14.

6 D. McRae, 'The Smiths' Anti-Apartheid Benefit', *NME*, 3 January 1987, p. 28; G. Martin, 'Angst', *NME*, 26 September 1987, p. 58.

7 B. Boyd, 'Paddy Englishman', *Irish Times*, 'Arts' section, 20 November 1999, p. 5.

8 For journalistic references to Morrissey's Irishness, see F. Worrall, 'The Cradle Snatchers', *Melody Maker*, 3 September 1983, p. 27; P. du Noyer, 'Oh, Such Drama!', *Q* (August 1987), p. 58. For interviews in which the band's Irishness is cited, see N. McCormick, 'All Men Have Secrets', *Hot Press*, 4 May 1984, p. 19; N. Adams, 'Johnny Too Bad', *No. 1*, 25 August 1984, p. 32; B. McIlheney, 'The Thoughts of Chairman Marr', *Melody Maker*, 3 August 1985, p. 33; C. Darling, 'Marr Needs Guitars', *BAM: Bay Area Music Magazine*, 3 July 1987, p. 18. For examples of the Claddagh ring, see Smash Hits, 'Morrissey', *Smash Hits*, 3–16 January 1985, p. 48; The Smiths, 'Bigmouth Strikes Again', *Smash Hits*, 4–17 June 1986, p. 60; J. Slee, *Peepholism: Into the Art of Morrissey* (London: Sidgwick and Jackson, 1994), title pages; M. Frith (ed.), *The Best of Smash Hits: The 80s* (London: Sphere, 2006), p. 59. For the word 'Eire', see the run-off groove of The Smiths, *Hatful of Hollow* (Rough Trade, 1984).

9　For details of The Smiths' Irish tours, see J. Rogan, *Morrissey and Marr: The Severed Alliance* (London: Omnibus Press, 1992), pp. 316–29.

10　See J. Marr, 'It's Our Most Enduring Record', *Uncut* (March 2007) p. 48; S. Lowe et al., 'Now My Chart Is Full', *Q/Mojo Special Edition: The Smiths and Morrissey* (2004), p. 134; S. Goddard, *The Smiths: Songs That Saved Your Life* (London: Reynolds & Hearn, 2004, 2nd edition), p. 106.

11　Goddard, *The Smiths*, p. 58.

12　For an account of The Smiths' musical styles, see Goddard, *The Smiths*.

13　For lyrical citations of English places, see 'Miserable Lie', 'Suffer Little Children' (*The Smiths*, Rough Trade, 1984), 'The Headmaster Ritual', 'Rusholme Ruffians', 'What She Said' (*Meat is Murder*, Rough Trade, 1985), 'Panic' (Rough Trade, 1986), 'Is It Really So Strange?', 'London' (*Louder Than Bombs*, Sire, 1987). For an example of Morrissey's citation of English towns in Smiths interviews, see S. Garfield, 'This Charming Man', *Time Out*, 7–13 March 1985, p. 19. Several record sleeves, including 'Heaven Knows I'm Miserable Now' (Rough Trade, 1984), 'Barbarism Begins At Home' (Rough Trade, 1985), *The Queen Is Dead* (Rough Trade, 1986) and *Strangeways, Here We Come* (Rough Trade, 1987) evoke distinctively English locales.

14　Like the members of The Smiths, MacGowan and Rowland were both born in England to Irish parents, a point that these musicians addressed in their interviews at this time. See, for example, M. McAnailly-Burke, 'Pogue Lore', *Hot Press*, 30 January 1986, p. 10; B. McIlheney, 'Burning the Midnight Oil', *Melody Maker*, 2 November 1985, p. 19.

15　I take this notion of 'routes' from Paul Gilroy, who points to the validity and inexorability of diasporic, hybrid musical forms that exceed the narrow frames of a fixed – and supposedly authentic – ethnic music, and thus confound 'any simplistic . . . understanding of the relationship . . . between folk cultural authenticity and pop cultural betrayal.' See P. Gilroy, *The Black Atlantic: Modernity and Double Consciousness* (London: Verso, 1993), p. 99.

16　See, for example, P. Ullah, 'Second-Generation Irish Youth: Identity and Ethnicity', *New Community*, Vol. 12, No. 2 (1985), pp. 317–19; A. Arrowsmith, 'Writing "Home"': Nation, Identity and Irish Emigration to England' (unpublished PhD thesis, University of Staffordshire, 1998), pp. 214, 219, 220, 221, 236, 237.

17　F. O'Toole, 'Nowhere Man', *Irish Times*, 'Weekend' section, 26 April 1997, p. 1.

18　See, for instance, P. Nolan, 'I've Something To Get Off My Chest', *Hot Press*, 2 July 2008, p. 41; B. Boyd, 'Paddy Englishman', p. 5; www.jmarr.com ('Q&A', March 2001); J. Marr, interview with the author, Manchester Night and Day café, 4 December 2006.

19　In the early 1990s, the singer publicly flirted with the iconography of British nationalism. Interestingly, this project was launched in Dublin, where the singer appeared wearing a Union Flag badge in the shape of 'mainland' Britain. See K. Cummins, *The Smiths and Beyond* (London: Vision On, 2002), no pagination.

20 J. Waters, 'Those Charming Men', *Irish Times*, 'Weekend' section, 25 April 1992, p. 3.

21 J. Rogan, *The Smiths: The Visual Documentary* (London: Omnibus Press, 1994), pp. 10–15.

22 Boyd, 'Paddy Englishman', p. 5.

23 McCormick, 'All Men Have Secrets', p. 18; Boyd, 'Paddy Englishman', p. 5.

24 Boyd, 'Paddy Englishman', p. 5.

25 K. Cameron, 'Who's the Daddy?', *Mojo* (June 2004), p. 79.

26 See Rogan, *Morrissey and Marr*, pp. 112–14; Talking Music, *The Interview: The Smiths* (Speek CD, 1998).

27 S. Goddard, 'Crowning Glory', *Uncut* (January 2006), p. 52; www.jmarr.com, March 2001, 'Q & A'.

28 S. Dalton, 'Getting Away With It', *Uncut* (April 1999), p. 52; www.jmarr.com (March 2001) 'Q & A'; McIlheney, 'The Thoughts of Chairman Marr', p. 33; Rogan, *Morrissey and Marr*, p. 114; Talking Music, *The Interview*.

29 B. Boyd, 'Johnny, We Never Knew You', *Irish Times*, 'Arts' section, 8 May 1999, p. 6.

30 B. Boyd, 'Johnny Take A Bow', *Irish Times*, 'The Ticket' section, 31 August 2007, p. 9.

31 R. Purden, 'Mancunian Marr Is Still Proud of his Irish Roots', *Irish Post*, 'Ri-Ra' section, 7 July 2007, p. 3. In his post-Smiths career, Marr composed a song called 'The InBetweens', which he explains was informed by this particular experience (Marr, interview with the author). See Johnny Marr and the Healers, *Boomslang* (New Voodoo Limited, 2003).

32 R. Purden, 'Keeping Up With The Smiths', *Irish Post*, 1 September 2007, p. 17. See also Rogan, *Morrissey and Marr*, pp. 114, 124.

33 Purden, 'Keeping Up With The Smiths', p. 17; Rogan, *Morrissey and Marr*, pp. 144–5.

34 A. Male, 'Get the Message', *Q/Mojo Classic: Morrissey and the Story of Manchester* (2006), p. 79; Marr, interview with the author.

35 Goddard, *The Smiths*, p. 25.

36 Purden, 'Keeping Up With The Smiths', p. 17, my emphasis.

37 Male, 'Get the Message', p. 79; Marr, interview with the author.

38 Ullah, 'Second-Generation Irish Youth', pp. 317–19.

39 Arrowsmith, 'Writing "Home"', pp. 214–37.

40 Savage, 'Rough Emeralds', p. 11.

41 Rogan, *The Smiths*, p. 10.

42 The first recording of this track was originally broadcast as part of a radio session for the *John Peel Show* (BBC Radio One, 21 September 1983), and this is the version that I discuss here.

43 A.F. Moore, *Rock: The Primary Text. Developing a Musicology of Rock* (Buckingham: Open University Press, 1993), p. 92.

44 B. Gilmore cited in T. Murray, 'Curious Streets: Diaspora, Displacement and Transgression in Desmond Hogan's London Irish Narratives', *Irish Studies Review*, Vol. 14, No. 2 (May 2006), p. 239.

45 B. Gray, 'Curious Hybridities: Transnational Negotiations of Migrancy through Generation', *Irish Studies Review*, Vol. 14, No. 2 (May 2006), p. 209.

46 I take this term, 'home triad', from Ian MacDonald's account of The Beatles. See MacDonald, *Revolution in the Head: The Beatles' Records and the Sixties* (London: Pimlico, 1995, 2nd edition), p. 366.

47 S. Whiteley, *The Space Between the Notes: Rock and the Counter-Culture* (London: Routledge, 1992), p. 125.

48 As Moore has explained, while certain rock bands have used acoustic, 'folksy' styles to convey a nostalgic yearning for an absent 'home', they have conversely deployed 'riff-based rock' to connote transportation to the cities of the metropolitan centre. See Moore, *Rock: The Primary Text*, p. 92.

49 G. Smyth, *Space and the Irish Cultural Imagination* (Basingstoke: Palgrave, 2001), p. 160.

50 Marr, interview with the author. The homology implied here – between a certain migrant mindset and a specific musical mood – is clearly one that Marr feels is valid.

51 Marr, interview with the author. See also Martin Roach, *The Right to Imagination & Madness: An Essential Collection of Candid Interviews with Top UK Alternative Songwriters* (London: Independent Music Press, 1994), p. 317.

52 Purden, 'Mancunian Marr Is Still Proud of his Irish Roots', p. 3.

53 Marr cited in Kevin Cummins, *Manchester: Looking for the Light through the Pouring Rain* (London: Faber and Faber, 2009), p. 147.

54 Marr, interview with the author.

55 See Kevin O'Connor, *The Irish in Britain* (Dublin: Torc Books, 1974), pp. 146–7.

56 John Robb, *The North Will Rise Again: Manchester Music City 1976–1996* (London: Aurum, 2009), p. 207.

57 Ibid., p. 207.

58 See Arrowsmith, 'Writing "Home"', pp. 237–8.

59 F. Owen, 'Home Thoughts from Abroad', *Melody Maker*, 27 September 1986, p. 16.

60 This track was included on *The Queen Is Dead*.

61 Stringer, 'The Smiths', p. 19.

62 See R. Day, *The Queen is Dead* (Woodford Green: International Music Publications, 1988), p. 13.

63 See Goddard, 'Crowning Glory', pp. 60, 52.

64 Owen, 'Home Thoughts from Abroad', p. 16.

65 B. Keaney, *Don't Hang About* (Oxford: Oxford University Press, 1985), p. 104 (my emphasis). See Goddard, *The Smiths*, p. 165.

66 See E. Hughes, '"Lancelot's Position": The Fiction of Irish-Britain', in A.R. Lee

(ed.), *Other Britain, Other British: Contemporary Multicultural Fiction* (London: Pluto Press, 1995), p. 153. For a reference to the band's 'miserablism', see Goddard, *The Smiths*, p. 97.

67 'Stretch Out And Wait' was originally released on the twelve-inch single of 'Shakespeare's Sister' (Rough Trade, 1985). 'The Queen Is Dead' served as the opening track on the album of the same name.

68 'How Soon Is Now?' was originally released as an extra-track on the twelve-inch single of 'William, It Was Really Nothing'.

69 *The Tube* (Channel 4, 25 October 1985).

70 N. Hubbs, 'Music of the "Fourth Gender": Morrissey and the Sexual Politics of Melodic Contour', in T. Foster, C. Siegel and E.E. Berry (eds), *Bodies of Writing: Bodies in Performance* (New York: New York University Press, 1996), p. 267.

71 Hubbs, 'Music of the "Fourth Gender"', p. 267.

72 E. Van Poznak, 'Morrissey: The Face Interview', *The Face* (July 1984), p. 32. See also Rogan, *Morrissey and Marr*, p. 71; D. Fricke, 'Keeping Up with The Smiths', *Rolling Stone*, 9 October 1986, pp. 32–3; McCormick, 'All Men Have Secrets', pp. 18–19; I. Birch, 'The Morrissey Collection', *Smash Hits*, 21 June – 4 July 1984, p. 40; Rogan, *The Smiths*, pp. 87, 83; The Smiths, *Meat is Murder* tour programme (London: Smithdom, 1985), no pagination; The Smiths, 'I Started Something That I Couldn't Finish' (*The Smiths: The Complete Picture*, DVD). See also the matrix messages on 'William, It Was Really Nothing', *Hatful of Hollow*, 'The Boy With The Thorn In His Side' (Rough Trade, 1985), and 'Bigmouth Strikes Again' (Rough Trade, 1986).

73 This track appears on *The Queen Is Dead*.

74 For an account of Wilde's ambivalent status *vis-à-vis* England and Ireland, see T. Eagleton, 'Mm . . . he was Irish, actually', *Fortnight*, Vol. 277 (October 1989), pp. 29–30.

75 *Earsay* (Channel 4, 7 July 1984). I refer to the unedited 45-minute interview, not all of which was included in the original broadcast.

76 B. Hoskyns, 'The Smiths: These Disarming Men', *NME*, 4 February 1984, pp. 13, 41; Worrall, 'The Cradle Snatchers', p. 27. While such comments might be considered naive, utopian and self-serving (not least from a marketing point of view), they also point to an anti-segregationist standpoint that exceeds ethnic specificity. It's worth noting, though, that The Smiths were often felt to be circumscribed around issues of 'race', especially after Morrissey made some troubling comments about black music in 1986, prompting claims that the singer was racist (Owen, 'Home Thoughts From Abroad', p. 16). Such charges met an unequivocal response that was underlined by other aspects of the group's work, not least their 1984 concert with the reggae group Misty in Roots for the multi-culturalist Greater London Council, and their support for Artists Against Apartheid (and refusal to allow their work to be sold in South Africa), as well as their interest in black music and invocation of certain black styles (see D. Kelly, 'Exile on

Mainstream', *NME*, 14 February 1987, p. 44; Rogan, *The Smiths*, p. 54, 154; G. Byrne, 'The Tune Smith', *Hot Press*, 12 March 1987, p. 21; Morrissey, 'Portrait of the Artist as a Consumer', *NME*, 17 September 1983, p. 11; Darling, 'Marr Needs Guitars', p. 18; Purden, 'Keeping Up With The Smiths', p. 17; McRae, 'The Smiths' Anti-Apartheid Benefit', p. 28). The band's audience also included certain black and Asian listeners, some of who identified with their sense of 'outsiderness' (see N. Zuberi, '"The Last Truly British People You Will Ever Know": Skinheads, Pakis and Morrissey', in H. Jenkins, T. McPherson and J. Shattuc (eds), *Hop on Pop: The Politics and Pleasures of Popular Culture* (Durham, NC: Duke University Press, 2002), pp. 541, 546; T. Christian, *My Word* (London: Orion, 2007), p. 65; R. Huq, 'Morrissey and Me', *New Statesman*, 10 December 2007, www. newstatesman.com/writers/rupa_huq (accessed 17 March 2008).

77 J. McLeod, *Beginning Postcolonialism* (Manchester: Manchester University Press, 2000), pp. 214–15.
78 C. O'Riordan, interview with the author, Dublin, 24 November 2005.
79 A. Jones, 'The Blue Romantics', *Melody Maker*, 3 March 1984, p. 35.
80 J. Campbell, 'Escape from the Margins', *Guardian*, 'Review' section, 19 November 2005, p. 11.
81 G. Byrne, 'The Manchester Martyr', *Hot Press*, 11 April 1986, p. 24.
82 W. Graham, 'Johnny Jumps Up!', *Hot Press*, 11–30 May 1979, p. 17, my emphases.
83 J. Henke, 'Oscar! Oscar! Great Britain Goes Wilde for the "Fourth-Gender" Smiths', *Rolling Stone*, 7 June 1984, p. 45.
84 Hubbs, 'Music of the "Fourth Gender"', p. 266.
85 T.P. Coogan, *The Troubles: Ireland's Ordeal 1966–1995 and the Search for Peace* (London: Hutchinson, 1995), p. 197.
86 P. Bishop and E. Mallie, *The Provisional IRA* (London: Heinemann, 1987), p. 339.
87 Anonymous, 'Denning Calls for Use of Treason Law', *The Times*, 18 October 1984, p. 2. See also T. Kavanagh, 'Hang the IRA Bombers Says Big Sun Poll', *The Sun*, 19 October 1984, p. 1. Interestingly, The Smiths would later praise Guy Fawkes on the matrix message of *Strangeways, Here We Come*.
88 Daily Mail Reporters, 'Moment of Grief for Maggie', *Daily Mail*, 15 October 1984, p. 3, my emphasis. For a full account of the operation, see Bishop and Mallie, *The Provisional IRA*, pp. 337–40.
89 I. Pye, 'A Hard Day's Misery', *Melody Maker*, 3 November 1984, p. 31.
90 Ibid., p. 31.
91 See S. Sutherland (ed.), 'Backlash', *Melody Maker*, 17 November 1984, p. 16; R. King, 'Running Scared?', *Manchester Evening News*, 9 November 1984, p. 39.
92 Marr, interview with the author.
93 R. O'More, 'Spit In Your Eye', *An Phoblacht*, 22 November 1984, p. 15.
94 Stuart James cited in Rogan, *The Smiths*, p. 98.
95 Rogan, *The Smiths*, p. 98.
96 G. Brown, 'Laughter in Paradise!', *Sounds*, 14 June 1986, p. 16.

97   Slee, *Peepholism*, p. 85.

98   Brown, 'Laughter in Paradise!', p. 16.

99   Goddard, 'Crowning Glory', p. 60; Goddard, *The Smiths*, p. 177.

100 D. Laing, *One Chord Wonders: Power and Meaning in Punk Rock* (Milton Keynes: Open University Press, 1985), p. xii.

101 C. Courtneidge, *Cicely* (London: Hutchinson, 1953), pp. 130–9.

102 M. Slobin, *Subcultural Sounds: Micromusics of the West* (Hanover, NH: University Press of New England, 1993), p. 87.

103 See Goddard, *The Smiths*, p. 176. MC5 represented, for Hardy and Laing, 'a political strand of the underground music of the sixties' that 'prefigured the concerns of the punk movement of the seventies' (P. Hardy and D. Laing, *The Faber Companion to 20th-Century Popular Music* (London: Faber and Faber, 1995, revised edition), p. 629).

104 Slobin, *Subcultural Sounds*, p. 87.

105 S. O'Hagan, 'What Are Your Favourite Songs by The Smiths?', http://blogs.guardian.co.uk/music/2007/05/what_are_your_favourite_songs.html (accessed 6 May 2007). See also Savage, 'Rough Emeralds', p. 11.

106 Slee, *Peepholism*, p. 41.

107 M. Dunn and N. Ferrari, 'Smiths' "Sick" Royal Disc Rapped', *The Sun*, 16 June 1986, p. 13.

108 Goddard, *The Smiths*, p. 180.

109 Darling, 'Marr Needs Guitars', p. 20; Kelly, 'Exile on Mainstream', p. 45. One of The Smiths' road crew later informed the band: 'if I told you what we found on that stage you'd never go out and play live again' (Goddard, *The Smiths*, p. 180).

110 J. Savage, *England's Dreaming: Sex Pistols and Punk Rock* (London: Faber and Faber, 1991), p. 366.

111 Lydon cited in *The Filth and the Fury* (Julien Temple, 2000).

112 S. Reynolds, 'Songs of Love and Hate', *Melody Maker*, 12 March 1988, p. 33.

113 C. Clerk, 'Sore Heads and Fairy Tails', *Melody Maker*, 28 November 1987, p. 15.

114 R. Elms, 'Pogue in the Eye', *The Face* (March 1985), p. 32.

115 D. Easlea, 'Don't Stand Me Down', *Record Collector* (April 2002), p. 51; C. Roberts, 'Grand Stand', *Uncut* (May 2002), p. 76.

116 This is a term that has been used to denigrate second-generation Irish people who seek to identify with Irishness, particularly when this identification has taken overt or essentialist forms. See S. Campbell, 'Beyond "Plastic Paddy": A Re-Examination of the Second-Generation Irish in England', *Immigrants and Minorities* Vol. 18, Nos. 2&3 (1999), pp. 266–88.

117 J. Savage, 'Androgyny: Confused Chromosomes and Camp Followers', *The Face* (June 1983), p. 23.

118 B. Rolston, '"This Is Not A Rebel Song": The Irish Conflict and Popular Music', *Race and Class*, Vol. 42, No. 3 (2001), p. 65.

119 See D. Miller, 'The Media and Northern Ireland: Censorship, Information

Management and the Broadcasting Ban', in G. Philo (ed.), *Glasgow Media Group Reader, Volume 2: Industry, Economy, War and Politics* (London: Routledge, 1995), pp. 48, 57; Anonymous, 'Pogues Fall from Grace with Government', *NME*, 19 November 1988, p. 3.

120 See L. Henshaw, 'Censored', *Melody Maker*, 11 March 1972, pp. 24–5; Anonymous, 'Mail Bag', *Melody Maker*, 4 March 1972, p. 15; M. Plummer, 'If Paul McCartney really wants to do something for Ireland, why doesn't he stop singing about it and come here?', *Melody Maker*, 4 March 1972, p. 42; J. Wiener, *Come Together: John Lennon In His Time* (London: Faber and Faber, 1985), pp. 210–11; Anonymous, 'Mail Bag', *Melody Maker*, 24 June 1972, p. 64; Anonymous, 'Mail Bag', *Melody Maker*, 1 July 1972, p. 48.

121 Rogan, *The Smiths*, pp. 97, 78.

122 A. Brah, *Cartographies of Diaspora: Contesting Identities* (London: Routledge, 1996), p. 209.

123 Savage, 'Rough Emeralds', p. 11.

124 Boyd, 'Paddy Englishman', p. 5.

125 www.jmarr.com ('Q&A', March 2001).

126 I take these terms from Paul Gilroy's allusion to Rakim. See Gilroy, '"It Ain't Where You're From, It's Where You're At": The Dialectics of Diaspora Identification', *Third Text*, Vol. 13 (1991), pp. 3–15.

4

'HEAVEN KNOWS WE'LL SOON BE DUST': CATHOLICISM AND DEVOTION IN THE SMITHS

Eoin Devereux

'In six months time, they'll be bringing flowers to our gigs' (Morrissey, 1983)[1]

Introduction

In this chapter I focus on the Catholic and broader religious dimensions of The Smiths. In doing so, I locate the significance of their Catholicism and their fans' obvious devotion in the context of recent debates concerning the apparent nexus between popular music and religion. What we might term as either the 'theological' or 'occultural' turn within analyses of contemporary music provocatively suggests that the sacred continues to be a feature of popular culture. Instead of seeing pop, rock or dance music as a secularising force and as a polar opposite to the religious and the sacred we can, it is suggested, see a significant overlap between the two.

Popular culture has regularly been the target of moral panics about its supposed capacity to negatively influence younger minds. It has been variously understood as a force of corruption, a promoter of materialism and hedonism, and as a powerful source of secularisation. However, writers such as Partridge,[2] Flory and Miller,[3] Lynch[4] and Sylvan[5] reject the presumption that secularisation goes hand in hand with the obvious decline in organised or institutionalised religions, and instead emphasise the degree to which the sacred remains in evidence within contemporary popular culture.

In a major study, Partridge[6] argues that what we are witnessing is not a blanket secularisation of western society but rather its *re-enchantment* and its *re-sacralisation*. The convergence of the secular and the sacred has resulted in a new hybrid form which he terms 'Occulture'. Sylvan[7] has gone further in arguing that popular music has, in fact, a distinct religious function. He holds that in a secular world it provides a sense of community, meaning and an experience of the sacred or the numinous. It offers music fans a sense of identity, of belonging, a means of escape and (sometimes) transcendence. The 'occultural' or 'theological' turn has given rise to a wave of studies that have attempted to identify the religious dimensions of a variety of music genres such as trance, rap, and country and western as well as heavy metal.[8] Using a research approach that can be broadly defined as ethnographic, a variety of settings such as rave clubs, free music festivals and 'traditional' rock concerts have been examined with a view to assessing the degree to which the sacred and the religious are in fact present.

It is in the light of these arguments that I want to examine how the Catholic aspects of The Smiths as well as the quasi-religious behavior of their fans are an essential part of understanding the band. I will do this in three ways. First, drawing upon band interviews, I discuss how The Smiths, and Morrissey in particular, related their experiences of growing up in a Catholic environment. Second, a detailed examination of The Smiths' creative output demonstrates that their Catholic upbringing cast a long and lasting shadow over their work. Catholic motifs are in abundance as markers of The Smiths' distinctiveness. As well as being white, northern and working class, they were Catholic, which was a badge of difference the band wore on their sleeves. While Catholic themes predominate, there is also evidence of a wider concern with religious themes in several of their songs – whether for humorous or more serious, political reasons. Third, an analysis of a sample of fan discourses reveals that when fans explain their intense relationships with The Smiths they invariably do so through a religious lens. Fan discourses about The Smiths are littered with references to how they have achieved personal redemption and salvation through their devotion to the band and to Morrissey in particular. It is hardly surprising that fans perceive themselves in this way, because from the outset media commentary was replete with religious references and metaphors in its efforts to explain both the phenomenon of Morrissey and that of the band's fans. Cultic discourses are a constant in terms of how both are portrayed.[9]

Vividly Catholic or vaguely Catholic?

With the exception of Simpson's[10] and Smith's[11] attempts to explain Morrissey's psycho-history by explicit reference to his puritanical Catholic upbringing and his supposed 'erotophobia', the Catholic and religious dimensions of The Smiths' story have been seriously underplayed within academic discourse.[12] Interviews with Morrissey, Johnny Marr and Andy Rourke all demonstrate the significance of The Smiths' Catholic backgrounds in terms of their formative influences and self-identities. With the exception of Morrissey, all of the members of The Smiths served their time as altar boys and recall their Catholic backgrounds in a positive light. With reference to the Catholic symbols that adorned his early milieu, Marr reflects: 'It's in me very deeply and I'm very happy to be that way'.[13] In another interview, he described his family home as having 'a lot of Catholicism . . . I remember it as being fairly Gothic really'.[14] Andy Rourke also recognised the strong influence of Catholicism on himself and The Smiths. In a 2007 interview, he remembered how he and Marr traded off serving as altar boys in their local church for free rehearsal time after helping out with mass on Sundays.[15]

Morrissey's Catholic background came into focus in many interviews with the band. In common with many other Catholics of the time, his upbringing was: '[s]olemn, sedate. But never intimate.'[16] Most accounts of his Catholic upbringing are in agreement that his family were initially quite traditional in their observance of Catholic rules and rituals. He was baptised a Catholic and sent to St Wilfred's and St Mary's, which were Catholic-run primary and secondary schools respectively. It is not without some irony that the first-century English saint after which Morrissey's primary school was named was said to be desperately unhappy at home as a teenager and in later life had a penchant for music. However, the singer has indicated in a number of interviews that the Morrissey family's adherence to Catholicism faltered quite significantly in the mid-1960s. In one interview, he referred to his family home as being '[q]uite vividly Catholic. Then it became vaguely Catholic.'[17] In the same interview, however, he acknowledged the lasting power of a repressive Catholic childhood especially when it came to inculcating guilt and worthlessness. He described his experiences as follows:

> The Catholic Church has nothing in common with Christianity. I can remember being at school on Mondays and being asked 'Did you go to church yesterday?' And if you hadn't you literally had the arms twisted off you. It's 'We'll sever your head for your own good. You'll learn my son'.[18]

Morrissey has also spoken numerous times in interviews about the sadism of the Catholic Church. He told one interviewer in 1997 that he would go to confession on a weekly basis and 'invent sins that he hadn't committed, "to please the priest"'.[19] The Catholic Church was particularly expert at generating feelings of guilt amongst its faithful, and especially amongst children.[20] According to Morrissey:

> It is probably the worst thing you can do to a child, to make it feel guilty, and guilt is astonishingly embedded in Catholic children without them knowing why. It's a ferocious burden to carry. How evil can children be?[21]

The Morrisseys' 'break' with Catholicism seems to have hinged on two key happenings – namely the breakdown in Peter and Elizabeth Morrissey's marriage and the death of two close family members. In a detailed interview with the Irish magazine *Hot Press* in 1984, Morrissey accepted that although he was to a large extent the victim of Catholic repression, he noted there was a significant lapse in his early childhood:

though I came from a monstrously large family who were quite absurdly Catholic, when I was six there were two very serious tragedies within the family which caused everybody to turn away from the church, and quite rightly so, and from that period onwards there was just a total disregard for something that was really quite sacrosanct previous to the tragedies. So yes, I experienced the severe, boring fear, but then I also experienced the realities of life.[22]

When asked whether he had in fact any religious beliefs, he replied:

I do, but not quite as dramatic as I should have by that absurd Catholic upbringing. I could never make the connection between Christian and Catholic. I always imagined that Christ would look down upon the Catholic Church and totally disassociate himself from it. I went to severe schools, working class schools, where they would almost chop your fingers off for your own good, and if you missed church on Sunday and went to school on a Monday and they quizzed you on it, you'd be sent to the gallows. It was like 'Brush your teeth NOW or you will DIE IN HELL and you will ROT and all these SNAKES will EAT you'. And I remember all of these religious figures, statues, which used to petrify every living child. All these snakes trodden underfoot and blood everywhere. I thought it was so morbid.[23]

Given Morrissey's other pronouncements at the time in which he stated that he considered himself a socialist,[24] his interpretation of the role of the Catholic Church as an agent of working-class oppression is interesting. It is important to note also that in some interviews Morrissey went so far as to say that he had no religious beliefs whatsoever and that he did not believe in an afterlife at all. In response to a 1985 question in *Star Hits* about whether he believed in an afterlife, he stated:

Not really. I can't think of any reason why I should. You're born, you live, you die and that's the end.[25]

The fear of living forever in Heaven (and in boredom) was a significant source of fear to the young Morrissey.

'Guy Fawkes was a genius': The Smiths and Catholicism

The decision by The Smiths to include a reference to a much-hated Catholic revolutionary figure in the etching of the vinyl version of the LP *Strangeways, Here We Come* provides us with a clue as to their self-identities. The etching states that 'Guy Fawkes Was A Genius' in reference to the Yorkshire man who in 1605 plotted with others to blow up the British Houses of Parliament.[26] Whatever about Morrissey's misgivings about his Catholic childhood – and there were many – it is of significance that a celebratory reference is made to a figure that in an English context was both anti-Establishment and Catholic. The creative work of The Smiths is replete with religious and specifically Catholic discourses. Their use of both intensifies at the latter end of their short career and is in evidence on *The Queen Is Dead* in particular. Despite its agnostic edge, Morrissey's worldview is a decidedly Catholic one and it is a crucial part of understanding The Smiths.

As the band's wordsmith, Morrissey drew upon an extensive lexicon of Catholic colloquial expressions in his songwriting, such as 'Heaven Knows', 'Heavenly', 'God Knows', 'Lord Knows' and 'Oh God'. The shaming and guilt-inducing processes associated with mid-twentieth-century (Irish) Catholicism are in evidence in many songs, especially in reference to the body and sexual expression, and sexual incapacity in particular. The loss of child-hood innocence in the face of sin and corruption is a core theme on the band's first album. Furthermore, there are abundant references in Morrissey's lyrics to the Devil, to Hell, to Heaven, to evil, to the sacred, to the unholy, to sin, to loss of faith, to devotion, to lies and to lying as well as to death. In spite of various invocations of God, there is a disproportionate emphasis on the Devil, on temptation and on sin, which arguably typifies Jansenist or puritanical Catholic thinking.

Death and dying (young) are constant themes, especially as a result of giving in to suicidal impulses. The focus on suicide is of particular inter-est because within the Catholic tradition suicide was, until very recently, deemed to be a mortal sin. Those who had committed suicide were refused burial in consecrated ground and were believed to face eternal damnation. Nevertheless, in Morrissey's lyrical world, death is regularly constructed as being a release from the misery endured in the here and now, and many of his male and female protagonists are preoccupied with dying young (see, for instance, 'Rusholme Ruffians', 'There Is A Light That Never Goes Out'). Side by side with these are Gothic discourses referring to graves, cemeteries, the fear of being buried alive and to ghouls and ghosts. The hereafter is alluded to in several songs, not least the 'mystical time zone' of 'A Rush and A Push and the Land is Ours', and 'the next world' of 'The Death of a Disco Dancer'. A small amount of light relief is provided by reference to religious themes. In 'Stop Me If You Think You've Heard This One Before', for example, Morrissey tells us that 'the pain was enough to make a shy bald Buddhist reflect and plan a mass murder'. Morrissey also paraphrases long established sayings such as 'Idle hands are the Devil's tools' (in 'What Difference Does It Make?'), 'Remember man you are but dust' (in 'Pretty Girls Make Graves') and 'These are the riches of the poor' (in 'I Want The One I Can't Have'). Morrissey's negative forma-tive experiences in Catholic working-class schools are alluded to in 'You've Got Everything Now' – 'Back at the old grey school' – and examined in detail in 'The Headmaster Ritual' – 'Belligerent ghouls run Manchester schools'. In the latter song, he wreaks revenge on those who inflicted a blinkered Catholic education on him.

Morrissey's lyrics demonstrate clever word plays full of religious allusion. The central protagonist in 'Pretty Girls Make Graves' is severely constrained by Catholic guilt in the face of the offer of bodily pleasure. In spite of repeated calls to 'give up to lust', the central speaker will not 'rise for anyone'. This implied allusion to erectile incapacity arguably points to the subject's puritanical Catholicism. Reynolds and Press[27] have interpreted this song as being an example of the male's fear of being sexually devoured.

Many of the male characters who populate The Smiths' songs share a close relationship with their mothers. The subject of 'Rubber Ring' states 'Oh, smother me mother'. The boy with the thorn in his side, referred to in the song of the same title, has been metaphorically speared like Jesus during his crucifixion. Reynolds and Press see Morrissey as '"castrated" by those invisible threads that attach him to his mother's apron, and thus incapable of any other attachments; Morrissey, with only misery for company, forever licking that "unnameable narcissistic wound" in the wordless falsetto that climaxes his greatest songs.'[28]

Hymns are also a source of inspiration. In 'These Things Take Time', Morrissey borrows from the first line of the 'Battle Hymn Of The Republic' by Julia W. Howe. Her 1861 lyric, 'My eyes have seen the glory of the coming of the Lord' becomes 'Mine eyes have seen the glory of the sacred Wunderkind'. In writing about the Moors Murderers, he inverts the meaning of the title of the traditional hymn 'Suffer Little Children' which originally meant to 'allow', but in the context of the horrific actions of Ian Brady and Myra Hindley the song title now literally means to 'suffer'. In the same song, one of the murdered children's mothers speaks of her child's 'sacred head'. The sacred also appears in 'The Hand That Rocks The Cradle' in reference to the child's bedroom ('sacred shrine') and to his frightened mental state ('sacred mind'). In this song, the abuser speaks of 'protecting' and 'praying' with the child whilst at the same time abusing his position of power. He uses 'words as old as sin' in order to control and abuse the child.

The Queen Is Dead is perhaps the most important example of how The Smiths engaged with religious themes. Here, organised religion is criticised and lampooned. It is the focus of serious social commentary as well as humorous observation. 'There is a Light That Never Goes Out' is arguably one of the most 'hopeful' songs that The Smiths composed. Ironically, there is a suggestion of hope and immortality through an early death through suicide ('to die by your side, is such a heavenly way to die'). In the satirical 'Frankly Mr Shankly', Morrissey makes it clear that faced with the alternatives of being 'righteous or holy', he would choose being 'famous' every time. In the album's title song – which amounts to a state of the nation address by Morrissey – we

are told that all the church want to do is to lay their hands on their congrega-
tion's money ('the church who'll snatch your money'; 'the church – all they
want is your money'). Money is also collected and counted in a church in a
later song on the album, 'Vicar In A Tutu', in which Morrissey takes considerable poetic licence by imagining a dancing vicar in the (Catholic) Church of
the Holy Name on Oxford Road in Manchester.[29] From an imagined vantage
point on the church's roof, the lead-lifting protagonist sees the cross-dressing
vicar annoying his clerical superior – 'the monkish monsignor' – before
preaching the following day in his unusual garb. In 'Bigmouth Strikes Again',
Morrissey once again demonstrates his ability to sing from a range of gender
perspectives. He sides with the martyred French Catholic Saint Joan of Arc
in expressing his sense of shame to his lover. The song rehearses the victim
narratives that are in evidence in many other Smiths songs, such as 'What She
Said' and 'Accept Yourself'.[30]

    In the Catholic tradition, death and the prospect of dying are ever present.
The emphasis on the Gothic is in evidence in 'Cemetry Gates', where the
song's characters discuss the issue of plagiarism amongst the headstones –
influenced no doubt by Morrissey's real-life practice of strolling through local
graveyards with Linder Sterling.[31] 'I Know It's Over' sees Morrissey drawing
a parallel between getting into an empty bed and being buried alive ('Oh
Mother, I can feel the soil falling over my head'). Death thus threatens to take
the song's protagonist before he can ever express himself sexually. The song
suggests a relationship which is equally about mothering and smothering and
thus reinforces a theme that had been alluded to previously in 'Rubber Ring'
and 'That Joke Isn't Funny Anymore'.

'Some kind of religious character': media and fan discourses

Religious discourses surfaced quite early in media coverage of The Smiths
and their fans. Music journalists were not alone in constructing both in this
fashion as Morrissey himself made explicit use of religious terminology in
talking about his lifestyle and the band's devoted fan-base. The most potent
example of the representation of Morrissey as a religious figure is to be found
in an edition of the *New Musical Express* (*NME*) in July 1985. The cover featured a picture of Morrissey replete with halo and stigmata. Mixing the lyrics
of the Christmas hymn 'Good King Wenceslas' and two distinct religious
roles, the paper's headline posed the question 'Feast of Steven: Morrissey
– Fallen Angel or Media Megagod?' Meanwhile, the accompanying article
referred to Morrissey as the 'Pope of Pop'[32] and joked that he was capable of
'walking on water'.[33] In the course of the interview, Morrissey commented
on the fervent response that The Smiths had received on their 1985 British
tour, suggesting that 'some of the dates were quite religious'.[34] Mindful of

Benjamin's notion of 'aura',[35] which is said to be a feature of authentic works of art and which provokes feelings of reverence from admirers, the two photographs used to illustrate the article are of particular significance. Shot by Douglas Cape in The Haçienda Club in Manchester, Morrissey is portrayed as having a halo – an item which is the preserve of saintly figures. The use of stigmata draws a parallel between Morrissey and, at the very least, the famous Italian Saint Padre Pio, but it could arguably also be interpreted as an attempt to represent Morrissey as a Christ-like figure who, as the article suggests, is capable of miraculous acts.

Apart from the obvious references to Morrissey's much publicised celibacy, the singer's alleged near monastic existence came in for repeated comment. His own statement made in 1983 that he was 'just inches away from a monastery'[36] provided a cue to music journalists who sought to make sense of his (very) private life. The Face, for example, wrote of Morrissey's 'monastic introversion' while Melody Maker and Q both referred to his 'monastic existence'.[37] In some interviews, Morrissey chose to draw attention to his ascetic way of life. In an interview with Time Out in 1985, for example, he argued that: 'The tabloids hound me. What makes me more dangerous to them than anybody else is the fact that I lead something of a religious lifestyle. I despise drugs and cigarettes. I'm celibate and I live a very serene lifestyle.'[38] Colloquial phrases such as 'Good Heavens' and 'Heavenly' are regularly found in Morrissey's responses to several interview questions. He talks of records such as Klaus Nomi's 'Death' as being 'Biblical' – a phrase which he also uses to explain his personal devotion to Wilde. In 1984, for example, he told Smash Hits that: 'As I get older, the adoration increases. I'm never without him. It's almost biblical. It's like carrying your rosary around with you.'[39]

In 1983, NME wrote of Morrissey 'singing in excelsis'[40] and a clear parallel is drawn between him and 'the great men of religion'.[41] His complexity, however, means that he is 'both missionary and heathen' all rolled into one. As if to contradict this position, Morrissey is quoted in the same interview as stating: 'I live a saintly life . . . He [Johnny Marr] lives a devilish life. And the combination is wonderful. Perfect.'[42]

Elsewhere, the work of the band is described as being that of 'spreading The Smiths gospel'.[43] Johnny Marr stated that The Smiths just wanted to 'convert everyone to our way of thinking' and for Morrissey and himself pop music was 'almost a spiritual thing'.[44] It was Morrissey who first described Smiths fans as being 'apostles'. In 1984, he told Melody Maker:

> I get terribly embarrassed when I meet Smiths apostles – I hate the word fan. They seem to expect so much of me. Many of them see me as some kind of religious character who can solve all their problems with the wave of a syllable. It's daunting. The other night we all went to the Haçienda, and for the entire night I

was simply sandwiched between all these Smiths apostles telling me about their problems and what should they do to cleanse themselves of improprieties. . . . Lots of people march away thinking I'm a totally empty headed sieve because I have not said, 'Go forth and multiply' or something! But if people saw me otherwise, as the hard-assed rock 'n' roller, then I'd just go to bed and stay there.[45]

In the same article, the religious aspects of The Smiths – and their live work in particular – were also outlined. In addition to being described as 'hysterical', fans of The Smiths are 'diehard devotees'[46] who have turned Morrissey into a 'near religious figure'.[47] He, in turn, rewards Smiths fans by 'blessing the faithful with flowers, transcending the group to whom he is utterly devoted and always ready to champion'.[48] The construction of a typical Smiths concert as having sacred and religious overtones was a strong and recurrent theme in how the band were portrayed by the music press – a template which would foreshadow how Morrissey's solo performances were interpreted in the years following.

Saved by The Smiths

Religious discourses are also employed by fans of The Smiths in telling stories about their own individual experiences of fandom.[49] The fact that some fans see themselves in these terms is interesting in that the term fan – an abridged version of the Latin word *fanaticus* – in its original usage meant 'of or belonging to the temple, a temple servant, a devotee'.[50] Smiths fans construct themselves as devotees, followers or apostles. Individual fan narratives contain common themes of redemption and salvation in terms of how individual affective relationships with The Smiths evolved.[51] Parallels are regularly drawn between the experiences of religious conversion and the processes involved in becoming a Smiths fan. Fans see themselves as making pilgrimages to sites such as the Salford Lads Club in order to make a more 'authentic' connection with the band. In the 'Smiths Room' at the Salford Lads Club, for example, hundreds of fans have left 'post-it' notes and letters behind. Like petition notes at a Novena, they invariably thank Morrissey and The Smiths for saving their lives. One note from a Serbian fan states 'Now my heart is full' whilst another fan writes 'I am a resurrection'. Morrissey's Catholic background is regularly cited by his immigrant Latino fans as being a key reason why they have developed an intense connection with him.[52]

Morrissey is variously deified, canonised or cast in the role of preacher. In 2006, for example, the *Guardian* newspaper published a fan essay in conjunction with interviews with five Smiths fans. In 'The Songs That Saved My Life', the founder of Smiths fanzine *Smiths Indeed* stated that the band was a source of personal redemption for him when he was a teenager.[53] In the face of loneliness and social isolation, The Smiths were his 'only solace'.[54] In becoming a self-described 'superfan',[55] he began to assemble a 'shrine-like collection of memorabilia'[56] concerning the object of his fandom. He writes of contacting 'like-minded Smiths apostles'[57] through the *NME* with the view to setting up a fanzine, which eventually went on to have some success over a three-year period. In the accompanying interviews, other fans speak of their devotion to, and adoration of, the band. One describes how, when she was younger, a religious friend told her that her fandom 'was just a substitute for believing in God'.[58] She stated: 'At the time I was incensed, but I suppose that it [being a Smiths fan] was like being in a tribe, believing in something that united you.'[59] Another interviewee spoke of the 'pilgrimages'[60] that fans make to the Salford Lads Club in Manchester. The process of becoming a Smiths fan was described by another interviewee as 'kind of like getting a religion. It's something inside of you that never leaves.'[61]

Religious discourses are also used extensively by Antti Nylén in his essay 'Me and Morrissey'.[62] Described as a 'long-time devotee',[63] Nylén writes in response to the publication of Mark Simpson's book *Saint Morrissey*. In his hagiography, Simpson, we are told, 'canonises Morrissey prematurely'.[64] Nylén argues that the process of becoming a Morrisseyite is a traumatic one. Morrissey fans are 'a metastasis of the idol, formed of the same substance and eternally defined by the originator'.[65] Morrissey is a source of protection in an evil world. 'When you say yes to Morrissey,' Nylén argues, 'in a radical way, you say no to the world and its requirements. The experience is poignant, but above all sublime and relieving. It gives the retreat value and principle.'[66] We could, however, argue against this supposed asceticism in that expressions of devoted fandom (including Smiths fandom) typically involve significant levels of conspicuous consumption (and material/worldly celebration) which are used as markers of fandom.[67] Indeed, the devotional and the promotional aspects of Morrissey fandom neatly dovetailed on his Winter tour in 2004 when 'Morrissey' rosary beads were on sale for £18 sterling.[68]

The sense of isolation and alienation which is part of (but not confined to) the adolescent experience is referred to in many fan narratives about The Smiths,[69] and Nylén's account is no exception. His conversion to vegetarianism – partially attributed to Morrissey – was, he tells us, 'not unlike a religious experience'. Morrissey, for his part, is not a saint but a preacher who has given us a 'vegetarian sermon'. Nylén's own literary awakenings are as a result of his adoration of Morrissey the wordsmith. As the writer of The Smiths' lyrics, Morrissey is, in Nylén's view, the successor to Charles Baudelaire – the founder of literary Dandyism. He sees Dandyism emerging from a specifically Catholic context in that the dandy is in fact a saint. He suggests that 'Catholic culture [unlike its Protestant opposite or other] idolises abstinence, strict rules, turning one's back on the world, personal strife and sacrifice'.[70] In its

Jansenist/Puritanical phase, suggests Nylén, 'Catholicism, like dandyism, like Morrissey, relates to the world with contempt and masochism'.[71] In presenting Morrissey as a Dandy, Nylén rejects Richard Smith's arguments about his alleged erotophobia: Morrissey's decision to be celibate is instead seen as a radical statement in a (pop) world obsessed with sex.[72]

Conclusion

So where do The Smiths fit in terms of the 'theological' or 'occultural' turn discussed at the start of this chapter? In common with many other recording artists in the 1980s (such as U2 or The Cure) the religious and the sacred are a pivotal part of understanding the band, their creative output and the response of fans. Far from representing a secular opposite to religious belief and practice, there were many sacred moments in the world of The Smiths. Morrissey's (self- and media) construction as an aura-laden 'authentic' star and the band's self-identification with their Catholic backgrounds, both point to the centrality of the religious and the sacred. In recognising this we need to go beyond their (obvious) Catholic formation, their extensive use of Catholic themes and their occasional critiques of organised religion. In particular, we need to focus on the way in which The Smiths were – and continue to be – received by their fans (a point explored by Karl Maton in his chapter). Fan narratives, as we have seen in this chapter, repeatedly refer to the redemption and salvation that occurs through developing intense forms of relationships with the band and Morrissey in particular. Smiths' concerts were the scenes of intense devotional behaviour by fans – a pattern that has intensified if anything throughout Morrissey's solo career. The connection that many Smiths fans feel with their anti-hero Morrissey is based upon his ability to confront the profound and often dreadful questions that so much popular culture evades. The quasi-religious appeal of The Smiths ironically may rest on the fact that they addressed the unpalatable existential realities of human existence and provided consolation[73] to their fans. Smiths fandom was/is not a religion (in the formal sense of the term) but it does have many parallels with religious belief and practice. Fan response to The Smiths (in the shape of self-described pilgrimages, shrines and conversions) tells us that in an occultural rather than a secular world the sacred and the (quasi-) religious continue to be present within popular cultural forms.

Notes

1 D. McCullough, 'Handsome Devils', *Sounds*, 4 June 1983.
2 C. Partridge, *The Re-Enchantment of The West: Alternative Spiritualities, Sacralization, Popular Culture and Occulture* 2 vols (New York: T & T Clark International, 2005).

3 R.E. Flory and D.E. Miller (eds), *Gen X Religion* (New York: Routledge, 2000). Flory and Miller provide further evidence of the presence of religion and quasi-religion within popular cultural forms amongst the 'Generation X' in the USA. Fay demonstrates how Goth subculture has a quasi-religious dimension. Hayward shows how, in spite of the usual Conservative criticisms of rock and pop music, some evangelical churches in the USA have, in fact, appropriated rock music as a way of making Christianity more attractive.

4 G. Lynch, 'The Role of Popular Music in the Construction of Alternative Spiritual Identities and Ideologies', *Journal for The Scientific Study of Religion* Vol. 45, No. 4 (2006), pp. 481–8; G. Lynch, *Understanding Theology and Popular Culture* (London: Blackwell, 2005); and G. Lynch, *Between Sacred and Profane: Researching Religion and Popular Culture* (London: I.B. Tauris, 2007).

5 R. Sylvan, *Traces of the Spirit: The Religious Dimension of Popular* Music (New York: New York University Press, 2002), and R. Sylvan, *Trance Formation: The Spiritual and Religious Dimensions of Global Rave Culture* (New York: Routledge, 2005).

6 Partridge, *The Re-Enchantment of The West.*

7 Sylvan, *Traces of the Spirit.*

8 See, for example, G. St John, 'Electronic Dance Music Culture and Religion: An Overview', *Culture and Religion*, Vol. 7 No. 1 (2006) pp. 1–25; G. Lynch and E. Badger, 'The Mainstream Post-Rave Club Scene as a Secondary Institution: A British Perspective', *Culture and Religion*, Vol. 7, No. 1 (2006), pp. 27–40; C. Partridge, 'The Spiritual and the Revolutionary: Alternative Spirituality, British Free Festivals and the Emergence of Rave Culture', *Culture and Religion*, Vol. 7, No. 1 (2006), pp. 41–60; M.L. Simon, 'Intersecting Points: The "Erotic as Religious" in the Lyrics of Missy Elliot', *Culture and Religion*, Vol. 10, No. 1 (2009), pp. 81–96; M. Grimshaw, '"Redneck Religion and Shitkickin' Saviours?" Gram Parsons, Theology and Country Music Author(s)', *Popular Music*, Vol. 21, No. 1 (2002), pp. 93–105; J.R. Howard, 'Contemporary Christian Music: Where Rock Meets Religion', *Journal of Popular Culture*, Vol. 26, No. 1 (1992), pp. 123–30; J.R. Howard and J.M. Streck, 'The Splintered Art World of Contemporary Christian Music', *Popular Music*, Vol. 15, No. 1 (1996), pp. 37–53; J. Gow, 'Rockin', Rappin', and Religion: Programming Strategy on Z Music Television', *Popular Music and Society*, Vol. 23, No. 1 (1999).

9 See, for example, A. Powers, 'In Thrall To The Trickster', *LA Times* Entertainment Section, 2007 p. 10. She writes of Morrissey's 'rabid cult', and fans are described as 'zealous' and 'devotees'.

10 M. Simpson, *Saint Morrissey* (London: SAF, 2003).

11 R. Smith, 'The God That Failed?: Morrissey', in *Seduced and Abandoned: Essays on Gay Men and Popular Music* (London: Cassell, 1995), pp. 64–8.

12 The Catholic backgrounds of the four members of The Smiths have been largely ignored within academic treatments of The Smiths. Two important exceptions are

worth noting. Antti Nylén's (2005) paper 'Catholicism, Anti-Modernity, Dandyism: Morrissey', which was read at a seminar on The Smiths in Helsinki on 14 May 2005, examines Catholic and Christian themes in Morrissey's songs but is focused predominantly on his solo work. Gavin Hopps examines Morrissey's renewed interest in religious themes in *Morrissey: The Pageant of His Bleeding Heart* (New York: Continuum Books, 2009).

13 *Rí-Rá*, 7 July 2007, p. 3.

14 C. Bohan, 'The Smiths are Dead', *Sunday Tribune*, 30 September 2007, p. 19.

15 R. Purdon, 'Keeping Up With The Smiths', *Irish Post*, 1 September 2007.

16 S. Mackenzie, 'After The Affair' *Guardian*, 2 September 1997.

17 D. Kelly, 'The Further Thoughts of Chairman Mo', *NME*, 8 June 1985.

18 Ibid.

19 Mackenzie, 'After the Affair'.

20 In an interview with Nicholas de Jongh in 1985 Morrissey referred to his 'starched Catholic upbringing' which resulted in 'guilt at every corner. I could always think of more reasons for not believing in God.' He added that '[p]eople in church seemed gagged by religion. It's a muzzle. I was soon tired of all the foul disasters being the will of God.' Echoing the lyrics of 'The Headmaster Ritual', Morrissey speaks of his experience of Catholicism as a 'cemented doctrine' which he states had a 'heavy embrace'. Nicholas de Jongh, 'Boy With A Thorn in His Side', *Guardian*, 4 October 1985, p. 17.

21 Mackenzie, 'After the Affair'.

22 N. McCormick 'All Men Have Secrets', *Hot Press*, 4 May 1984.

23 Ibid.

24 See '20 Questions', *Star Hits*, 1985. Morrissey responded to the question 'Are you a socialist?' as follows: 'I am. I don't belong to any particular party but were I to be stripped down, as it were, I would be shoved in the socialist box. Why? Just the very obvious things of coming from a working-class background, being exposed to hardships and the reality of life. I think all socialists are absolute realists.' Notwithstanding this response, Morrissey's attitude to the socialist cause is best described as ambivalent. The Smiths' involvement in Red Wedge owed more perhaps to Johnny Marr's political convictions than Morrissey's. Johnny Marr played with Billy Bragg for some of the Red Wedge gigs in 1986. In 2006 Marr recalled how he and his wife 'drove The Smiths up to Newcastle and we gate-crashed the . . . Red Wedge concert. We had no equipment with us, so we hijacked The Style Council's gear and got on stage unannounced. We played the best 20 minutes of our lives. I was so proud. It was partly a sense of vindication and partly just "Great! We're Back"' (Johnny Marr, 'The Smiths: Johnny Marr Looks Back', *Independent*, 24 February 2006).

25 '20 Questions', *Star Hits*, 1985. The parallel with the lyrics of 'Cemetry Gates' – 'they were born, and then they lived and then they died' – is worth noting here.

26 This practice is repeated elsewhere by The Smiths. In the etching for 'The Joke Isn't Funny Anymore' we find reference to 'Our souls, our souls, our souls'.

27 S. Reynolds and J. Press, *The Sex Revolts: Gender, Rebellion and Rock 'n' Roll* (Cambridge, MA: Harvard University Press, 1995), p. 90.

28 Ibid., p. 214.

29 There are no vicars within the Catholic tradition.

30 The theme of victimhood is a recurring one within The Smiths' canon and within Morrissey's solo output. Indeed, when the *NME* reviewed *Vauxhall And I* (1994), the publication included a cartoon of Morrissey being burnt at the stake. The review – written by Stuart Bailie – speaks of the new record which 'smells like . . . human flesh at the stake'. Specific reference is made to Morrissey's alleged Joan of Arc complex. We are told of his 'Christ trip' and of his difficult path to sainthood. Bailie states that 'Steven has revealed his Joan of Arc complex before, but now it's like he's passed right through the flames into this fascinating ascension trip. His trail to sainthood is hindered with the usual devils – unreliable friends, lost love, liars, innocence-abusers, stupid folk – but it's the critics above all that currently trouble him, so deeply hurt the fellow'. Stuart Bailie, 'His Astra's Voice', *NME*, 1994.

31 Morrissey and Linder's traverses through Manchester graveyards featured in the 1987 *South Bank Show* special on The Smiths.

32 Kelly, 'The Further Thoughts of Chairman Mo', p. 24.

33 Ibid.

34 Ibid.

35 L. Schofield-Clarke, 'Introduction to a Forum on Religion, Popular Music and Globalisation', *Journal for the Scientific Study of Religion*, Vol. 45, No. 4 (2006), pp. 475–9.

36 Radio interview with Morrissey, available as twelve-inch picture disc, Red Door Records (1983).

37 E. Van Poznack, 'Morrissey: The Face Interview', *The Face* (July 1984); I. Pye, 'A Hard Day's Misery', *Melody Maker*, 3 November 1984; P. Du Noyer, 'Oh, Such Drama', *Q* (August 1987).

38 S. Garfield, 'This Charming Man', *Time Out*, 7–13 March 1985.

39 I. Birch, 'The Morrissey Collection', *Smash Hits*, 21 June–4 July 1984, p. 40.

40 D. Durell, 'The Smith Hunt', *NME*, 24 November 1983.

41 Ibid.

42 Ibid.

43 W. Shaw, 'Glad All Over', *Zig Zag* (February 1984).

44 Shaw, 'Glad All Over'; Marr, 'The Smiths'.

45 Pye, 'A Hard Day's Misery'.

46 S. Reynolds, 'Bands of the Eighties' Supplement, *Melody Maker*, 23 September 1989.

47 Pye, 'A Hard Day's Misery'.

48 Ibid.

49 The use of religious discourses has of course continued in terms of how both Morrissey's solo career and his fans are described. One Morrissey fan – Rachel Elder – writes of Morrissey being 'eternal' and of making her 'pilgrimage' to the stage in order to touch the hand of her hero. See 'Why Morrissey Matters?', www. blacktable.com. In describing Morrissey's Latino fans, Arellano writes of Morrissey performing 'some grand ethnic genuflection to his adoring fans, letting them know that he knows. They always respond in ecstasy; grateful.' Arellano's account of one Morrissey fan's devotion is 'a lesser example of what Latino Morrissey fans feel for their God. They dress like him (rockabilly chic to British mod), carry around his favourite flowers (gladioli), and cite his songs as answers to every problem they might have.' He refers to 'New Wave's Sermon on the Mount' and also describes his own 'conversion' to becoming a dedicated Morrissey fan. See G. Arellano, 'Their Charming Man: Dispatches from the Latino Morrissey Love-In', *Orange County Weekly*, Vol. 8, No. 2 (September 2002), pp. 13–19. Morrissey continues to be referred to in religious terms – his status ranging between Pope (The Pope of Mope), high-priest, prophet, saint and monk. For an example of the latter, see D. DiMartino, 'The Loneliest Monk', *Raygun*, March 1994.

50 J. de Kloet and L. van Zoonen, 'Fan Culture – Performing Difference', in E. Devereux (ed.), *Media Studies: Key Issues and Debates* (London: Sage, 2007), p. 324.

51 For an account of the role that music (including the music of The Smiths) plays in the affective or emotional lives of university students, see A. Wells, 'Popular Music: Emotional Use and Management', *Popular Culture*, Vol. 24, No. 1 (1990), pp. 105–17.

52 See for example A. E. Cepeda, 'The Light That Never Went Out', www.treblezine. com 4 December 2005. Cepeda makes reference to what he terms the 'strict Roman Catholic tradition' that Latino fans and Morrissey have in common. The Catholic connection as one of the key reasons for Morrissey's appeal to Latino immigrant fans is also referred to by J. Oransky in 'Latin American Idol'. See www.papermag. com, 25 February 2006.

53 M. Taylor, 'The Songs That Saved My Life', *Guardian*, 3 April 2006.

54 Ibid.

55 Ibid.

56 Ibid.

57 Ibid.

58 R. Mal, cited in Taylor, 'The Songs That Saved My Life'.

59 Ibid.

60 K. Lloyd, cited in Taylor, 'The Songs That Saved My Life'.

61 P. Evans, cited in Taylor, 'The Songs That Saved My Life'.

62 A. Nylén, 'Me and Morrissey', *Eurozine*, 24 August 2004.

63 Ibid., p. 1.

64 Ibid., p. 3.

65 Ibid., p. 4.

66 Ibid., p. 5.

67 For a brief account of the more materialistic aspects of Morrissey fandom, see E. Devereux, 'Being Wild(e) About Morrissey: Fandom and Identity', in M. Corcoran and M. Peillon (eds), *Uncertain Ireland* (Dublin: Institute of Public Administration, 2006).

68 See www.passionsjustlikemine.com/gigs/moz-gio411eur-r.htm (accessed on 28 January 2010).

69 See, for example, Smith, 'The God That Failed?', pp. 64–8.

70 Nylén, 'Me and Morrissey', p. 10.

71 Ibid.

72 This point is also made by S. Hawkins in *Settling The Pop Score: Pop Texts and Identity Politics* (Aldershot: Ashgate, 2002).

73 For an extensive treatment of this theme *vis-à-vis* Morrissey, see A. Nylén *On Consolation* (Helsinki: n.p., 2009).

5

'SING ME TO SLEEP':
SUICIDE, PHILOSOPHY AND THE SMITHS

Kieran Cashell

I am going to kill myself because I cannot continue to live, because I cannot bear the weariness of falling asleep and waking up. (Charles Baudelaire, suicide note, 30 June 1845)[1]

What we see when awake is death, what we see asleep is sleep. (Heraclitus of Ephesus)[2]

During his period as 'voice' of The Smiths, Morrissey made several statements in relation to suicide. Perhaps the most unambiguous of these was made in response to Michael Aston's interview questions for the Dutch magazine *Oor* in November 1986.[3] Addressing Aston's challenge to defend his alleged view that suicide constitutes 'an act of bravery',[4] the singer answered,

I think the recurring phrase is that it's the 'coward's way out.' But I think it's the strongest decision that any individual can possibly make, as obviously it's very frightening . . . But I admire people who take their own lives.[5]

But can suicide be prevented? Through his phrasing of the ubiquitous question, Aston provocatively suggested that Morrissey address this issue personally. The singer responded that it is impossible to help anyone who is truly suicidal. The concept of life presupposes meaning; 'when meaning shatters', as Julia Kristeva has observed, 'life no longer matters'.[6] How can you possibly help someone whose life has *ceased to matter*? The suicidal cannot be consoled, Morrissey continued, by the 'standard awful lies that people throw at individuals who are struggling', because such sanctimony – coming, incidentally, from those who have never doubted the value of life – is clearly ineffectual; it is, perhaps, part of the problem. Despite (or, more accurately, *because of*) a prevailing culture of aggressive optimism, Morrissey insisted that suicide represents an enormous display of 'self-will', an uncompromising, yet thoroughly legitimate, reaction to real unhappiness: 'I'd rather say, in essence, well, the despair you feel is true, and it's common.'

Aston persisted. Alluding to an incident where two fans of The Smiths who, prior to their suicide, had written extensively to Morrissey,[7] he asked: 'do you feel a sense of achievement in touching them?'[8] And the singer, perhaps perversely to some, replied, 'Yes'.[9] However, the bereaved family, it should be emphasised in this instance, directed no ill will toward Morrissey. In spite of their grief, some of the victims' relatives contacted the singer to inform him that the records of The Smiths had been 'a great source of comfort during bad times [and] they were grateful for that'.[10] Apt nevertheless to be mis-construed as a vindication of nihilism – or worse, as incitement to self-harm – Morrissey's views may appear irresponsible to those unsympathetic to any pessimistic questioning of the value of life. And indeed predictable allegations of romanticising suicide were directed against The Smiths.[11] Morrissey was accused of having a 'gift for inspiring suicide'.[12] It is crucial, however, that this view of suicide should not be considered a morbid endorsement of self-killing. Although inchoate and perhaps ultimately unsatisfying, Morrissey's remarks, however epigrammatic, suggest a sensitive and sympathetic but especially, I will argue in this chapter, *philosophical* conception of suicide.

Critical investigation has exposed the inadequacy of the conventional explanations of suicide.[13] The dominant sociological and psychological approaches, in particular, have been indicted for failing to appreciate the phenomenological structure and ethical significance of suicide.[14] In accessing this critique, the general objective of this chapter is to draw attention to an alternative 'counter-hegemonic'[15] matrix that has the capacity to ethically vin-dicate what, according to the conventional paradigms, is widely considered a transgressive attitude to suicide.

And Morrissey's statements serve as a point of departure for the philoso-phy of suicide developed here. Yet I also seek to leaven this development with reference to how the issue is thematised in the songs of The Smiths. Although it is suggested in several songs, in 1985 the band recorded two tracks that explicitly invoke suicide.[16] In March of that year 'Shakespeare's Sister', a manic helter-skelter of psychobilly and suffrage inspired by a Virginia Woolf essay,[17] was released, and six months later, on the B-side of the luminous track 'The Boy With The Thorn In His Side', a composition called 'Asleep' appeared.

A nocturne for voice and piano, 'Asleep' occupies an atypical place in The Smiths' discography. In the absence of the distinctive sound of the complete ensemble, and, more significantly, without Marr's signature guitar-playing, 'Asleep' cannot really be considered a paradigmatic Smiths song. Apart from some subtle atmospheric effects, it has a similar musical form to the nineteenth-century *Lied*. Yet this chromatic minimalism is appropriate to the mood of what is essentially a suicide note set to music. It would be unjust, however, for analysis to detach the lyric from the melody. 'Asleep' is a unity of music and word, an 'audial picture'[18] that, like the Schubertian *Lied*, allows Marr's composition to complement the phatic intensity of Morrissey's lyric. Because it is compatible with Morrissey's statements – but also, more importantly, because it epitomises the philosophy of suicide defended in this chapter – I shall focus exclusively on 'Asleep'. It is not my intention to endorse the stereotypical perception of The Smiths as 'morbid and miserable', but the song will be treated as a subtly encoded and darkly radical – yet perhaps ultimately redemptive – philosophy of suicide.

Toward a philosophy of suicide: the incapacity of prevailing theories

At the beginning of *The Myth of Sisyphus*, Albert Camus observed that, because it leads inevitably to the fundamental question 'is life worth living?' suicide is the 'one truly philosophical problem' – the prerequisite infra-structural *a priori* that requires engagement with anterior to every empirical inquiry.[19]

> Judging whether life is or is not worth living amounts to answering the fundamental question of philosophy.[20]

Confronting suicide, Camus suggests, means accepting that the possibility of intentionally accomplishing one's own death reveals a philosophically ultimate structure. This is the case *not* because we are compelled to assess the meaning of life against the horizon of 'my death' (*à la* Heidegger), but rather because suicide brings *my own existence*, and specifically the *value* of that existence, into ineluctable focus.[21]

If, as Slavoj Žižek has reiterated,[22] Camus's disturbing caveat remains of serious philosophical significance it is because his challenge, once pro-posed, cannot be dismissed without bad faith. If no compelling reason not to commit suicide can be provided, indeed, if life cannot supply any conclusive counter-defences against the *why not* of suicide, then the inviolable value of life is thereby threatened and many paradigmatic cultural discourses held to ransom for unconditionally accepting that human life is *a priori* meaningful. Yet philosophy, *qua* the inheritance of critique, remains concerned precisely with daring to challenge what is generally accepted to be unchallenge-able – ultimately, the idea that life is worth living. It is because it leads into the intractable snare of this *aporia* that suicide remains a characteristically philosophical problem.

As has been acknowledged, the prevailing quantitative and clinical models are incapable of delivering a convincing explanation of suicide.[23] Although providing invaluable empirical evidence, the quantitative approach remains descriptive.[24] As Eglin has noted, '[l]ooking for laws in large numbers is its methodological orientation'.[25] An explanation based on phenomenological interpretation exceeds its regional framework. The sociological apparatus, exemplified by Durkheim's classic typology *Suicide: A Study in Sociology* (1897),[26] in relegating qualitative existential factors such as subjective intentionality, moral agency, interiority and personal identity to the periphery of analysis, remains circumscribed by quantitative limitations. 'Since virtually all sociological theories of suicide are designed to explain patterns in official suicide statistics', Peter Eglin concludes, 'the whole Durkheimian enterprise is called seriously into question'.[27]

The other dominant mode of inquiry, the clinical paradigm, is restricted by the assumption that suicide is the inevitable result of mental illness.[28] Edwin S. Shneidman's *The Suicidal Mind* (1996)[29] theorises suicide, on the basis of this assumption, as the 'tragic' result of psychological dysfunction. Exemplifying the psychopathological hypothesis, this study has been criticised as a diagnostic sublimation of conventional opinion in a way that scientifically legitimates the common-sense insistence that no 'normal' person would take their own life.[30] This medical interference in the realm of human subjective life effectively puts a normative moratorium on admitting to suicidal feelings.

Because it has repeatedly defended suicide as a volitional act, Matthew Pianalto and Thomas Szasz argue that the philosophical tradition has construed the question of self-determined death in an alternative mode – a mode, in that it is sensitive to the qualitative factors that led the individual to suicide as a *solution* to existential despair, that must remain irreducible to quantitative and clinical explanations. Part of a general clinical ideology favouring psychopathological explanations for all subjective life, the now hegemonic psychiatric view of suicide is not, Pianalto argues, theoretically fundamental.[31] Founded on the assumption that suicide-ideation is an inevitable consequence of abnormal mental processing, this position is less the result of scientific research than a philosophically challenged, unreflective faith in the value of human life.[32] 'The person who kills himself', Szasz insists, 'sees suicide as a solution. If the observer views it as a problem, he precludes understanding it.'[33]

Understanding suicide philosophically is contingent on resisting the disinterested attitude traditionally associated with the theoretical perspective *per se*. Philosophy, in this regard, could be defined precisely as that concern with what cannot be reduced to theory undiminished. As Kierkegaard recognised, the theoretical perspective is oriented to a conception of observer-independent objectivity based on scientific models of epistemic value that are deficient in relation to the existential issues that affect individual lives and are, to that extent, *ipso facto*, irreducible to the abstract generics of any theoretical schema.[34] Understanding suicide demands a specificity that, precisely because it acknowledges the incommensurable 'particularity and complexity'[35] of subjective experience, defies the 'tendency to objectify'. Such a tendency, according to Pianalto, results in the 'depersonalisation' of the subject and should therefore be condemned from an ethical viewpoint.[36]

Because it remains a possibility attending human existence as such, the effort to make sense of suicide demands adopting a subjective – that is, personal, irreducibly individual, even solipsistic – perspective. Suicide 'can become the most penetrating and personal of problems', Pianalto claims. It 'may take the form of a dreadful question we must ask ourselves, because we know that suicide is for each of us a possibility of our existing as we do'.[37] This suggests that suicide is intimately, albeit disturbingly, bound up with subjective life and is thus a problem that can only be addressed adequately through a modality sensitive to the phenomenological *thisness* of subjective reality. However, there is, again, more at stake here. In accepting the *why not* of suicide as a fundamental ontological issue, any serious attempt to understand suicide must involve a self-analysis that risks distressing endearingly held attitudes concerning the inviolable value of life.

It is according to this conceptual environment that Morrissey's elliptical statements about suicide, which may at first resemble a transgressive neo-romantic endorsement of heroic suicide, can be defended from a philosophical perspective. Despite their gnomic economy, Morrissey's remarks suggest such a subjective and, indeed, existential confrontation with suicide. In an interview not long after the breakup of The Smiths, he revisited the issue:

> Because I had such an intense view about taking one's life, I imagined that this must be my calling, suicide, nothing more spectacular or interesting. I felt that people who eventually took their own lives were not only aware that they would do so in the last hours or weeks or months of their life. They had always been aware of it. They had resigned themselves to suicide many years before they actually did it. In a sense I had.[38]

Speaking in 1984 to *Hot Press*, Morrissey had already observed that '[p]eople who have never been close to [suicide] cannot hope to understand it'; on this occasion he added, 'to me it's quite honourable in a way, because it's a person taking total control over their lives and their bodies'.[39] Asked if he ever seriously considered taking his own life, Morrissey replied, '[a]bout 183 times, yes', before continuing: 'I think you reach the point where you can no longer think of your parents and the people you'll leave behind. You go beyond that stage and you can think only of yourself.'[40]

From a clinical perspective, such sentiments, expressed by a person regarded as having influence over an impressionable social group, may appear irresponsible. According to the philosophical matrix, however, these views may instead represent a sensitive understanding achieved through the personal confrontation with the *why not* of suicide. Moreover, by acknowledging a subjective reality repressed by the obligatory optimism of contemporary

western society, The Smiths provided an existential image radically opposed
to the affirmative character of popular culture. Not only do Morrissey's
outspoken admissions contribute to our understanding of suicide *as such*
therefore, but The Smiths also seem to have supplied crucial support to many
vulnerable people by providing a vivid expression of suicide-ideation that
they have strongly identified with.

Before this begins to sound overly speculative, it should be observed that
there is significant ethnographic evidence to support such claims. 'Often [The
Smiths] become the only hope, the only consolation, the only thing in this
world that makes sense', one fan writes. Morrissey, he continues, 'approached
suicide, but clawed past it and made a success of life. Quite naturally therefore,
we assume that by following his example we can "boot the grime of this world
in the crotch dear".'[41] 'I have a very good friend', an American fan claimed,
'who was saved by hearing "Rusholme Ruffians."'[42] Morrissey should take
solace in news like this'. Similar sentiments are reiterated in music magazines
and fanzines.[43] Perhaps it is time for those who claim to be sincerely committed to suicide-prevention to take note of this phenomenon; for, in light
of such evidence, it is becoming increasingly apparent that it is the 'expert'
perspective – insensitively dogmatic, convinced of its own right-minded good
conscience – that represents the truly irresponsible view of suicide.[44]

Pianalto has claimed that the expert view conceals a serious presupposition.
Because it assumes suicide to be the inevitable consequence of the irrational
thought processes of a depressive disorder, the 'expert view' presupposes that
the 'victim' was in a state of diminished responsibility. This now hegemonic
attitude has the effect, Pianalto suggests, of excommunicating the suicide
from 'the moral dimension of the [normal] human world'.[45] Not accepting
suicide as the rational decision of an autonomous agent is determined by
the yet more fundamental moral conviction that suicide is *a priori* wrong.
Pianalto concludes that the 'suicidologist's foundation' is, therefore, exposed
as 'moral, and not scientific'. The psychopathological hypothesis not only fails
to provide an adequate understanding of suicide, therefore, but is actually a
sublimated form of moral disapproval.

'Denouncing suicide', as Schopenhauer wrote, is nothing but a surrepti-
tious denial masked by the 'crass optimism' that, despite overwhelming evidence to the contrary, unquestioningly supports the positive value of life; the
particular form of this denunciation revealingly expresses a prior unease that
it may be life itself that is already denounced by the very existence of suicide.
This explains the righteous anger – or infectious anxiety – that discussion of
suicide often provokes: the perception that the person who orchestrates their
own death has unfairly opted out of the competition of life. Yet suicide represents the *most competitive* gesture, because it invalidates the competition itself
and exposes the competitors' goal as pointless; he who chooses suicide is the

deserter, who, in the words of Milan Kundera, 'refuses to grant meaning to the battles of his contemporaries'.[46]

Judging the act of suicide *wrong* is, Schopenhauer concludes, 'ridiculous', for it was evident to him 'that there is nothing in the world to which every man has a more unassailable right than to his own life and person'.[47] A person contemplating suicide therefore may be completely (and almost certainly is) indifferent to the prevailing attitude of opprobrium concerning suicide, for the very readiness of the subject to choose death over continued life signifies that the restrictions associated with every moral prohibition have ceased to matter: 'for what admonishment' the philosopher asks, 'can frighten a man who is not afraid of death itself?'[48]

Perhaps an ethical response adequate to suicide ought to involve the suspension of moral judgement itself – the acknowledgement, in Pianalto's words, that 'no moral argument has been offered against suicide that does not' in the final analysis 'resort to dogmatism'.[49] The problem associated with suicide *is* ethical, but only to the extent that the act itself radically subverts the presupposition that life is *a priori* valuable. By undermining the moral framework that sustains the inviolability of human life, the act of suicide may indeed invalidate the entire ethical ground according to which any value judgment makes sense.

Sing me to sleep: suicide in the songs of The Smiths

So far we have concentrated on Morrissey's statements about suicide, elaborating his unconventional views in the context of the philosophical critique of the standard theoretical approaches to the 'issue'. The remainder of this chapter will explore the theme of suicide in the songs of The Smiths. However, as it corresponds closely to the philosophy of suicide outlined above, this exploration will concentrate on 'Asleep' –Morrissey's most sincere treatment of despair in song.

A disconsolate melody unravelling from an old upright piano is carried aloft by the wind toward a darkened bedroom. Once it fades in, a voice intones 'Sing me to sleep', and softly repeats in an almost imperceptible, yet identifiably, Mancunian[50] accent, 'sing me to sleep'. As so often in the songs of The Smiths, this voice pleads – or, more accurately, *prays* – asking to be sung to, but actually singing to itself, while the wind-chilled arpeggios evoke a deepening darkness.

The morally significant ethical indifference of the suicidal subject is captured in 'Asleep', where the voice repeats, 'Don't feel bad for me, I want you to know / Deep in the cell of my heart, I will feel so glad to go'. This is a calm and reasonable request. Do not, the voice peacefully yet insistently asks, feel sorrow on account of my death. Rather, be glad for me, for death is preferable to the prospect of a continued life that has ceased to matter. The social fact of suicide compels us to acknowledge that there is an indisputable truth in this: when someone expresses such metaphysical sadness, tells us that life is bereft of value, who are we to argue? Is it possible to dissuade the suicidal? Just '[s]ing me to sleep' the voice requests, '[a]nd then leave me alone'. It is important to acknowledge that the person who commits suicide really does feel like this: it is not pretence or the result of a delusional psychosis. The rational, intentional aspects of suicide, as acknowledged by Morrissey, need to be generally recognised: 'I really *want* to go', the voice repeats.[51]

Simon Goddard observes that the metaphorical transposition of sleep and death in 'Asleep' recalls one of the most memorable disquisitions on suicide in literature: the third soliloquy from Shakespeare's *Hamlet* (III, i, 56–88). 'To die, to sleep', Hamlet says, ''tis a consummation / Devoutly to be wish'd.'[52] Indeed, the single thing preventing Hamlet from suicide is the divine prohibition ''gainst self-slaughter'. However, the sleep-death affinity engaged in 'Asleep' has a more ancient philosophical heritage. Several of the extant fragments of Heraclitus[53] (known by the sobriquet 'the melancholic' in antiquity[54]) develop a fascinating, if typically obscure, relationship between sleep and death.[55] Most pertinent to 'Asleep' is fragment 21 (the second epigram cited at the beginning of the chapter), which implies that if in the waking state we are aware of death, when asleep we *forget* death and can, therefore, sleep more soundly.

Although the Heraclitean identification of being-awake with consciousness of death ultimately amounts to a *disassociation* of sleep and death, this, paradoxically, renders the fragment amenable to interpretation in a way that elucidates the image of suicide suggested by 'Asleep'. Exegesis of the fragment in this context, indeed, may suggest that suicide is motivated by a desire to evade *death* (and not life, as might be presumed) through engaging a state of permanent sleep that cancels the ubiquitous awareness of death that mars waking life.

Consciousness of death, Heraclitus says, is annulled in sleep. According to Heidegger and Eugen Fink's interpretation, the Heraclitean fragments constitute statements about the 'essence' of the human condition.[56] The sleeping state is an attunement to what they call the 'dark region' of existence, 'an experience of being returned to the dark ground'.[57] Associating sleep with somnolent forgetting, they suggest that the desire for nocturnal darkness is a longing for the narcosis of amnesia: 'Night is a kind of *lethe*', Fink proposes.[58] 'The knowledge of the wakeful concerning sleep is a manner of the dark flux of life where the I is extinguished for itself in a reduced manner.'[59] The desire to escape death through accessing sleep, a desire ultimately fulfilled by acquiescing to oblivion, and embalming the ego in darkness, resurfaces in 'Asleep' through identification with suicide.[60] As the cyclic piano motif returns to its deepest note in 'Asleep', the melody finds its own dark ground. Acting as a drone, this is the dormant note that, while unplayed, nevertheless rings on – its soft boom sustained in a silent dimension that draws the entire motif back to its somnolent substrate – simultaneously its inaudible point of departure and its ultimate destination.

The music-box detail of 'Auld Lang Syne', which constitutes the coda of the song, relieves the melody's cycle by announcing a change of state. A narrative effect of this detail is to co-ordinate 'Asleep' seasonally at New Year's Eve. Highly significant for this context, such a setting suggests, without explication, several phenomenological reasons why the subject singing to us, having experienced despair, has embraced suicide as a mode of escaping an inescapable condition. A celebration of calendar over chronology, New Year's Eve has been interpreted as a collective resistance to linear time expressed in the 'orgiastic' abandon of socio-symbolic categories – a *fort-da* game with the reel linking the past to the future.[61] Is it plausible to read this closing detail of 'Asleep' as a metaphor of transformation, symbolising the passage from one phase of existence to another?[62]

Does the voice in 'Asleep' not communicate, however, a painful entrenchment in the present, a life withdrawn from any viable future? Being alone at New Year's Eve is particularly sorrowing. Any loneliness is likely to be amplified on hearing the revellers' merriment, the muffled singing, the unseen fireworks popping dully in the still dark skies outside. For the person who has voluntarily cut off the possibility of a future, therefore, the dawn of a new year – an occasion marked out on the calendar-cell for anticipation, optimism and resolution – gives no cause for celebration. The prospect of new beginnings provides no solace: there are just the numb memories – 'a little interior of gray mirrors'[63] – that have led to the final decision, a past life that is in the process of passing away into permanent oblivion.

To this extent, is it possible to consider 'Asleep' an epilogue to the earlier 'How Soon is Now'? Having stood alone all night, and having eventually left, alone, to the countdown that only marked the final stages of his life, having gone home . . . So we are brought home in 'Asleep', into the person's bedroom, toward the deathbed. Sparing us the final scene, however, the music-box tympanum announces that the moment of sleep is approaching. After that, the silence of the run-out track seems a more complete consummation.

Is there another, darker celebration at work here? New Year's Eve, symbolising the demise of an old form of life and the ushering in of a new one, becomes an appropriate trope for the philosophy of suicide evaluated above. Why? Set into the interregnum between waking and sleep that 'Asleep' adumbrates, the coda emphasises the song's occupation of liminal space. Yet it is not quite accurate to consider 'Asleep', according to this emphasis, the marker of a transitional passage from one state to another. Rather, the 'Auld Lang

Syne' motif, in the context of accepting precisely that there will be no future, allows us to define the locus of the song as a kind of eternal present – an atemporal condition that Walter Benjamin, in his last writings, identified as 'Now-time' (*Jetztzeit*): 'a present which is not a transition, but in which time stands still and has come to a stop'.[64] 'We have grown very poor in threshold experiences', Benjamin writes. '"Falling asleep" is perhaps the only such experience that remains to us'.[65]

This is the lacuna that 'Asleep' occupies. New Year celebrations are 'orgiastic' precisely because they privilege the *presence* of the present, arrested and divorced (albeit for a temporary period) from past and future determinants. Yet 'Asleep' remains forever suspended, alone, in the 'atemporal dimension' of Benjaminian 'Now-time', invoking a transcendent site, crystallised at the threshold of the past and the future, where 'thinking suddenly stops in a configuration pregnant with tensions' – and, in this *Now*, illuminated only by that which will be, as Benjamin puts it, in an *Augenblick*, 'irredeemably lost', the subject of the song wants to experience – and wants us to identify with – this suspended state, by invoking the caesura between consciousness and sleep.

As the piano motif fades in with the wind, rises in cadence, and gradually withdraws, this suspended *Now*, forever repeated in the circular track of the song, transcends the classical ontological oppositions in the manner suggested by Benjamin, by remaining perfect and crystalline: outside the demands of life, beyond the command of death, arrested in an 'intermediate epiphanic place'.[66] In this way 'Asleep' answers the question, 'How Soon is Now?'

Time's tide will smother you: suicide as escape

In an existentialist-inspired discussion, Arndt Seifert interprets suicide as the ultimate self-determined 'project', when all possibilities of transforming the self have been nullified in despair.[67] Seifert regards despair as a condition in which the sustaining life-project seems to have led to a cul-de-sac, a present which is, precisely, *not a transition*. 'When all projects have become emptied of meaning, the suicide may finally embrace a last project, a trap – self-destructive in kind, yet one which seems to afford that dramatic possibility of self-expression (in the staging of the act of suicide)'.[68]

Kierkegaard's analysis in *The Sickness unto Death* identifies despair as a structural modality of the human condition.[69] Even if the majority remain innocent of their personal despair, Kierkegaard claims, it nevertheless continues to exert a clandestine, stressful influence over their lives.[70] We instinctually repress despair, exercising convoluted resources to distract from its oppressive presence. For Kierkegaard, however, this denial merely reinforces its subterranean impact. If one remains in denial regarding despair, there is no possibility of freedom from it.

Despair, Emmanuel Levinas proposes in an early essay, ought therefore to be thematised as a failure to 'claim responsibility for ourselves',[71] a failure leading to a kind of schizoid condition of self-conflicted confrontation which manifests itself as a shameful revelation of previous self-deceptive behaviour. Nevertheless, the existentialist tends to view this as 'a fundamental condition of self-deception which is experienced by all human beings who have not yet achieved genuine selfhood'.[72] What is genuine selfhood? If the question *Who am I?* yields contradictions, such as, 'I am not myself', then, intensely aware of what previously lay dormant, clandestine despair may surface in the specific form of a crisis of identity. 'I am, I am, I am', as the protagonist of *The Bell Jar*, as if gazing into a vacuous mirror, continually reassures herself.[73]

Levinas characterises the true model of despair in terms of such a shame-inducing self-vs-self confrontation. This solipsistic, specular conflict exposes an elemental deficiency at the heart of the human predicament that inaugurates an equally fundamental desire to *escape*, described simply as 'an effort to get out of an unbearable situation'.[74] Yet is despair not the experience of entrenchment *par excellence*? Indeed: Levinas identifies it as the 'fact of being riveted to existence'.[75] For the dreadful truth revealed by the suicidal crisis is that we are unable, inevitably, to escape from ourselves. I cannot evade this experience of 'internal antagonism' because it comes from *within me* – my instinctual capacity to rid myself of that which causes trauma therefore is gridlocked in this particular case: the 'revolting presence of ourselves to ourselves appears insurmountable'.[76] The one thing a person in despair cannot do, Kierkegaard had already observed, is 'get rid of himself'.[77] An instinctual need to escape is counteracted by the equally basic 'binding presence of the I to itself'.[78]

Such a vicious inertia generates *nausea* – a sensation which Levinas considered highly symptomatic of the condition of existential entrenchment. In despair, we are assaulted, he says, by a nausea that leaves us exhausted, we are 'enclosed in a tight circle that smothers'.[79] Elicited by the inevitable failure of the instinct to escape existential entrenchment, this nausea will later be modified by Levinas as a metaphysical passivity and will be thematised 'through the description of insomnia'.[80] We can easily make the link to the frustrated longing for sleep that this state of passive paralysis inevitably evokes and recognise thereby its affinity with the view of suicide expressed in 'Asleep'.

Articulated around metaphors of fatigue and somnolence, 'Asleep' is a subtle meditation on despair in the existential sense. The already-discussed dormant bass note of the melody is resonant of the entrenchment in existence discussed by Levinas. In despair, we feel anchored to an unendurable life with no hope of extradition: no escape route can alleviate its cramped, sinking chamber. Yet all my being yearns for escape. More than nausea, I would suggest, therefore, that the experience of despair can be compared to an asthma attack. For, like an asthmatic gasping for breath, despair is the condition of inescapability *per se*, a condition closely associated with isolation and de-personalisation, and captured by Sylvia Plath in the image of the bell jar, in which she imagined herself confined, 'stewing in [her] own sour air'.[81]

The subject in despair suffers a condition comparable to life-internment that is only relieved through the solipsistic violence of self-destruction that actually relieves this unbearable, claustrophobic condition. Suicide can be understood as an attempt to escape the claustrophobia of despair. And, indeed, motifs of claustrophobia recur in Morrissey's lyrics ('Well I Wonder', 'That Joke Isn't Funny Anymore', 'I Know It's Over' and 'Rubber Ring').[82] The claustrophobic condition of despair is also obliquely depicted in 'Asleep' when the voice, recognising its internment in life, longs, 'deep in the cell' of his being, for 'another world . . . a better world'.

'Asleep', signalling the moment of departure from the waking world, also signifies escape from claustrophobic inertia of despair into the nocturnal region. However, the faint little coda adumbrates a fragile optimism that, in choosing death, paradoxically, a new possibility has been discerned in the hermetic paralysis of claustrophobic despair. Glimpsing the paradox here may elucidate the meaning of Benjamin's aporetic formulation: 'Only because of the hopeless is hope given to us.'[83] For Benjamin (who, in 1940, committed suicide from an overdose of morphine – an opiate, incidentally, named after the Roman god of sleep),[84] as for the Hamlet-like subject of 'Asleep', there may be something after this moment, some post-mortem *Nachleben*, waiting at the strait-gates, at the limits of truth; and even if there isn't, then a comatose state is a preferable condition: 'There is another world / There is a better world.' This paradoxical hope, the hope left among the ills in Pandora's box, is complemented by Marr's addition of the fifth note of the scale to the arpeggio which strengthens the resolve of the chord and brightens it, as Morrissey sings his valediction: 'Well, there must be / Well, there must be . . . / 'Bye Bye'.

Must there? Projecting into the future means cancelling the uncertainty associated with its 'not-yet' modality, giving nothingness a salient form. Anxiety, Kierkegaard claims, is forward-directed: death is always, already, ahead of us, waiting at the door. It is exactly when the attempt to ignore the *moribundus sum* fails, for whatever reason, that despair effloresces. And my mirror image becomes a *memento mori*. For the subject entrenched in despair therefore, the future cannot have the significance of the 'not yet' – it has become the dark void of the never. And the desire for oblivion, for escape into a 'better' state of pure nothingness undetermined by the future 'to-come' of death, and dissociated from the past, has eclipsed every anticipatory project.

'To despair over oneself', Kierkegaard warns, is 'to will to be rid of oneself'.[85] That is why he identifies despair as the *sickness unto death*; when it shows itself, the spleen of despair may appear to the desperate as a death wish.[86] When the subject becomes aware of the unconscious will-to-death driving their despair, suicide may appear not only as the only coherent intention that makes sense, but as an inevitable destiny.[87] However, as Michael Watts remarks, the suicidal crisis *can* be disciplined and self-destruction ultimately rejected as the *only* solution to despair. For, as Kierkegaard argued, it is when I become *conscious* of my despair that it can be controlled, and its true function revealed. If it is acknowledged, although traumatic, despair can actually provide the necessary will to precipitate a dramatic *Aufhebung* (cancellation and transcendence) of the present existential impasse. If I can turn the potency of the will-to-death revealed by despair into an affirmative power to transcend the self I no longer identify with, the will can be overpowered and I can counter-will into existence the self I need to become.[88] Yes, there is another world – there *must*, by logic, be; but, as Benjamin recognised, it is *here* and it is *now*. And this, more than anything else, represents the tragedy of suicide.

By the time we begin to listen to 'Asleep', it is already too late: the instant of death has already come – and gone. The moment when 'Sing me to sleep' was uttered by a living voice has now passed. What we are now listening to, like the ghost in *Hamlet*, we realise with a shock, is a dead, spectral voice. The title signifies that the person who is singing to us in the song is now finally sleeping. And we have to admit that he (or, indeed, she) to whom this dead voice once belonged is now, at last, having achieved sleep, relieved. It is dawn and (s)he is glad to be gone. Yet somehow, uncannily, the voice remains.

The voice from beyond the record: the saving songs of The Smiths

'Rubber Ring', the song that precedes and audibly merges with 'Asleep' on its original release, refers to the 'songs that saved your life', a deeply resonant concept that has had a profound effect on many listeners. The singer cautions us, from the perspective of an imagined amnesiac future, not to forget certain songs that once perhaps offered support through dark times. Ending with a reflexive reference to his own mediated voice surfacing from the record-player in the penumbra of the bedroom, Morrissey asks: 'Can you hear me?'

Goddard is convinced that Morrissey's address to his imagined listeners of the future, grown up now and perhaps over the worst, is intended to be understood as post-mortem, 'a haunting reprimand from the other side'.[89] This interpretation is substantiated by careful listening, revealing that 'Asleep', if not actually part of the same song, at least constitutes a close sequel to 'Rubber Ring'. As the latter comes to an end, a woman's voice is heard repeating in accented English, 'You are sleeping; you do not want to believe; you are sleeping . . .' to the sound of the wind that ushers in 'Asleep'.[90]

Songs like 'Rubber Ring / Asleep' demonstrate that The Smiths were trying to craft songs that, like emotional rescuing equipment, have redemptive potential. 'Any time in my life that I felt that it might be the end', as one eulogist puts it, 'when I've felt like I'm in some sort of life-threatening situation, I go to "Asleep" and I get lost in it. It submerges me, enfolds me. It's the most embryonic feeling.'[91] As absurd as this might sound, it seems to have been Morrissey's ambition: to touch people, as he himself had been touched:

> I think it primarily stems from feeling quite isolated and believing that the people who make the records you buy are your personal friends, they understand you, and the more records that you buy . . . the closer you get to these people. And if you are quite isolated and you hear this voice that you identify with, it's really quite immensely important.[92]

He later acknowledged that '[t]here's something about vinyl and words and a voice on record that's very grabbing'.[93]

It is not insignificant that Morrissey refers to *vinyl* when emphasising the phatic semiotics of the recorded voice. One reason why the analogue recording remains so captivating is because it represents what the American philosopher C. S. Peirce classified as an indexical sign. That is to say, the vinyl record is a non-arbitrary, homologous simulacrum that is associated with its referent *by direct physical connection*.[94] A living human voice has causally affected the material surface of the record, leaving traces engraved in its surface. When the stylus engages the groove, it picks up, and the player electronically amplifies, this sonographic intaglio. However, every time it is replayed, due to the action of the needle, the record suffers and the track deteriorates. Yet this means that each repetition paradoxically becomes a unique and unrepeatable, inestimably valuable *moment*, the significance of which can again be appreciated according to the Benjaminian concept of the 'Now of recognisability' invoked above.

'Asleep' represents a resonant, but perplexing, instance of Benjamin's hypothesis. If the voice evokes a liminal *topos* 'in which time stands still and has come to a stop', it should also be acknowledged that Benjamin identified the 'Now of recognisability' with *awakening*.[95] Although his writings display an uncharacteristic consistency precisely regarding the motif of awakening, it would be to misconstrue this aspect of Benjamin's project to consider it, in Enlightenment terms, a metaphor for rational demystification. Rather, the concept of philosophical awakening in Benjamin, as in Heraclitus, is more than a rhetorical appeal to the waking–sleeping rhythm and its metaphorical cadences.[96] The Now of recognisability is prompted, Benjamin insists, by catastrophe – by what he refers to as a 'state of emergency', such as that initiated, *par excellence*, by the suicidal crisis. It is important, therefore, not only to distance the Benjaminian Now from the sleep–death nexus, but also to avoid any unproblematic identification with 'awakened consciousness'.

As it appears in his last writings, and specifically 'On the Concept of History' (a text composed, it should not be forgotten, in the last months before Benjamin's suicide), the Now is best understood as 'emergence', 'epiphany' or, perhaps, 'efflorescence' – a singularity manifested the moment the elusive event, with a shock, 'flares up',[97] as it passes away. For, as Benjamin suggests, in the Now of recognisability, 'what in the next moment is already irretrievably lost', as if spot-lit for a nanosecond, crystallises as an *image*.[98]

Having perhaps ingested a quantity of some retail pharmaceutical, thus invalidating an entire industry committed to healthcare, the languid, yet already stiffening figure in 'Asleep', spot-lit and lost, desires to sleep forever in the single bed where, as in a grave, he lies. As the shadows thicken, the frail music weakens.

Longing for sleep implies desire for a more profound awakening. Levinas quotes Husserl: 'Sleep, on close inspection, has meaning only in relation to wakefulness, and in itself bears the potentiality for awakening'.[99] Suspended in the threshold before sleep, a liminal, hypnotic state uncannily captured by the haunting voice addressing us 'from the corner of the room', does the desire for the amnesia of sleep not ultimately evoke a transcendental desire for a deeper, anamnetic awakening? Affirmation of another, better world would certainly seem to suggest so. Benjamin associated the eidetic *Now*-time with redemption, specifically, with 'rescue from oblivion'.[100] Nothing, he maintained, no event that has *ever* occurred, however 'inconsequential', should be regarded as permanently lost.[101] And nothing could be closer to the sentiments of 'Asleep / Rubber Ring'.

It is tempting (if hubristic) to conclude that Morrissey's connection with suicidal people by way of song was probably more effective at 'saving lives' than any government-funded suicide-prevention initiative. His acknowledgement that it is impossible to help the truly suicidal is, because it indicates an understanding of the intolerable condition of despair, the very admission of failure that may prove effective in this context. For many, it is the sincerity and concern communicated in the songs of The Smiths that, as we have seen, enables such profound identification with their emotional index. Yet it is also significant, and not inconsistent, to observe that it is precisely the *anonymity* of the voice in 'Asleep' – a preservation of privacy emphasised by Foucault in his defence of suicide[102] – that is pertinent. Indeed, it is perhaps only because it remains *sans identité* that the voice allows itself to be identified with. Here, the words of contemporary French philosopher Alain Badiou are relevant: 'To the question "Who speaks?"', the song replies: 'No one.' 'There is just a voice, an anonymous voice.'[103] It is thus with 'Asleep': there is just this voice, this anonymous voice. What the words of 'Asleep' verbalise has less significance than the phatic redemptive *gesture* of the voice itself – the effect of a living human voice possessing the semiotic capacity to *touch*. This voice ultimately only says: 'here I am . . . can you hear me?' For the subject of 'Asleep', it is too late. Yet the voice, reaching out, remains awake.

Notes

1 C. Pichois and J. Ziegler, *Baudelaire* (trans. G. Robb) (London: Vintage, 1991), p. 122.
2 Heraclitus (Diels / Kranz) Fragment 21, as translated in R.D. McKirahan, *Philosophy Before Socrates* (Indianapolis, IN and Cambridge: Hackett, 1994), p. 119.
3 M. Aston, 'Morrissey: Interview', *Oor* (November 1986). Reprinted and translated as 'The Lost Interview' in *Q/Mojo: The Smiths and Morrissey Special Edition* (May 2004), pp. 52–7.
4 These are Aston's words. He may have been referring to a statement made in an interview with Ian Pye for the *New Musical Express* (*NME*) some months before (June 1986). 'Although it's very hard for many people to accept, I do actually respect suicide because it is having control over one's life. It's the strongest statement anyone can make, and people aren't really strong. You could say it was negative leaving the world but if people's lives are so enriched in the first place then ideas of suicide would never occur. Most people as we know lead desperate and hollow lives.' Quoted in L. O'Brien, 'Sing me to Sleep', *NME*, 8 November 1986, p. 22; also J. Robertson, *Morrissey: In His Own Words* (London and New York: Omnibus Press, 1988), p. 26.
5 Aston, 'Morrissey: Interview', p. 56.
6 J. Kristeva, *Black Sun* (trans. L.S. Roudiez) (New York: Columbia University Press, 1989), p. 6.
7 On this incident, see O'Brien 'Sing me to Sleep', pp. 22–4. 'Amongst the constant fan mail he receives, some comes from people who are "incredibly depressed", and there were two recent instances of young people who wrote to him on a daily basis and afterwards killed themselves' (p. 22). See also D. Bret, *Morrissey: Scandal and Passion* (London: Robson Books, 2004), p. 74.
8 Aston, 'Morrissey: Interview', p. 56.
9 He continued: '[B]ecause quite largely people in such situations are untouchable by the human race, and nothing makes sense to them. So I think it's quite remarkable.' Ibid.
10 Press Officer Pat Bellis in O'Brien, 'Sing me to Sleep' p. 22.
11 Bret, *Morrissey*, p. 68.
12 This situation, Simon Goddard reports, was exacerbated by The Smiths' song 'Asleep', released as a B-side in September 1985 and criticised for 'promoting a "suicide-chic"'. S. Goddard, *The Smiths: The Songs That Saved Your Life* (London: Reynolds & Hearn, 2002), p. 156. Ironically, however, Goddard was one of those commentators who, at the time, contributed to the accusations. See *Smiths Indeed* 10 (Winter 1988).

13 M.C. Pianalto, *Suicide and the Self*, MPhil thesis (University of Arkansas, 2004). Available as pdf file at http://comp.uark.edu/~mpianal/Suicide%26TheSelf.pdf (accessed on 25 May 2004).

14 Ibid.

15 This is Stuart Hall's term for oppositional reading: S. Hall, 'Encoding / Decoding', in Hall et al. (eds), *Culture, Media Language: Working Papers in Cultural Studies, 1972–1979* (London: Hutchinson, 1980), pp. 128–38.

16 It should also be noted that Morrissey, as a solo artist, recorded a song entreating the addressee not to resort to suicide: 'Angel, Angel, Down We Go Together' (on *Viva Hate* [1988]), could not be more explicit in its request – 'Angel, don't take your life . . . I love you more than life'.

17 The song was allegedly influenced by *A Room of One's Own* (1929), Woolf's critique of the patriarchal subjection of women prevented from reaching their literary potential. See V. Woolf, *A Room of One's Own* (San Diego, New York and London: Harvest Books, 1929). See Goddard, *The Smiths*, pp. 142–5 for discussion of this and other putative 'influences'.

18 W.H. Poteat, *Polanyian Meditations: In Search of a Post-Critical Logic* (Durham, NC: Duke University Press, 1985), p. 71.

19 A. Camus, *The Myth of Sisyphus*, trans. Justin O'Brien (London: Penguin, 2000), p. 11.

20 Ibid.

21 Ibid., p. 18.

22 S. Žižek, *On Belief* (London and New York: Routledge, 2001), p. 102.

23 Pianalto, *Suicide and the Self*.

24 Ibid. See also his webpage *Suicide and Philosophy: An internet resource for the philosophical study of suicide and its meaning for us.* http://comp.uark.edu/m~pianalto/suicide.htm (accessed on 31 October 2006).

25 See P. Eglin, 'Suicide', in R.J. Anderson and W.W. Sharrock (eds), *Teaching Papers in Sociology* (York: Longman, 1985) (unpaginated).

26 E. Durkheim (1897), *Suicide: A Study in Sociology* (trans. J.A. Spalding and G. Simpson) (London and New York: Routledge, 1952).

27 Eglin, 'Suicide'.

28 C.M. Smyth, C. MacLachlan and A. Clare, *Cultivating Suicide? Destruction of Self in a Changing Ireland* (Dublin: Liffey Press, 2003).

29 E.S. Shneidman, *The Suicidal Mind* (New York and Oxford: Oxford University Press, 1996).

30 Typically, people who take their own life have been diagnosed as clinically depressed – as suffering from a bipolar or schizoid disorder – so it is very easy to be convinced, after the event, that suicide is the result of a preventable and treatable illness – that suicidal persons require the kind of preventative care that only an interventionist agency like the institution of clinical psychiatry and its pharmacopoeia can provide. Pianalto, *Suicide and the Self*. See also *Suicide and Philosophy*.

31 Pianalto, *Suicide and the Self.*

32 Tacitly determining that 'victims' of psychological dysfunction are not responsible for their actions, the mental illness hypothesis indicates a refusal to consider suicide a voluntarily undertaken rational action: 'The only socially acceptable view of suicide', Thomas Szasz agrees, 'is as a "cry for help", uttered by a person who has a mental illness (depression) and denies that he is ill'. T.S. Szasz, 'Straight Talk About Suicide', *Ideas on Liberty*, 52 (September 2002), p. 34.

33 T.S. Szasz, 'Suicide as a Moral Issue', *The Freeman*, Vol. 49 (July 1999), pp. 41–2.

34 S. Kierkegaard, *Concluding Unscientific Postscript* (trans. H.V. Hong and E.H. Hong) (New York: Princeton University Press, 1989); M. Watts, *Kierkegaard* (Oxford: Oneworld, 2003), pp. 79–88; P. Gardiner, *Kierkegaard: A Very Short Introduction* (Oxford: Oxford University Press, 1988), pp. 92–6.

35 M.C. Nussbaum, *Love's Knowledge: Essays on Philosophy and Literature* (London and New York: Oxford University Press, 1990), p. 5.

36 Pianalto, *Suicide and the Self.* It is worth noting that Irish philosopher and psychiatrist Maurice O'Connor Drury (1907–76) strongly advocated such a revolutionary non-objectifying, non-judgemental and anti-reductive mode of therapeutic analysis; he claimed that an ethical therapeutics should acknowledge the subjective difference, and irreducible *thisness* of the 'patient'. Perhaps ultimately 'un-understandable', the person, he termed an 'individual enigma'. 'The truth is that . . . human beings are not meant to study each other as objects of scientific scrutiny, but to see each other as an individual subject that evolves according to its own laws.' Quoted in T. Duddy, *A History of Irish Thought* (London and New York: Routledge, 2002), pp. 305–8.

37 Pianalto, *Suicide and the Self.*

38 Morrissey, in Robertson, *Morrissey: In His Own Words*, p. 36.

39 Morrissey, in Goddard, *The Smiths*, p. 143.

40 Morrissey, in Robertson, *Morrissey: In His Own Words*, p. 26.

41 *Smiths Indeed*, 10 (Winter 1988), unpaginated.

42 SavBag, the letters page, *NME* 29 November 1986.

43 With particular reference to The Smiths, see *NME*, 8 November 1986; *NME*, 29 November 1986, p. 50; *NME*, 6 December 1986; see also *Smiths Indeed* issues 8 (1988); 9 (1988); 10 (1988); 11 (1989).

44 See Szasz, 'Straight Talk About Suicide', p. 34. Indeed, the expert view, canvassed by clinical-psychologist journalists calling for early intervention in newspapers, is founded on the view of suicide that Pianalto critiques. Their reduction of the problem of suicide to mental health statistics, and their confusion of suicide and parasuicide (attempted suicide or self-harm), betrays a serious misunderstanding. See, for instance, the article by Tony Humphries, 'We Need to Watch out for the Signals', *Irish Examiner*, 6 May 2005. Suicide, as Pianalto describes it, indicates the vulnerability of the subject in despair. It should not be understood as a

failure of the individual, therefore, but rather a failure of the socio-symbolic value systems (the very systems that promote the ideological construct of 'the expert') to meet the desire for acceptance and simultaneously accommodate the individual's demands for the expression of difference. Pianalto and several others have argued that suicide is associated with the problem of identity formation. In the extreme case, where identity formation leads to an irreconcilable conflict, suicide comes into the horizon of possibility as a solution. See M.J. Chandler, C.E. Lalonde, B.W. Sokol and D. Hallett, 'Personal Persistence, Identity Development, and Suicide: A Study of Native and Non-Native North American Adolescents', *Monographs of the Society for Research in Child Development*, Vol. 68, No. 2 (2003), p. 115. Suicide can therefore be understood according to this as a response to the conflict between social integration and the expression of individuality. See also K. Keohane and C. Kuhling, *Collision Culture: Transformations in Everyday Life in Ireland* (Dublin: Liffey Press, 2004) for a study that, not unproblematically, addresses these factors in the contemporary Irish context.

45 Pianalto, *Suicide and the Self.*

46 M. Kundera, *The Curtain: An Essay in Seven Parts* (trans. L. Asher) (London: Faber & Faber, 2007), p. 112.

47 A. Schopenhauer, 'Suicide', *The Essential Schopenhauer* (London: Unwin Books, 1962), p. 97.

48 Ibid., p. 98.

49 Ibid.

50 This is not insignificant. As Goddard points out, the band had recently moved back to Manchester. Goddard, '*The Queen is Dead*: Twenty Years On', *Uncut* (January 2006), p. 50. Goddard quotes Marr: '[In London] we were all isolated in flats, with no good hang-out, so I bought a hang-out back up here and everything fell into place creatively. It was all very insular. We just shut up shop, moved back and became incredibly Mancunian again. Even more Mancunian, if that's possible'.

51 Pianalto characterises suicide as an ethically legitimate response to despair, a response perceived by the subject to be volitional and freely undertaken. In order to understand the problem, he believes, suicide must be comprehended as a freely undertaken act. His aim from the beginning, he tells us, has been the effort 'to construe the problem of suicide as it pertains to human beings as agents (rather than as brains, a mass of psychological fodder, or as social products)'. Pianalto, *Suicide and the Self.*

52 'To die, to sleep,' he repeats, 'To sleep, perchance to dream: ay there's the rub, / For in that sleep of death what dreams may come / When we have shuffled off this mortal coil / Must give us pause . . .'. Bereft, clothed in his 'customary suits of inky black', in many respects, the brooding, pallid figure of Hamlet represents the quintessential melancholic.

53 Heraclitus of Ephesus was active circa 500 BCE.

54 G.S. Kirk and J.E. Raven, *The Presocratic Philosophers* (Cambridge: Cambridge University Press, 1964), p. 184. He was more commonly referred to as 'the obscure' and 'the riddler'. See also J. Barnes, *Early Greek Philosophy* (London: Penguin, 1987), p. 106.

55 Fragment 26 suggests that, as a torch is kindled to light a path in darkness, so in sleep, death is dimly touched by light, in the same way as, when awake, the sleeper in us is, in its turned-inward darkness, briefly lit. McKirahan, *Philosophy Before Socrates*, p. 119. Also M.R. Wright, *The Presocratics* (Bristol: Bristol Classical Press, 1985), pp. 6, 58.

56 M. Heidegger and Eugen Fink, *Heraclitus Seminar* (trans. C.H. Seibert) (Evanston, IL: Northwestern University Press, 1993), p. 149.

57 Ibid., p. 148.

58 Ibid., p. 147.

59 Ibid.

60 See also M. Proust, *A la Recherche du temps perdu*, for a similar meditation on the annihilation of the ego in sleep. *Swann's Way* (trans. C.K. Scott Moncrieff and T. Kilmartin) (London: Penguin, 1984), pp. 5–6.

61 G. Agamben, *Infancy and History: The Destruction of Experience* (trans. L. Heron) (London and New York: Verso, 1993), p. 76.

62 This interpretation was reinforced during Morrissey's 2006 live shows where the band, prior to playing 'How Soon is Now?', performed 'Auld Lang Syne' in the same frail, dreamy style to mimic a xylophone or music-box melody.

63 S. Plath, 'Insomniac', in T. Hughes (ed.), *Poems Selected by Ted Hughes* (London: Faber & Faber, 1985), p. 25. Incidentally, there is an episode in Plath's thematically relevant novel *The Bell Jar* which features 'Auld Lang Syne'. S. Plath, *The Bell Jar* (London: Faber & Faber, 1966), p. 57.

64 W. Benjamin, 'Theses On the Philosophy of History', *Illuminations* (trans. H. Zohn) (London: Fontana, 1973), p. 252–3; see also *The Arcades Project* (trans. H. Eiland and K. McLaughlin) (Cambridge, MA: Belknap Press, 2001), pp. 462–3, 475; and 'Central Park' (trans. E. Jephcott & H. Eiland), *The Writer of Modern Life* (Cambridge, MA: Belknap Press, 2002), p. 160.

65 Benjamin, *The Arcades Project*, [M°, 24] p. 856.

66 G. Agamben, 'The Phantasms of Eros' in *Stanzas* (trans. R.L. Martinez) (Minneapolis and London: University of Minnesota Press, 1993), p. 25.

67 A. Seifert, 'A Theory of Projects: Its Application to Death and Suicide', *Philosophy and Phenomenological Research*, Vol. 39, No. 2 (1978), pp. 208–18.

68 Ibid., p. 213.

69 S. Kierkegaard, *The Sickness Unto Death* (trans. W. Lowrie) (New York: Princeton University Press, 1968).

70 Ibid., p. 181.

71 E. Levinas, *On Escape* (trans. B. Bergo) (Stanford, CA: Stanford University Press, 2003), p. 63.

72 Watts, *Kierkegaard*, p. 175.

73 Plath, *The Bell Jar*, pp. 152, 233; see also 'Suicide off Egg Rock', in *Poems Selected*, p. 10.

74 Levinas, *On Escape*, p. 58.

75 Ibid., p. 66.

76 Ibid.

77 Kierkegaard, *Sickness Unto Death*, p. 151.

78 Levinas, *On Escape*, p. 64.

79 Ibid., p. 67.

80 J. Rolland, in ibid., p. 82. Interestingly, Giorgio Agamben maintains that melancholy was classically associated with the insomniac state and not, as latter exegetes assume, with the somnolent. Agamben, *Stanzas*, p. 14.

81 Plath, *The Bell Jar*, p. 178. Images of claustrophobia recur throughout the novel: 'I was so scared, as if I were being stuffed farther and farther into a black, airless sack with no way out' (p. 123).

82 'Gasping, dying, yet somehow still alive' ('Well I Wonder'); 'Time's tide will smother you' ('That Joke Isn't Funny Anymore', where, incidentally, Morrissey also refers to 'people who feel so very lonely, their only desire is to die'); 'Oh Mother I can feel the soil falling over my head' ('I Know It's Over'); 'Oh so smother me, mother' ('Rubber Ring'). Such metaphors, in Morrissey's lyrics, are often associated with an overbearing, specifically maternal influence.

83 W. Benjamin, 'Goethes Wahlverwandtschaften', *Gesammelete Schriften* I. 1 (Frankfurt: Suhrkamp 1980), p. 201. This explains Blanchot's confusing claim that suicide is, ultimately, an affirmative act. 'He who kills himself' he writes, 'is a great affirmer of the *present*' because he still has the hope and strength to execute this extreme act, a hope and strength that is essentially, and paradoxically, life-affirming: 'suicide retains the power of an exceptional affirmation.' M. Blanchot, *The Space of Literature* (trans. A Smock) (Lincoln: University of Nebraska Press 1982), p. 103.

84 Benjamin's suicide note provides an interesting epitome of the ideas in this context. 'In a situation with no way out, I have little choice but to end it. My life will finish in a little village in the Pyrenees where no one knows me.' Benjamin, in M. Brodersen, *Walter Benjamin: A Biography* (trans. M.R. Green and I. Ligers) (London: Verso, 1996), p. 257. See also J. Parini, *Benjamin's Crossing* (London: Anchor, 1988). It has been observed that Benjamin's entire body of work can be read as a complex response to, and preparation for, suicide: he was intensely affected by the suicide-pact of his friends Fritz Heinle and Rika Seligson in August 1914. See M. Jay, 'Walter Benjamin, Remembrance and the First World War', H. Geyer-Ryan, P. Koopman and K. Yntema (eds), *Benjamin Studien 1: Perception and Experience in Modernity* (Amsterdam/New York: Rodopi, 2002), pp. 187–8.

85 Kierkegaard, *The Sickness Unto Death*.

86 Ibid.

87 See, again, Plath, *The Bell Jar*, p. 123.

88 Watts, *Kierkegaard*, p. 180.

89 Goddard, *The Smiths*, p. 153.

90 According to Goddard, Morrissey sourced this weird sample from a record connected with parapsychologist Konstantin Raudive's madcap study of the voices of the dead, *Breakthrough: An Amazing Experiment in Electronic Communication with the Dead* (1971). The particular piece selected by Morrissey was a cryptic message from Raudive's late colleague Professor Gebhard Frei rendered into English by Nadia Fowler.

91 D. Banhart, in 'Last Night I Dreamt That Somebody Loved Me . . .' *Uncut* (March 2007), p. 39.

92 Morrissey, in Goddard, *The Smiths*, p. 153.

93 Aston, 'Morrissey: Interview', p. 56.

94 C.S. Peirce, 'Logic as Semiotic: the Theory of Signs', in *Philosophical Writings of Peirce* (ed. J. Buchler) (New York: Dover, 1955), p. 108.

95 See, for instance, Benjamin, 'Theory of Knowledge', in *Selected Writings* 1 (ed. M. Bullock and M.W. Jennings) (Cambridge, MA: The Belnkap Press, 1996), p. 276, for the first instance of this concept. Also *The Arcades Project* [N 3a, 3], [N 18, 4], [K1, 1], [K1, 2], [K1, 5], [K1a, 9] 'The first tremors of awakening serve to deepen sleep' pp. 389, 399, 464, 486; 'Paris, Capital of the Nineteenth Century', in *The Arcades Project*, p. 13. The concept of awakening as it operates in Benjamin's philosophy of history derives from the Overture of Proust's *A la Recherche du temps perdu. Swann's Way*, pp. 7–8.

96 'Sleep is a way in which we come into the proximity of being dead', Eugen Fink observes, 'and is not merely a metaphor for death'. Heidegger and Fink, *Heraclitus Seminar*, p. 147.

97 Benjamin uses the word *Aufblitzen* rendered by Zohn as 'flares up briefly', 'Theses on the Philosophy of History', p. 248.

98 Benjamin, *The Arcades Project* [N9, 7], p. 473.

99 Husserl, in Levinas, 'Philosophy and Awakening', *Discovering Existence with Husserl* (trans. R.A. Cohen and M.B. Smith) (Evanston, IL: Northwestern University Press, 1998), p. 176.

100 M. Löwy, *Fire Alarm: Reading Walter Benjamin's 'On the Concept of History'* (trans. C. Turner) (London and New York: Verso, 2005), p. 35. Benjamin's idea is parsed as follows: 'every past, victim, every attempt at emancipation, however humble and "minor" will be rescued from oblivion . . . that is to say recognised, honoured and remembered.'

101 'Nothing that has ever happened should be regarded as lost for history', Benjamin, 'Theses on the Philosophy of History', p. 246.

102 M. Foucault, 'Un plaisir si simple', *Dits et ecrits*, 3, pp. 777–9, quoted in D. Macey, *Michel Foucault* (London: Reaktion Books, 2004), p. 124. See also Heraclitus,

Fragment 89 which puts this concept in context: 'For the waking there is one common world, but when asleep each person turns away to a private one' (McKirihan, *Philosophy Before Socrates*, p. 118).

103 A. Badiou, *The Century* (trans. A. Toscano) (Cambridge: Polity, 2007), p. 94.

6

'A BOY IN THE BUSH': CHILDHOOD, SEXUALITY AND THE SMITHS

Sheila Whiteley

While there is a well-established litany of songs that engage with illicit sex, not least within the popular domain, those that seek to engage with the pre-pubescent body are often veiled in metaphor or couched in mythology, such as the Oedipal motif of Jim Morrison's psychodrama 'The End'. As I discuss in my essay 'Nursery Crymes',[1] one of the problems in identifying pop's evocation of this issue revolves around age. How young is too young, and what is the perceived boundary between songs which express a carnal desire for the mother, and those which express a similar lust for the child? Is there a distinction between songs which perform under-age desire such as Tatu's 'All The Things She Said',[2] those which focus on the boundaries of legality (Sam Cooke, 'She Was Only Sixteen'), and those which express a more predatory obsession such as Eminem's 'Guilty Conscience'?[3]

My concern in 'Nursery Crymes' was to explore the problematic relationship between image, age and musical performance. More specifically, I was interested in the erotic potential and appeal of child artists such as Brenda Lee,[4] Annabella Lwin[5] and Frankie Lymon,[6] not least the attraction of what can be described as an adult performance by a child and how this engages with the paedophiliac gaze. Clearly, there is a distinction to be made between songs performed by people who have committed sex offences, and those that somehow suggest an unlawful love.[7] Similarly, songs which describe paedophiliac abuse, such as 'Centipede', where Sonja Aurora Madan (of Echobelly) explores the paradox of being abused ('you're the evil world of the nursery rhyme') and loving your abuser ('you're my only friend, don't be cruel to me') are not necessarily autobiographical. Rather, like Smiths songs that hint at this issue, the use of 'I/Me/You' within a fictionalised mini-narrative – in which the author takes the leading role – heightens dramatic effect[8] and, as Madan reflects, is 'written in a voyeuristic sense'.[9]

Morrissey's sexual orientation has attracted attention from the outset of his career, and his insistence that 'it's all within the lyrics' was given a specific focus in 1983 when *The Sun* claimed that the BBC was holding an emergency meeting to decide whether a song about child abuse should be broadcast on the David Jensen Show. According to correspondent Nick Ferrari, the lyrics to 'Handsome Devil' – the B-side to The Smiths' first single, 'Hand In Glove' (1983) – contained 'clear references to picking up kids for sexual kicks'.[10] While this was subsequently recognised as tabloid-led sensationalism, the BBC took the precautionary measure of removing a specially recorded six-minute version of another song, 'Reel Around The Fountain', from the David Jensen Show.[11] It was the first of Morrissey's many tussles with the press and the establishment, and it is this tension between his often cryptic though provocative lyrics and his overt and public confrontations that provides particular insights into his personal politics. The former, with their multiple connotations, are open to interpretation; the latter provide an anchoring contextualisation. What emerges is an outspoken and controversial figure whose views on environmentalism, racism, sexuality, gender politics,[12] drugs and terrorism have made him one of the most interviewed musicians of his time. Secretive about his personal life yet politically outspoken, 'an ordinary, working-class anti-star who nevertheless loves to hog the spotlight, a nice man who says the nastiest things about other people, a shy man who is also an outrageous narcissist';[13] these seemingly contradictory traits situate Morrissey as both challenging and controversial.

This mood of confrontation is explicit in The Smiths' album titles: *Meat Is Murder, The Queen Is Dead, The World Won't Listen, Strangeways, Here We Come.* They read like banner headlines, demanding attention, exuding attitude. The politicised lyrics are equally compelling, locking into the social and cultural divide caused by Thatcherism, focusing attention on domestic violence, child murder, animal rights and bullying, and peppered with subtle references to such iconic figures as Shelagh Delaney, Oscar Wilde, James Dean and Jack Kerouac. To an extent, there is a possible comparison with the 1960s counter-culture, where musicians were recognised as central to its political aims, voicing dissent and opposition to the dominant ideologies surrounding war, marriage, education and the exploitation of developing countries by capitalist states.[14] What attracted me to that scene, both at the time and today, were the lyrics and the musicality, and while I had subsequently welcomed punk's confrontational stance (not being a fan of the excesses of 'prog rock'), I missed that sense of musicianship. Hence my love for The Smiths. Certainly there was little in The Sex Pistols' 'gobbing' and in-yer-face delivery that compares to Morrissey's somewhat flat and introverted vocal style. His attack was far more subtle, far more sophisticated, and coupled with the undoubted prowess of Johnny Marr's guitar playing – with its emphasis on melody and texture – The Smiths promised a new and relevant sense of direction. There was an indisputable musicality, and you were either passionately for or against them. As John Peel said of their first session on his BBC radio show, 'there was a sense of completeness. Where the hell did they come from?'[15] The fascination continues not least because there is always something new to find: connections, interactions, references and cross-references that relate to my own fascination with dialogics and the understanding that 'meaning is situated both socially and historically, that it works through dialogue – echoes, traces, contrasts, responses – both with previous discursive moments and, at the same time, with addressees real or imagined.'[16]

The concept of dialogic exchange provides a particular insight into intertextuality and how meaning in popular music is produced at many different levels. A textual analysis of lyrics and musical style provides one important methodological trajectory, but meaning is also produced through dialogue within the textures, voices and structures; between producers and addressees; between discourses, musical and other. Add to this a concern with sexuality and gender, the singing style, the visual gesture, the image and, significantly, the ideological interests that support dominant interpretations, and it is apparent that how one 'tells' the story is crucial to its interpretation. In effect, the story told is one among many, and while musical analysis, and research into historical and cultural data remain important, meaning is always at issue. There is no one scientifically 'true' account of the music, but rather a sense of collective complicity: is this story plausible,[17] is *my* interpretation plausible, and *is* the report in *The Sun* simply sensationalist journalism?

Handsome devils or fallen angels?

My initial discussion focuses on four tracks that appear to contain paedophiliac connotations, so relating to my particular interest in sexuality and to issues concerning child-centred lyrics: the relationship between image, age and musical performance (the persona created in interpreting a particular song) that situates the artist/song as problematic, as inviting questionable pleasures in their audience. Not least, I am interested in the relationship between the erotic (love of, or instinct for, life, *eros*) and the thanatic (love of, or instinct for, death, *thanatos*). Both evoke and celebrate sensuality, both work in the imagination. But, as A.S. Byatt points out, it is arguably the case that the liberation of passions can lead to 'refinements of pleasure, of ecstasies of perception, of courtesies and reciprocities undreamed'[18] and hence to the liberation of those passions which take pleasure in the hurt of others. Within human nature, death and its relationship to pleasure are not necessarily distinct. The one can have an uneasy and perverse relationship to the other. Indeed, it is difficult not to surmise that 'shameful things, shameful secrets, desires . . . (which) are kept secret and separate . . . fester in body and brain'.[19] You cannot unsee what you have seen. You cannot unhear what you have heard. You cannot un-experience what you have experienced – not least if you were brought up a Catholic boy.

Representations of eroticised children are commonplace, and appear in the work of writers such as Lewis Carroll, whose fascination with and suppressed longing for the innocent world of the child was equalled only by his desire to 'escape from the improper implications of passion introduced into his world by the adult women around him'.[20] While Carroll's photographs of naked girls (including Alice Liddell, whose fictional adventures are chronicled in *Alice in Wonderland* and *Alice Through the Looking Glass*) suggest a paedophiliac obsession with underage flesh, the implications of illicit desire was given a more explicit focus in Vladimir Nabokov's controversial novel *Lolita* (1959). As Jeremy Irons (who played the predatory male lead Humbert Humbert in Adrian Lyne's film of the book) explains, '[i]ts power comes from moments when you want the love between the man and the girl to succeed, when their happiness seems untouchable',[21] so inviting readers to reassess their relation to their own sexuality, while engaging with libidinous fantasy.

While paedophiles provide the most extreme example of child abuse, it has become disconcertingly apparent that there is no such thing as 'the innocent eye' in contemporary society. Films, books, art, the media and popular music continue to have an ambivalent attitude towards representations of children-as-adults, adults-as-children, and in the profit-driven world of advertising, fashion and music, the image and culture of the young are appropriated for the high pleasure quotient they evoke. Youthful allure is a sellable commodity and is all too often exploited as a marketing ploy with little thought of the consequences. Today, with the tabloids insistent that paedophiles lurk on every street corner, populating the web with sites that offer horrendous excursions into child abuse and pornography, we are all too aware of the problems surrounding texts that hint at paedophiliac desire. As such, the question arises as to whether Morrissey's lyrics touch a raw nerve in their evocation of illicit sex, whether they tend more towards libidinous fantasy, or whether they are a celebration of child-molesting, as *The Sun*'s reaction claimed.

With these thoughts in mind, I want to return to The Smiths and the tracks 'Handsome Devil', 'This Charming Man', 'Reel Around The Fountain', and 'The Hand That Rocks The Cradle'. As fans are aware, Morrissey's lyrics work like a personal diary in their sense of observation but are, like Morrissey himself, enigmatic. As the novelist Will Self has explained, Morrissey 'encapsulates deep thought, glosses it with irony and then repackages it with emotion.'[22] The question that arises is the extent to which this is true of the songs that have been perceived as potentially paedophiliac.

There is little doubt that Morrissey was acutely aware of Manchester's social and cultural environment[23] and, as such, it is unlikely that he would have been insensitive to the underage rent boys who haunted the arches close to UMIST (University of Manchester Institute of Science and Technology) and what is now ironically dubbed (C)anal Street. The inclusion of 'I Want A Boy For My Birthday' (a cover of the 1963 B-side by 60s girl-group The Cookies, and the first song to be committed to tape by Morrissey and Marr) in their early set lists[24] teased the listener by playing with the connotations associated with same-sex desire.[25] Thus, while the gender reorientation and shift in sexual dynamic can be offset by the argument that this was simply a cover version, there is an obvious tension between the straight heteroconformity of the original and Morrissey's queered performance. As such, the word 'boy' takes on more problematic connotations, insinuating a space of possibility that includes boyfriend as well as the age-based associations of 'boy' and its relationship to the innocence of childhood.

These problematic associations are compounded in 'The Hand That Rocks The Cradle', where lyrics such as 'I once had a child . . . and I never even asked his name' and 'your mother she just never knew' situate nostalgia within a disturbing frame of reference, resonating with the plaintive 'I didn't know it was going on' of domestic child abuse. As the opening number of their stage debut at the Manchester Ritz in October 1982,[26] 'The Hand That Rocks The Cradle' was immediately controversial. It was to have been the title of the band's first album, and the decision to change it to *The Smiths* might well have been informed by the tabloid scandal mentioned earlier. Written in the first person singular, the lyrics read like a poetic monologue of illicit desire, while posing and reposing the enigma of identity: who is the protagonist, who is the abused? As is characteristic of Morrissey's lyrics, identity is never revealed. Rather, the opening lines create an underlying unease – 'please don't cry for the ghost and the storm outside' – a plea which anticipates the elegiac 'Suffer Little Children', the final track on the album, where the lines 'you might sleep but you will never dream' of the Moors murderers are set against the sound of child-like laughter.[27] As Rogan comments, 'The Hand That Rocks The Cradle' evokes not only 'the innocence of childhood but also the genuine terror that childlike imaginings can inspire'.[28]

Citations from Al Jolson's 'Sonny Boy' ('climb upon my knee, sonny boy') cast a dark shadow over the original. Surely this was a simple song of affection for a three-year-old boy. But what is affection and where does the longing to protect lead, when 'you are all that matters'? To a vow of 'never, never, never again' before returning to 'the shrine', 'like a moth to the flame', promises forgotten? What haunts most are the child's eyes – beautiful yet sad – and the way in which Morrissey's monochromatic vocal creates a web of melancholia which sits, uneasily, on Marr's melodic guitar line. It is a song that situates innocence ('your untouched, unsoiled wondrous eyes') within a context that implys possession ('I once had a child'), but while Morrissey's stylised performance juxtaposes detached observation with phrases that hint at suppressed desire ('I'm here and here I'll stay/Together we lie, together we pray') there is a clear distinction to be made between the constructed narrative of the lyrics, which structures the experience of the song, the characterisation inherent in the performance, and the performer as mediated by the press. Thus, while it is tempting to conflate the experience described in the song with the author (not least in a singer-songwriter context), they are not necessarily synonymous. Rather, there is an analogy with a self-penned drama in which the author takes the leading role: it may relate to observation or personal experience but it is, nevertheless, fictionalised.

Even so, the ambiguity in Morrissey's lyrics and the dramatic use of 'I'/'me' within the context of lyrics which 'could be said to contain paedophiliac leit-motifs'[29] invites speculation, and 'The Hand That Rocks The Cradle' was not alone in attracting controversy. As Rogan comments, '[it] seems remarkable that Morrissey failed to detect the paedophiliac connotations in "Handsome Devil"'[30] not least when sexual favours are aligned with a successful outcome in exams. Yet while the association with sado-masochism ('I crack the whip and you skip, but you deserve it'), homoeroticism ('Let me get your head on the conjugal bed') and the tension between the overt and the implied ('and when we're in your scholarly room, who will swallow whom?') can imply a predatory undertow, there is a clear distinction between 'Morrissey's fascina-tion for the loss of spiritual/sexual innocence'[31] and his personal views on pae-odophilia – 'We do not condone child molesting. We have never molested a child', the singer explained in 1983, adding: 'I wish I could laugh about this . . . but I can't because it's very serious, it's just a little bit too serious', referring to the claims that had been 'fabricated by Gary Bushell who was our arch enemy, and [who] went out of his way . . . to contact certain people at "The Sun" to write something totally denouncing about us'.[32] Maybe, as Rogan suggests, it was the 'archness and literary playfulness [that] actually nettled [Morrissey's] detractors'[33] or, indeed, the naked male that featured on the sleeve of The Smiths' debut single.[34] More likely, it was the indeterminacy surrounding the term 'boy' within an arguably provocative and homoerotic context that provoked outrage, but as Morrissey stated at the time, 'I'm certainly not going to change the way I write because I think it's essential. If I have to be accused of anything, it's because I write strongly from the heart . . . if you dare get too personal, and I don't mean *offensively* personal but just *too* close, then it's what a "strange" person, let's get him on the guillotine.'[35]

Morrissey's literary playfulness is at its most pronounced in 'This Charming Man', which had replaced 'Reel Around The Fountain' as the group's second single, climbing to number twenty-five in the British pop charts in November 1983, this time attracting more favourable attention from the press. As *New Musical Express* (*NME*) writer Danny Kelly com-mented, it was 'one of those moments when a vivid, electric awareness of the power of music is born or renewed'.[36] Mike Smith's description of the song highlights its rapturous feel:

> At one level, it is an immaculate pop song (two minutes and forty-three seconds of pure joy). The infectious r&b groove (laid down by bass player Andy Rourke and drummer Mike Joyce) is complemented by Marr's guitar which, with thirteen tracks at his disposal, weaves in and out of the texture with incredible skill and dexterity. The construction of the song is simple with two basic sections. The verses alternate between minor and major every four bars, lending the song a constant feel of melancholic tension and satisfying resolution; the chorus, which is dominated by Rourke's descending bass line, also serves as the closing section. The whole arrangement is punctuated by dramatic instrumental stops, with the band being led back in by Morrissey's vocal which generates both a musical and narrative excitement about the 'desolate' hillside rendezvous.[37]

The cryptic phrases, with their erotically nuanced subtext, are enigmatic. Who is 'this charming man' in his 'charming car'? The juxtaposition of the 'punctured bicycle on a hillside desolate' with the smooth leather upholstery of the passenger seat and the reflective 'will Nature make a man of me yet?' hints at a sexual rite of passage and elicits a sense of identification which is triggered by the foregrounding of personal involvement characteristic of The Smiths' early songs: 'All men have secrets and here is mine', as Morrissey sang in the opening line of 'What Difference Does It Make?'

Sex in cars is something Morrissey would return to later in The Smiths' career, most notably in 'That Joke Isn't Funny Anymore' (1985): 'and on cold leather seats / well it suddenly struck me / I just might die with a smile on my face after all'.[38] Whether based on personal experience or simply journalistic observation (and Morrissey spent much of his adolescence writing letters to the *NME*), such songs nevertheless express a homoerotic longing which is clearly at odds with his Catholic upbringing. Returning to Byatt's observation that 'shameful things, shameful secrets, suppressed desires (which) are kept secret and separate . . . fester in body and brain',[39] it is relevant to note, in this context, that Morrissey has always refused to talk about the homoerotic connotations and references in his songs. The enigma surrounding his sexuality is matched by the enigma surrounding his muses and, as such, it is unlikely that we will ever know the identity of his protagonists if, indeed, they are based on actual encounters. The 'Handsome Devil' and 'Charming Man', like that of the enigmatic 'you' of 'Reel Around The Fountain' are thus cloaked in mystery, but there remains an underlying knowingness, an eroticism which raises the question of whether the lyrics indicate a personal reminiscence of 'how you took a child, and you made him old', and whether they can be interpreted as conveying paedophiliac connotations.

'I dreamt about you last night . . .' The simplicity and directness of the lyrics work like the 'once upon a time' of fairytale and myth, transporting the listener into a narrative that taps into a past experience. It is both reflective and wistful ('you can pin and mount me like a butterfly', but 'take me to the haven of your bed' was 'something that you never said'), reminiscing on a relationship that was transitory or, at best, on the protagonist's terms. The allusions to sexual submission ('Slap me on the patio, I'll take it now') are juxtaposed with phrases that suggest an underlying longing which is heightened by repetition of the pivotal phrase ('fifteen minutes with you, I wouldn't say no'). There is, then, the suggestion of a powerful and life-changing experience that continues to preoccupy the thoughts of the narrator. Certainly there is no animosity. Rather, the subtle changes in the refrain suggest a mood of yearning which shifts from 'I'll take it now' to 'I'll take it slowly', as if to suggest that the time spent together was too brief, that 'the main thrust of the song is still, on an emotional level, one of unexpurgated love'.[40] It would seem, then, that 'Reel Around The Fountain' has a nostalgic soft-focus which works against an interpretation of child-abuse. There is no monster who actively procures children, making them old, sexually knowing. Rather, there is the suggestion of an affirmative sexual awakening, which challenges dominant perceptions about the protagonist ('people see no worth in you, but I do') and the negative associations of the sexual act ('they were so wrong'). Is this, then, about the archetypal paedophile who society actively condemns? Is this the face we should fear?

Arguably, interpretation is conjectural. In common with films and novels, songs can actively engage the sympathy of the listener or arouse antagonism. It is part of the stock in trade of the skilful song writer, not least one with literary aspirations, and Morrissey's choice of words invites speculation.[41] By locating his narrative within a social setting, he constructs a scenario 'of physical desire spiked with tremendous humour . . . [and] erotic intent.'[42] For his admirers, his lyrical style is 'special, singular, monstrously good';[43] for his critics, 'perverted filth'.[44] The ambiguity of the lyrics is given a particular edge by the tone and melodic contouring of the vocal line, where Morrissey's monochromatic, sung-spoken phrasing and the offsetting of vocal pitches with the chords to which they belong suggest a detached and often ironic stance. But as Morrissey has a tendency to taunt with his lyrical expression, there is always a double-edge to his songs. Clearly, there is no empirical evidence to help interpretation. We know neither the age of the boy nor that of the sexual protagonist; we only infer 'his' sex, because it is Morrissey who narrates 'the tale'. Interpretation, then, is subjective. My personal feeling is that the song reflects on a socially taboo subject in a way that causes us to reflect on how a seemingly perverse experience can, with hindsight, evoke a nostalgic yearning; a song which makes us sit back and think.

Is it a case, then, of how 'the tale were told'? Is it because pop music is still considered too lightweight to tackle moral issues that Morrissey attracts such controversy? Returning briefly to 'Suffer Little Children' (the one track on the album that is unequivocally concerned with extremes of abuse), Morrissey had reported that as a child he had been deeply affected by the Moors murders, which had taken place on the outskirts of Manchester on Saddleworth Moor in the mid-1960s. The realisation that Pauline Reade, Lesley Ann Downey, John Kilbride and Edward Evans were only a few years older than he left a lasting impression. Given Morrissey's deeply embedded social conscience and his personal relationship to Manchester and the north-west, it is not so surprising that he should turn to the Moors murders. Given his gift for narrative, it is also not surprising that his lyrics would relate to the different personae – the victims, the mother of one of the victims, and the murderers (Ian Brady and Myra Hindley) – in an elegiac lament ('Oh Man-ches-ter, so much to answer for'). The poignancy of the lyrics lies in their detail ('Lesley Ann with your pretty white beads'), stark realism ('dig a shallow grave'), reported speech ('whatever he has done, I have done'), the juxtaposi-tion of sadism ('Edward see those alluring lights, tonight will be your very last night') and grief ('I know my son is dead'), and the plea of the child to 'find me' – a reference to the fact that the location of Keith Bennett's grave has never been found.[45] The mood is established in Marr's introduction, where the alternating Dmaj7–Amaj7 chord structure suggests a rocking motion, which cradles the flat, monochromatic vocal line evocative both of reportage and a funereal lament for the victims. It is, as Morrissey confirms, 'a memorial to the children and to all like them who have suffered such a fate'.[46] But what of the other songs under consideration?

Reassessing the evidence

It is interesting to note that the article on child molesting to which Rogan and others have subsequently referred did not in fact appear in *The Sun* on 25 August 1983, but rather featured in the edition of 5 September 1983 under the title '"Ban Child-Sex Pop Song" Plea to Beeb'. As the *NME* commented (24 September 1983) 'two weeks' ago, *The Sun* ran a news story by their showbiz correspondent, Nick Ferrari . . . [whose] spot-the-pervert accusations alleged that 'Handsome Devil' contained clear references to picking up kids for sexual kicks'[47] and claimed that the BBC were holding an emergency meeting to decide whether or not it should be broadcast on the David Jensen Show. The report also claimed that 'as part of their live act, [The Smiths] also do a version of 'Climb Upon My Knee, Sonny Boy' about picking up a seven-year-old in a park',[48] and alleged that Morrissey had said: 'I don't feel immoral singing about molesting children'.[49] *Sounds* 'then ran a damning indictment of the band in their gossip column *Jaws* – penned by Gary Bushell, a fervent enemy of the Mancunian Quartet . . . [who was also] blamed by The Smiths' record company, Rough Trade, for giving *The Sun* its derogatory and misleading information in the first place.'[50]

While Bushell subsequently accused Dave McCullough (his rival and ardent fan of The Smiths) of being the first to interpret the band's lyrics as paedophiliac – thus instigating the controversy – the accusation that Morrissey condoned child-molesting was sufficiently inflammatory for the BBC to ban the scheduled broadcast of 'Reel Around The Fountain' (which Ferrari had confused with 'Handsome Devil') from the David Jensen show, as mentioned earlier. According to producer Mike Hawkes, this was purely a precautionary measure, and when 'fellow producer John Walters learnt of The Smiths' plight, and the circumstances surrounding the band, he . . . offered them a second John Peel session as compensation . . . so ensuring two BBC promotional broadcasts in the space of three weeks.'[51] As Rogan observes, 'the paedophile drama ultimately proved advantageous to the Smiths, for not only did it provide them with national publicity but secured the unexpected bonus of a recording session'.[52]

Nevertheless, Ferrari's article and its misquoted date of publication provide an interesting insight into the way in which otherwise unconnected events can be given a sensationalist spin, not least in homophobic tabloids. On the day of the supposed Smiths article, the front page of *The Sun* was dominated by a report of a homosexual attack on a young boy in Brighton and the headline feature of music magazine *Sounds*, 'Mind Molesting', conveniently aligned the two reports: 'To the anger and embarrassment of many *Sounds* staffers, the band's sicko songs were first brought to the world's attention and in fact *praised* by [*Sounds* journalist] Dave McCullough who described them as "the kind of ultra-violent grime rock 'n' roll needs." Try telling that to the mother of the six year old Brighton boy recently mob-raped by paedophiles.'[53]

McCullough's review of The Smiths' University of London Union gig in the 14 May 1983 edition of *Sounds* had described the band as 'MONSTROUSLY GOOD', and featured a photo of Morrissey with the caption 'THE SMITHS. Under 16s are advised to avoid their gigs'. The predatory connotations were clarified in his identification of Morrissey as a lyricist 'from the brink . . . Most of his word-packed lyrics are about child molesting, and more mature sexual experimentation.'[54] As Rogan observes, '[s]ignificantly, McCullough saw nothing distasteful, disconcerting or immoral about Morrissey's lyrics and even the lines he misheard ('Climb upon my knee Sonny Boy', the coda to 'The Hand That Rocks The Cradle', which he interpreted as a 'come on to a seven year old in a park') were applauded for their 'originality and humorous outrage'.[55] His enthusiasm for Morrissey's subject matter was further evidenced in the 4 June 1983 edition of *Sounds*. 'The subject of child-molesting crops up more than a few times in Smiths songs. They are hilarious lyrics, more so because they suddenly touch on the personal.'[56]

McCullough's reference to the personal – the inference that the subject matter hints at the autobiographical within the context of 'child-molesting' – is clearly both problematic and inflammatory, and possibly fuelled Ferrari's allegations in *The Sun*. It is also evident that Ferrari's report drew heavily on McCullough's misquotation of the lyrics in 'The Hand That Rocks The Cradle' and his identification of 'child-molesting' lyrics in 'Handsome Devil'. As Dorrell commented at the time, the article was both 'garbled and inaccurate',[57] and served to both instigate and support a blanket connection between homosexuality and paedophilia. Nevertheless, Morrissey's explanation of its subject matter did little to clarify his intentions as a lyricist:

> the message of the song is to forget the cultivation of the brain and to concentrate on the cultivation of the body. 'A boy in the bush . . .' is addressed to the scholar. There's more to life than books you know but not much more – that is the essence of the song. So you can take it and stick it in an article about child-molesting and it will make absolute perfect sense. But you can do that with anybody. You can do that with Abba.[58]

As Rogan observes, his explanation is 'at worst evasive, and at best curiously obscure and dismissive' not least because 'the rational tone of these lines contrasts markedly with the explicit innuendo and seething lust dramatized earlier'.[59] What is interesting, however, is that Morrissey, Bushell and Ferrari 'failed to voice the crucial point that writing about child molestation (intentionally or not) is not the same as proselytizing or prompting such conduct'.[60] Thus, while there are enough vagaries in all four songs discussed to mount a reasonably damning prosecution argument of paedophiliac content,[61] I would agree with Goddard that the accusation that Morrissey condoned child-molesting is both malicious and ludicrous,[62] and that *The Sun*'s conflation of the lyrics with paedophiliac abuse reveals a more sinister, homophobic agenda.

It is nevertheless possible that the controversy surrounding *The Sun*'s accusations made Morrissey reflect on his self-image, not least where children were concerned. The Smiths subsequently made numerous appearances on children's TV shows (such as ITV's *Datarun* and *Charlie's Bus*) in which they engaged in light-hearted banter with young children. This was quite untypical for 'alternative' rock bands of the period, especially one on an 'indie' label like Rough Trade. *Splat!* (a regular slot in *Charlie's Bus*) featured a group of children, including Elvis Costello's son, who joined Morrissey and Marr on an open bus ride to Kew Gardens. After responding to such questions as 'Where did the Smiths get their name from?' and 'Where are we going?' they then wandered around Kew, to the strains of 'Heaven Knows I'm Miserable

Now' before being joined by Sandie Shaw for an acoustic version of 'Jeane'.[63] ITV's choice of accompanying songs is interesting. The *Datarun*[64] clip actually begins with 'Reel Around The Fountain', and the children from Morrissey's old school (where the session was filmed) sang the chorus to 'This Charming Man', albeit 'comically out-of-sync'[65] when Morrissey and Marr performed a short acoustic version of the song. It is, of course, conjectural as to whether these early 1984 appearances were an attempt to 'correct' the tabloid misreading of late 1983 but, in retrospect, it does appear a strange choice of songs for a children's TV show. Clearly, the association of education and growing up ('how you took a child and you made him old') is subtly nuanced, and even Johnny Marr called the lyrics of 'This Charming Man' 'flummoxing' when asked to comment on the song's implicitly erotic overtones.[66] Nevertheless, the fact that similarly ambiguous lyrics had been the subject of controversy at the BBC, and cited as 'condoning child-molesting' in *The Sun*, is a reminder that interpretation is speculative. ITV saw no such threat to their programming. Rather, it would seem that their response to The Smiths' notoriety was more tongue-in-cheek. As Simon Goddard writes, the programme 'ended with two puppets dancing to "What Difference Does It Make?" while reading a copy of *Melody Maker*'.[67] Then again, any interpretation can only be conjectural . . .

Postscript: interpreting sexuality and queerness

The framing of childhood/puberty in popular music remains problematic. As Biddle and Jarman-Ivens note, the 'figure of the boy – specifically the adolescent boy – operates as a site of slippage, as he sits on the border between childhood and adulthood. His juvenility performs an important role in his sexualization, since he is man enough to be desired and desiring, and yet boy enough to be unthreatening.' They continue, '[i]t is those moments where the performativity of masculinity becomes legible that masculinity "itself" becomes legible: in the scenario where man/boy is played out, masculinity "as such" operates . . . to consolidate the power already in place . . . resolutely connecting pleasure and the performance of pleasure to an enactment of being taken up by another's will.'[68] It is, perhaps, this sense of domination in conjunction with lyrics which suggest a longing for illicit sex that connect most strongly to the performative 'as if' of Morrissey's lyrics. It also provides a possible explanation of why a homophobic tabloid such as *The Sun* could so easily link together two unconnected narratives of 'picking up kids for sexual kicks'. While there is no-one specific to whom Morrissey's lyrics refer, they nevertheless foreground issues of gender and sexuality, and configurations of masculinity in particular, which can be exploited by unscrupulous and sensationalist journalism.

The complex relationship between music, sexuality and gender remains and continues to taunt and provoke controversy due, largely, to its association with identity politics, society and the self. Most recently, the sleeve of Morrissey's 2009 album *Years Of Refusal* (which features the singer holding a baby), has prompted the question, 'Is that his baby on the cover?' and 'He's grabbing that baby's crotch!'[69] It is apparent that both Morrissey's and masculinity's relationship to popular music are again centre stage, placing a particular emphasis on personal, individual relationships through lyrics which juxtapose a belligerent confidence with a troubled and unsettling sexuality, so expressing and throwing into relief different sexual subject-positions. As Hubbs observes, '[f]rom both artistic and commercial perspectives, it's not difficult to imagine why Morrissey might wish to resist containment in the binary categories of contemporary sexual subjectivity – particularly when the one most eagerly offered (by the media) is that of homosexuality'. What is apparent throughout his work with The Smiths and with subsequent solo albums, is that his songs are 'about queer erotics and experience'[70] and for this reason alone, they will continue to provoke attention from a tabloid press whose focus on morality is all too often couched in homophobic vitriol.

Notes

1 S. Whiteley, *Too Much Too Young: Popular Music, Age and Gender* (London: Routledge, 2005), pp. 19–62.

2 In 1999, Britney Spears became an overnight sensation, appearing in the video for her first single, '. . . Baby One More Time' as a playful schoolgirl, complete with mini-skirt, pigtails and sexualised dancing – the embodiment of the classic schoolgirl fantasy image which, along with baby doll routines, is a mainstay of strip culture. 'In 2003, it seemed Russian girl band Tatu went one better. Dressed in matching school uniforms, the band kissed and fondled their way through the video for their debut English-language single, "All the Things She Said". Whereas Spears's performance passed relatively un-noted, Tatu attracted intense media attention for the visualization of their ode to teenage lesbian infatuation. Daytime TV hosts Richard Madeley and Judy Finnegan denounced them as "sick, paeodophiliac entertainment" and called for the song to be banned' (S. Kerton, 'Too Much Tatu Young. Queering Politics in the World of Tatu', in S. Whiteley and J. Rycenga (eds), *Queering the Popular Pitch* (New York: Routledge, 2006), p. 155).

3 The piano hook for Britney Spears's song '. . . Baby One More Time' is borrowed from Eminem's 'Guilty Conscience', where the second verse focuses on a man who is struggling to decide whether or not to sexually abuse a fifteen-year-old girl.

4 In June, 1957, Brenda Lee, 'the little girl with grown-up reactions' released her single 'Dynamite'. It was recorded when she was thirteen years old, but her vocal

delivery abounds with an overtly physical and self-conscious sexual energy that belies her age. What makes her 'sexy' is the sense of 'knowingness' behind what might appear to be innocent lyrics, the erotic pause before a punch line pregnant with innuendo – 'one hour of love tonight just knocks me out like dynamite' with the implication of post-orgasmic exhaustion. See Whiteley, *Too Much Too Young*, p. 1.

5 Annabelle Lwin, the fourteen-year-old Anglo-Burmese lead singer of Bow Wow Wow, was managed by Malcolm McLaren and was exploited as the embodiment of exotic under-age sex. His marketing plans included photographs in a magazine called *Chicken* – 'a magazine for adults that features kids as objects. Chicken, for those in the know, is slang for underage boys or paedophile jailbait'. See S. Reynolds and J. Press, *The Sex Revolts: Gender, Rebellion and Rock 'n' Roll* (London: Serpent's Tail, 1995), pp. 41–2.

6 Frankie Lymon's recording of 'Why Do Fools Fall in Love' reached No. 1 in the UK Charts in 1956 and went on to sell two million copies world-wide. As a twelve-year-old with no previous musical experience and a subsequent reputation for under-age sex, he evidenced an example of an ingénue who could be moulded to perfection by an unscrupulous management.

7 For example, despite Gary Glitter's conviction as a sex offender, it would be misleading to interpret his hit songs of the early 1970s ('Wanna Be In My Gang?' ('I'm the Leader of the Gang') and 'Doing Alright With The Boys') as signifying grooming and personal sexual conquests.

8 For a more detailed discussion of Morrissey's influence on Sonja Aurora Madan, see S. Whiteley, 'Trainspotting: The Gendered History of Britpop', in A. Bennett and J. Stratton (eds), *Britpop and Englishness* (Andover: Ashgate, 2010).

9 A. Raphael *Never Mind the Bollocks: Women Rewrite Rock* (London: Virago, 1995), p. 45.

10 J. Rogan, *Morrissey and Marr: The Severed Alliance* (London: Omnibus Press, 1992), p. 173.

11 The issues surrounding the publication of Ferrari's article will be discussed in detail later in the chapter.

12 Another theme of such early songs as 'Pretty Girls Make Graves', 'Heaven Knows I'm Miserable Now', 'Wonderful Woman' and 'Rusholme Ruffians' is an apparent revulsion towards women, which appears to be at odds with Morrissey's early endorsement of feminist texts.

13 J. Stringer, 'The Smiths: Repressed (but Remarkably Dressed)', *Popular Music*, Vol. 11, No. 1 (1992), pp. 16–17.

14 See S. Whiteley, *The Space Between the Notes: Rock and the Counter-culture* (London: Routledge, 1992).

15 *Live Forever* DVD, 2003.

16 R. Middleton, 'Introduction', in R. Middleton (ed.), *Reading Pop: Approaches to Textual Analysis in Popular Music* (Oxford: Oxford University Press, 2000), p. 13.

17 Ibid., pp. 13–14.

18 A.S. Byatt, *Babel Tower* (London: Random House, 1996), p. 204.

19 Ibid., p. 65

20 B. Dijkstra, *Idols of Perversity: Fantasies of Feminine Evil in Fin-de-Siecle Culture* (Oxford: Oxford University Press, 1986), p. 189.

21 N. Hasted, 'Playing with the Devil Within', *Independent*, 'Eye On Friday' section, 8 May 1998, p. 4.

22 Quoted in *Live Forever*, DVD, 2003. The novelist also appears in another Channel 4 documentary, *The Importance of Being Morrissey*, broadcast in June 2003.

23 Morrissey's awareness of this part of Manchester is something that he discussed in interviews, see, for example, F. Owen, 'Home Thoughts from Abroad', *Melody Maker*, 27 September 1986, pp. 15–16.

24 As singer for The Nosebleeds, Morrissey had also covered the Shangri-Las' 'Give Him A Great Big Kiss' at their 1978 gig at The Ritz, Manchester. See Rogan, *Morrissey and Marr*, p. 99.

25 According to Dale Hibbert, the band's original bassist, Morrissey had considered an overtly gay aesthetic for the group: 'not in a Tom Robinson, effeminate way, but more in an underlying kind of macho type way'. Marr, however, refutes this, saying such a 'manufactured image' would be tantamount to clumsiness on Morrissey's part. Even so, the presence of a male dancer, dressed in red high-heels (a friend and former pen pal of Morrissey's from his journalism days, James Maker) gave the band a controversial image. See S. Goddard, *The Smiths: Songs That Saved Your Life* (London: Reynolds & Hearn, 2002), p. 27.

26 Ibid., p. 55.

27 The sound of laughter also appears on 'What Difference Does It Make' (also on the album) which suggests an underlying sense of resignation which could be linked to *The Sun*'s article on Morrissey and his awareness that self-defence does little to offset the damage caused by such an attack.

28 Rogan, *Morrissey and Marr*, pp. 139–40.

29 Ibid., p. 173.

30 Ibid., p. 176.

31 Ibid., p. 174.

32 Morrissey cited in D. McCullough, 'Handsome Devils', *Sounds*, 4 June 1983, p. 6; M. Whitehead, 'The Smiths', *The Underground*, No. 2 (1983), no pagination.

33 Rogan, *Morrissey and Marr*, p. 177.

34 Morrissey had borrowed the photo of the naked male from 1970s erotic photographer Jim French. His enthusiasm ('I adore this photo. It blends with the record and evokes both passion and sorrow . . . It's time the male body was exploited') (Rogan, *Morrissey and Marr*, p. 163) suggests an underlying evangelism that complements the homoerotic connotations of the song.

35 Morrissey quoted in D. Dorrell, 'The Smith Hunt', *NME*, 24 September, 1983, p. 6.

36 Quoted in Goddard, *The Smiths*, p. 49.

37 M. Smith, 'Morrissey, Manchester and The Smiths' (unpublished undergraduate dissertation, Salford University, 2005), p. 4.

38 As Mike Smith observes, 'the erotic potential of a rendezvous with a stranger in a car is curiously contemporary, thanks to the new fad of outdoor sex, in public, or "dogging" as it is known' (ibid, p. 6).

39 Byatt, *Babel Tower*, p. 65.

40 Goddard, *The Smiths*, p. 63.

41 The line 'I dreamt about you last night' is a direct quotation from Salford playwright Shelagh Delaney. The butterfly line ('take and mount me like a butterfly') was borrowed from feminist writer Molly Haskell's *From Reverence to Rape*, and may also relate to one of Morrissey's favourite actors, Terence Stamp, who played the role of the psychotic butterfly collector in the film adaptation of Ian MacEwan's novel *The Collector*, where the innocent victim is a young woman.

42 Goddard, *The Smiths*, p. 63.

43 D. McCullough, 'Out to Crunch: The Smiths, University of London Union', *Sounds*, 14 May 1983, p. 33.

44 Anonymous, 'Mind-Molesting', *Sounds*, 10 September 1983, p. 6.

45 The search for the remains of Keith Bennett, the third of the five Moors murder victims, who was killed in 1964 by Myra Hindley and Ian Brady, was officially ended by the police in July 2009, 45 years after his death.

46 Rogan, *Morrissey and Marr*, p. 203.

47 Dorrell, 'The Smith Hunt', p. 6.

48 Rogan, *Morrissey and Marr*, p. 173.

49 Dorrell, 'The Smith Hunt', p. 6.

50 Ibid., p. 6 It is not insignificant that *Sounds'* rejection of Morrissey was written by Gary Bushell. As Simon Goddard notes, his aggressive attitude toward The Smiths can be traced back to McCullough's feature article in *Sounds*, when he had 'provoked Morrissey into slandering his colleague. "The British press is an art form," said the singer, before commenting that "Bushell was an exception to the rule"' (Goddard, *The Smiths*, p. 60). As retribution, Bushell reportedly armed Ferrari with all the misinformation the latter needed to concoct his allegations in *The Sun*.

51 Rogan, *Morrissey and Marr*, p. 178.

52 Ibid., p. 178.

53 Anonymous, 'Mind Molesting', p. 6.

54 D. McCullough, 'Out to Crunch', *Sounds*, 14 May 1983, p. 4.

55 Rogan, *Morrissey and Marr*, p. 174.

56 McCullough, 'Handsome Devils', p. 13.

57 Dorrell, 'The Smith Hunt', p. 6.

58 Morrissey, quoted in ibid, p. 7.

59 Rogan, *Morrissey and Marr*, p. 176.

60 Ibid., p. 177.

61 Goddard, *The Smiths*, p. 61.

62 Even so, the reality of paedophliac obsession continued to trouble Morrissey. 'Ambitious Outsiders' (*Maladjusted*, 1997), possibly inspired once again by the Moors Murders, is an explicitly predatory and spiteful song about child murderers scavenging for potential victims, this time in the suburbs: 'Top of the list is your smiling kids . . . And we knows when the school bus comes and goes'.

63 Goddard, *The Smiths*, p. 92.

64 The clip is available at www.youtube.com/watch?v=rolR4Ou8t8w (accessed on 6 April 2008).

65 Goddard, *The Smiths*, p. 46.

66 Ibid., p. 41.

67 Ibid., p. 46.

68 I. Biddle and F. Jarman-Ivens, Introduction, in F. Jarman-Ivens (ed.), *Oh Boy! Masculinities and Popular Music* (New York: Routledge, 2007), p. 8.

69 www.brooklynvegan.com/archives/2008/12/morrissey_new_a. html#comment-372334 (accessed 2 August 2009). The baby pictured with Morrissey is Sebastien Pesel-Browne, who is the son of Charlie Browne, Morrissey's assistant tour manager. Sebastien's mother met Charlie at a Morrissey concert in Boston.

70 Hubbs, 'Music of the "Fourth Gender"', p. 85.

7

'THIS WAY AND THAT WAY': TOWARD A MUSICAL POETICS OF THE SMITHS

Jonathan Hiam

A heartless hand on my shoulder
A push – and it's over
Alabaster crashes down
(Six months is a long time)
I tried living in the real world
Instead of a shell
But before I began
I was bored before I even began

As the climax to 'Shoplifters of the World Unite' (1987), the above passage distils the disengagement and disaffected nihilism that characterise the song as a whole. It summarises the mundane and dull 'now, today, tomorrow, and always' of the song's first two verses, the music of which seems directed toward nowhere as the band thumps out a single, gritty chord. Yet there is something about this passage that is jarring and disconcerting as well. The dry resignation of the first four lines and the apathy and disinterest conveyed in the last four arrive sounding urgent, even desperate, as if the musical setting – now angular, full, powerful, and low pitched – has somehow betrayed them. The song becomes uneasy with itself, uncomfortable and uncertain in its own purpose. The effect on the listener is uncanny: how can boredom feel urgent and disengagement desperate? Yet it is urgency and desperation that are at the centre of the song's poetic message. It is a visceral message, one that moves beyond the irony of the lyrics or the aggressive emotional signifiers of the music, emerging from the structural interplay between the song's musical form and its words. Such structural interplay, as I will demonstrate, characterises The Smiths' music as a whole. As close analysis reveals, it is also the defining element of the band's powerful and deeply meaningful songs.

Much analysis of The Smiths' music reflects the once common tendency in popular music scholarship to marginalise consideration of a song's musical elements in favour of an interpretation based largely upon lyrics. This is understandable to a degree in dealing with The Smiths, given the unusual strength of Morrissey's words and the particular, if not peculiar, performative actions he brings to song lyrics. Yet analyses of The Smiths' music that treat the music as secondary to the words sacrifice an interpretive richness that can only be achieved through a more concerted analytical technique. The strongest interpretations of The Smiths' music undoubtedly are those that treat both the lyrics and the music as equal, playing one off the other as a means by which to tease out a genuine musical poetics.[1]

Clearly, that which Morrissey brought to The Smiths – lyrical invective, sexual ambiguity, theatrical performance, an unusual singing style, dark wit, and a relationship with popular culture and politics that both validated and challenged the public – had much to do with the band's success during the 1980s. Morrissey's continued success as a solo performer, a success dependent still upon many of these same features, has pushed the locus of The Smiths' reception ever more firmly onto him. This has had the unfortunate effect of obscuring the equally significant contributions to the band's aesthetic made by Andy Rourke, Mike Joyce and, especially, Johnny Marr, a fact that demands serious reconsideration. Although some due attention has been given to Marr's particular talents, it was the musical contributions of all three that defined the absolutely unique sound of the band – the key to their success. Any attempt at historicising The Smiths' role in popular music, therefore, must fully consider the completeness of their total musical *sound*, a consideration that begs a closer examination of how their songs work on the one hand as pure superficial sound, and on the other as musical–textual objects.

Although I have separated Morrissey from the other members of The Smiths, it is only by way of balancing what I would call his 'popular semiotics'. For his role as a musician is indeed equal to that of his band mates, as the sound of The Smiths is dependent as much on his singing style and vocal timbre as it is on Marr's eclectic guitar, Rourke's dynamic bass, or Joyce's creative drumming. As a standard rock quartet – lead singer, lead guitar, bass and drums – The Smiths were built to sound along fairly conventional lines. In reality, however, their timbre and stylistic eclecticism generated an aesthetic that set them apart from many of their musical peers. Morrissey's singing – often ornamented by yelps, yodels and barks – articulates the finest of diction, and his sometimes throaty vocal timbre, however melodious, pushes the limits of acceptable pitch. Likewise, Marr's playing often adopts unusual, even unidentifiable effects and techniques, such as the 'wah-wah' heard on 'The Queen Is Dead' or the thin but gritty distortion on 'London'. These effects hardly go unnoticed, not simply because they are interesting enough sounds on their own, but because they sound nothing like so much of the synth-laden pop tunes with which The Smiths shared the radio waves during the

1980s. Add to this the unusual 'found sound' that Morrissey layered onto a number of tracks, such as the sound of children playing heard at the close of 'What Difference Does It Make?', or the bizarre, 'You are sleeping, you do not want to believe' loop at the end of 'Rubber Ring', and the strangeness of The Smiths' music stands in even starker relief to most of the bands populating the contemporaneous hit parades.

This surface amalgamation of timbre, individual style, and found sound, however significant in defining The Smiths' unique sonic profile, bears less responsibility in deriving possible musical meaning than that of the seemingly ineffable and cognitively intensive poetics of the aforementioned musical-textual play. What follows in this essay is an attempt to locate that poetics through a combined musical and textual analysis of three of The Smiths' songs: 'Shoplifters Of The World Unite', 'I Want The One I Can't Have', and 'Stretch Out And Wait'. To aid these analyses, track timings are used wherever possible to serve as points of reference. Generally speaking, a very basic understanding of musical terminology should suffice in following the analyses presented below. However, as a discussion of musical form, in particular, is integral to this essay, I should first devote some space to it here.

Musical form in most popular song commonly follows one of the following formal schemes: AABA, twelve-bar blues, verse–chorus, or some hybrid form incorporating elements of two or more of these forms.[2] The AABA form typically consists of 32 bars of music with an introduction of four bars. The 'A' section is usually eight bars long and recognisable as the song itself, as the tune or textual phrase that is the song's most memorable part. It is also harmonically discrete – that is, it opens and closes in the same key. The 'A' section is then repeated, sometimes with the same words, sometimes not, but always with the same music. The eight bars of the 'B' section, often known as the 'bridge' or 'middle eight', provide new music as a means of contrast and variety. The 'B' section may modulate to another key, but almost always sets up a return to the original key in the final 'A' section. The Smiths utilised the AABA form, albeit with their own peculiar twists, in a number of their songs. 'Panic' serves as a particularly good example (Example 1).[3] As with any formal construction, adherence to a given model varies in strictness depending on the prerogatives of the songwriters or musicians. Nonetheless, a song's form is usually readily discernable after only a few hearings.

Example 1   AABA form in The Smiths' 'Panic'

| Panic on the streets of London ... (0:03) | **A** | Burn down the disco | (1:02) | **B** |
| Hopes may rise on the Grasmeres ... (0:26) | **A** | On the Leeds side-streets that you slip down (1:24) | | **A** |

There are few, if any, examples of the twelve-bar blues in The Smiths' output.[4] However, there are numerous songs written in verse–chorus form, including the three under consideration in this essay. Simply defined, the verse–chorus is a form in which the verse or set of verses alternate with the chorus; the verse introduces a different text each time, while the chorus retains its text with each reiteration. Likewise, the verse and the chorus each have music distinct from one another. The most defining feature of the verse–chorus form is the ability for one to remember the chorus, often known as the 'hook'. Therefore, while it is not uncommon for different verses of a song to use different music each time, it is extremely rare for the chorus to do so – it would undermine its ability to be remembered.

Many of The Smiths' verse–chorus songs indeed have very memorable choruses; 'Girlfriend In A Coma', 'You Just Haven't Earned It Yet, Baby', and 'Sheila Take A Bow' are but a few. 'There Is A Light That Never Goes Out', arguably containing The Smiths' most memorable hook ('And if a double-decker bus / Crashes into us . . . ') provides a clear example of how a standard verse–chorus works (Example 2). Here, there are two sets of two verses each, and each set is followed by the chorus. The song concludes with a coda, during which 'There is a light and it never goes out' repeats nine times over the music of the verse.

In spite of the preceding examples, The Smiths' songs are rarely so straightforward in their formal design. As the following analyses illustrate, the manner in which The Smiths manipulate and play with musical form is a decisive element in their music. In other words, the band's manipulation of musical form, particularly with regards to the relationship between the poetic content of the text and the structural events within the music, are critical to comprehending musical meaning in their work. Even beyond consideration of musical form, although inseparable from it, the following analyses address

Example 2 Verse-chorus form in The Smiths' 'There Is A Light
That Never Goes Out'

Take me out tonight Where there's music and there's people...	Verse 1	Take me out tonight Take me anywhere, I don't care...	Verse 3
Take me out tonight Because I want to see people...	Verse 2	Take me out tonight Oh, take me anywhere, I don't care...	Verse 4
And if a double-decker bus...	Chorus	And if a double-decker bus...	Chorus
		Oh, There Is A Light And It Never Goes Out (9x)	Coda

The Smiths' subtle creation of homologous relationships between a song's words and its musical elements, such as melody, harmony and rhythm. The sum of all of these relationships may have the effect of 'revealing' a meaning not otherwise perceptible by consideration of the lyrics or music separately, or the effect of powerfully reinforcing the meaning claimed by the textual surface.

Desperation and betrayed nihilism in 'Shoplifters Of The World Unite'

To return to the opening example, 'Shoplifters Of The World Unite', let us first consider the meanings inherent in Morrissey's text (Example 3). The opening lyrics, 'Learn to love me / Assemble the ways / Now, today, tomorrow and always' paint a picture of a life in which even love seems to be a product of routine; dull, repetitive and seemingly endless, like an assembly line. The confession by the song's voice ('My only weakness is a list of crimes / My only weakness is . . . well, never mind') elicits the profile of a flippant petty criminal, struggling to get by in a world otherwise apathetic toward his or her very existence. Certainly, criminality here could include homosexuality and other social taboos that might lead to a sense of personal alienation. In any case, the sensibility of the song is indeed one of total indifference. The world is pointless, if not pointlessly violent ('But last night the plans for a future war / Was all I saw on Channel Four'), and boring as a result. Morrissey's call for a shoplifters' revolution can be taken as either a genuine but feeble clarion for insurgency, or as ironic futility.[5] Either way, the tone of his voice gestures toward a feeling of powerlessness and alienation.

On the surface, the music seems to support such a bleak worldview. The dull repetition embodied by the lyrics at the opening of each verse is reflected in the music as a singular, repetitive E chord, which changes only briefly to accentuate the close of each metrical unit. Likewise, the melody itself is some-what dull. It passes by at a slow to moderate pace, with each syllable given its own note. It, too, seems subject to routine. In short, the melody is ostensibly as uninteresting as the life characterised by the song.[6]

The song unfolds in verse–chorus form, which, as we have seen, dictates that the music changes with the onset of the chorus. And indeed it does. The powerful, syncopated groove on G differentiates the transcendent possibilities of the revolution called for by the chorus, ironically or not, from the static nature of the verses. So far, the song makes sense, musically and textually. But, with the arrival of 'A heartless hand on my shoulder / A push – and it's over', something changes. The song arrests the listener's expectations, unconscious or otherwise, creating a strong sense of tension in the process. The unease born thereof betrays the passive disinterest projected by the song to this point, and forces the listener to feel something other than indifference.

Example 3   Lyrics and musical form of The Smiths' 'Shoplifters Of
The World Unite'

Learn to love me	verse	Instrumental	(1:20)	(verse)
Assemble the ways	a music			a music
Now, today, tomorrow and always				
My only weakness is a list of crimes				
My only weakness is...well, never mind				

Shoplifters of the world (0:23)	chorus	Instrumental	(1:43)	(chorus)
Unite and take over	b music			b music
Shoplifters of the world				
Hand it over, hand it over, hand it over				

Learn to love me (0:40)	verse	A heartless hand on my shoulder (2:00)	
Assemble the ways	a music		(verse or chorus?)
Now, today, tomorrow and always		A push – and it's over	b music
My only weakness is a listed crime		Alabaster crashes down	
But last night the plans for a future war		(Six months is a long time)	
Was all I saw on Channel Four		I tried living in the real world	
		Instead of a shell	
		But before I began	
		I was bored before I even began	

Shoplifters of the world (1:03)	chorus		
Unite and take over	b music		
Shoplifters of the world		Shoplifters of the world (2:22)	chorus
Hand it over, hand it over, hand it over		Unite and take over	b music
		Shoplifters of the world	
		Unite and take over	
		Shoplifters of the world	
		Take over	

The tension in this case is very real, as the text and the music are at structural odds with one another. As Example 3 illustrates, a breach in the verse–chorus form occurs precisely at this point in the song (2.00). Immediately leading up to this event, the instrumental verse that follows the second chorus gives way to an instrumental chorus, where Marr's guitar solo builds to a climax. But where we might expect a musical return to the 'a' music of the verse, the band repeats the 'b' music of the chorus and the text re-enters not with the words of the chorus, 'Shoplifters of the world . . . ', but as words fit for another verse. Consequently, as if taken by surprise, the 62 syllables of the verse, 'A heartless hand on my shoulder' sound compressed into the musical space of the chorus, the text of which, to this point, has sustained a syllable count of only 32. Only after twenty-two seconds of sonic urgency and formal disorder do the music and the text firmly realign themselves at the chorus (2.22), after which they remain synchronous through to the song's close.

This particular event, a breach in the song's form, gives way to the real poetic crux of the song. The haste and instability created at that point of formal disjuncture give way to a sense of desperation and intensity: too many words in the wrong space at the wrong time. Furthermore, the violence and bleakness of 'heartless', 'push', 'crashes' and 'bored' only reinforce that feeling. The voice, it seems, which has thus far put forth a sense of unflappable emotional disconnect, has been penetrated to reveal a true state of uneasiness and fear. If there is irony to be found here, it is to be experienced at this musical moment when the ironic indifference of the surface is rendered false by the assertion of very real, if unspoken, human emotions.

Confusion and frustration in 'I Want The One I Can't Have'

Unlike 'Shoplifters Of The World Unite', 'I Want The One I Can't Have' makes no attempt at indifference; the song embodies confusion and frustration almost as straightforwardly as its title admits. Whereas the structural interaction between the text and music of 'Shoplifters . . . ' creates a 'revealed' meaning, the formal interplay of 'I Want The One I Can't Have' reinforces an emotional sensibility that is otherwise clearly articulated by the text.

'I Want The One I Can't Have' draws together lyrics that address three seemingly unrelated subjects: a thwarted sexual desire ('I want the one I can't have / and it's driving me mad'); the simple material achievement of ordinary folk ('A double-bed / and a stalwart lover, for sure / these are the riches of the poor'); and teenage homicide ('He killed a policeman when he was thirteen / and somehow that really impressed me') (Example 4). Each of the three subjects is comprehensible as a short, discrete theme, but taken together they make for a very confusing text. Any attempt to draw a coherent relationship among them is nonsensical, if not frustrating. As we will see, these central poetic conceits – confusion and frustration – are embedded in the relationship between the song's musical form and its relationship to the text.

'I Want The One I Can't Have' has four distinct musical ideas (Example 4). The first, labelled 'a', is the music heard at the opening of the song. It is four bars of energetic and highly danceable music, characterised by Rourke's upward bass and Marr's rhythm guitar (0.04–0.27) (the opening four seconds present the effect-laden guitar lead-in that sounds somewhat like a helicopter). The next section of music, 'b' (0.27–0.37), is characterised by two presentations of rising, shimmering chords. 'C' is built out of two bars of an unresolved chord. The remaining identifiable section I have labelled 'a1', as it is identical to the 'a' music, without those first two bars of Rourke's bass.

Formally speaking, 'I Want The One I Can't Have' makes little sense; its musical design is itself confusing. On first hearing, the song sounds like a typical verse–chorus form: 'I want the one I can't have / And it's driving me mad / It's all over, all over my face' serves as the chorus, those words always accompanied by the 'b' music. Likewise, the verses utilise the 'a' music, although this sometimes occurs in the aforementioned abridged version.

Example 4   Lyrics and form of 'I Want The One I Can't Have'

On the day that your mentality (0:08) a
Catches up with your biology
'come round   +1

I want the one I can't have   (0:27) b
And it's driving me mad
It's all over, all over, all over my face

(instrumental)   (0:37) c

On the day that your mentality (0:42) a1
Catches up with your biology

I want the one I can't have   (0:52) b
And it's driving me mad
It's all over, all over, all over my face

A double bed   (1:03) a
And a stalwart lover for sure
These are the riches of the poor

A double bed   (1:13) a
And a stalwart lover for sure
These are the riches of the poor

(instrumental)   (1:21) c

And I want the one I can't have (1:25)   b
And it's driving me mad
It's all over, all over my face

(instrumental)   (1:35) c

A tough kid who sometimes swallows nails   a1
                                          (1:41)
Raised on Prisoner's Aid
He killed a policeman when he was thirteen   b
                                          (1:51)
And somehow that really impressed me
And it's written all over my face

(instrumental)   (2:01) a
Oh, these are the riches of the poor
These are the riches of the poor

(instrumental)   (2:11) a
Oh, these are the riches of the poor
These are the riches of the poor

(instrumental)   (2:19) c

I want the one I can't have   (2:24) b
And it's driving me mad
It's written all over my face

(instrumental)   (2:34) c

On the day that your mentality   (2:38) a1
Catches up with your biology

And if you ever need self-validation (2:48) b
Just meet me in the alley by the
Railway station
It's all over my face
Oh ...

(instrumental)   (2:59) c

However, a close consideration of the musical form results in the following pattern:

a, b, c, a1, b, a, a, c, b, c, a1, b, a, a, c, b, c, a1, b, c

This highly irregular scheme is at odds with the text, which follows a slightly more predictable pattern, loosely approximating a verse–chorus form:

Verse–verse–instrumental – chorus / verse–verse–instrumental – chorus / instrumental / verse–verse–verse–instrumental–chorus / instrumental–verse–verse.

A remarkable feature of this song, though, is that the unruly semantics of this musical-textual free-for-all pass by almost unnoticed. There are two reasons for this. First, the frenetic tempo effectually masks the variety of disjunctions and seemingly illogical internal repetitions within the music. Second, the chorus arrives at regular intervals in real time (0:04, 1:03 and 2:01), creating an audible phantom of regularity and thus suggesting to the ear a normalised and predictable form. The confusing nature of 'I Want The One I Can't Have', however, is still present, poetically embedded in its musical structure, perceptible to varying degrees, and demonstrative of the repressed sexual confusion alluded to in the lyrics.

If the confusion of this song is therefore more subtle, the frustration is highly palpable – and audible. From the start, the song toys with harmonic tension, thwarting its resolution as a means by which to aurally convey this frustration. The song's richest musical action is also its most critical, and it can be heard four seconds into the song with the arrival of a robust G-major chord, the song's tonic. G major is the first chord of the harmonic progression of the 'a' music, and its three arrival points (0:04, 1:03 and 2:01) are the only moments in the song where harmonic tension finds resolution. With each resolution the effect is one of release, and, given the boldness of the chord's 'majorness', it has a gladness about it that befits the highly danceable rhythm of the bass and drums, adding to the sense of satisfaction, even celebration. The first instance, at the song's very outset, is the subtlest of the three occurrences (0:04). Its arrival is announced by the drums, and resolves the almost imperceptible E-major sound of the introductory 'helicopter' guitar effect that makes up the song's opening moments.[7] This resolution establishes the 'home key' of G major, the chord on which the song should cadence or return to at critical formal junctures.

Therefore, it is all the more aurally frustrating when at critical formal shifts the song moves to the 'a1' music rather than returning to the 'a' music, as it does at 0:43, 1:41 and 2:13. The definitive feature of the 'a' music, its initial G-major chord, is omitted by the 'a1' music, which differs from the 'a' music in this respect only. Through the omission of the G-major chord, the 'a1' music thwarts the harmonic resolution of the final chord of the 'c' music, which always occurs immediately prior to the 'a1' music. This action creates a very real sense of frustration, musically perceptible by the listener and in accordance with the song's lyrical theme of sexual frustration.

Clearly, 'I Want The One I Can't Have' is among The Smiths' most sophisticated songs formally and textually. What is particularly fascinating is how the song engages multiple levels of musical cognition (i.e. musical form *and* real-time perception) to render its sophistication palpable and meaningful to a pop sensibility. Even if, as will be touched at this essay's conclusion, the final 'text' derived itself somewhat accidentally, it typifies the rich possibilities inherent in the majority of the band's musical output.

Anxiety in 'Stretch Out And Wait'

As in 'I Want The One I Can't Have', frustration also plays a significant role in 'Stretch Out And Wait', although in this case as a means to a different end.[8]

Example 5   Form of 'Stretch Out And Wait'

On the high-rise estate   Verse
What's at the back of your mind?
On a three-day debate on a high-rise estate
What's at the back of your mind?

Two icy cold hands conducting away
It's the Eskimo blood in my veins.
Amid concrete and clay and general decay
Nature must still find a way.

So ignore all the codes of the day
Let your juvenile impulses sway.
This way and that way, this way and that way
God, how sex implores you

To let yourself lose yourself.   (0:50)   Bridge

Stretch out and wait, stretch out and wait.   Chorus
                                                (0:54)
Let your puny body lie down, lie down
As we lie you say,

As we lie you say, Stretch out

Stretch out and wait, stretch out and wait.
Let your puny body lie down, lie down
As we lie you say,

Will the world end in the nighttime? (1:22) Verse
I really don't know.
Will the world end in the daytime?
I really don't know.
Is there any point ever having children?
Oh, I don't know.

What I do know   (1:46)   Bridge
Is we're here and it's now

So stretch out and wait, stretch out and wait. Chorus
                                                (1:51)
There is no debate, no debate, no debate.
How can you consciously contemplate
When there's no debate, no debate.
Stretch out and wait

Stretch out and wait   (2:10)   Chorus
Wait, wait
Wait

(instrumental)   (2:28)   Coda

The text of 'Stretch Out And Wait' expresses a pastoral sensibility, which calls for contemplative relaxation (Example 5). Yet the events that unfold within the musical structure call the aesthetic posture of the surface into question. In the case of 'Stretch Out And Wait' especially, the subtle harmonic and rhythmic events within the musical structure are responsible for engaging the song's text in a poetically meaningful interplay.

The opening passage is set in the key of E (I), and the sense of calm and peacefulness established in the opening passage by the gentle rhythmic sway and friendly melody is undermined by two harmonic features: the question, 'What's at the back of your mind?' is accompanied by a move from B (V) to G-sharp (iii).[9] In effect, this motion serves as a type of deceptive cadence, thwarting the listener's harmonic expectations, while at the same time exploiting the minor mode to affect a sense of melancholy, which, in turn, mirrors a sense of unease and contributes to a growing feeling of anxiousness. Here, too, the harmonic *rhythm* plays a role in undermining the sense of stasis. The strong first beat of each of the first four metrical units emphasises these harmonies: I–IV–iii–IV. The dominant chord (B) occurs on the weak beat of each of these bars and does not resolve to the tonic until bar five, at which point the progression quickly repeats itself. In other words, a subtle sense of harmonic instability is created and cycled through for the first fifty-one seconds of the song. This has the twin effects of non-resolution and forward propulsion, both of which play a part in further establishing a feeling of anxiousness; an anxiousness that sits 'at the back of your mind'.

The sense of forward motion intensifies through the repetition of the words, 'This way and that way and this way and that way' (0:42). It is here that we arrive at a temporary release from the building tension, for 'this way and that way' leads us to the realisation of 'juvenile impulses'. Set off musically by a hemiola (a metrical pattern that pits a feeling of two against that of a three) the liberating powers of youthfulness and sex provide an escape from hang-ups and anxieties. 'Let yourself lose yourself', also highlighted by a hemiola, is indeed the climax of this idea, both metaphorically and literally. The move to the exotic-sounding C-major seventh chord stands out to the listener and harmonically represents the 'losing of oneself', in this case through sexual release.

With the arrival of the first chorus, the sense of anxiousness returns (0:55). The modulation to a minor key affects a feeling once again of melancholy and here too, as in the opening, this is prolonged through a deceptive cadence on the tonic. It occurs precisely at 'as we lie you say' and heightens one's sense of expectation of what actually is to be said (1:03). Furthermore, 'as we lie you say' intensifies this sensation by moving through some surprising harmonies, VII–V$\frac{4}{2}$–V–III, before returning to the tonic. This progression creates a false feeling of modulating back to the home key of E major, and instead remains true to the local tonic of C-sharp minor seventh. Likewise, the repetition of 'as we lie you say' reinforces this anticipation. Fulfilment is further thwarted by the chorus's internal repetition of 'Stretch out and wait', which interrupts the thought (1:10). There is also an added 'Stretch out and wait' before the repetition of the chorus proper, even further intensifying expectations.

The arrival of the second verse finally realises the anticipated statement in the form of a question, 'Will the world end in the nighttime?' (1:23). Yet, even as the listener has been waiting for this moment, it almost comes too soon. The move from chorus to verse is abrupt with nothing to signal a formal shift; the song nervously breaches etiquette and then asks for the contemplation of nothing short of the apocalypse.

The second verse is akin to the first in as much as it relies on a cyclic forward motion. Harmonically, the phrase progresses, i–iv–(V)–vi–cadential $\frac{6}{4}$–VII, and repeats itself with each presentation of a question and answer (1:31). This progression operates in a way similar to that of the opening four bars of the song through repetition, forward motion, and non-resolution. (In fact, the harmonies are in a sense in an inverse relationship with those of bars 1–4, thus strengthening the functional unity of the song). The effect is one of increased momentum that, to great relief, is subsumed by the modulation in the second bridge.

Here again, the bridge material provides a relief to the song's building tension. After three repetitions of the question remain unanswered, 'Will the world end . . .', 'I really don't know', the listener finally gets, 'What I do know is we're here and it's now' (1:46), which leads the way to a shift in poetic meaning. The first chorus presented the idea 'Stretch out and wait' as an act during which one is asked to engage in contemplation (as it turns out, a contemplation of the end of the world, metaphorically or otherwise). The second chorus accepts the 'here and now' of life and furthermore dismisses the act of contemplation ('How can you consciously contemplate when there's no debate?'). This is achieved musically by a return to the home key of E and to the 'a' music of the song's opening. Through the return of the chorus to the peaceful opening music used by the first verse, the song has synthesised the dialectic. It has come full circle; contemplation has rendered itself unnecessary and to 'Stretch out and wait' is to wait for blissful nothing. Perhaps.

It is in the final section of the song that The Smiths' gift for musical ambiguity fully emerges. Beginning with the onset of the second chorus, the text breaks up into repetitions of the phrase 'Stretch out and wait' (2:17). This process of fragmentation also occurs musically with the repetition of the two-bar phrases of 'a1'. The result is that once again a feeling of heightened anticipation is created, this time through the acceleration, by way of fragmentation, of both the musical and textual material.

The final bars deliver a witty conclusion to the song with a wordless and unresolved question. As the accompanying motive for the question 'Will the world end . . . ' the music at the onset of the coda recalls the questioning voice of the second verse, 'Will the world end . . . ?' (compare 1:23–1:30 with 2:28–end). Hence, in effect, the penultimate two bars ask the same question, without text, and are answered by an unresolved chord (Am add9), whose sound leaves us unsettled (2:32). In the end we 'really don't know' and are left to further contemplate the end of the world.

Coda

The brief analyses above demonstrate the richness of The Smiths' songs as musical compositions, a factor that must be considered when accounting for the particular appeal of the band to such a wide popular audience. In as much as Morrissey has offered a seemingly endless supply of material for critics and scholars of gender, politics and class, so too has the band as a whole presented a body of musical work worthy of further study by musicologists and pop music critics. But as I have also attempted to show, any such analysis should not favour the study of the musical elements over that of the song words, or vice versa. Doing so would ignore what is indeed the most powerful facet of The Smiths' music – the interplay between the two.

This chapter raises the inevitable question of compositional intentionality, one which any well-trained new critic or empirical musicologist would
quickly cast aside.[10] Yet the issue of intentionality in the case of Morrissey and
Marr is too enticing to ignore. As Simon Goddard reveals, the pair frequently
wrote songs apart from one another, bringing together the music and the
words after they had been composed.[11] If that is the case, then indeed the mis-
matched formal schemes of 'I Want The One I Can't Have' and 'Shoplifters Of
The World Unite' are easily accounted for and the consequent poetic meanings might best be considered 'happy accidents'. At the same time, Morrissey
and Marr often wrote face to face as well, leaving us to wonder if indeed intentionality does matter in the case of The Smiths. In either case, I would suggest
that further analyses of The Smiths' music are required to more completely
understand the unique visceral meaning inherent in their songs, meaning
which has set The Smiths apart as arguably the most creative practitioners of
popular music of their era.

Notes

1 I define musical poetics here as the totality of acoustically perceptible means by
   which The Smiths create musical meaning. For further discussion on music/text
   analysis in popular music, see A.F. Moore, *Rock: The Primary Text. Developing a
   Musicology of Rock* (Buckingham: Open University Press, 1993); G. Boone and J.
   Covach (eds), *Understanding Rock: Essays in Musical Analysis* (New York: Oxford,
   1997); W. Everett (ed.), *Expressions in Pop-Rock Music: A Collection of Critical and
   Analytical Essays* (New York: Garland, 2000). See also S. Frith, 'Why Do Songs
   Have Words?', *Music For Pleasure: Essays in the Sociology of Pop* (Cambridge:
   Polity Press, 1988), pp. 105–28, and W. Everett (ed.), *Rock Music: Critical Essays on
   Composition, Performance, Analysis, and Reception* (New York and London:
   Garland, 2000).
2 For an introduction to the forms typical of rock and pop, see J. Covach, 'Form in
   Rock Music: A Primer', in D. Stein (ed.), *Engaging Music: Essays in Music Analysis*
   (Oxford: Oxford University Press, 2005), pp. 65–76.
3 As clear as this formal scheme may be in 'Panic', the textual elision of the lines
   'Because the music that they constantly play / On the Leeds side streets that you
   slip down' has the aural effect of masking the return of the 'A' section of music.
4 'Is It Really So Strange?' might be an exception to this.
5 'Shoplifters Of The World Unite' references T. Rex's 'Children Of The Revolution'
   (1974) by 'lifting' the music in a very general, but readily identifiable way. Certainly,
   this adds a layer of possible interpretation, but at the very least The Smiths
   are paying homage to one of the rock icons of their youth. The same might be
   said about Marr's guitar solo, which garnered him comparisons, not always
   favourable, to Thin Lizzy. In any event, Marr's solo is one of the few straightforward

guitar 'breaks' he ever recorded with The Smiths, making it interesting for this fact alone.

6 Morrissey's declamatory singing style has not gone unnoticed in print. The narrow range typical of his melodies and his exaggerated diction, for example, are addressed by Nadine Hubbs, among others. See N. Hubbs, 'Music of the "Fourth Gender": Morrissey and the Sexual Politics of Melodic Contour', in E. Berry, T. Foster and C. Siegel (eds), *Bodies of Writing, Bodies in Performance* (New York: New York University Press, 1996), pp. 266–96. Hubbs argues that Morrissey's highly individualised singing style is a key component of his ability to differentiate himself from both his own band and other pop singers. Likewise, Julian Stringer notes that Morrissey's singing style takes on the manner of the English gent, contributing to a sense of 'Englishness' crucial to The Smiths' overall aesthetic. See J. Stringer, 'The Smiths: Repressed (But Remarkably Dressed)', *Popular Music*, Vol. 11, No. 1 (1992), pp. 15–26.

7 This opening version of 'a', in fact, adds a single bar of music, to which Morrissey sings, 'come round' – a small detail not repeated elsewhere in the song and therefore especially confusing in its musical function.

8 I refer to the original version of 'Stretch Out And Wait', which was released on the twelve-inch single of 'Shakespeare's Sister' (1985). An alternate version was included on the compilation *The World Won't Listen* (1987).

9 The analysis of 'Stretch Out And Wait' uses the conventional Roman numeral system of labelling harmonies. Upper-case numerals refer to a major-mode harmony while lower-case numerals refer to a minor-mode harmony, so 'I' refers to a major chord built on the first step of the seven-step diatonic scale, while 'ii' refers to a minor chord built on the second step. Furthermore, each chord has a lexical name as well, which can be used interchangeably with the roman numeral. For a major key, they are as follows: I: tonic; ii: supertonic; iii: mediant; IV: subdominant; V: dominant; vi: submediant; vii: subtonic.

10 At the same time, any musical analysis must make claim to a fixed musical 'text'. As has become customary in popular music analysis, a particular recording serves as the musical text on which to base theoretical study. In the case of The Smiths, the recording-as-text model seems particularly valid, as their live performances rarely subjected their songs to drastic revisions or manipulations. In other words, The Smiths' live renditions of their songs tended not to stray too far from the recorded versions.

11 S. Goddard, *The Smiths: Songs That Saved Your Life*, (London: Reynolds & Hearn, 2004), pp. 186–7.

8

'I DON'T OWE YOU ANYTHING':
THE SMITHS AND KITCHEN-SINK CINEMA

Cecília Mello

The music of The Smiths enjoys a fruitful relationship with cinema which long surpasses the five years in which the band was together. It is well known that Morrissey had the habit of elegantly interweaving numerous cultural references into the fabric of his lyrics, and that cinema was one of his greatest sources of inspiration. The films known as 'kitchen-sink' dramas left an especially indelible imprint on his writing for The Smiths, and Morrissey also cultivated a lesser but nonetheless consistent attraction to the glamour of Hollywood. Thus it is no surprise that Pat Phoenix and Shelagh Delaney rub shoulders on Smiths record sleeves with Elvis Presley and James Dean. Conversely, the music of The Smiths has, since the 1980s, been used by cinema in varied and poignant ways, in a reciprocal and symbiotic movement in which one medium borrows from another. This chapter seeks to examine how the kitchen-sink dramas of the early 1960s influenced Morrissey's writing, and proposes that beyond the literal references in his lyrics there lies a sensibility at the heart of these films akin to the one found in his poetic impulse. It also expands the argument with some concluding thoughts on how cinema has 'returned the favour' by employing The Smiths' songs in various ways.

Morrissey's demotic

Morrissey's writing during the time of The Smiths seems to have been fuelled by a nostalgic admiration for British films, novels, plays and television programmes, especially from the post-1956 period. He mined this cultural past for material and filtered it into his lyrics, which in turn gained a life of their own. This nostalgic 'looking back' has to be understood against the background of the severe social and economic change that unfolded during the years of the Thatcher administration (1979–90), which saw the steady erosion of manufacturing jobs, the massive widening of the north–south divide and the gradual de-industrialisation of the country. The dismantling of the working classes in Britain during the 1980s meant that Morrissey was writing during what can be seen as the end of an era. His lyrics sought refuge from the severity of the changes in the country's social tapestry by turning back to the post-war years, and to the British working-class cultural icons of a 'lost' past: 'There's so much buried in the past to steal from, one's resources are limitless. I'm not saying everything I write has been written before but most of the way I feel comes from the cinema. I fed myself on films like *A Taste of Honey, The L-Shaped Room*.'[1] Made on the cusp of the irreversible changes of the late twentieth century, the kitchen-sink dramas seemed to preserve the last gasp of a working class being annihilated in the 1980s.

The uniqueness of Morrissey's lyrics did not go unnoticed by the specialist press after the release of The Smiths' first recordings in 1983. During interviews, he was frequently asked about the motivation for his writing: 'Lyrics that are intellectual or obscure are no use whatsoever',[2] he said to *Melody Maker* in 1983. He repeatedly affirmed in interviews a rejection of obscure and metaphorical language in favour of simplicity or, in other words, the presence of a demotic impulse in his writing:[3] 'We could never be obscure, because I use very fundamental language in my lyrics. I use very simplistic words, but hopefully in quite a powerful way.'[4] Morrissey claimed that 'simple' or 'basic' language was a lot more effective in popular music than what he called 'eso-terical' and 'mysterious' language, and it is no wonder he greatly admired the work of George Formby, an ambassador of ordinariness whose songs fascinate precisely because of their simplicity.

Morrissey's declarations should be taken with a pinch of salt. Despite the prevalence of what he calls 'fundamental language' in his lyrics, they also undoubtedly extended the vocabulary of pop, and can be complex and oblique. Couplets such as 'What she asked of me at the end of the day, Caligula would have blushed'[5] and 'Farewell to this land's cheerless marshes, hemmed in like a boar between arches'[6] are simple and yet not, simultane-ously. Morrissey was also eloquent and witty in interviews, drawing from a vocabulary rather more extensive than that of everyday language. Wilde was, after all, on his side. Therefore, his lyrics stand above the simplistic and banal writing of the bulk of pop music, yet they possess, even in their most florid tonalities, an elegant simplicity in tune with the everyday quality of their landscape, far from the obscurities of, for instance, Kurt Cobain's lyrics for Nirvana. Morrissey's demotic impulse was, therefore, a combination of simplicity and complexity, fuelled by his ability to extract poetry out of everyday language.

Morrissey's impulse to employ a language closer to the everyday for poetic purposes, and to write from his own working-class experience, was analogous to that of the writers from whom he liked to borrow. It is no wonder that the work of Alan Sillitoe (from Nottingham), Shelagh Delaney (from Salford) and Keith Waterhouse (from Leeds), all of whom adapted their novels or plays to the screen in the early 1960s, had such a strong impact on his writing. Ultimately, Morrissey could identify with the world that was unveiled in the kitchen-sink films and in the literary works from which they originated, and was inspired by it. In order to grasp the close semiotic bond between kitchen-sink cinema and Morrissey's lyrics, it is crucial to consider the appearance of films, novels, plays and television programmes in the British post-war landscape, which sought to find a new language, closer to the everyday, in which to articulate reality.

Kitchen-sink dramas

From the 1940s onwards, British cinema gradually began to provide space for a wider range of social characters and experience, a shift that saw the working classes, until then often relegated to minor or stereotyped roles, begin to take centre stage. This 'movement towards social extension',[7] noticeable in numerous post-war films and television programmes, could be seen as a natural corollary of the spirit of egalitarianism of the war years. Perhaps no other moment of British history produced a parallel effect, or at least not as intensely. The Second World War affected the everyday lives of people in the country regardless of class, gender or race. The nation seemed to be united, and by 1940 the phrase 'people's war' already suggested a change in perception. Peter Clarke explains: 'Whether it should be called "a people's war" . . . depends on how ambitiously that claim is meant. It was partly a description of the blurring of obvious class distinctions brought by a sense of shared crisis. . . . But in the summer of 1940 the authenticity of this emotion can hardly be dismissed.'[8]

The 'people's war', while not eroding the class system in the country, at least increased the visibility of the working classes during the post-war period. This was more than ever reinforced by the five years of Labour Government that followed the end of the war (1945–51). In the 1950s populist tendencies seemed to dominate all art forms in one way or another, and 'working-class culture' ceased to be viewed as a contradiction. The kitchen-sink dramas, therefore, belong to a broader period of cultural transition linked to the severe historical impact of the Second World War. In fact, they can be seen as one of the many 'responses' to the new historical conjuncture produced by the war, which called for the articulation of a new language – or new languages – better suited to address and respond to post-war reality.

The social extension of representation which characterised kitchen-sink realism was in many ways a reflection of the changes in the world of theatre and literature in the 1950s. It was during this period that writers from a less

privileged social stratum set out to write about their backgrounds, questioning general assumptions of class and affluence. It would be fair to say that
the general climate of reconstruction and the increasing economic power of
the working classes during the 1950s contributed to a democratisation of the
production of literature and drama, and to the populist inclination of the new
novels and plays. The writers credited with reinvigorating the British novel
and theatre did so by staying close to their origins, letting their own everyday
experiences reflect in their writing. In other words, what was being unveiled in
the 1950s was the language of the working classes, appealing precisely because
it was from a class not normally associated with the world of letters. This
newfound vitality, therefore, came from the impact of the 'insider's point of
view' in relation to a particular class, and from the sense of authenticity that
it afforded.

The main titles in the kitchen-sink cycle consist exclusively of literary and
theatre adaptations. The two films which inaugurated the cycle, *Look Back
in Anger* (Tony Richardson, 1958) and *Room at the Top* (Jack Clayton, 1959),
were adapted from the play by John Osborne and the novel by John Braine
respectively, both associated with the 'angry young man' movement.[9] A
couple of years later a new wave of writers – mainly from the north of England
– started to enjoy some popularity thanks to the success and the impact
of the 'angry young men'. Alan Sillitoe, David Storey, Keith Waterhouse
and Shelagh Delaney brought the language and experience of the northern
working classes to the centre of their novels and plays, and later collaborated
with directors such as Lindsay Anderson, Tony Richardson and Karel Reisz to
adapt them for the screen.

The kitchen-sink cycle has been extensively studied by researchers of
British film, and invariably features as a chapter in numerous historical over-
views of the subject. In his 1978 book *A Critical History of the British Cinema*,
Roy Armes suggested that the directors associated with the kitchen-sink
dramas – Lindsay Anderson, Karel Reisz and Tony Richardson – were, as
John Grierson before them, middle-class observers making sympathetic films
about the working class, and who never put into question their own privileged
status.[10] This view, which in itself very much dominates most accounts of the
kitchen-sink cycle, was articulated by John Hill in *Sex, Class and Realism:
British Cinema 1956–1963* (1986) in a more complex manner, offering the
seminal work on the period. Hill suggests that rather than simply possessing
a progressive quality, the kitchen-sink films, as products of an outsider's look,
'may well have obscured as much as they enlightened, and obstructed as much
as they initiated the potential for social change and reconstruction.'[11] Building
on Andrew Higson's essay 'Space, Place, Spectacle: Landscape and Townscape
in the "Kitchen-sink" Film', published by the journal *Screen* in 1984,[12] Hill
detects in the aestheticisation of squalor a mark of enunciation,[13] and thus of

the outsider/observer look, the authorial voice being inscribed, for instance, in descriptive shots of location divorced from the narrative.

Despite this commonly held view, I believe that the kitchen-sink films reflect the fusion of the insider's (the writer's) vision with that of the middle-class directors, rather than exclusively the outsider/observer look.[14] Indeed, those 'marks of enunciation' detected by Hill and Higson especially in *Saturday Night and Sunday Morning* and *A Taste of Honey* can be traced back to the original novel and play, and could not be attributed to the vision of the middle-class director. Moreover, it is also worth considering how Alan Sillitoe – and Shelagh Delaney to a certain extent – occupied a vantage point when writing their first works, for they had the ability to stand inside and outside their class experience, and inside and outside the perspective of the 'common man'. Sillitoe was living in Majorca on an air force disability pension when he wrote *Saturday Night and Sunday Morning*, already distanced from the world where he grew up. Delaney's first play had references to Shakespeare and Ibsen, and her subsequent works strayed far from the world of *A Taste of Honey*. The dualism of their position, however, does not undermine the point of view of the insider vividly felt in both works, for Arthur, the lathe operator of *Saturday Night and Sunday Morning*, and Jo, the gauche working-class teenager of *A Taste of Honey*, were still at the time of writing a great part of Sillitoe and Delaney. Morrissey himself seems to embody this very tension between the insider and the outsider perspectives. While he was undoubtedly the product of working-class immigrants, he was also the boy who grew up cosseted by a bookish mother, sheltered to some extent from the full ravages of Thatcherism. He occupied, therefore, the same vantage point of those he admired and identified with, able to stand inside and outside his class experience.

The voice of the working class

Before returning to the subject of Morrissey's lyrics, it is also essential to consider how popular music gradually replaced cinema in the 1950s and 1960s as the most important arena of expression for the voice of the working classes. From the 1960s onwards, it was indeed pop music and not literature, theatre or cinema that could most effectively speak for the young working classes. Or rather, it was through pop music that the young working classes could most effectively speak for themselves. Pop music appeared to not even have to strive to be demotic, precisely because it was already so in essence, meaning that it had the potential to be simple and effective enough to speak to everyone.

The first indigenous near-pop movement in Britain was skiffle. It followed the first wave of rock, or the American rock'n'roll invasion of 1956. Skiffle was indigenous as a wave but consisted basically of a re-reading of American folk music from the turn of the century. In the words of Nik Cohn, it was 'knockabout American folk song thumped out any old how on guitar and washboard. Its major attraction was that any musical ability was entirely irrelevant. All you needed was natural rowdiness.'[15] The appeal of skiffle to working-class teenagers lay in the feeling of authenticity that came with American folk music, the music of the common people. Moreover, skiffle preceded punk's 'do-it-yourself' ethos by twenty years, in that musical talent was not a prerogative in its formula.

The skiffle wave did not last very long, but it was crucial in opening a channel between young working-class people and music-making. Moreover, one of the most important bands of all time had its genesis in a skiffle band, The Quarrymen. In the words of Robert Hewison, The Beatles 'showed that it was possible to be listened to, and be young, provincial and working-class'.[16] In short, they ascertained the voice of pop as the true voice of the working classes. And they came from a place which had been revealed through the realism of the kitchen-sink dramas, the north of England, and spoke with a regional accent. The Beatles soon breached the north–south divide in England, and later attained global status, but Paul McCartney was to maintain what is vaguely referred to as 'a northern sensibility'. Significantly, he shared with Morrissey an admiration for *A Taste of Honey*, and decided to include on The Beatles' first album *Please Please Me* (1963) a version of Bobby Scott's and Rick Marlow's song 'A Taste Of Honey', written for the Broadway production of the play.[17] Tony Richardson's film adaptation (1961) of Shelagh Delaney's play had made a big impression on McCartney, and in 1967 he composed 'Your Mother Should Know', a song inspired by the character Geof's concerned remark to Jo when he realises that she is pregnant, a phrase that is included in both the play and the film. In so doing, he pioneered Morrissey's habit of quoting from kitchen-sink films in his lyrics, and hinted at the impact they would still have twenty years on.[18]

Ultimately, The Beatles changed the face of pop music in Britain and opened doors for various other bands from similar backgrounds, turning the 'voice of the pop singer' into the legitimate arena for the voice of working-class youth. From the 1960s onwards, the north of England, official kitchen-sink territory and seen as the place of authenticity as opposed to London, bred a number of innovative bands whose songs echoed their working-class background. In 1983, it was the turn of The Smiths, as Morrissey brilliantly acknowledged in the *New Musical Express* (*NME*) a year later: 'To me popular music is still the voice of the working class, collective rage in a way, though not angst-ridden. But it does really seem like the one sole opportunity for someone from a working-class background to step forward and have his or her say. It's really the last refuge for the articulate but penniless humans.'[19]

Kitchen-sink ballads

Morrissey found his refuge in pop music; he had the opportunity to step forward and have his say, choosing to articulate elements of his own reality while rejecting music that said nothing to him about his life.[20] His lyrics echoed the northern landscape and voices articulated and unveiled by the realism of the kitchen-sink dramas, in which he could identify elements of his own working-class northern upbringing and of his essential gaucheness:

> I'm afraid that they [the kitchen-sink films] probably remind me of my child-hood because I lived in lots of those circumstances and I also think that . . . I gaze upon them fondly because it was the first time in the entire history of film where regional dialects were allowed to come to the fore and people were allowed to talk about squalor and general depression and it wasn't necessarily a shameful thing. It was quite positive . . . people were allowed to be real instead of being glamorous and Hollywoodian, if that is a word, and I sincerely hope it isn't.[21]

The kitchen-sink dramas' articulation of the real or, in other words, their aspiration to realism, helped to shape Morrissey's writing style on more than one level. Most perceptibly, Morrissey had the habit of quoting, literally or almost literally, from the films' dialogue in his lyrics. As Morrissey himself acknowledged, an essential facet of the kitchen-sink dramas' realism came from the novels and plays on which they were based: the realism of language. The nature of their dialogues, the use of regional language and their delivery in a regional accent meant that the characters became more 'real' when they opened their mouths, for they spoke in the vernacular. In other words, the kitchen-sink films, in their search for contemporaneity, authenticity and youthfulness, borrowed from the Northern writers the language of the insider and its revelatory impact. And Morrissey chose on a number of occasions to borrow the voice of these characters, bringing them back to life in his lyrics.

The influence of the kitchen-sink cycle on Morrissey's writing, however, is more complex than the bits and pieces of dialogue he 'took on loan' could suggest. It is important to notice how the visual impact of his lyrics also finds a parallel in the 'familiar kitchen-sink iconography' created by the cycle, mainly through the use of black and white photography in northern locations. These films made recurrent use of images of gasometers, railway viaducts, cobbled streets, factory chimneys, oily canals and shots of the townscape, and the creation of this recognisable 'kitchen-sink territory' certainly contributed to their appeal. Morrissey also recurrently employed a similar imagery in his lyrics, thus bringing them close to the world of the films he so admired.

On yet another level, the feeling of disillusionment which permeates the lives of the kitchen-sink characters also finds a parallel in Morrissey's lyrics.

The land of the kitchen-sink dramas is a dreamless land, and its dwellers seem to be trapped in a trajectory of disillusionment, failure and resignation. The title of Shelagh Delaney's play *A Taste of Honey* can be applied allegorically to this trajectory: 'My title, *A Taste of Honey* – which everybody at one time in their lives experiences – comes from the Bible where Jonathan says to Saul, "I did but taste a little honey with the end of the rod that was in mine hand, and lo I must die."'[22] Kitchen-sink characters such as Jo from *A Taste of Honey*, Arthur from *Saturday Night and Sunday Morning*, Billy from *Billy Liar* and Colin from *The Loneliness of the Long Distance Runner* are denied access to the 'honey' for most of their lives. Their moment of enlightenment – the 'taste of honey' in their lives – is ephemeral and comes under the risk of punishment.[23] This essential dreamless quality of the kitchen-sink world can be found at the heart of many of Morrissey's lyrics, and he himself was seen during his years with The Smiths as the official voice of gauche and disillusioned youth. He sang about small-town frustration, lost dreams and complicated loves, against a backdrop of fairgrounds, iron bridges, railway arches, old grey schools, cemeteries, humdrum towns, disused railway lines and desolate hillsides.

Finally, and perhaps most importantly, the 'everydayness' which inextricably bonds form and content in Morrissey's lyrics is also in tune with the sensibility found at the heart of the kitchen-sink dramas. For underlining kitchen-sink realism lay an impulse to find worth in ordinary things and people not usually seen as fit subjects for drama, and to portray them in a plainer language, accessible and closer to the everyday. This impulse is expressed in the phrase itself, which originally was applied to the realist tendencies in painting during the 1950s, and soon came to describe the new realism of theatre and film. The kitchen-sink symbolises the ordinary, the banal, the uninteresting, the everyday. To make drama out of it meant to subvert the acceptable conventions of what should and should not deserve an artistic treatment. The main characters of the kitchen-sink dramas were, after all, ordinary people leading ordinary lives, resigned to disillusionment in a land where dreams had 'a knack of just not coming true'.[24]

The references to kitchen-sink films in Smiths lyrics, album covers (all designed by Morrissey) and pop videos are too numerous to list in full.[25] Amongst the films that inspired him were *Saturday Night and Sunday Morning* (Karel Reiz, 1960), *A Taste of Honey* (Tony Richardson, 1961), *The L-Shaped Room* (Bryan Forbes, 1962), *Billy Liar* (John Schlesinger, 1963) and *Poor Cow* (Ken Loach, 1967). One of the finest examples of how the atmosphere of the kitchen-sink dramas was incorporated by Morrissey into the fabric of his lyrics can be found in 'William, It Was Really Nothing' (1984). This song was inspired by the character Billy Fisher, played by Tom Courtenay in the 1963 film adaptation of Keith Waterhouse's novel *Billy Liar*. In the words of Simon Goddard, 'Morrissey's genius in "William. . ." was to distil an entire 90-minute Sixties kitchen-sink drama into less than 20 lines of pop prose.'[26] Billy was an expert daydreamer, but when faced with the possibility of going after real dreams he fails to take the train to London and goes back to his family home. Morrissey's lyrics perfectly encapsulate the feeling of failure in Billy's life, dragged down by a humdrum town that crushed his aspirations to become a writer. In 'Morrissey: The Escape Artist', Jon Savage suggests that, in his life, Morrissey offered 'an alternative ending' to Billy's story: 'He is the Billy Liar who caught the train'.[27] And by doing so, he firmly occupied the vantage position previously held by Sillitoe and Delaney, able to stand inside and outside his class experience. However, as Savage points out, it might be the 'knowledge that leaving brings loss'[28] that prevented Billy from taking the train to London. Indeed, Morrissey's longing for the past seems to spring from a sense of loss, and from the inescapable feeling of in-betweenness that 'taking that train' has brought. Billy's desire to escape with Liz (Julie Christie) to London, his relationship with his boss and his trips to the cemetery also inspired other lyrics by Morrissey (respectively 'London', 'Frankly Mr Shankly', and 'Cemetry [sic] Gates').

Characters from other kitchen-sink films, such as Arthur from *Saturday Night and Sunday Morning* and Jo from *A Taste of Honey*, share with Billy similar feelings of frustration and disenchantment. Lyrics such as 'What a terrible mess I've made of my life' ('You've Got Everything Now'), 'But we cannot cling to the old dreams anymore' ('Still Ill'), 'Life is never kind' (I Don't Owe You Anything'), 'You will leave me behind' ('These Things Take Time'), 'But I once had a dream and it never came true' ('Accept Yourself'), 'Haven't had a dream in a long time' ('Please, Please, Please, Let Me Get What I Want'), 'I know it's over' ('I Know It's Over'), 'Never had no one ever' ('Never Had No One Ever'), 'No hope, No harm, Just another false alarm' ('Last Night I Dreamt that Somebody Loved Me'), 'We tried, and we failed' ('Jeane'), 'Heaven knows I'm miserable now' ('Heaven Knows I'm Miserable Now'), and 'I don't have much in my life' ('Unloveable') are further examples of how the hopelessness of the kitchen-sink dramas, and an ensuing nostalgia for something which seems permanently lost, reverberate through Morrissey's lyrics. Michael Bracewell called this achievement 'a revolutionary reworking of English pop, strip-mining the half-forgotten icons of Englishness in the face of post-punk alienation as a stylism mask, and re-routeing, through their resonance, the power of the romantic imagination back to the undefended self – gauche, ordinary, lonely, misunderstood or frustrated.'[29]

Morrissey was also especially fond of *Coronation Street* and in his teens used to write scripts for the soap, which were all kindly rejected by the company producing the show, Granada. The seminal character Elsie Tanner, played by Patricia Phoenix, was celebrated by Morrissey on the cover of The Smiths' single 'Shakespeare's Sister'. *Coronation Street* was Britain's first soap opera and depicted life in a working-class community in Manchester. Aimed at working-class viewers, it began transmission in 1960, bringing regional accents to television for the first time. Furthermore, it purposely reinforced an idealised view of a traditional working-class community, one already being undermined in the early 1960s. Morrissey, therefore, nurtured a nostalgic fondness for a programme which was in itself a form of nostalgia, perhaps wishing to celebrate what was irretrievably lost in the 1980s.

This nostalgic impulse, counterbalanced by a great dose of irony, is at the root of 'The Queen Is Dead', which opens with a sample from *The L-Shaped Room*. In this sequence, Mavis (Cicely Courtneidge) sings 'Take Me Back To Dear Old Blighty' to the lodgers of a boarding house in London during their Christmas celebration. Sonia, one of the lodgers, is fittingly played by Patricia Phoenix, Morrissey's 'Shakespeare's Sister'. They form an impossible community of working-class misfits, brought together under the same roof but still marginalised and isolated. The characters and the film itself seem to be caught between two worlds, one which nostalgically looks back to an idealised past, and the other which announces the irreversible changes of the post-war period. Morrissey chose to sample 'Take Me Back To Dear Old Blighty', a popular and sentimental British wartime song written in 1916 and revived during the Second World War, but as sung by an ageing lesbian to her equally segregated housemates:

> Take me back to dear old Blighty!
> Put me on the train for London town!
> Take me over there,
> Drop me ANYWHERE,
> Liverpool, Leeds, or Birmingham, well, I don't care!

This crucial moment in Forbes's film amalgamates nostalgia and irony in an effective way. Home and country are one and the same in the song intoned by Mavis, which speaks of a yearning to return to Britain, ending with the cry 'Hurry me home to Blighty, Blighty is the place for me!'. The veracity of this feeling of yearning for something lost is evident in the melancholic undertones of the sequence, which has Mavis struggling to remember the words, and ends in a tearful chorus of all the lodgers (the one sampled by Morrissey). What had passed out of existence in the early 1960s was that idealised view of the traditional and homely working-class community, then celebrated on television by *Coronation Street*. This was a time of change, and *The L-Shaped Room* seems to be conscious of this irrevocability. It is, therefore, no surprise that the film adds a dose of irony to this sequence, for those who seem to yearn for something lost never quite had it in the first place. It is a form of nostalgia for something unreal, never experienced, and all the more painful for that. Morrissey creates a perfect symmetry between *The L-Shaped Room* and his lyrics by deepening the nostalgic and ironic fabric of the film's sequence. He opens the song with a movement in the opposite direction: Mavis sings 'take me back', but he bids farewell to Blighty, or to its 'cheerless marshes'. Perhaps Morrissey would also feel nostalgic for that idealised community of the wartime song, and he would not have been out of place in that Notting Hill boarding house Christmas party. But he writes during Thatcher's 1980s, when even that yearning could seem utterly misplaced.

A Taste of Honey

Of all of Morrissey's influences, the most pronounced and discussed came from Shelagh Delaney, and especially from *A Taste of Honey*. Both the play and the film had an enduring impact on Morrissey, who once declared to the *NME*: 'I've never made any secret of the fact that at least fifty percent of my reason for writing can be blamed on Shelagh Delaney who wrote *A Taste of Honey*.'[30] Born in Salford to a working-class Irish Catholic family, Delaney wrote her first play, *A Taste of Honey*, when she was seventeen, and in 1958 it was accepted by Joan Littlewood's Theatre Workshop and presented at the Theatre Royal in Stratford, in the East End of London. The play was later adapted into a script by Shelagh Delaney and Tony Richardson, who directed the film in 1961. *A Taste of Honey* is the story of a young girl, Josephine, played in the film by the Liverpudlian Rita Tushingham, who struggles on her way to adulthood, quite abruptly brought upon her by an unexpected pregnancy. It is also the story of Jimmy (Paul Danquah), the black sailor with whom Jo has a brief affair, and of Geof (Murray Melvin), the young and effeminate textile design student who befriends Jo in the second part of the film, and with whom she develops a platonic relationship. The three characters, a clumsy working-class girl, a black sailor and a young homosexual, were essentially three gauche individuals caught between childhood and adulthood, and in whom the young Morrissey could identify elements of his own reclusive condition.

Delaney's justification for writing *A Taste of Honey* accords with the generally accepted idea that theatre in the 1950s was in need of rejuvenation. It was the artificiality of plays at the time that concerned her, and the divorce from the real made explicit through their choice of subjects and their style: 'We used to object to plays where factory workers come cap in hand and call the boss "Sir". Usually North Country people are shown as gormless, whereas in actual fact they are very alive and cynical.'[31] *A Taste of Honey* brought with it an environment and characters which had rarely been seen on stage before the 1950s, revealing what could be called 'a hidden real': 'I see the theatre as a place where you should go not only to be entertained but where the audience has contact with *real* people, people who are *alive*.'[32]

In the play, all the characters are very much alive in their use of language.

Delaney's dialogues are extremely articulate, sometimes even poetic, but without straying too far from everyday language. Her assertion that North Country people are 'in actual fact . . . very alive and cynical' – and her mission to write a play portraying them in such a way – is evident in the many humorous dialogues that punctuate *A Taste of Honey*. In this sense, Morrissey's spoken and written language echoes the very eloquence of *A Taste of Honey*'s characters, and especially the expressiveness of Jo's mother Helen, the greatest source of humour in the play and the film.[33] As well as the revelation of a language which is alive, the film, shot almost entirely on location in Manchester and Salford, exposed an environment of squalor which still existed in many parts of the country in the late 1950s, unveiling the northern industrial landscape through recurrent images of factory chimneys, dirty canals, railway arches, fairgrounds and cobbled streets.

Morrissey's fascination with Delaney and with *A Taste of Honey* found its way to the front cover of some of The Smiths' singles and albums, such as the Sandie Shaw version of 'Hand In Glove', for which Rita Tushingham appeared on the cover, the album *Louder than Bombs*, which featured a 1961 picture of Delaney from the *Saturday Evening Post*, and the single 'Girlfriend In A Coma', which included another picture of Delaney, this time taken from a 1961 edition of *A Taste of Honey*. The precocious author was also the inspiration behind The Smiths' song 'Sheila Take A Bow', in which Morrissey wonders how 'someone so young' could 'sing words so sad'.

Morrissey's celebration of the play and the film, however, came mainly from his incorporation of the voices of Jo, Geof and Jimmy into his lyrics. Theirs were the young, authentic and witty vernacular voices of Salford, which rang so true for Morrissey. Songs such as 'You've Got Everything Now' ('As merry as the days were long'), 'Barbarism Begins At Home' ('Must be taken in hand') and 'Shoplifters Of The World' ('Six months is a long time') contain quotes, reworked or not, from *A Taste of Honey*, in both its theatrical and cinematic renditions.[34] This chapter also takes its title from a line in the play's first act, 'I don't owe you a thing'.[35] Jo's blunt statement, directed at her mother, was reworked by Morrissey in the 1984 song 'I Don't Owe You Anything'.

Other songs have an even closer connection with the film's plot and atmosphere. The most overt example can be found in 'This Night Has Opened My Eyes', which encapsulates the aftermath of Jo and Jimmy's separation. Morrissey called it 'a *Taste of Honey* song – putting the entire play to words'.[36] In fact, the lines come mainly from the play's second act, when Jo discusses with Geof her brief affair with Jimmy, trying to come to terms with her unexpected pregnancy. The lines 'That river, it's the colour of lead', 'You can't just wrap it in a bundle of newspaper and dump it on a doorstep', 'Oh well, the dream's gone, but the baby's real enough', and 'I'm not sorry and I'm not glad'[37] were slightly reworked and incorporated into the lyrics (notably, the 'bundle of newspaper' of the play became the *News of the World* in Morrissey's version). 'This Night Has Opened My Eyes' seems to sum up Morrissey's demotic impulse: it skilfully weaves, through the poetry of everyday language so dear to Delaney and himself, the kitchen-sink landscape ('In a river the colour of lead') and the hopelessness of its dwellers ('The dream has gone').

The attentive viewer of *A Taste of Honey* will also be able to recognise pieces of the play and the film even in those songs which are less overt in their borrowing. One very good example can be found in the film's prelude sequence, not present in the original play, and which effectively introduces Jo's main features. She is first seen as a clumsy girl playing netball in the schoolyard. She is hopeless and is constantly being reprimanded by her teacher, who in this way also isolates her from the other girls: 'Come on, Jo, come on, move with it!' Once back inside the toilets she is seen washing her hands and talking to a friend, a blonde girl who mechanically combs her hair. The shot reveals their reflection in the mirror as they talk to each other:

> Friend: You're not much good at netball, are you Jo?
> Jo: No, I'm bad on purpose.
> Friend: Are you going dancing tonight?
> Jo: I can't.
> Friend: You never go anywhere do you Jo?
> Jo: I haven't got any clothes to wear for one thing. And for another. . .
> Friend: What?
> Jo: We might be moving home again.
> Friend: Like a couple of gypsies, you and your mother.
> Jo: So what!

The other girls leave the bathroom and Jo, now alone, washes her face and makes a soap bubble as she stares at the mirror. Her main features are clearly established in this short sequence: the netball game denotes her gaucheness and clumsiness, the lack of fashionable clothes and the fact that she is moving houses reveal her social class, and the soap bubble stands for her childlike manners. Jo's declaration, 'I haven't got any clothes to wear for one thing', was ingeniously reworked by Morrissey in The Smiths' song 'This Charming Man': 'I would go out tonight/But I haven't got a stitch to wear'.

Jo and her mother Helen move into a new place in the film's second sequence. It is a shabby and comfortless flat or, in other words 'a room with a cupboard bare' with 'ice on the sink where we bathe', as Morrissey sang in 'Jeane'. The very reference to death in the song, 'how can you call this a home when you know it's a grave?', finds a parallel in Jo's description of the bed as 'a coffin only not half as comfortable'.[38] In the subsequent sequences of the film, Jo will taste a little of her honey, and that comes in the form of Jimmy, a sailor on leave whom she meets one day on the bus. The two spend long afternoons walking around Salford canals and making plans for their future. This is how they say goodbye one day in the outdoor steps of a steep street:

> Jo: Dream of me!
> Jimmy: Dreamt of you last night. Fell out of bed twice!
> Jo: Ta-ta. I love you.
> Jimmy: Why do you love me?
> Jo: Because you're daft!

The simplicity and grace of Jimmy's lines 'Dreamt of you last night. Fell out of bed twice!' were incorporated by Morrissey in 'Reel around the Fountain', which opens The Smiths' 1984 debut album: 'I dreamt about you last night/ And I fell out of bed twice.'

Jo and Jimmy's love affair also inspired 'Hand In Glove', first released as a single in May 1983. The lines 'and if the people stare, then the people stare' refer to their interracial relationship, which could still shock British society in the 1950s, and the disillusionment of the final declaration, 'I'll probably never see you again', is a direct quote from the play and the film's dialogue, in which Jo pessimistically reveals to Jimmy how she feels about their future.[39] Jimmy indeed has to leave Jo behind, and as she stares at his ship sailing down the canal she knows that she has tasted her honey.

The Smiths twenty-four times a second

If Morrissey's use of cinema derived mainly from his fixation with the grime of the kitchen-sink dramas, their melancholy characters and landscape, cinema's use of The Smiths can suggest a different story. Since 1985 the band's songs have appeared in around thirty films and television programmes, and despite a few exceptions a clear pattern can be identified. It was in *Pretty in Pink* (Howard Deutch, 1986) that 'Please Please Please, Let Me Get What I Want' made its debut on the big screen, on a very brief (twenty-five seconds) scene in which the character Duckie (Jon Cryer) sits in his shabby bedroom in a sulk, suffering from his unrequited love for his friend Andie Walsh (Molly Ringwald). The film, a quintessential 'teen' flick produced by John Hughes, also includes in its soundtrack tunes by British bands New Order and Echo and the Bunnymen, and borrows its title from a Psychedelic Furs song. The discreet inclusion of 'Please Please Please . . . ' in *Pretty in Pink* pioneers the use of this particular song in cinema, either in its original or cover version.

Simon Goddard comments on how Morrissey's plea 'Please, please, please let me get what I want, this time' could relate autobiographically to his wish that the 'good times' which had come, for a change, in his life would linger.[40] The song was written in 1984, after The Smiths had attained relative success, so Morrissey could indeed be singing about having tasted his honey and not wishing it would fade away. There is an emphasis in his verses on how this is the first time in his life that something good has a chance of coming his way, reinforcing the precarious and ephemeral quality of this moment of enlightenment, which Morrissey prays the Lord will let him enjoy. The song thus applies itself well to both melancholic and wishful moments in films, relating to both the feeling of being stuck and being on the cusp of something good.

Ferris Bueller's Day Off (John Hughes, 1986), another of the 'Brat Pack' offspring, follows *Pretty in Pink*'s lead and includes an instrumental version of the song as covered by The Dream Academy. It is played in its entirety during a memorable sequence inside the Art Institute of Chicago, visited by Bueller (Matthew Broderick), Cameron (Alan Ruck) and Sloane (Mia Sara) on their day off. The sequence, which provides a relaxation of the film's narrative drive, was described by John Hughes as 'self-indulgent', and derives from the director's fond memories of visiting the museum as a teenager.[41] It is also a comment on the fragmented nature of film itself, alternating increasingly closer shots of Cameron's puzzled face with Seurat's pointillist masterpiece, 'A Sunday Afternoon on the Island of La Grande Jatte' (1884), composed of small dots which must be seen from a distance in order to form a picture, just as film is composed of shots and frames added together by the editing and the projector. The instrumental version of 'Please Please Please . . .' adorns this contemplative sequence in this by and large upbeat film, offering a counterpoint to the rather stereotypical miserabilist view of The Smiths.

The song was subsequently used in its original version during the prom scene in another American teen film, *Never Been Kissed* (Raja Gosnell, 1999), in which journalist Josie Geller (Drew Barrymore) enrols in her old high school as an undercover reporter, and in the crass parody *Not Another Teen Movie* (Joel Gallen, 2001), as covered by Muse. Most notably, though, it was used in two British films from 2006 set in the 1980s, *Starter for Ten* (Tom Vaughan) and *This Is England* (Shane Meadows). In *Starter for Ten* the song provides the soundtrack for the character Brian Jackson's moment of despair after cheating on the game show *University Challenge* and returning to his mother's home in Southend. Brian is a working-class scholarship student who enrols in his first year at the University of Bristol, and who ends up in the team for *University Challenge*. The film deals with class issues and is a distant inheritor of the kitchen-sink dramas, but despite a few moments of disillusionment a hopeful atmosphere prevails. Brian, after all, has already earned his ticket to a first-class education and left his working-class home, unlike Jo, Arthur or Billy. It is fitting that 'Please Please Please . . .' is heard precisely when he seems to have lost the good times he had in his first year in Bristol. There is an element of defeat, but the film's optimistic ending suggests that his prayers were answered.

Director Shane Meadows's films are rooted in the working-class Midlands and are much closer inheritors of the realist impulse of the kitchen-sink dramas. *This Is England*, like *Starter for Ten*, is also set in Thatcher's 1980s, but the inclusion of 'Please Please Please . . .' in the soundtrack functions not only as a gesture back to that moment of British history which saw the appearance of The Smiths, but also to the kitchen-sink milieu which so inspired Morrissey. *This Is England* tackles the skinhead subculture through the story of a young boy named Shaun (Thomas Turgoose), who befriends a gang of skinheads in a small coastal town in Lincolnshire, and ends up involved with acts of racism and violence. The song is heard in the film's final sequence, as covered by Clayhill, and punctuates a transformative and poignant moment in Shaun's life, as he throws into the sea the English flag which had been give to him by Combo (Stephen Graham), the psychotic leader of the gang. The scene directly quotes François Truffaut's masterpiece ending of *Les 400 Coups* (1959), in which Antoine Doinel (Jean-Pierre Léaud) runs away from the borstal he had been sent to and reaches the sea for the first time in his life, wetting his feet in the water, only to then turn away from it and look at the camera. Similarly, Shaun walks to a beach reminiscent of the coast of Normandy in Truffaut's film and throws his flag into the sea, finally turning and staring at the camera, thus breaking, like Doinel before him, the fourth wall which preserves cinema's illusion. There is, however, a note of redemption and confidence in Shaun's symbolic act which somehow contrasts with the uncertainty of Doinel's future, and this is reinforced by the choice of 'Please Please Please . . .' in the soundtrack.

Other songs by The Smiths have been used in recent films, such as *Closer* (Mike Nichols, 2004), which features 'How Soon Is Now?' playing inside a strip club, the comedy *Forgetting Sarah Marshall* (Nicholas Stoller, 2008) with 'Heaven Knows I'm Miserable Now', and *The History Boys* (Nicholas Hytner), another British film from 2006 set in the 1980s, and which uses the instrumental version of 'This Charming Man' at the beginning of the film, when the (working-class) boys of the title have just received their A-level results and learned that they will be competing for a place at Oxford or Cambridge. The song is used to underscore a moment of buoyancy about moving on up in life, suggesting the potential of class mobility, which contrasts with the noted immobility of the kitchen-sink characters.

Finally, the 2009 film *(500) Days of Summer* (Marc Webb) also provides a counterpoint to The Smiths' use of cinema, for while Morrissey has drawn on films about failure and constraint this is in turn a film about possibilities. Both 'There Is A Light That Never Goes Out' and 'Please Please Please . . .' are used in different moments of the film, and here, unlike other cases, the band is actually named and becomes part of the plot. Tom (Joseph Gordon-Levitt) meets Summer (Zooey Deschanel) at work and, while at first dismissing her to his colleagues as conceited, realises he's falling in love with her after a meeting in the lift: he is listening to 'There Is A Light That Never Goes Out' in his earphones, dutifully ignoring her, and she starts a conversation about how she loves The Smiths, singing along to the song. From that moment, Tom is convinced that he has found his soul mate, and in a subsequent scene he plays 'Please Please Please . . . ' on his office computer in an attempt to call Summer's attention. Thus, The Smiths work as that first thing which awakens Tom to his love for Summer, united as they are in their love for the band. Things do not go according to plan, but the prevailing mood of the film, to which The Smiths lend themselves, is one of hopefulness.

People see no worth in you; I do

Cinema's use of The Smiths, therefore, is far from being confined to films or sequences about disillusionment and failure, and can be read as a useful counterpoint to the stereotypical view of the band as 'miserablist'. In a similar vein, the close semiotic bond between Morrissey's lyrics and the kitchen-sink dramas is far deeper than the feeling of hopelessness the words he borrowed could suppose. As Mark Simpson points out, he 'took much more than mere words from A Taste of Honey; he took its world, its language and its voice, made them his own and in the process fashioned something new and yet time-less.'[42] At a time when the voice of pop music had been cemented as the voice of working-class youth, ironically against the severe reality of the demolition of the working classes in the 1980s, Morrissey found in the demotic impulse of the kitchen-sink dramas an endless source of inspiration. Conversely, the realism of films like A Taste of Honey revealed its enduring impact through Morrissey and The Smiths. It would, therefore, be fair to say that Morrissey owes to the kitchen-sink films only as much as they owe him, for they have been kept alive through his lyrics as much as they have inspired them. Thus, whenever someone hears song words such as 'I would go out tonight, but I haven't got a stitch to wear' or 'I dreamt about you last night, and I fell out of bed twice', it is also Jo and Jimmy that can be heard in the distance, the clumsy working-class girl from Salford and her boyfriend who could almost seem undeserving of artistic treatment. Michael Bracewell called Morrissey's impulse a return to the glamour of the ordinary, suggesting the existence of a cyclical movement:

> In its return to the cat's cradle of English ordinariness, the impact on English pop of Morrissey's writing and performance could be likened to the revolution caused in English theatre in 1956 by John Osborne's Look Back in Anger. The sophisticated tragedy and the ironic comedy of manners had been usurped. And a return to the glamour of the ordinary, in the face of honed sophistication,

could be achieved only by a writer who knew how to lift poetic truths out of the mass of common experience.[43]

If this is indeed a cyclical movement, it is interesting to note that in 2006, almost twenty years after The Smiths split up, the Sheffield band Arctic Monkeys took the name of their highly successful debut album from Arthur Seaton's declaration of individuality in the film *Saturday Night and Sunday Morning*: 'Whatever people say I am, that's what I'm not'. In true Morrissey fashion, they borrowed the voice of a 1960s working-class hero and used it as a champion and standard, echoing therefore the impact of that (also northern and vernacular) voice.

Morrissey was attracted to Jo and other kitchen-sink characters precisely for their ordinariness, and he consciously chose to celebrate them in a language closer to the everyday, but no less effective or poetic. This aspiration was emblematically stamped in Morrissey's choice of band name, 'The Smiths', which was, in his words, 'the most ordinary name and I thought it was time the ordinary folk of the world showed their faces'.[44] And what he saw and heard in the kitchen-sink films he later celebrated were precisely the faces and the voices of ordinary people, living in ordinary towns and speaking in regional dialects. Ultimately, Morrissey's lyrics for The Smiths remain the finest example – in British pop – of a conscious wish to write about the everyday lives of ordinary people. William Wordsworth once wrote in his *Lyrical Ballads* that a tale could be found in every thing.[45] He too dedicated his verses to those not normally seen as fit subjects for poetry, and sought to employ a simple language for poetic purposes.[46] Wordsworth's impulse finds a parallel in the kitchen-sink dramas' sensibility and demotic aspiration. Morrissey's own writing denotes, despite the oceanic distance between the two writers, a similar impulse. 'People see no worth in you', he sings to the addressee in 'Reel Around The Fountain', before affixing a redeeming (and highly revealing) caveat: 'I do'.

Notes

1 Morrissey, quoted in E. Van Poznak, 'Morrissey: The Face Interview', *The Face*, 51 (1984), p. 33.

2 Morrissey, quoted in F. Worral, 'The Cradle Snatchers', *Melody Maker*, 3 September 1983, p. 27.

3 Demotic comes from the Greek word which means 'of the people', and here denotes the everyday language that is spoken on the streets, or in other words the language of the common people.

4 Morrissey, quoted in N. McCormack, 'All Men Have Secrets', *Hot Press*, 4 May 1984, p. 19.

5 The Smiths, 'Heaven Knows I'm Miserable Now', Single A-side (May, 1984).

6 The Smiths, 'The Queen Is Dead', *The Queen Is Dead* (1986).

7 Raymond Williams, 'A Lecture on Realism', *Screen*, 18 (1977), p. 63.

8 P. Clarke, *Hope and Glory: Britain 1900–1990* (London: Penguin, 1996), p. 207.

9 The appearance of John Osborne's *Look Back in Anger* and Colin Wilson's *The Outsider* in 1956 prompted the creation of the phrase 'Angry Young Man' as a label of convenience by the press. One of the first articles to use the phrase was a review of both *Look Back in Anger* and *The Outsider* by J.B. Priestley, published in the *New Statesman* in 1956. It was later applied to other writers with similar styles and themes. The main characteristics of the Angry Young Man movement are an alliance with literary realism and a rejection of subjectivism and the language of modernism; a lack of political commitment; and an interest in the issue of class mobility.

10 Roy Armes, *A Critical History of the British Cinema* (London: Secker and Warburg, 1978).

11 J. Hill, *Sex, Class and Realism: British Cinema 1956–1963* (London: British Film Institute, 1986), p 3.

12 Andrew Higson, 'Space, Place, Spectacle: Landscape and Townscape in the "Kitchen-sink" Film', *Screen*, Vol. 25 (1984), pp. 2–21.

13 A mark of enunciation is the product of an address, which presupposes a subject who enunciates. In a film like *A Taste of Honey*, a mark of enunciation would be any moment in which the point of view (the enunciation) of the director, who in this case is the middle-class outsider, stands out from the supposedly objective narrative of the film.

14 C. Mello, 'Everyday Voices: The Demotic Impulse in English Post-war Film and Television' (PhD dissertation, University of London, 2006).

15 N. Cohn, *Awopbopaloobopalopbamboom: Pop From the Beginning* (London: Pimlico, 2004), pp. 63–4.

16 R. Hewison, *Too Much: Art and Society in the Sixties 1960–75* (London: Methuen, 1988), pp. 66–7.

17 Bobby Scott, who was the musical director of Broadway's *A Taste of Honey*, originally composed the song in 1960. Rick Marlow added the lyrics in 1962. See also I. MacDonald, *Revolution in the Head: The Beatles' Records and the Sixties* (London: Pimlico, 1998), p. 61.

18 Another notable example of the referencing of kitchen-sink films in pop music can be found in the band Television Personalities (1978–present day). Singer/songwriter Dan Treacy referenced popular culture in his lyrics, naming the song 'Look Back In Anger' (1981) after John Osborne's play and 'Geoffrey Ingram' (1981) after the character in *A Taste of Honey* (both from their debut album *And Don't The Kids Just Love It*).

19 Morrissey, December 1984, quoted in D. Kelly, 'The Mad Chatter', *NME*, 9 April 1988, p. 13.

20 Morrissey sings in 'Panic' (1986): 'Because the music that they constantly play, it says nothing to me about my life'.

21 Morrissey on Australian Radio, 1985, quoted in M. Simpson, *Saint Morrissey* (London: SAF Publishing, 2004), p. 58.

22 S. Delaney, *A Taste of Honey* (London: Methuen, 1982), p. xvi.

23 In 2005, the writer Tony Parsons declared that the prevailing mood of his latest novel, *Stories We Could Tell* (2005), came from 'that feeling you get from the films of the time [the kitchen-sink films], like *A Taste of Honey* or *Saturday Night and Sunday Morning*. That working-class feeling, that you've had your fun and now this is what the rest of your life looks like' (S. Mackenzie, 'Let's Get Personal', *Guardian* 'Weekend' section, 27 August 2005, p. 19).

24 The Smiths, 'Accept Yourself', *Hatful Of Hollow* (1984).

25 For a song-by-song account of The Smiths and the sources of Morrissey's lyrics see S. Goddard, *The Smiths: Songs that Saved Your Life* (London: Reynolds & Hearn, 2nd edn, 2004).

26 Goddard, *The Smiths*, pp. 102–3.

27 J. Savage, 'Morrissey: The Escape Artist', *Village Voice: Rock & Roll Quarterly* (Summer 1989), reprinted in J. Savage, *Time Travel: Pop, Media and Sexuality, 1977–96* (London: Chatto & Windus, 1996), p. 258.

28 Ibid., p. 264.

29 M. Bracewell, *England is Mine: Pop Life in Albion from Wilde to Goldie* (London: Flamingo, 1998), p. 219.

30 Morrissey, quoted in I. Pye, 'Some Mothers Do 'Ave 'Em: Interview with Morrissey', *NME*, 7 June 1986, p. 30.

31 Quoted in Henry Popkin (ed.), *The New British Drama* (New York: Grove Press, 1964), p. 10.

32 Delaney, *A Taste of Honey*, p. xx.

33 Helen was wonderfully played by Dora Bryan in the film adaptation of the play.

34 See Delaney, *A Taste of Honey*, pp. 84, 49 and 24. In *A Taste of Honey* Delaney quotes Shakespeare's *Much Ado about Nothing* in Act 2, Scene 1: 'He shows me where the bachelors sit, and there live we as merry as the day is long.' In Act 2, Scene 2 of *A Taste of Honey* Helen says 'There I was standing on a chair singing away merry as the day is long. . .'. And Morrissey in 'You've Got Everything Now' reworks Delaney's quote into 'As merry as the days were long, I was right and you were wrong'.

35 Delaney, *A Taste of Honey*, p. 8.

36 Morrissey, quoted in Pye, 'Some Mothers Do 'Ave 'Em', p. 30.

37 Delaney, *A Taste of Honey*, pp. 54, 55, 75.

38 Ibid., p. 21.

39 Ibid., p. 38.

40 Goddard, *The Smiths*, p. 106.

41 Clip from interview with John Hughes, www.youtube.com/watch?v=p89gBjHB2Gs (accessed on 30 August 2009).

42 Simpson, *Saint Morrissey*, p. 57.

43 Bracewell, *England is Mine*, p. 222.

44 Morrissey, live on the television show *Data Run*, 1984, quoted in Goddard, *The Smiths*, p. 20.

45 Here is the tenth stanza of Wordsworth's poem 'Simon Lee': 'O reader! had you in your mind / Such stores as silent thought can bring, / O gentle reader! you would find / A tale in every thing. / What more I have to say is short, / I hope you'll kindly take it; / It is no tale; but should you think, / Perhaps a tale you'll make it'. In William Wordsworth and Samuel Taylor Coleridge, *Lyrical Ballads and Related Writings*, ed. W. Richey and D. Robinson (Boston and New York: Houghton Mifflin Company, 2002), pp. 66–7.

46 See William Wordsworth's 1802 'Preface to Lyrical Ballads' in *Lyrical Ballads, with Pastoral and Other Poems, in Two Volumes*. Vol. 1 (London: T.N. Longman and O. Rees, 3rd edn, 1802), reprinted in Richey and Robinson (eds), *Lyrical Ballads and Related Writings*, pp. 390–411.

9

'A DOUBLE BED AND A STALWART LOVER FOR SURE':
THE SMITHS, THE DEATH OF POP AND THE NOT SO
HIDDEN INJURIES OF CLASS

Colin Coulter

The ashes are all about us

As the closing monologue of a documentary concerned with the frequently
vacuous medium of popular music, it would be difficult to script a more
dramatic or indeed profound one. Many people reading this are doubtless
familiar with the particular scene that ends the episode of the *South Bank
Show* devoted to The Smiths and broadcast posthumously in October 1987.[1]
Indeed, quite a few could probably recite it word for word. Here we encounter
Morrissey, reclined in an elegant Queen Anne chair, sporting, for reasons best
known to himself, the jersey of the French national rugby team and evidently
amused by the escalating extravagance of what has doubtless been an endless
stream of pronouncements. The singer informs us that the demise of popular
music is entirely inevitable and indeed imminent and that The Smiths mark
'the end of the line'. In a haunting sequence, memorable even by the standards
of someone blessed with the gift of the telling phrase, he observes that 'the
ashes are all about us if we could but notice them'.[2] The credits roll immediately against a backdrop of Stephen Wright's iconic shot of gladioli flouncing
from the hind pocket of Morrissey's Levi's and accompanied by a soundtrack
of 'Stop Me If You Think You've Heard This One Before'.

This is a rather telling, if perhaps somewhat predictable, choice of song that
is presumably intended to chastise and deflate the distinctly apocalyptic talk
that has just gone before. The selection of 'Stop Me . . . ' to close the documentary evidently seeks to consign the notion that The Smiths mark the end
of pop to the realm of rock'n'roll mythology. It implies, in other words, that
Morrissey's dire warnings mark little more than a rehearsal of that familiar
tale in which musicians insist that popular culture could not possibly imagine
the world without them. The gentle scepticism of those who produced the
South Bank Show is of course not entirely unreasonable. The narratives that
form around popular music abound, after all, with morbid tales of the end

of days. The recurrent figure of the chosen one, the seer, with an appetite for self-destruction is merely the most familiar embodiment of a wider set of stories that speak from, and to, the dark heart of popular culture. Against this particular backdrop, it is entirely understandable that some might regard the notion of The Smiths as marking the end of pop as simply another rollicking sequel to a hoary old pop cultural legend; understandable, but thoroughly mistaken nonetheless. While the construction of The Smiths as the last great (English) pop band appears merely to retell a familiar tale, it differs possibly from other renditions in two crucial senses – in its substance and its influence. Each of these will be considered in turn.

I know it's over

In *Mystery Train*, his influential reading of American popular music, the critic and academic Greil Marcus contends that popular culture is innately optimistic. It is, he insists, marked by a youthful disbelief in mortality and a perennial curiosity about the 'next big thing'. While all of this is entirely true, the complete opposite is perhaps even more so. Among the multiple tales that embroider popular music, the ones that are most compelling and most recurrent are those that deal not with beginnings but rather with *endings* – the endings of careers, of sanities, of lives. One of the forms in which these narratives are cast might be termed eschatological. In other words, in some of these stories the demise of bands, of songwriting partnerships, most dramatically of individuals, is conceived as an almost necessary moment of annihilation that prepares the ground for something else. To take the perhaps obvious example of another great Manchester band, the heartrending suicide of Ian Curtis becomes the moment of self-destructive transcendence that enables the ecstatic autism of Joy Division to become the haunted hedonism of New Order. Endings and Beginnings are bound together in the order of things.

The stories that are told around The Smiths are of a rather different kind. In these death narratives, the seemingly natural cycle of popular culture – that of endings and beginnings in presupposition of one another – is dramatically broken. The confused and acrimonious implosion of the band in the late summer of 1987 is taken to mark some fundamental moment of rupture in the order of things. The death of The Smiths is conceived as signalling – to pilfer an obvious metaphor – the absolute end of pop cultural history.

That resolute sense of finality that characterises the stories that surround The Smiths marks them as different in substance perhaps to the others that make up the lore of popular music. What further identifies the difference of these death narratives is their enduring influence. It is really quite remarkable how many people genuinely seem to believe that after Morrissey and Marr parted company, pop music – or at least *a certain version* of pop music

– ceased to be possible. This particular tale of the end of days is rendered and read in a great many different ways. It is merely implicit, for instance, in the blistering denunciation that John Harris provides of the collusion of popular musicians in the anointment of Tony Blair.[3] The role that The Smiths would seem to play in his fine text *The Last Party* is that of spectres at the feast of Britpop. The songs crafted by Morrissey and Marr are implicitly held to have attained a standard of aesthetic integrity that none of the often far more commercially successful guitar bands that came after them could ever possibly hope to come close to. Even the blur of financial and pharmaceutical excess that marked the height of Britpop could not conceal the reality that a certain version of popular music had already been perfected and exhausted.

While the notion that the still lamented demise of The Smiths drew the curtain down on popular music exists between the lines of Harris' text, it finds a rather more explicit rendition in the writings of Mark Simpson. In an article published in the *Guardian* in November 1999 to coincide with a forthcoming and ill-fated Morrissey tour, Simpson eloquently sought to capture the true cultural significance of the singer.[4] The essay concluded on a dramatic note that clearly echoed the edition of the *South Bank Show* broadcast a dozen years earlier. Readers were advised to grasp what was seemingly considered to be possibly their last chance to catch the erstwhile Smiths singer live so that they might experience at first hand the man who had 'killed pop. With his genius.'

It could of course be said in objection at this point that Mark Simpson might not represent an entirely reliable narrator on these matters. As a journalist, he works within an idiom often regarded as given more to speculative hyperbole than to measured critical judgement. And he is of course a very public and unabashed devotee of The Smiths. It comes as little surprise then to hear Simpson offer a hearty version of that particular tale suggesting that something was fundamentally altered within popular culture the day that Johnny Marr quit the band. What is rather more remarkable perhaps is that this view seems to be held not only by fans[5] of the band but by some of their sternest critics as well.

In their impressive and undervalued 1999 book *Discographies*, Jeremy Gilbert and Ewan Pearson set out to interpret, critique and, above all, celebrate the various dance cultures that flourished in the aftermath of The Smiths breaking up. While Gilbert and Pearson acknowledge the demise of The Smiths as a defining moment in the evolution of popular culture, their intention here is neither to mourn nor praise the band. In *Discographies*, The Smiths are held to represent an orthodox and thoroughly reactionary understanding of what popular music is for.[6] The songs of Morrissey and Marr are repeatedly identified as the embodiment of what is clearly regarded – although never precisely named – as an essentially modern(ist) conception of representation. In other words, the work of The Smiths is considered to operate upon the assumptions that there exist certain essential truths and experiences and that the role of popular music is to speak these truths to, or perhaps more accurately *for*, the audience.

Gilbert and Pearson consider this discernibly modern idea of what popular culture exists to do as incarcerating experience within the circuit of what is essentially patriarchal authority. It is entirely inevitable then that they should shed few tears at the passing of The Smiths. For Gilbert and Pearson, the demise of the band represented a welcome development that heralded and enabled a broadening of the field of popular cultural practice and experience. The subsequent flowering of the 'second summer of love', they insist, marked the realisation of a (re)new(ed) understanding of the potential and purpose of popular music. The enduring certainties of 'the truth' were to be exchanged for the transient rush of the moment; the presumed veracity of the word bartered for songs often with no words at all; the constraints and imperatives of experience and identity displaced with more fluid and autonomous notions of self.

The contentions that Gilbert and Pearson provide are bold ones that take us into the very heart of the major theoretical debates of recent times. Although impressive, their thesis is so riddled with problems that it is difficult to know where to start. So maybe we should start with the most glaringly obvious, namely that it is almost impossible to recognise The Smiths in their descriptions of the group. In *Discographies*, the band appears as the essentially patriarchal voice of profoundly restrictive notions of truth and being. It might be that Gilbert and Pearson managed somehow to get The Smiths mixed up with another group entirely. Led Zeppelin perhaps. Or maybe even Mötley Crüe. But it really would be difficult to produce a more profoundly inaccurate depiction of the band.

It has to be acknowledged that The Smiths certainly did – as Gilbert and Pearson contest – trade explicitly in notions of the truth and its cognates (authenticity, sincerity, nature ...). The emotional power and longevity of the songs derive largely from the fact that they offer explicit and exquisite accounts of demonstrably lived experience. The sheer first-person authenticity of the likes of 'Accept Yourself', 'I Know It's Over' and 'Well I Wonder' are not the least of the reasons that they remain utterly spellbinding a quarter of a century later. And the claim that The Smiths were guided by, and indeed guides to, 'the truth' was of course central to the rhetoric that Morrissey spun around the band. Take, for instance, his recurrent claim early on that The Smiths simply 'followed nature' or his classic binary that people have the choice of either entering the world conjured up in his songs or the rather less edifying prospect of pursuing Diana Ross instead.[7]

While the abiding certainties that Morrissey pronounced were invariably

compelling and entertaining – and it must be said that his splenetic judgements on Margaret Thatcher, the House of Windsor and Bernard Matthews[8]
have worn rather well – these barely scratch the surface of the cultural politics
of The Smiths. What is most powerful and enduring perhaps about the songs
that Morrissey and Marr wrote with, and occasionally for, one another is an
understanding that truth and being are problematic, changeful and multiple.
The prodigious body of work that The Smiths compiled during their five years
together features, therefore, a marked and recurrent sense of ambivalence.[9] It
is precisely their inability to recognise this particular and essential attribute
of The Smiths that renders Gilbert and Pearson blind to both the aesthetic
wonder and the progressive politics of the band.

The ambivalence that pervades the work of The Smiths has of course over
the years drawn the attention of many commentators, sympathetic and hostile
alike. The discussion of these tensions within the songs has, however, tended
to focus rather narrowly upon matters of sexuality. The lyrics have been
scoured incessantly for clues as to what or who precisely Morrissey is or is
not. This recurrent and, in many respects, understandable preoccupation with
issues of sexuality has meant that other forms of social identity that inform the
songs have often been somewhat neglected. I would like, therefore, to direct
our attention now to another mode of being and becoming that represents an
indispensable motif running through the work of The Smiths but nonetheless
tends at times to be overlooked, namely that of social class.

The riches of the poor

As is the case with all genuinely great popular music, the work of The Smiths
is both utterly timeless and yet precisely and palpably of its time. The songs of
Morrissey and Marr were of course written in very specific and indeed har-
rowing historical circumstances. The recording career of the band coincided
more or less precisely with the second term in power of Margaret Thatcher.
It was in this middle period in office that Thatcher revealed the full extent
of both her political ambition and cultural prejudice. Emboldened by the
popular acclaim that greeted her squalid imperial excursion in the South
Atlantic, Thatcher began to implement a revolutionary political agenda that
would render British society transformed and, in many quarters, trauma-
tised.[10] At the very heart of an evidently overstocked personal demonology
were the institutions and individuals who acted in the name of organised
labour. The Thatcherite obsession to challenge and ultimately vanquish the
'enemy within' inexorably led to confrontation with the most powerful and
militant of the trades unions. In a vicious industrial dispute that would span
an entire year, the full repressive power of the British state was brought to bear
on a series of coal-mining communities. The material assault on the miners

was mirrored in a rather broader ideological onslaught against the poor and the powerless.[11] Cheered on by the braying scribes of the tabloid press, Thatcher and her acolytes sought incessantly to demonise and demean those who had been the victims of the neoliberal policies pursued by Westminster. Ordinary folk who could no longer find work as a succession of factories and pits folded were denounced as scroungers and instructed to 'get on their bikes' and find jobs elsewhere. Them truly was rotten days.[12]

The songs of The Smiths derive and retain much of their meaning and indeed a great deal of their force from the very particular historical context in which they were conceived. In the back catalogue of the band, the values and imperatives of Thatcherism are challenged and ultimately turned on their head. The (im)moral heart of the Thatcher project drew of course from the pilfered ideal that 'there is no such thing as society'.[13] The records of The Smiths represent in part an endeavour to critique and resist the atomised and instrumental vision of society that Thatcherism sought to inflict. It was readily apparent from the outset that the aesthetic agenda of the band would centre upon a distinctive and highly stylised version of northern working-class communalism that had, if it had ever existed at all, long since passed away. Those astounding lyrics that Morrissey wrote summoned up an entire imaginary in which were resurrected that warmth, community and modesty that had been annihilated by the possessive individualism of Thatcher's barbaric second term. In these songs, we are invited to a place in which it is again possible that each household appliance might be greeted as a new science and where it is possible to remain blissfully unaware of nine-year-old thugs peddling drugs. In these songs, in other words, we are called back to a prelapsarian state in which the communal and the collective have not been decimated by the petit bourgeois instrumentalism of the grocer's daughter from Grantham.[14]

The standard bearers of the Thatcher 'revolution' were of course the *nouveaux riches* who were not exactly bashful about flaunting their newfound wealth. At the time, the 1980s were heralded as the 'style decade' in which greed was good and in which the devil was entitled to the hindmost. While the values and imperatives of Thatcherism would in time convert a great many people, neither Morrissey nor Marr would be among them. In their songs, we encounter a complex but nonetheless cogent cultural agenda that inverts the logic and morality of the entire Thatcher project. The values and characters celebrated in those singular lyrics that sprang from Morrissey's imagination could scarcely be more removed from the greed and the alleged glamour of the hero(in)es of Thatcherism. In the songs of The Smiths, we are introduced to the glamour of grime, instructed in the poetry of the prosaic, informed of the epiphany of the everyday.

The commitment and connection to common folk and ordinary circumstances had of course already been disclosed before The Smiths had even signed a record deal. The decision to christen the band after what was – and what remains[15] – the most common surname in England was a bold and indeed humorous one.[16] In naming his band The Smiths, Morrissey issued an explicit challenge to a pop mainstream that in the early 1980s reflected more perhaps than any of the other culture industries the ostentation and emptiness of the Thatcher era.[17] The nature and ambition of this challenge would only become fully apparent though when the band released their debut single. At the time, 'Hand In Glove' sounded like the opening salvo of an entire cultural manifesto delivered in three minutes twelve seconds flat, and more than a quarter of a century has done little to diminish the vitality and bravado of the track.[18] The lyrics of the song ridicule and reject the hierarchies of value that had held sway since Thatcher had come to power. With characteristic vitriol, Morrissey dispenses with the orthodoxy that wealth is a measure of worth and insists that it is in fact the impoverished who are worthy of our respect. As he would subsequently underscore in interviews,[19] those who may appear poor in the conventional material sense are in reality the most likely to have more valuable, spiritual riches. Yes, we may be hidden by rags, but we've something they'll never have.

The veneration of those whom mainstream society often despises that we first encounter in 'Hand in Glove' signals a thread that runs through The Smiths' songbook. The characters and contexts that Morrissey seeks to invest with a certain unconventional glamour are often drawn from a very specific cinematic template. It has been widely acknowledged that the words that the singer wrote, particularly in the early days of the band, owed a great deal to that sequence of social realist British movies released as the 1950s turned into the 1960s. These 'kitchen-sink' dramas were in their day genuinely revolutionary in their depiction of the actual hardships of ordinary people's lives and in their use of working-class actors delivering lines in their own vernacular. As Cecília Mello shows in her chapter, the characters and concerns of these social realist movies feature strongly in the recordings that The Smiths made at the beginning of their career. One that springs readily to mind is an often overlooked track that graces the flipside of the group's breakthrough seven-inch single, 'This Charming Man'. The relatively simple composition 'Jeane' is in effect a kitchen-sink drama put to music. To a stomping beat, the narrator of the song recounts the squalor of the home that (s)he[20] shares with the title character. There is ice on the sink where they bathe and despite the 'greedy grace' with which Jeane attempts to 'tidy the place', it will 'never be clean'. All of her best efforts to transform the hovel into a home will probably come to nought and the place will likely prove to be their 'grave'.

On first listen, 'Jeane' may appear a somewhat slight and perhaps even disposable track, not least when judged against the stellar standards of the rest of Morrissey and Marr's compositions. Indeed, this may well be one of the songs that spring to the minds of those who would seek to denounce and deride The Smiths as repetitive and depressing.[21] A few further listens, however, reveals 'Jeane' to be a rather more substantial and uplifting recording than might initially appear to be the case.[22] In large measure, the value and power of the song derive precisely from its existence within a wider and decidedly particular body of work. In the songs of The Smiths, we are enticed into a fully realised cultural world that centres upon a great number of concerns but not least a recurrent valorisation of the struggles, triumphs and catastrophes of ordinary working-class people. Once we take the time to listen to the lyrics of the other songs, marvel at the sheer audacity and wordplay of the interviews and stay up late to watch yet another rerun of those inestimable kitchen-sink movies then the value and even meaning of a seemingly minor track such as 'Jeane' begin to become rather clearer. As soon as we locate the song in its rightful place as a text that only really makes sense within a broader and more ambitious cultural imaginary, then we start to hear 'Jeane' anew. The struggle to transform the hovel into a little palace appears genuinely heroic; the effort to ensure that all the bills are paid 'cash on the nail' seems an enterprise of true valour; above all, perhaps, the doomed tryst of the ill-starred lovers begins to appear utterly and ineffably romantic.

While the valorisation of a certain version of working-class identity shone through the records, it was even more apparent on their sleeves. More perhaps than any other band ever, The Smiths assembled a body of cover art that was, and indeed remains, both instantly and arrestingly identifiable.[23] The sleeves of the band's singles in particular evidently set out to construct a whole sequence of radical and subversive cultural agendas. One of the most recurrent and memorable types to be cast as a cover star of The Smiths' forty-fives was that of the tough, spirited, northern working-class woman.[24] The sleeve of the ill-realised single 'Shakespeare's Sister', for instance, features the actress Pat Phoenix, who most famously played the unrepentantly wanton siren Elsie Tanner during the golden age of television's very own kitchen-sink drama, *Coronation Street*. In addition, the image that graces the cover of the irrepressibly jaunty 'Girlfriend In A Coma' is that of the Salford playwright Shelagh Delaney, who authored the social realist classic *A Taste of Honey* and whose fingerprints are all over the early lyrics of The Smiths. Perhaps the most remarkable and striking of this particular genre of cover image, however, is the one that appears on the sleeve of the band's first top ten single. 'Heaven Knows I'm Miserable Now' features a shot of Viv Nicholson, who secured celebrity and then infamy in the 1960s when she won the football pools only to squander her fortune on wild spending and men of questionable character.[25] The cover image records Nicholson returning to her home in Castleford, West Yorkshire, a working-class community that has clearly been blighted both by traditional poverty and modern urban planning. It shows Nicholson

standing in the middle of a potholed road that runs through a shamble of terraced houses, her expression sullen and indomitable, her hairdo a ramshackle
beehive.[26]

The sheer power of the sleeve derives in part of course from its utter incongruity. The choice of an image that so profoundly marks the prevalence of
poverty as the cover of a single that for a time nestled in the top ten signals
an obvious rebuke on the part of The Smiths to their fellow chart contenders,
who in the main were then – as they remain now – given to the superficial,
and betrothed to idle wealth. The resonance of the sleeve also owes a great
deal, however, to the very particular historical context in which it appeared.
'Heaven Knows I'm Miserable Now' disturbed the torpor of the charts at
the precise moment that marked the height of the miners' strike. As the full
material and ideological might of the state bore down on working-class men
outside Orgreave coking plant, that unforgettable image of Viv Nicholson
bore down from the singles racks of Woolworth's and other reliable outlets.
When regarded in its appropriate historical context, therefore, the cover shot
assumes both a greater significance and the shape of what it really was – a
declaration of faith in the value and shabby dignity of ordinary folk at a time
when entire working-class communities faced annihilation. The release of
'Heaven Knows I'm Miserable Now' should then be remembered not only as
one of The Smiths' finest – and funniest – musical moments but also as one of
their most astute and important political interventions.

Sick, dull, plain

The songs of The Smiths clearly feature a highly stylised and nostalgic veneration of the northern working classes. If this widely acknowledged attribute
were all there was to the cultural politics of the band they may well of course
have been consigned to the status of a mere curio amid the agitprop of the
polarised 1980s. The appeal of the group has in fact endured in part precisely
because they offer a vision of what it is to be subaltern in capitalist society in
all of its complexity. The songs that The Smiths committed to vinyl underscore
not only the essential virtue of being working class but also its abiding and
essential indignities. Indeed, this distinct sense of ambivalence often appears
in the same lyric. This is arguably the case in the track 'I Want The One I Can't
Have', which features the remarkable lines: 'A double bed and a stalwart lover
for sure / These are the riches of the poor'. At first glance, the sentiments
articulated here appear to be a fairly familiar and conventional declaration of
the presumed warmth and authenticity of working-class lives. A closer look
suggests, however, a rather less comforting reading. As Morrissey would subsequently underline in interviews,[27] the song was intended to suggest that the
wedding day marks the moment when working-class people are encouraged

to regard themselves as special – a status marked by the acquisition of the matrimonial bed – but is in reality the final time when they will be enabled or allowed to do so. The lines that leap out from the lovelorn gem that is 'I Want The One I Can't Have' represent at one and the same time then both a celebration of cosy intimacy and an indictment of the snares of domesticity. It would be hard to imagine anything more double-edged.[28]

The tone of ambivalence that defines the ways in which the issues of social class are dealt with in the work of The Smiths may be attributed in part to the biographical details of the band's lyricist. While the young Steven Patrick Morrissey emerges as a conflicted boy in many regards, this is true not least in relation to his class status. The singer was of course the child of poor immigrants who fled the misery of 1950s Ireland in order to make a fresh start in one of the more deprived districts of Manchester. In early interviews in particular, Morrissey was at pains to establish his working-class credentials with constant references to having grown up 'penniless' and in 'dire poverty'.[29] In the main, journalists were content to accept on face value this particular narrative and often identified the 'first-hand' authenticity with which Morrissey detailed working-class life.[30] The precise details of the singer's background before he joined the band transpire, however, to be a little more complicated than this familiar version of events would seem to allow. In the year that their youngest son turned eleven, the Morrissey family left their terrace in Hulme and moved into another council home in the district of Old Trafford.[31] The house at 384 King's Road would of course assume a central place in the mythology of The Smiths once Johnny Marr came knocking in search of a songwriting partner, and the location has since become a place of pilgrimage for fans.[32] Those who have paid a visit to the house in which the words of 'Suffer Little Children' were written often remark that it is rather different to the cramped terrace in which they imagined the young Morrissey to have passed his formative years.[33] In what appears – at least to the casual cultural tourist –to be a quiet and tree-lined suburb, the singer was sheltered from some of the perils of the world by a bookish and ambitious mother said to have airs and graces.[34] This enduring maternal support would enable Morrissey to nurture his creative talents free from pressure to find gainful employment and cosseted from the full ravages of the 'dole age' that raged around him.[35]

It might be said, therefore, that the insights into the epiphanies and indignities of working-class life that we find in the songs of The Smiths are delivered from a vantage point that is quite particular and distinctly liminal. While the background of the band's singer and lyricist is evidently working class, it is hardly conventionally or even typically so. These biographical tensions are in part responsible for the profound sense of ambivalence that informs and enlivens the cultural world of The Smiths. One critical expression of this is to be found in the competing versions of subjectivity and sexuality that

Morrissey appears to endorse at different times. There are of course multiple ways of being both working class and male. There is, however, one particular version of working-class masculinity that appears perennially able to assume hegemonic status. This readily familiar rendition of what it means to be a man prescribes the values of emotional distance, physical violence and (hetero) sexual conquest.

In his lyrics and interviews, Morrissey set out to ridicule and reject many of the abiding imperatives of hegemonic (working-class) masculinity. Indeed, at times it seemed that the singer was intent on nothing less than disassembling the entire category of gender identity altogether. As the prophet of the 'fourth gender',[36] Morrissey endeavoured to map out a more progressive way of being a working-class man. Heavily influenced by feminist writers, the singer championed the causes of emotional literacy and intelligent wordplay. In what were perhaps more conservative times than our own, these calls for more fluid and progressive ways of being a man were genuinely subversive and not, therefore, without their dangers. It really did take strength to be gentle and kind.

The enlightened version of working-class masculinity that Morrissey sought to promote coexisted from the outset of course with another, starkly different understanding of what it means to be a man. In some of his lyrics, The Smiths' frontman appears to endorse those very kinds of male subjectivity that he is otherwise and more frequently eager to denounce. On occasions, there are glimpses of admiration for those males who know what they want and know how to get it, even – or perhaps especially – through recourse to physical violence.[37] A number of these characters suggest themselves – the 'tough kid who sometimes swallows nails', the 'tattooed boy from Birkenhead' and of course an entire gallery of 'sweet and tender hooligans' whom no jury in the land could ever bring itself to convict. When Morrissey gazes upon the tattooed toughs who stalked the fairgrounds of his childhood and would later stalk the fairgrounds of his imagination he does so with a palpable homoerotic longing.[38] While thuggish violence invokes a profound revulsion, it still remains at some level 'all a tremulous heart requires'.[39] His gaze though is perhaps also directed by another form of envy or desire, one that suspects that the emissaries of this violence are in some way authentically working class in a way that he can never possibly be. It is this recurrent sense of being torn, or possibly even inadequate, that has both blighted Morrissey's existence and gilded his art.

The sense of personal humiliation and ontological damage that pervade Morrissey's singular lyrics clearly chime with the concerns that appear in the writings of the sociologist Richard Sennett. In a book entitled *The Hidden Injuries of Class*, co-written in 1972 with Jonathan Cobb,[40] Sennett offers a vision of bourgeois society that he has refined and developed in a sequence of subsequent texts.[41] In his eyes, the multiple iniquities of capitalism assume the guise not merely of material exploitation but also of emotional and psycho-logical damage. The age of capital pits people together in a 'contest for dignity' that expresses itself in a pervasive 'morality of shaming and self-doubt'.[42] The principal casualties of this hegemonic moral economy are of course working-class people who are judged against the standards of others and more often than not found wanting. The inevitable outcome of these judgements is that ordinary folk are often the bearers of profound psychological wounds that find expression in retarded and divided conceptions of self.

In the songbook of The Smiths, those abiding psychological scars that are the often concealed and unspoken wounds of bourgeois society begin to flail into public view. The words that Morrissey added to the incandescent music of Johnny Marr often deal with the jarring themes of disease, decay and despair. The sense of suffering and suffocation that pervades the work of the band has often been read through the lens of a misbegotten sexuality. Commentators have tended to listen to the songs for clues as to the precise constellation of Morrissey's (un)interest in the opposite or, rather more plausibly, the same sex. While this fixation with the singer's sexuality remains entirely under-standable, it has unfortunately tended to conceal another equally crucial and fascinating aspect of his subjectivity.

The sense of longing and loss that runs through the songs of The Smiths reflects not only the wounds of the lovelorn but also the scars of the subal-tern. While the damage that arises out of being working class is a recurrent subtext of the songs, it is expressed rather more explicitly in the enormous body of interviews that Morrissey gave to the music press. Perhaps more than any other pop cultural figure of his day, the singer was renowned for giving good copy. Indeed, Simon Garfield goes so far as to suggest that Morrissey's interviews were responsible for more record sales than his songs.[43] In con-versation with music journalists, the singer would hold forth on a great many issues but would return time and again to the theme of the humiliations that were inflicted upon him growing up as a working-class boy. What is most significant perhaps about these passages is that the bile that Morrissey issues invariably reflects an outrage not only at what happened to him but also at what happened – and continues to happen – to people *like* him.

In interviews, the lyricist would repeatedly employ the specific and explicit language of what was evidently a keenly developed sense of class conscious-ness. And he was of course rather less than bashful about naming the names of those he deemed responsible for the various social ills that he so astutely divined. In conversation with music journalists, Morrissey would with no little relish take aim at an entire gallery of establishment figures and institu-tions. The self-identified socialist[44] would reserve particular venom of course for the unearned and unwarranted privilege of the monarchy.[45] Even over a quarter of a century later, his withering comments on the royal family could hardly fail to reduce anyone with an ounce of political judgement to tearful mirth.[46] And Morrissey was also wont to recount with no lack of colour the very particular miseries that are often the lot of the (second-generation) Irish Catholic. It is significant though that in his critique the singer seeks to depict the machinations of the Vatican as being animated not by an abstract morality but rather by a very precise political programme. It is the ambition of all organised religion, he asserts, to 'keep the working classes humble and in their place'.[47]

Some of the more memorable tirades that Morrissey directed towards the establishment world were targeted at the education system.[48] In a host of magazines, the singer would depict the secondary school that he attended as a place of ritualised horror and humiliation. He once commented to the Irish publication *Hot Press* that he had gone to 'severe schools, working class schools, where they would almost chop off your fingers for your own good'.[49] In time, of course, Morrissey would exact a stunning revenge on an education system that denounced and dismissed both him and others of his kind as entirely 'hopeless'.[50] On the startling opening track of the *Meat Is Murder* album, the singer reveals that he has neither forgiven nor indeed forgotten. Against the backdrop of a relentless rhythm, Morrissey denounces the 'belligerent ghouls' who 'run Manchester schools' and dismisses them as 'spineless swines' with 'cemented minds'. The palpable anger that drives 'The Headmaster Ritual' arises in part out of very specific and autobiographical experience.[51] It should also, however, be acknowledged as the expression of a rather wider and more political sensibility, one that is appalled at living in a society that venerates the few while seeking to humiliate the many.

Never had no one ever

The profound ambivalence that characterises the ways in which Morrissey talks about who he is almost inevitably finds echoes in the ways in which he writes about where he is from. There are few bands as indelibly associated with their city of origin as The Smiths.[52] When we listen to those exquisite songs, we are taken by the hand and brought on an impromptu tour of Manchester. For many of us who had the ill fortune to be born elsewhere, The Smiths were in fact our first, and sometimes only, introduction to the city that often seems the very epicentre of popular music. It is first and foremost because of the lyrics and sleeve notes that grace the work of the band that we know and even find inexplicably glamorous the likes of Ardwick or Ancoats. If it were not for the artwork of *The Queen Is Dead* most of us would never even have heard of Salford Lads Club let alone have made the pilgrimage there in order to recreate Stephen Wright's glorious group shot.[53] The intimate and

inextricable association between The Smiths and Manchester has in the main
– or at least in the course of time – served the city rather well. The songs that
Morrissey and Marr wrote with one another imbued the place with a certain
sense of glamour and wonder. It was for many outsiders at least often rather
difficult to listen to The Smiths without falling head over heels for the city
from which they sprang. The resonant and in some respects loving evocation
of Manchester that we find in these songs is apparent not only in their composition but also in their delivery. While Morrissey would occasionally affect
the airs of the archetypal English gentleman,[54] these social pretensions would
evaporate the moment that he opened his mouth to sing. The songs of The
Smiths are of course delivered in a particular version of the rich local vernacular. If you hear the way Morrissey pronounces the word 'guts' on 'I Know It's
Over', for instance, it is almost impossible to miss that you are in fact listening
to a working-class Mancunian.

The sense of place that appears in the songs of The Smiths also, however,
takes other rather darker and less complimentary forms. While Morrissey
would at times in interviews stress his close ties to Manchester, he would
perhaps rather more often underline his feelings of disconnection from the
city.[55] In the lyrics that he scripted for the band, the singer introduces us
to some of the bleaker moments of personal and collective experience in
Manchester. The first song that he and Johnny Marr collaborated on was,
after all, a heartbreaking contemplation of the infamous infanticide that
took place in the 1960s on Saddleworth moor adjoining the city. This sense
of Manchester as a place of imminent and actual catastrophe would recur
throughout the entire body of work that the pair created. One of the more
haunting and cryptic expressions of Morrissey's feeling of alienation from his
native city can be found on a curious piece that features on the album conventionally regarded as The Smiths' masterpiece. On 'Never Had No One Ever',
we find the narrator ruminating against a funereal beat on the feeling of when
'you walk without ease, / On these streets where you were raised'. The inability of Morrissey to find or recognise himself in his hometown would never
perhaps be expressed with greater clarity or economy.[56]

Although the profound feelings of alienation that mark the disposition
of Morrissey evidently give rise to a certain despondency, they also nurture
a conviction that the good life is out there somewhere. The very particular
world of The Smiths plays host to a series of fantasies of escape that inevitably draws upon a familiar set of cultural figures and templates. On the cover
of the promotional twelve-inch single of 'Barbarism Begins At Home', we
are introduced once more to the iconic personality of Viv Nicholson. While
in her previous appearance Nicholson had marked the grinding poverty of
her youth, here we find her on a very different mission. Jauntily attired in a
curious ensemble of crocheted mini dress and peaked hat, and posing outside

the local colliery, she appears to be waving goodbye to a previous life and on the verge of taking the packed suitcase beside her to somewhere else entirely more glamorous.[57]

On other occasions, this particular dream that there must be a better world draws upon the conventions of Morrissey's favourite social realist movies. One of the themes prevalent in the genre of the kitchen-sink drama is the desire to flee the parochial constraints of northern working-class life for the supposed cosmopolitan freedoms of London.[58] In the 1963 John Schlesinger film adaptation of *Billy Liar*, for instance, the title character has the opportunity to escape to the capital in the company of the sexually liberated Liz. As the night train for London is about to leave, however, Billy insists on going to get some milk from a vending machine in a deliberate attempt to miss the departure. Although Morrissey would empathise with these fictional characters who had – to borrow one of his favourite phrases – their 'tails trapped in the door', he would not ultimately allow himself to share their fate. In songs such as 'London', 'Half A Person' and 'Is It Really So Strange?', the singer would rehearse the kitchen sink storyline of the misfit dreaming of a fresh start in the capital. And his genius would of course take Morrissey to London and indeed a great deal farther afield.[59] As Jon Savage would observe after the demise of The Smiths, the band's front man was in effect 'the Billy Liar who caught the train'.[60]

In time, however, it would transpire that the promise of escaping who you are and where you are from can never quite be fully realised.[61] One of the issues addressed in *The Hidden Injuries of Class* is the fate that awaits upwardly mobile working-class people. Sennett and Cobb suggest that those who appear to have succeeded in climbing the social ladder often continue to feel judged and found wanting by the standards of those born into privilege. It is the fate of the upwardly mobile working-class person, they argue, to be caught in a state of limbo between different social worlds. In a sense, this is perhaps the tragedy that has befallen Morrissey. Among the many sources of the singer's ambition and energy was a desire to evade the judgement of those who would seek to humiliate him and to return their scorn many times over. And there can be few cultural icons that have with greater style and zest turned the tables on those who would seek to torment them. As Nick Kent among others has noted, Morrissey's entire career has at times appeared to revolve around an understanding of fame as a form of revenge.[62] But a whole social order constructed upon judgement and humiliation cannot of course be unmade simply through the acquisition of celebrity and wealth. That he will always remain in part that loathed and self-loathing working-class boy would be dramatically brought home to Morrissey when the mismanaged financial affairs of The Smiths eventually and inevitably landed the four band members in court. In his final ruling, the High Court judge famously derided the singer as 'devious, truculent and unreliable'.[63] With his characteristic combination of perspicacity and paranoia, Morrissey identified the cultural undertow of the comments delivered in court. Three years after the trial ended, he spoke of the experience to an *Irish Times* journalist, noting 'I was working class and I was made to feel like a peasant'.[64]

While Morrissey can never genuinely escape the place that he is from, nor can he ever return there either.[65] There is, after all, always someone there to remind him that in the days when he was hopelessly poor, they just liked him more. The sense of being trapped between different worlds – of being drawn this way and that way – appears in many of the songs of The Smiths. It represents a dominant theme, for instance, of the track that fans often regard as the band's finest moment, namely 'There Is A Light That Never Goes Out'. I would like though to turn our attention towards another, lesser known but no less exquisite composition. It is perhaps the most telling illustration of their prowess that Morrissey and Marr often consigned to the status of B-sides songs that would for most other songwriting partnerships represent their greatest achievement. A case in point is a spellbinding tale of unrequited love entitled 'Back To The Old House'.

In this pristine early acoustic number, Morrissey relates his conviction that he would 'rather not go' back to the home of his youth. There are 'too many bad memories', not least of golden opportunities squandered, waiting there for him. As Sean Campbell has illustrated, however, this air of conviction that the narrator can never go home anymore is questioned somewhat by the music that accompanies his voice.[66] There is a contrapuntal tension, Campbell points out, between the guitar playing and the lyrics that suggests that the sentiments expressed at the outset of the song are less steadfast than they might at first appear. This sense of ambivalence is confirmed in the closing verse of the song. Here the narrator confesses that he really 'would love to go' back to these enchanted and haunted places of his childhood but alas he 'never will'. In both its words and its music, 'Back To The Old House' represents the song that perhaps more than any other in The Smiths' back catalogue speaks of the pain of being able neither to leave nor to return. The anxiety of feeling lost in the world that defines this particular track articulates not merely the heartaches of the individual but also the miseries of the wider social order. The marked ambivalence that attends the sense of place in Morrissey's lyrics intimates that the personal mobility revered in bourgeois society often ultimately transpires to be an illusion. While you may never feel at home on the streets where you were raised, neither can you ever genuinely escape them.[67] In giving expression to this particular bind, the songs of The Smiths disclose the kernel of a genuinely revolutionary sensibility, one that rests on the conviction that the transformation of the individual presupposes that of the collective.

Rubber ring

When we return again and anew to the songs of Morrissey and Marr we encounter, therefore, a body of work rather different to the caricatures that critics would often seek to foist upon us. As intimated earlier, the likes of Gilbert and Pearson advance what is perhaps a rather more sophisticated version of a more common depiction of The Smiths as a band that offer a restricted and repetitive understanding of both musical practice and cultural subjectivity. As the discussion above will hopefully have illustrated, however, nothing could possibly be further from the case. While the songs that Morrissey and Marr composed often trade in certain eternal truths, they also and more frequently rest upon the assumption that our identities and biographies draw from a great many complex and often contradictory sources. The work of The Smiths declares, in other words, that we are many different things at different times and perhaps even at the same time. This sense that subjectivities are multiple and conflicted finds expression in the manner in which the songs deal with a range of issues but not least, as we have seen, in the way they depict social class. In the lyrics that Morrissey wrote, working-class people are at one and the same time the heroic survivors of a brutal social order and the boorish authors of mindless violence, both enhanced and enslaved by the ties of community and simultaneously unable to leave or to remain where they were raised. The sequence of ambivalences that run through the songs of The Smiths reveal a band that are rather more complex than their many detractors seem willing or even able to recognise. In constructing subjectivity as multiple and changeful, the songs of Morrissey and Marr assemble a cultural politics starkly different to that ascribed to them by the likes of Gilbert and Pearson. Indeed, if we look a little more closely here a certain irony begins to suggest itself. It might perhaps be that the songs of The Smiths not only diverge from the version of cultural politics that Gilbert and Pearson ascribe to them but also in fact bear more than a passing resemblance to another version that the authors of *Discographies* themselves explicitly endorse.

If this is really the case then why is it that Gilbert and Pearson seem to find it so difficult to recognise, let alone appreciate, the nature and value of The Smiths? It might well be of course that the pair are simply not that familiar with the work of the band. While this is perhaps the most obvious answer, it is also, as usual, the least interesting. I would suggest that the failure of Gilbert and Pearson to appreciate The Smiths owes rather less to the gaps in their record collection than to the gaps in their theoretical vision.

The ideological frame of *Discographies* is that provided by the writings of Ernesto Laclau and Chantal Mouffe. While the work of Laclau and Mouffe[68] draws upon various philosophical traditions, it represents above all perhaps an endeavour to reformulate Marxism in order to make it relevant to the nature of what is often termed 'late capitalism'. The idea of 'radical democracy' that they seek to advance reflects in part an exhaustion of belief in the notion of the revolutionary moment and the revolutionary subject. It expresses, in other words, the conviction that there simply will not be some 'glorious day' precisely because the heroes of Marxist fable, the working class, are unable to produce such a moment. This scepticism leads Laclau and Mouffe to construct a cultural politics that insists that power and subjectivity are multiple. The vision of 'radical democracy' asserts, in other words, that there are many places where people choose to resist power and there are a great many sources upon which people can draw in order to do so.

It should be acknowledged of course that the advocates of 'radical democracy' have offered invaluable insights into the ostensibly 'new times' of late capitalism. In seeking to underline that modes of both oppression and resistance are multiple and indeed ubiquitous, Laclau and Mouffe have made an important contribution to the aspiration of a renewal of socialist theory. An essential problem, however, with the notion of radical democracy is that in seeking to develop a model of subjectivity that acknowledges class as merely one of a number of sources of selfhood it can easily write class out of the narrative altogether. And this is precisely what Gilbert and Pearson end up doing. That *Discographies* consigns social class more or less to the status of an anachronism is no mere aberration but rather emblematic of a broader sociological current. Over the last generation, many of the most prominent figures within the social sciences have lined up to assert that class no longer really matters and that those who regard it as important are in the throes of some peculiar, antiquarian passion. Nothing of course could be further from the truth. As Beverley Skeggs[69] has noted, one of the greatest ironies of contemporary sociology is that while there is a growing body of theoretical writing that insists that class has little bearing upon today's society, there is at the same time a growing body of empirical evidence that indicates that class is as central as ever to the ways in which ordinary people actually live their lives. The notion of social class remains, therefore, an indispensable tool for understanding the social world and our place within it.

It is for this reason not least perhaps that The Smiths deserve to be remembered with both clarity and conviction. Among the many achievements of the band was the construction of a cultural politics that managed both to acknowledge that subjectivity is multiple and changeful and that social class is absolutely central to it. In the songs of The Smiths, we encounter the indignities and epiphanies, the alienation and community that mark experience in the age of capital. While those sublime tracks may well have been recorded a very long time ago, they also have a timeless quality that gives them a distinctly contemporary edge. When we listen to 'The Headmaster Ritual' or 'Nowhere Fast' or 'This Night Has Opened My Eyes' we are reminded of precisely that which we are meant to forget – that we continue to live in a world in which social class still exerts a profound and often debilitating influence. It is among a great many other things their status as the narrators of this secret history that makes The Smiths so very important and so very dangerous.

In view of the radical cultural politics of The Smiths, it is little wonder that there have been various attempts to airbrush the band out of the picture altogether. Perhaps the most explicit of these came in the cultural moment that heralded both the political ascent and the cultural emptiness of the New Labour project. The choreographed succession that was 'Britpop' was, however, entirely doomed from the outset, principally for two reasons. Firstly, the guitar bands that were supposed to have taken the place of The Smiths in the mid-1990s in the main appeared to have no genuinely critical political agenda. The often reactionary cultural politics of Britpop was reflected most vividly perhaps in the particular versions of working-class masculinity that it sought to package. While the figure of the 'New Lad' would play well for a while with middle-class audiences keen to rub shoulders with a bit of rough under controlled circumstances, this version of what it means to be a working-class man would never quite manage to displace entirely the troubled and troubling figure who forms the lyrical and metaphorical heart of The Smiths.[70] With the passage of time, it would become ever more apparent that the boorish and illiterate simulations of someone like Liam Gallagher are a very pale substitute for the timeless wordplay of a genuine working-class autodidact like Steven Patrick Morrissey.

The second reason that the cultural moment of Britpop never quite managed to erase entirely the memory of The Smiths is simply that none of the bands that sheltered under its umbrella ever managed to scale the same creative heights. There were of course a few genuinely great records that emerged from the era. The classic long-player *Different Class* by Pulp, for instance, would certainly deserve such an accolade. The supposedly golden age of Britpop would ultimately fail, however, to produce a band that was sufficiently gifted or prolific to take the place of The Smiths. Those who lived through the reign of the eighteenth pale descendant of some old queen or other were, needless to say, never going to be even vaguely convinced by the Eighteenth Brumaire of Brett Anderson. Indeed, the debacle of Britpop merely served to jolt us from our reverie and recall what it is that we have been missing since Morrissey and Marr went their separate ways. And what we have been missing of course is the band that killed pop. With their genius.

Notes

Thanks to Sean Campbell, Rob Moore, Marion Kelly and Pieni Mehiläinen for their helpful comments on a previous version of this chapter.

1 S. Goddard, *The Smiths: Songs That Saved Your Life* (London: Reynolds & Hearn, 2004, second edition), p. 160.

2 The documentary would be the context in which Morrissey would express most explicitly his conviction that The Smiths would mark the death of a certain version of pop but it was not the only occasion when he would do so. See, for example, his characteristic hyperbole in the following interview: I. Pye, 'Some Mothers Do 'Ave 'Em', *New Musical Express*, 7 June 1986.

3 J. Harris, *The Last Party: Britpop, Blair and the Demise of English Rock* (London: Fourth Estate, 2003).

4 M. Simpson, 'The Man Who Murdered Pop', *The Guardian*, 5 November 1999. The claim that Morrissey's work with The Smiths signalled the death of pop is developed more fully in Simpson's uneven but often brilliant book *Saint Morrissey* (London: SAF Publishing, 2004). See especially pp. 12–28.

5 The view that the work of The Smiths exhausts some version of popular music also appears in complementary form elsewhere. See, for instance, M. Bracewell, *England is Mine: Pop Life in Albion from Wilde to Goldie* (London: Flamingo, 1997), p. 226; P. Reid, *Morrissey* (Bath: Absolute Press, 2004), p. 83; J. Rogan, *Morrissey and Marr: The Severed Alliance* (London: Omnibus Press, 1992), p. 18.

6 J. Gilbert and E. Pearson, *Discographies: Dance Music, Culture and the Politics of Sound* (London: Routledge, 1999). Chapter 7 is particularly pertinent to the discussion here.

7 Morrissey would of course employ a range of celebrities to signify a cultural world bereft of the integrity summoned in his work. On other occasions, for instance, the fate of those unable to grasp the joys of The Smiths would be a lifetime of 'saying yes to Madonna'. See D. DiMartino, 'We'll Meat Again: Doing It Smiths Style', *Creem*, February 1985.

8 Bernard Matthews was and remains the owner of a major food processing corporation best known for its poultry products. When The Smiths were at their peak, Matthews was probably the most recognisable face of the meat industry in England. Morrissey's revulsion at the Norfolk-based agribusiness was immortalised in the run-out groove of the single 'Sheila Take A Bow' which bears the imperative 'Cook Bernard Matthews'.

9 J. Stringer, 'The Smiths: Repressed (But Remarkably Dressed)', *Popular Music*, Vol. 11, No. 1 (January 1992), pp. 15–26, p. 17.

10 S. Hall and M. Jacques (eds), *The Politics of Thatcherism* (London: Lawrence and Wishart, 1983); S. Hall and M. Jacques (eds), *New Times: The Changing Face of Politics in the 1990s* (London: Lawrence and Wishart, 1989).

11 N. Zuberi, *Sounds English: Transnational Popular Music* (Urbana and Chicago: University of Illinois Press, 2001), p. 40.

12 The phrase 'them was rotten days' is etched on the vinyl of *The Queen Is Dead*. It was borrowed from dialogue in the kitchen-sink movie *Saturday Night, Sunday Morning* (Karel Reisz, 1960).

13 The phrase was coined by the neoliberal intellectual Friedrich von Hayek and adopted by Thatcher in an interview published in, of all places, *Woman's Own*, 31 October 1987.

14 S. Lowe, 'England Made Me', in *Q/Mojo Morrissey and The Smiths Special Edition*, p. 97; K. Swayne, 'If I Ruled the World', *No. 1*, 7 January 1984; N. Zuberi, *Sounds English*, p. 63.

15 See 'The Top 500 Irish & British Surnames', *The Observer*, 15 April 2007.

16 Goddard, *The Smiths*, p. 20.

17 Lowe, 'England Made Me', p. 97.

18 Goddard, *The Smiths*, p. 36.

19 'Morrissey Answers Twenty Questions', *Star Hits*, 1985.

20 One of the most beguiling traits of Morrissey's songwriting is that the identity of the narrator and narrated are often not disclosed. The sexual preference of the narrative cannot, therefore, be presumed in this case.

21 J. Pernice, *Meat is Murder* (New York: Continuum, 2003), p. 23.

22 The significance of the song to the band themselves is reflected perhaps in the fact that it was one of the compositions chosen for the collaboration with 1960s icon Sandie Shaw.

23 In the 2007 Michel Gondry movie *The Science of Sleep*, for example, there is a scene where the lead male character retires to his bedroom. The walls are covered with a clutter of pop cultural imagery. On the edge of the frame is the sleeve of the single 'How Soon Is Now?' The image of actor Sean Barrett on the cover simply demands the attention of the viewer and for a few seconds it is impossible to look at anything else.

24 Zuberi, *Sounds English*, pp. 20, 37–8.

25 Simpson, *Saint Morrissey*, p. 50; Zuberi, *Sounds English*, pp. 41–2.

26 M. Aston, 'Tease, Torment, Tantalise', *Q/Mojo Morrissey and The Smiths Special Edition*, p. 40.

27 B. Kopf, 'A Suitable Case for Treatment', *New Musical Express*, 22/29 December 1984.

28 Goddard, *The Smiths*, p. 135.

29 I. Pye, 'A Hard Day's Misery', *Melody Maker*, 3 November 1984; W. Shaw, 'Glad All Over', *Zig Zag*, February 1984.

30 A. Collins, 'The Flesh is Willing', *Q/Mojo Morrissey and The Smiths Special Edition*, 2004, p. 35; S. Reynolds, *Blissed Out: The Raptures of Rock* (London: Serpent's Tail, 1990), p. 21.

31 D. Bret, *Morrissey: Scandal & Passion* (London: Robson Books, 2004), p. 8.

32 P. Gatenby, *Morrissey's Manchester: The Essential Smiths Tour* (Manchester: Empire Publications, 2002); P. Gatenby, *Panic on the Streets: The Smiths and Morrissey Location Guide* (London: Reynolds & Hearn, 2007).

33 Reid, *Morrissey*, p. 69.

34 Rogan, *The Severed Alliance*, p. 62. N. Kent, *The Dark Stuff: Selected Writings on Rock Music* (London: Faber & Faber, 2007), p. 221.

35 Goddard, *The Smiths*, p. 77; E.Van Poznack, 'Morrissey: The Face Interview', *The Face*, July 1984.

36 J. Henke, 'Oscar! Oscar! Great Britain Goes Wilde for the "Fourth-Gender" Smiths', *Rolling Stone*, 7 June 1984.

37 Mark Simpson goes so far to suggest of Morrissey that 'the hooligan is his masculine muse'. See *Saint Morrissey*, p. 131. See also Reynolds, *Blissed Out*, p. 18.

38 N. Kent, 'Dreamer in the Real World', *The Face*, May 1985; Zuberi, *Sounds English*, pp. 52, 60.

39 The words are of course from the song 'Rusholme Ruffians', which is set amid the melodrama and carnage of a funfair. See Goddard, *The Smiths*, p. 127. See also Morrissey's comments on the efficacy of violence in a group interview with several fanzine editors, 'Trial by Jury', *Melody Maker*, 16 March 1985.

40 R. Sennett and J. Cobb, *The Hidden Injuries of Class* (New York: W.W. Norton, 1972). A more expressly feminist text that covers similar ground is C. Steedman, *Landscape for a Good Woman* (London: Virago Press, 1986).

41 See, for example, R. Sennett, *The Corrosion of Character: Personal Consequences of Work in the New Capitalism* (New York: W.W. Norton, 1999); R. Sennett, *Respect: The Formation of Character in a World of Inequality* (London: Allen Lane, 2003).

42 Sennett and Cobb, *The Hidden Injuries of Class*, pp. 147, 74.

43 S. Garfield, 'This Charming Man', in H. Kureishi and J. Savage (eds), *The Faber Book of Pop* (London: Faber and Faber, 1995), p. 595.

44 'Morrissey Answers Twenty Questions', *Star Hits*, 1985.

45 J. Berens, 'Spirit in the Dark', *Spin*, September 1986. Available at http://www.foreverill.com/interviews/1986/spirit.htm (accessed 4 March 2010).

46 Garfield, 'This Charming Man', p. 600.

47 McCormick, 'All Men Have Secrets', *Hot Press*, 4 May 1984.

48 Rogan, *The Severed Alliance*, p. 79; Simpson, *Saint Morrissey*, pp. 37–8.

49 McCormick, 'All Men Have Secrets'.

50 Pye, 'A Hard Day's Misery'; Kent, *The Dark Stuff*, p. 222.

51 Morrissey explained the personal context of the track to the late Tony Wilson on the television programme *Granada Reports*. The clip is available at www.youtube.com/watch?v=sCuqKzW6r7M (accessed 8 February 2010).

52 See, for instance, C.P. Lee, *Shake, Rattle and Rain: Popular Music Making in Manchester 1955 – 1995* (Ottery St Mary: Herdinge Simpole, 2002), especially chapter 9. See also *Q Classic: Morrissey & the Story of Manchester*, 2006.

53 Zuberi, *Sounds English*, pp. 35–6, 50–1.

54 In his profile of Morrissey, the journalist James Henke noted that the singer 'speaks with a very upper-crust accent'. See 'Oscar! Oscar!'. See also Stringer, 'The Smiths', p. 17.

55 Lowe, 'England Made Me', p. 97.

56 Goddard, *The Smiths*, p. 165.

57 J. Slee, *Peepholism: Into the Art of Morrissey* (London: Sidgwick and Jackson, 1994), pp. 24–5; Aston, 'Tease, Torment, Tantalise', p. 41.

58 For a fuller account of the influence of kitchen-sink movies on The Smiths, see Cecilia Mello's chapter in this volume.

59 Goddard, *The Smiths*, p. 212.

60 J. Savage, 'The Escape Artist: Morrissey's Manchester: Where He's Coming From', *The Village Voice* (Summer 1989), pp. 8–10, p. 8.

61 Reynolds, *Blissed Out*, p. 29.

62 Kent, 'Dreamer in the Real World'. See also Kent, *The Dark Stuff*, p. 219; Garfield, 'This Charming Man', p. 599.

63 Simpson, *Saint Morrissey*, pp. 161–2.

64 B. Boyd, 'Paddy English Man', *The Irish Times*, 20 November 1999.

65 Simpson, *Saint Morrissey*, p. 143.

66 See Sean Campbell's chapter in this collection for his account of the song.

67 Simpson, *Saint Morrissey*, p. 180.

68 E. Laclau and C. Mouffe, *Hegemony and Socialist Strategy: Towards a Radical Democratic Politics* (London: Verso, Second Edition, 2001).

69 B. Skeggs, *Class, Self, Culture* (London: Routledge, 2004).

70 Simpson, *Saint Morrissey*, pp. 158–9, 171.

10

LAST NIGHT WE DREAMT THAT SOMEBODY LOVED US: SMITHS FANS (AND ME) IN THE LATE 1980S

Karl Maton

Introduction

In the late 1980s a white, working-class boy from the south of England became the first from his family to enter higher education. By 1989 he had survived two attempts by the authorities of Cambridge University to move him on to other places of study, but was still struggling to fit into its rarefied atmosphere. His undergraduate supervisor was Graham McCann, who would later become, after being pushed out of the university for focusing on such 'unscholarly' topics as Marilyn Monroe and Woody Allen, a widely acclaimed writer on popular culture.[1] McCann suggested the student replace an examination in his final year of study with a research dissertation and asked, 'What are you interested in? What do you know about?'. 'Er . . . Manchester United, The Smiths . . . that kind of thing', the student replied. 'Why not do something on The Smiths, then? That would certainly be original.' In this chapter I discuss what happened when I did. In particular, I focus on the meanings The Smiths had for their fans. I discuss how fans often expressed intimate relationships with Morrissey but also intense feelings of loneliness and isolation, even from fellow Smiths fans – a highly individualistic form of subcultural membership. I also explore the experience of researching such an intense community when one is a member.

In *Apocalypse Now* (Coppola, USA, 1979), Martin Sheen's character 'Willard' narrates:

> It was no accident that I got to be the caretaker of Colonel Walter E. Kurtz's memory. . . . There is no way to tell his story without telling my own. And if his story is really a confession, then so is mine.

This study of Smiths fans was conducted in 1989–90, when I was nineteen, clumsy and shy – and a Smiths fan myself. It is research I never fully wrote up and did not return to for sixteen years. Why I put it aside for so long forms part of my focus, for there is no way of telling the fans' story without telling my own, and if theirs was often confessional, then so is mine.[2]

Well I wonder

The context to the study was both intellectual and personal. Intellectually, at the time of the research, published studies of fans of popular music were far from numerous. Sociological research had showed that the musical preferences of young people play a greater role in forming their sense of self and place in society than other areas of mass culture, such as their favourite film genre.[3] As Morrissey stated at the time, 'popular music is the last refuge of young people in the world. It's the only remaining art form. There's nothing else that touches them.'[4] However, in the late 1980s the affective significance of music in the lives of young people remained underexplored.[5] Studies of the political economy of the media revealed the factors shaping cultural production and semiotic analyses explored the meanings of cultural texts, but how popular culture was received was less well known.

The two principal traditions of work closest to doing so were studies of audiences and youth subcultures.[6] Briefly, until the late 1970s audience studies had often been influenced by a one-way conveyor belt model whereby meanings were viewed as unproblematically conveyed from the intentions of cultural producers into cultural products and thence on to their audiences. Studies typically neglected the ways consumers integrated culture into their everyday lives, except in terms of its uses to gratify such needs as entertainment or interaction. During the 1980s a series of qualitative studies influenced by the work of Stuart Hall had begun to explore audience reception, but these remained confined to television audiences.[7] A second tradition of work comprised studies of youth subcultures, most famously those associated with the Birmingham Centre for Contemporary Cultural Studies.[8] These were revealing more about the role played by music in the lives of young people. Above all, they highlighted the active construction of meanings, how young people are not simply passive sponges of media messages but rather actively integrate cultural products into their everyday lives, often altering and subverting their intended meanings. However, considerations of the role of music in the lives of youth were secondary in this work to a focus on whether the youth subculture in question was conformist or rebellious in relation to dominant middle-class culture. More generally, sociological studies of culture typically focused on how cultural activities reflected such identity positions as class, gender or ethnicity, rather than how those activities helped shape identities and the ways they are perceived. Thus, what a specific band or cult figure might mean for their fans and the role they played in fans' lives and identities were areas yet to be fully explored.

Why focus on The Smiths? Though 'mass figures' – cultural producers with large-scale commercial success – had already received critical discussion, cult figures with a smaller but more intense and obsessive following had attracted less attention. The Smiths were relatively successful commercially, at least in terms of chart placings. Leaving aside compilations, their albums *The Smiths, Meat Is Murder, The Queen Is Dead* and *Strangeways, Here We Come* all entered the British charts at number 1 or 2. However, they were anything but 'mass figures'. They released their records on the independent label Rough Trade (though signing a contract for EMI in 1986) and refused to make promotional videos, until 1986 when they agreed to three videos by the controversial director Derek Jarman.[9] Moreover, initially high chart placings reflected less a mass following than the passion of fans eager to possess their latest release. The Smiths were not a mass phenomenon but neither were they simply a minor fad – they were a 'cult' band in terms of the intensity of their influence on both the subsequent music scene and their fans but one that also managed to reach a mainstream audience. In particular, what made The Smiths and especially Morrissey different is that they articulated an alternative mode of thought and behaviour in relation to many of the concerns and issues faced by the young, one not obviously 'alternative' in the way that that label has itself become an institutionalised badge of teenage rebellion. Much of this ran against not only the fads and fashions of the prevailing music scene but also societal norms in general: celibacy, androgyny, a feminised masculinity, anti-commercialism, vegetarianism, dismissal of the standard pop-star lifestyle of 'sex, drugs and rock'n'roll', republicanism, valorisation of Englishness, and a penchant for such unfashionable accessories as National Health Service glasses and hearing aids.[10] (It is easy to forget from the perspective of the present that practices now widely accepted, such as vegetarianism, were anything but during the 1980s.) In particular, Morrissey's lyrics offered a distinctive voice. One of his own idols, Sandie Shaw, claimed: 'Nobody's ever written songs like that before . . . He's changed the pop idiom into something that is a social comment, a piece of literature. He's made it OK to actually be a lyricist.'[11]

The Smiths and particularly Morrissey were, then, exemplary illustrations of cult figures. The research was itself also timely. It was only two years since the band had split up. Morrissey was still struggling to develop a distinctive solo image, with a succession of musical collaborators having been quickly dispensed with and plans for a follow up to his successful debut album *Viva Hate* laying temporarily abandoned. The Smiths maintained a strong posthumous presence in the musical consciousness, aided by the release of the live album *Rank* and the UK release of the US compilation *Louder Than Bombs* in late 1988. For example, an advertisement for Pioneer Multiplay CD in Q magazine (December 1989) lists Smiths song titles, interspersed by enticements to 'slump back and savour any dirge from any disk in any order'. It was thus a golden opportunity to capture a sense of what The Smiths had meant to fans for whom the band had been a living presence.

There were also personal reasons for choosing to research The Smiths. Since my early teens, I had been deeply affected by the songs of The Smiths. They seemed to speak directly to my situation of alienation and despair, giving voice to my own sense of hope and disappointment, and isolation from my peers. Morrissey's views influenced my decision to become vegetarian and gave voice to my republicanism and anti-Thatcherism. I wanted to know: was it really so strange? Why should such a little thing as a pop band make such a big difference?

Studying The Smiths

The project was for a brief undergraduate dissertation to be completed within a few months alongside my study of other taught courses. However, the scale of the research I threw myself into was a case of serious overkill. The methodology for the study comprised, first, textual and semiotic analyses of the band's imagery and style, lyrics, album covers, photographs and liner notes. I spent many weeks in the British Library, the National Sound Archive, the British Newspaper library, and the archives of *Melody Maker* and *Record Mirror*, reading every available interview with or article on The Smiths, a corpus which grew exponentially as contacts with other fans revealed ever-more obscure sources. Secondly, I attempted to interview everyone connected to The Smiths: the band; managers; musical collaborators such as Sandie Shaw; journalists from music papers such as *Q*, *New Musical Express* (*NME*), *Melody Maker, Record Mirror* and *The Face*; authors of books on The Smiths; those who helped 'break' the band, such as John Walters, producer of the John Peel Show on BBC Radio One; and contemporary performers on the 'indie' music scene, such as Dave Gedge of The Wedding Present. My sometimes naive attempts to gain access to and then interview people of whom I was a fan met with mixed results and is a story unto itself. Thirdly, I embarked on an ethnographic study of (or, to be honest, a pilgrimage to) all the places in Manchester mentioned in The Smiths' lyrics and which I knew were formative in the biographies of the band. Finally, I engaged with fans of the band through written correspondence and a series of interviews. Here, I shall discuss the last of these: studying the fans.

My contact with fans began after I placed a notice in the 'small ads' sections of the *NME* and *Idols* magazine in late 1989. This advertisement said very briefly that I was seeking fans' opinions about The Smiths for a research project. Within weeks I received over fifty replies from the UK, across Europe, Scandinavia, the USA, Australia and Asia. Some letters were short, simply asking what I wanted to know. Many were long, probably the first essay-length analyses of Smiths fan culture, detailing how they had discovered the band, their thoughts and feelings, and how the band affected their lives. They often included poetry, drawings, photographs, fans' own lyrics, and such obscure facts as a list of the words etched on the run-off grooves of The Smiths' vinyl releases. I also received copies of a host of fanzines, including *Smiths Indeed* and *Colossus* (both from England), *Coversmiths* and *Stay Handsome* (both from Belgium), *Smiths' Ways* (Spain), *Hand In Glove* (Switzerland), *Fragile et Mystique* (France) and *Forever Ill?* (USA).

Fans who answered the advertisement were sent a series of questions about the basis of the appeal of The Smiths, the 'average' Smiths fan, the influence of the band on the fan's views, whether their feelings had changed over time, and how The Smiths compared to other contemporary musicians. In addition, correspondents from overseas were asked about the success of the group, press exposure, general perception of the band, and issues of access to Smiths records in their respective countries. These questions were typically personalised, depending on what each fan had written in their first letter. For those who had already addressed these questions, I further explored issues such as the role that The Smiths played in their lives, what the group meant to them, and their relationships with other fans. In this way, an ongoing correspondence was begun, often extending over several months via a series of letters. Finally, I also personally interviewed several 'hardcore' fans about their obsession.

The responses to my questions were overwhelming. I was suddenly engaged in often lengthy correspondence with over fifty highly articulate young people. It was as if they had been waiting for an opportunity to express their feelings about The Smiths, as if their desire to share their experiences had hitherto been repressed. In academic terms, the correspondence generated a considerable amount of rich qualitative data. Fans often wrote the equivalent of essays in reply to each question I asked, then without further prompting would quickly write again with supplementary answers to those questions or with answers to their own questions. As one fan put it, 'I couldn't possibly write every single feeling I have for him [Morrissey] onto a piece of foolscap' (David).[12] Some fans enclosed stamped addressed envelopes to encourage me to reply sooner. I was also sent questionnaires to answer myself; as I discuss further below, I was often viewed not as a student researcher but as a fellow and perhaps privileged fan. It is worth highlighting that this correspondence occurred before access to word processors or personal computers had become widespread. Fans' responses were not hastily written emails, blogs or entries on a web-based discussion group; they often took time and great care to hand-write or manually type many pages of considered thoughts and ideas, for which I retain a strong sense of gratitude and respect. Of all the areas this wide-ranging correspondence covered I shall focus here on two principal issues: how fans viewed themselves in relation, first, to The Smiths and, secondly, to other people. In writing about such issues, there is always a danger of appearing a critical outsider, sneering at the deluded beliefs of weaker minds. As I hope will become clear, that is far from my intention, for what follows applies as much to me as to any of the fans who were kind enough to write to me.

He knows I'd love to see him

In terms of fans' relations to The Smiths, it was, perhaps naturally, Morrissey who formed the primary if not nearly exclusive focus of fans' attention. Through my reading of academic studies of youth subcultures and audiences, I had been primed to expect fans to form a social community. In contrast, what Smiths fans focused on was an intimate and one-on-one relationship with Morrissey. In an interview, the singer had claimed that 'lyrically I speak for everybody, or at least I try to'.[13] According to these fans he also spoke *to* everybody, and to everybody *individually*. For example, one fan wrote:

> I knew what he was saying, and he was saying it to me. It's like having an invisible friend . . . you know he's there, but you can't see him. (Seán).

Typically, fans described not simply identification with or respect for Morrissey but also a strong sense of personal communication – 'It's as though Morrissey speaks to me through his lyrics' (Jacky) – and of understanding. As Sheila put it, in a sentiment often expressed:

> It was so comforting to know that I wasn't the only shy awkward person in the world. I felt Morrissey really understood me.

This apparently personal communication led to a form of empathic bonding between fans and 'their' Morrissey. They often wrote of 'relating' to or 'identifying' with Morrissey's lyrics, especially those describing dejection, loneliness, insecurity and low self-confidence: 'Nearly every song of his says something about me' (Maria). To his audience, it appeared that Morrissey understood them and knew how they felt – he is, they proclaimed, 'one of us' (Maria), 'a kindred spirit' (Peter), someone who 'has similar problems to me' (Claire). This sense of identification was encouraged by repeated references in Morrissey's interviews to his own background as a fan of pop groups: he was 'a pop fan who became a pop star' (Kathy). Indeed, fans often highlighted how events and feelings described by Morrissey were similar to their own: 'there has been an uncanny similarity between incidents and situations in songs, and my own life' (David). Sometimes this led to claims that he was not singing of similar events to their own experiences but must somehow know them personally. One fan, for example, concluded that 'I think Morrissey must have lived near me in Hastings for a while' (name illegible).

Morrissey was held to know each fan and in turn each fan felt they knew Morrissey. They often felt connected to his personal life and claimed to know his innermost feelings, thoughts and ideas. This was underpinned by a belief that Morrissey's lyrics and interview quotes were reliably autobiographical – knowledge of The Smiths' songs could thereby enable fans to know him personally:

> Morrissey is a close personal friend ... I've probably heard / read more of Morrissey's views / ideas and know more about him than most people do about even their closest friend. (David)

Unsurprisingly, relationships with Morrissey were thus described in intense, intimate and often heartfelt terms:

> He is the brother I never had, the father figure I always longed for and the friend I always wanted. I love him. (David)

Such feelings were not unknown to Morrissey himself. Though encouraging fans to regard him reverentially by repeatedly referring to his 'apostles' or 'disciples', Morrissey complained in 1984 that '[m]any of them see me as some kind of religious character who can solve all their problems with a wave of a syllable'.[14]

I want the one I can't have

Fans' feelings of intense intimacy were, however, cross-cut by a sense of Morrissey's aloofness. Despite being 'a close personal friend' who knew each individual fan, he remained somehow always a little distant and unknowable – there was always more to discover, something was being held back: 'His personality is a secret which he has managed to keep private' (Paul). Morrissey was thereby often viewed as what Richard Schickel describes as an 'intimate stranger'.[15] The theme of 'knowing but not knowing' or intimacy and strangeness was often repeated across fans' responses:

> Morrissey is an open book ... we got to learn more and more about him. And yet, throughout all this peeling off of layers, it seems as though we know nothing about him at all. (Seán)

For such fans, Morrissey appears to have perfected the art of transparent mystery, a quality Walter Benjamin defined as the essence of the cult image:

> True to its nature, it remains 'distant, however close it may be'. The closeness which one may gain from its subject matter does not impair the distance which it retains in its appearance.[16]

Although interviews with Morrissey had appeared with remarkable frequency in the music press throughout the 1980s, there remained somehow a sense that little was still known about him. As the music journalist Mat Snow put it, 'he told them a lot but suggested a great deal which he wasn't telling'.[17] Partly this reflected Morrissey's talent for reinventing, revising or obscuring his past. Authors such as Nick Kent complained of constant interference in their research from a panic-stricken Morrissey.[18] Similarly, a typical initial response from his colleagues and associates to my own enquiries was that offered by Sandie Shaw at the start of our interview about Morrissey: 'I know nothing about the man that I want to discuss'.[19] It also partly reflected the way Morrissey embodied contradictions and confusions; as one fan perceptively highlighted, he was 'supposedly depressive yet dancing wildly on stage, lonely yet surrounded by ardent admirers, miserable yet witty' (Kathy).

Though often claiming to have the most extensive and intimate knowledge possible, fans were left wanting more, proclaiming:

> I found him fascinating, but I couldn't quite make him out, despite reading anything about him I could get my hands on! (Sheila)

Though Walter Benjamin famously argued that 'the age of mechanical reproduction' had removed the aura of authenticity associated with cultural *products*, I would argue that such an aura remains or has been transferred to cultural *producers*. This fuels a hunger for more knowledge of the 'real' person behind the public persona. In the fans' correspondence, they often declared such sentiments as 'I often wonder what a day in Morrissey's life is like' (Jacky) and asked me questions about all areas of his everyday life, including whether he ate cereal for breakfast or preferred showers to baths. This phenomenon may also be the case for 'mass', and not just cult, figures. The hunger for insight into the private lives of public figures, even those associated with banal and mediocre cultural achievements (as evinced by the contemporary media obsession with so-called 'celebrities') would appear to suggest so. What perhaps distinguishes the cult figure from the mass figure, though, is the source of this interest: the fans themselves, rather than the media. Moreover, for fans of The Smiths this combination of intense connection and distance was in sharp contrast to how they viewed other contemporary musicians. One of the questions I asked was about their perceptions of Dave Gedge, lead singer of The Wedding Present, often portrayed by the contemporary music press as Smiths fans' second favourite band and whose songs painted a similar landscape of suburban life and adolescent love lost. Though often also fans of The Wedding Present, their responses made clear that they admired the group rather than seeing them as intimate companions. The fans' opinions of other, more commercially successful, bands were much less generous.

Fans thereby expressed admiration of others, but *possession* of Morrissey. As popular music helps one to assert or adopt an identity, it becomes an integral part of that identity. It is not so much the records that fans feel they own as it is the performers themselves. Morrissey was 'their' Morrissey. To not know something about him was, in a sense, to not know something of themselves. In similar fashion to how the culture industry 'perpetually cheats its consumers of what it perpetually promises', a situation in which 'the diner must be satisfied with the menu', Morrissey's talent for pregnant suggestion, beguiling transparency and clothed nakedness in his lyrics and interviews left fans wanting more.[20] His passionate articulation of alternative views bolstered this sense of possession through the influence he had on fans' views. Many stated that Morrissey had changed their outlooks or brought out hitherto hidden aspects of their personalities, inducing them to adopt anti-royalist stances and to at least consider vegetarianism. Such changes were described by fans in quite dramatic terms:

> He completely changed me within weeks. In the past year I have gone from being quite normal to an indie-freak, dyeing my hair and in general doing anything to be different. (Claire)

Such attribution and internalisation encourages feelings of possession, and possession encourages personalisation. Mick Middles, for example, explained that after his book on The Smiths was published he received at least twenty letters containing personal threats.[21] His criticisms of The Smiths were viewed by some fans as deriding their own values and outlook on life and not simply their favourite pop group. Commitment to a pop star is one of the earliest commitments one might make; in the case of cult figures, the experience is particularly intense. One is what one identifies with.

I won't share you

In contrast to their expressed feelings of personal intimacy with Morrissey, fans' descriptions of relations with other people, even other Smiths fans, were often couched in terms of loneliness and isolation. Repeatedly, fans wrote of their sense of disconnection from family and peers. Often this sense of difference fixed on their love of The Smiths – the band represented a shibboleth distinguishing those who understood from those who could not, and thus affected relations with others:

> When I first 'got into' Morrissey I was going out with this lad but I dumped him because he was very different to Moz and myself. (Maria)

If Maria is similar to other fans, it would not have been enough for 'this lad' to profess that he liked Morrissey, for 'Morrissey is someone you either love or hate. You can't just like him' (Joanne). Moreover, as Maria suggests, loving Morrissey was also, for many, to be *like* him.

In similar fashion to the paradox of intimate strangeness, being a fan of The Smiths provided a source of collective identity but of a highly individualist kind. The strong (if shifting and constantly negotiated) external boundary to be found around any distinctive youth subculture was here echoed *within* the subculture – the line was drawn around the individual rather than the group. What often attracted fans to The Smiths was their ability to capture a sense of difference and alienation. So the basis of shared attitudes and attributes among fans was paradoxically that each felt alone in the world. As one fan observed, 'there's a lot of lonely people in this country – bedroom recluses – He is one of us' (Maria). However, as this quotation suggests, Smiths fans were not simply isolated. Those I corresponded with and interviewed quite often (though not always) revealed a healthy social life. Like many other similar groups with shared interests, they also formed a loose network of associations through fanzines, meetings and other gatherings. In 1989, for example, over one thousand people attended The Smiths Convention, a series of events and tours around 'Morrissey's Manchester'. Each fan may have felt lonely but they were not always alone. Moreover, there was an expressed bond among fans:

> There is a kind of love and comradeship that I feel whenever I see someone who is wearing a Smiths T-shirt . . . you feel safe as if you know them. You know that they are probably very shy and vulnerable like yourself. (Claire)

Indeed, many wrote that fellow fans were very friendly, easy to talk to and sociable. However, for all this professed camaraderie, fans still maintained their unique sense of displacement; for example:

> I know there are many other wandering souls scattered about the place who feel this as well, but I feel different. (Seán).

Similarly, in response to questions about what characterised an 'average Smiths fan', fans typically claimed 'I don't think it's fair to say there's an "average Smiths fan"' but would then go on to offer such characterisations as 'a male . . . probably in his mid–late teens, who's a bit shy and unaware of himself, not very successful with girls and probably quite lonely . . . fairly intellectual' (Sheila).

Fans' feelings of identification with Morrissey were, therefore, not always reflected in feelings of identification with other fans, something regularly reflected in their letters by a strong distinction between 'real' fans, such as themselves, and those who were mere 'clones'. Fans were thereby able to enjoy the sense of solidarity given by the common interest of fan clubs, fanzines and so forth while presenting themselves as individuals and different. They shared what studies of youth subcultures refer to as 'maps of meaning' but often each felt alone within this community. Reading fans' letters was like hearing a chorus of voices singing a similar tune but each feeling they sang their own song solo – a shared singularity underpinned by feelings that they alone 'identified with' Morrissey. What Pierre Bourdieu describes as the cultural struggle for social distinction was thus underpinned by a particularly individual and personalised sense of belonging.[22] To adapt an expression of Karl Marx, Smiths fans described a subculture-in-itself but not a subculture-for-itself. Lest all this sound a deliberate strategy of self-promotion by fans wishing to attain distinction, I should emphasise that this sense of difference was not simply celebrated but was also the cause of pain, frustration, depression and resentment. As the intensity of the correspondence highlights, and as many fans made clear in their letters, loneliness was the last thing they wanted. For many followers of The Smiths at this time, then, being a fan was to be deeply involved in an isolating experience – making it a highly charged and personal affair.

I started something I couldn't finish

I have focused on only two issues arising from my correspondence with fans, itself but one aspect of the research as a whole. However, this focus is useful for understanding a further issue: the experience of conducting this kind of research on this kind of subculture, especially when you are one of its members. For the written results of all my research only touched on the issues I have explored here. Though I spent a considerable length of time analysing the rich data I gathered, relatively little of this work appeared in the undergraduate dissertation I submitted to the university.[23] Instead, it focused more on the images presented by The Smiths. The voices of fans had been if not silenced then forced into the background. Furthermore, I did not return to the data for another sixteen years, when finally prompted by the 2005 conference on The Smiths. This repression of the voice of the fans resulted from a combination of academic politics and the intensity of my own experiences in conducting the research.

In the late 1980s, writing about the experiences, feelings and thoughts of fans of an 'indie pop' band was not readily acceptable in academic circles. As a lecturer at my university made plain to me, 'Writing about lonely listeners is not academic work'. Cultural studies may have flowered but, in mainstream sociology, research into popular culture was often not considered a scholarly endeavour. As my supervisor, Graham McCann, put it, '[t]hey approach it as if they were talking about child sex abuse or various forms of sodomy in public schools'.[24] At the University of Cambridge, a course in the sociology of culture and media is now well established. At the time of my research, however, finding a course under which the dissertation could be submitted was problematic. Eventually, it was allotted to one entitled 'Deviance'. That the fans were then backgrounded in the finished product was not, however, simply the result of institutional conspiracy; it was easier to submit a dissertation centred on textual analysis, but this is not a simple case of suppression by the powers-that-be. More importantly, I found it extremely difficult to write about the feelings, thoughts and experiences of fans of The Smiths.

Today students conducting research projects attend lectures in research methods, learn about ethics and must submit detailed forms to committees overseeing their work. Research such as that I conducted would have to be approved by an ethics committee before it could even begin. When I was researching, however, I knew little of the personal impact of different research methods and even less of ethics. However, perhaps nothing could have prepared me for the kinds of intense responses I received and especially for how they triggered and echoed feelings of my own. I should emphasise that I do not want to underplay the sense of joy, the wonderful wordplay, use of irony and sheer fun expressed in many of the letters I received. Moreover, many showed a level of perceptive insight that scholars of cultural studies would have envied; for example:

> Morrissey is the antithesis of macho . . . This, I believe, has great appeal to females, who are directly victimized by rock and pop images, and to males, who are victimized by the pressure to live up to that kind of roughness and omnipotence. (Mariana)

Against the common conception at the time of the average Smiths fan as miserable and melancholic, it was not all doom and gloom. The Smiths and Morrissey clearly brought sweetness and light into the lives of many of their fans:

> He [Morrissey] demonstrates how somebody who is supposedly a bumbling introvert can adopt a defiantly confident, dogmatic figure on stage . . . and as such is an inspiring, 'life-affirming' person. (Francis)

The Smiths were also a source of considerable comfort. Morrissey was perceived as 'a spokesperson for anybody who felt insecure, lonely, dejected and lacking in self-confidence' (Paul) and to feel that you are not alone, that you are not the only one who feels this way, is a positive experience that should not be underestimated.

While describing a source of comfort, Paul's quotation highlights the kind of experience that was being comforted. Abuse from a violent father, thoughts of suicide, loneliness, isolation from peers, bookishness considered aberrant within a working-class environment, alienation from middle-class educational institutions, a deeply felt failure to fit the profile of the average teenager, all these and more I knew only too well. The letters I received touched often on such issues, things I had barely begun to come to terms with myself. I read heartbreaking accounts of unrequited love, suicide attempts and self-harm, often prefaced with the words 'I've never told anyone this before but . . .'. Sometimes fans believed that because I was doing this research at Cambridge University I must somehow be important, officially sanctioned and know Morrissey personally, so they felt they could write to me as if writing to him directly. I became a perceived conduit or at least surrogate for writing to Morrissey. Alongside requests for jobs at *NME* and personal introductions to Morrissey, came confessional, intensely personal accounts of lives often very much like mine. In short, the identity relations whereby fans felt intensely and intimately involved with Morrissey within a wider context of isolation from other people was reflected in an often intimate language describing deeply personal issues.

It was far more than I could handle at the time. I was nineteen years old. I was meant to be conducting a brief piece of research, an undergraduate dissertation to be completed alongside my study of five other courses. I had embarked on a project far bigger than was necessary. For someone also going through the emotional turmoil of experiencing relationships for the first time, trying to make the most of having left home, studying in an institution in which it was made clear I did not fit, the letters became overwhelming. Faced with my final exams in June, I let the correspondence fall away, something for which I still feel regret and sorrow. Insightful, articulate, too close to home and too near the bone, the fans gave me something that I won't forget too soon. Indeed, the box of their letters has remained with me, wherever I have gone. It has found a home in Cambridge, seven addresses in North London, Cambridge again, Leicester, Stoke-on-Trent, Wollongong in Australia, and now Sydney. Though my intellectual interests changed, I could not bear to leave the box behind, though until the conference I could not bear to open it. The box became something akin to that of Pandora – I feared what I would find of myself within. Had I changed at all? Nicholas Currie (the pop singer/songwriter 'Momus') told me in an interview that the secret of Morrissey's commercial success was to capture the sense of what it is like to be adolescent, and to have maintained it. One reason I did not return to the research for so long is that, though I'm older now (and a clever swine), I too remain in many ways the same as I was back then.

The story goes on

In conclusion, I have described how fans of The Smiths at the end of the 1980s often expressed perceptions of Morrissey as an 'invisible friend' who spoke to each fan individually but also as an intimate stranger one could never fully know, alongside feelings of a sense of isolation from other people, even fellow fans. This combination of seemingly paradoxical feelings, I argued, engendered a particularly individualist form of subcultural membership and a sense of personal possession. In short, being a Smiths fan was an intense experience. I also described the unexpected consequences of researching one's own kind, particularly in the face of such intensity.

Like all real-life stories, this one never ends. At the 2005 Smiths conference, another delegate glanced at my name badge and proceeded to introduce himself. He was Peter, one of the fans who had written to me sixteen years before. Over lunch he recounted how his life had changed since writing the letters I still possess . . . marriage, a career, children. Peter floated the idea of attempting to contact other fans who had written to me, or at least who had been fans of The Smiths back then. Whatever happened to these boys and girls least likely to? Do the feelings of isolation from peers and friendship with an intimate stranger continue or are they a teenage phase that people grow out of? Do those fans still dream that somebody loves them or did they come to replace such dreams with real friends, families and colleagues? In describing how their feelings had changed over the years, the fans I corresponded with had already hinted at such developments:

> My feelings for Morrissey began to change after I started University. For the first time, I had good, close friends. (Sheila)

Are the most impassioned songs to lonely souls so easily outgrown? How does fandom evolve over the life course? These are not simply personal issues but significant sociological questions.[25] They ask whether cult figures in popular music serve as a pressure valve for teenage discontent prior to adult assimilation, whether alienation is replaced by integration or finds different forms of expression, and whether popular music retains its power for identity formation throughout life or becomes more of a lifestyle consumer choice. Such questions remain of considerable significance for us all and reach from the structure of society to the innermost sense of ourselves. They retain their urgency even today. For now, I shall leave the last word to a fan:

> All our lives people will wonder about existence and the need for the warmth generated from another human being . . . Some people feel so shy and awkward that they think they could not communicate with another human being and that others could not possibly feel the same insecurity. Yet, I believe that there are thousands of people that share that same cold, hard core of loneliness . . . Yours, with avid sentimentality, Julie.

Notes

1 G. McCann, *Marilyn Monroe: The Body in the Library* (Cambridge: Polity Press, 1988); G. McCann, *Woody Allen: New Yorker* (Cambridge: Polity Press, 1990).

2 I wish to thank The Smiths fans involved in the study, those figures in the pop music industry who kindly agreed to be interviewed, Alexandra Lamont for help and support, and Graham McCann for teaching how a real rebel flies under the radar.

3 See, for example, D. Hebdige, *Subculture: The Meaning of Style* (London: Methuen, 1979); S. Frith, *Sound Effects: Youth, Leisure and the Politics of Rock'n'roll* (New York: Pantheon, 1981); S. Frith, *Music For Pleasure: Essays on the Sociology of Pop* (Cambridge: Polity Press, 1988).

4 M. Middles, *The Smiths: The Complete Story* (London: Omnibus Press, 1988), p. 31.

5 Here I am reconstituting the historical moment of my research in the late 1980s. At this time there were relatively few studies of pop music fans, a notable exception being F. Vermorel and J. Vermorel, *Starlust: Secret Life of Fans* (London: Comet, 1985). Studies of fans have subsequently grown in number. See, for example: L.A. Lewis (ed.), *The Adoring Audience: Fan Culture and Popular Media* (London: Routledge, 1992); H. Kruse, 'Subcultural Identity in Alternative Music culture', *Popular Music*, Vol. 12, No. 1 (1993), pp. 33–41; A. Raviv, D. Bar-Tal, A. Raviv and A. Ben-Horin, 'Adolescent Idolization of Pop Singers: Causes, Expressions, and Reliance', *Journal of Youth and Adolescence*, Vol. 25, No. 5 (1996), pp. 631–50; W. Brooker and D. Jermyn (eds), *The Audience Studies Reader* (London: Routledge, 2002); A. Bennett, J. Toynbee and B. Shank (eds), *The Popular Music Studies Reader* (London: Routledge, 2006); and M. Hills, *Fan Cultures* (London: Routledge, 2002). There is also a burgeoning literature on fans of individual bands and artists, such as J. Tate (ed.), *The Music and Art of Radiohead* (Aldershot: Ashgate, 2005). Nonetheless, compared to studies of (for example) television audiences, the role played by popular music in the lives of fans has still received *relatively* little scholarly attention; as Williams put it, 'little work within popular music studies has engaged directly with those who consume, listen to and use popular music as part of their everyday lives' (C. Williams, 'Does it Really Matter? Young People and Popular Music', *Popular Music*, Vol. 20, No. 2 (2001), p. 223).

6 What follows in the main text is a necessarily brief sketch of the intellectual state of play at this time; for more expansive accounts see any of the now numberless introductions to cultural studies.

7 See, for example, D. Morley, *The 'Nationwide' Audience* (London: BFI, 1980); D. Hobson, *'Crossroads'* (London: Methuen, 1982); I. Ang, *Watching 'Dallas': Soap Opera and the Melodramatic Imagination* (London: Methuen, 1985); D. Morley, *Family Television: Cultural Power and Domestic Leisure* (London: Comedia, 1986).

8 For example, S. Hall and T. Jefferson (eds), *Resistance Through Rituals: Youth Subcultures in Post-war Britain* (London: Hutchinson, 1976).

9 The Smiths had previously participated in a recording of 'This Charming Man' by the music programme *The Tube* (on Channel 4) and produced their own promotional video for 'The Boy With The Thorn In His Side'. However, neither represent

the kind of commissioned, professional 'music videos' of the kind associated in the 1980s with MTV.

10 Prior to 1986, the British National Health Service provided (where needed) free glasses to low-income groups and the young. They were extremely unfashionable and the source of ridicule among children. In 1986, the policy was changed to offering vouchers instead of providing glasses.

11 Interview with the author, February 1990.

12 All quotations from fans are from correspondence with the author, late 1989–early 1990. For reasons of anonymity, I have not given full names, but retain first names to enable fans to recognise their contributions.

13 Quoted in I. Pye, 'A Hard Day's Misery', *Melody Maker*, 3 November 1984, p. 31.

14 Ibid.

15 R. Schickel, *Common Fame* (London: Pavilion, 1985).

16 W. Benjamin, *Illuminations* (Glasgow: Fontana, 1992), pp. 236–7.

17 Interview with the author, November 1989.

18 See N. Kent, 'Dreamer in the Real World', *The Face*, 61 (May 1985).

19 Interview with the author, February 1990. This response did not preclude expansive discussion once an interviewee's initial caution was declared – the topic of Morrissey was thus both unapproachable and inexhaustible.

20 T.W. Adorno and M. Horkheimer, *Dialectic of Enlightenment* (London: Verso, 1976), p. 139.

21 Interview with the author, January 1990.

22 P. Bourdieu, *Distinction: A Social Critique of the Judgement of Taste* (London: Routledge, 1984).

23 K. Maton, *What Difference Does It Make? Sociology, Popular Culture and the Cult Figure*, unpublished undergraduate dissertation (University of Cambridge, 1990).

24 Quoted in C. Landesman, K. Maton and T. Young, Opening editorial, *The Modern Review* (Autumn 1991), p. 4.

25 For recent articles that are beginning to address these issues, see: L. Vroomen, 'Kate Bush: Teen Pop and Older Female Fans', in A. Bennett and R.A. Peterson (eds), *Music Scenes: Local, translocal, and virtual* (Nashville, TN: Vanderbilt University Press, 2004), pp. 238–53; A. Bennett, 'Punk's Not Dead: The Continuing Significance of Punk Rock for an Older Generation of Fans', *Sociology*, Vol. 40, No. 2 (2006), pp. 219–35.

11

'WHEN WE'RE IN YOUR SCHOLARLY ROOM': THE MEDIA, ACADEMIA AND THE SMITHS

Fergus Campbell

Some of the essays collected in this volume were conceived originally at a conference on The Smiths that was held at Manchester Metropolitan University (MMU) in April 2005. At the opening of the event, I had an interesting conversation with a researcher from Channel 4 News, who were filming a short piece for broadcast. While we discussed some of the questions that he wanted to ask conference participants, I asked him what it was about the event that was so interesting to Channel 4. He immediately replied that it was because we were 'bringing together two completely different worlds – academia and pop music'. This was certainly the case, although I did not think that this was as novel an idea as the researcher clearly did. However, it did occur to me later that the conference *was* in fact bringing together two very different worlds. These were not the realms of academia and popular music as the researcher had suggested but rather those of academia and the media.

The media response to *A Symposium on The Smiths* was both extraordinary and unexpected. The three organisers (Sean Campbell, Colin Coulter and myself) had arrived at the idea for the conference during several discussions in 2003, and felt that twenty years after the formation of The Smiths was an appropriate point to begin thinking about staging an event to reflect on them. As academics, we were used to staging formal conferences and did not expect this event to be particularly different from ones that we had organised before. The media response, therefore, took us somewhat by surprise. Altogether, there were more than fifty articles on the conference in national newspapers in Britain, and there was also significant coverage on national and international television, including Channel 4 News, BBC 3, CBC in Canada and DW TV in Germany.

Much of the media coverage would transpire to be extremely critical of what we were doing, and – as I later discovered – we were neither the first nor the last academics to be mocked by the media for daring to engage with pop music. In fact Peter Watson of *The Times* adopted a gently critical tone in his report of the first international conference on popular music held at the University of Amsterdam in June 1981, which was attended by 120 academics who were, he claimed, 'on the gravy train'.[1] Similarly, a conference on Morrissey held at the University of Limerick four years after the symposium in April 2009 was caricatured by Eoin Butler in the *Irish Times* as a meeting place for 'geeks' listening to lectures that lacked 'objectivity'.[2] Indeed, the hostility with which the media has responded to academics writing or even talking about pop culture is striking, and in this chapter I want to use the example of the media's response to the Smiths symposium to explore the more general – and often fraught – relationship between the media and the academia.

More to life than books

The media response to *A Symposium on The Smiths* can be divided into two main strands. The first wave followed the release of a press statement about the event on Monday 28 March 2005, and the following day there were articles published in five national newspapers. Intriguingly, the conference registered on the radar of the tabloid press. For the most part, the articles in the *Daily Star*, the *Daily Mirror* and *The Sun* were purely descriptive with each of them using a headline suggesting that The Smiths were being absorbed into the university curriculum: 'Mozzer master classes', 'Scholars to study Smiths', and – most wittily – 'Smiths Institute'.[3] All of them had short articles which broadly speaking were the same as that in the *Daily Star*: 'Rock legends The Smiths are to be studied by some of the world's leading academics'. What is revealing about these articles is where they were placed in the newspapers. In both the *Daily Star* and the *Daily Mirror*, the article on the conference was placed alongside a large photograph of pop singer Charlotte Church and her (then) new boyfriend, suggesting the 'showbiz' framing of the story. Perhaps the article in *The Sun* is most illuminating in this respect. The article on the conference was placed beneath a story on Arnold Schwarzenegger with the headline: 'Schwarzenegger has E.T. "living" in his belly'.[4] It would seem that the editor of *The Sun* believed that an academic conference on The Smiths was no less bizarre than the prospect of an extra terrestrial making a home in the torso of the Governor of California.[5]

As we might expect, there was a more serious response from the *Daily Telegraph* and *The Times*. Hugh Davies, writing in the *Telegraph*, located the conference in the context of 'a rash of intellectual scrutiny on American campuses of such diverse figures as Duke Ellington, Hank Williams, The Velvet Underground and The Doors':[6]

> After endlessly examining 'the enigma' of Bob Dylan and explaining why John Lennon is an 'icon', academics are turning their attention to The Smiths.

Scholars at a symposium in Manchester next week will compare the lyrics of the band's charismatic singer and songwriter Morrissey . . . to the works of the poets John Keats and W.B. Yeats.[7]

Similarly, Sean O'Neill was broadly favourable in his piece entitled 'Academics of the world unite for a gig with the Smiths'.[8] Most interestingly, he speculated as to the likely response of 'the fans', and reached the following conclusion:

Many, now in their serious forties, will be delighted that the finest minds will be trying to make sense of their youthful attachment.

The more solipsistic devotees, and they are many in number, will be appalled that the lyrics that so succinctly summed up the essence of their very personal bedroom angst will be publicly dissected and discussed.

Purely hedonistic fans are more likely to respond with bemusement.[9]

In the same newspaper, Caitlin Moran delivered a more critical response to the Symposium:

Although I'm sure . . . the three-day seminar of Smiths studies at MMU, will have a broader academic base than simply letting a load of ageing Smiths fans dress up like Morrissey and sad on about their favourite lyrics, one fears the worst.

While few under the age of 90 would argue that the Smiths' impact on British mores makes them just as worthy of academic analysis as Harold Pinter or James Joyce . . . the whole business of academic dissection of popular culture is, at best, flawed.

Despite universities being completely right to teach both how to split the atom and why the Beatles split up, the elements of popular culture they choose to examine are usually much of a muchness. Madonna, Elvis, the Beatles, Pink Floyd, the Smiths – in a nutshell, it's invariably stuff academics like . . . It does seem a slightly emotional non-academic trait. It's a bit like molecular biologists only holding seminars on . . . the fun molecules with amusing names.[10]

Moran's – admittedly tongue-in-cheek – point is somewhat contradictory. On the one hand, she acknowledges that the study of popular culture is just as 'worthy' as that of the literary giants. But she then goes on to suggest that the academic study of popular culture is flawed because academics choose to study those artists whom they admire. If this is the case – following the logic of Moran's argument – the serious study of James Joyce and Harold Pinter must also be flawed since their most notable biographers (Richard Ellman and Michael Billington) would appear to have affection for their subjects.[11] The notion that academics should not be permitted to have an investment in their subjects makes little sense, and Moran elides the critical point that all culture is worthy of study even if she and readers of *The Times* think otherwise.[12]

Moran concluded her article by suggesting the futility of the conference, and this tone was typical of the second wave of media commentary during the week leading up to and including the conference itself. In some ways, the extent of media attention during this period was particularly striking, given that it coincided with major news events such as the funeral of Pope John Paul II on 8 April and the wedding of Charles Windsor and Camilla Parker-Bowles the following day. Even so, an early fatwa was issued by the redoubtable Ann Widdecombe, Conservative MP and author, who told the *Independent* on 2 April: 'No respectable university would study a pop band; it must be an April Fool.'[13]

Widdecombe's point was developed further by two music journalists, James Cabooter and Paul Lester, on the first day of the conference, Friday 8 April. That evening, BBC 3 news broadcast a report on the conference by Andy Johnson, which was then discussed by these music journalists in the studio. When asked by the BBC presenter if Morrissey's lyrics were 'worth studying', Lester replied:

> I'm kind of appalled at the idea that one would study this at university level. I like the idea of taking things seriously but I don't think there are enough people taking the stuff seriously which we need in society. When I'm at home listening to The Smiths and I get a little bit stuck on – I don't know – track two, side one of *The Queen Is Dead* I don't think I'll call someone that attended that Smiths seminar the other week. But what I might need is someone to fix the stereo that breaks or the TV that's busted or 'God, I've just been to the toilet and I can't flush the chain'. That is what I personally require.
>
> [T]here is a genuinely serious demand for geezers who do hard graft. We don't need anymore fey narcissists with flowers in their back pocket . . . The future Morrisseys of this world will flourish without the need for a helping hand from the seminar in Manchester or wherever.

He then explained that he thought studying popular culture was 'not something that's meant to be done sanctioned by the government and the authorities and done in a hallowed university environment'.[14]

What is striking about Lester's comments, and the coverage on BBC 3 news more generally, is the assumption that the conference on The Smiths was the basis for an entire degree programme (sponsored by the government!) with the objective of training the youth of Manchester to become the new Morrisseys, Marrs, Rourkes and Joyces. Indeed, this negative comment appears to have emerged from a misconception about the function of third-level education. Broadly speaking, Lester and Widdecombe seem to suggest that universities exist solely for the instrumental purpose of training people to become electricians, plumbers, 'Morrisseys' and so on; and they fail to acknowledge that one of the most important functions of the university is to reflect on the nature of the world in an attempt to understand it better. This obviously involves both scientific research into, say, the causes and possible cures of diseases, as well as the investigation of the nature of history, culture, society, and so on.[15] What BBC 3 missed was that the conference was not an attempt to teach people how to become 'The Smiths' but to understand the context that the band came from, what their music means and why it continues to resonate with so many people.

Channel 4 News broadcast a more serious piece on the second day of the conference, Saturday 9 April, under the banner 'Profs Go Pop'. Lucy Manning began her report by explaining:

> Some said they put the miserable into Manchester. Others that they were the 80s' most influential band. But twenty years after the Smiths' heyday, who would have guessed they'd hit the heights of academia? At Manchester's Metropolitan University, only a few Morrissey style quiffs in sight, but many serious fans wanting to get serious about their music ... But is this academic enterprise taking things a little too far? With lecture titles including 'Remapping Manchester and The Smiths using psychogeographics', are Smiths fans taking themselves a little too seriously?

In some respects, the report was distinctly sympathetic. Channel 4 conducted an interview with the late Tony Wilson, for instance, who told Manning that:

> A song by Bob Dylan or The Smiths is not the same as a piece of Shakespeare or a piece of Keats, but you have to come to terms with the fact that it has the same level of emotional and intellectual resonance inside your brain so I'm all for academic study of it.[16]

But the Channel 4 report was – like other media responses – clearly based on the premise that academics are 'boffins' who trespass on the terrain of popular culture at their peril.

This was a line that was also pursued by the *New Musical Express* (*NME*). When the *NME* expressed an interest in attending the conference, the organisers were happy to welcome them. We had all in the past been readers of the paper, which has a history of engaging intelligently with pop music as well as politics and culture. In many ways, our idea for the conference was to try to develop further the analysis outlined by the *NME* in some of its earlier incarnations. However, it would become apparent that the current incarnation of *NME* is somewhat different to its predecessors. Rather than engaging with the conference itself, the paper simply dismissed the event in the most sneering manner. It described those attending the conference as 'Mozophiles and Moz-acolytes-turned-academics' and announced 'Come back, Klingon Studies – all is forgiven'. The journalist also caricatured a discussion of whether the test of a 'great' artist was to develop novel ideas or to refine the same set of ideas as 'a debate about Moz's genius. The gist being who was closer to genius: Picasso, Francis Bacon or Stephen [sic] Morrissey.' Finally, the paper reduced an illuminating conference discussion of sexuality in the songs 'Reel Around The Fountain' and 'This Charming Man' to what it described as a '*Trisha*-style confessional as the female members of the audience are asked for their feelings on Morrissey's desirability'.[17] In fact, this discussion addressed the question of how women responded to The Smiths, a point of significant interest given the prevailing conception of the band as appealing exclusively to reclusive males.

The *NME*'s response perhaps revealed just how much the weekly has changed since its heyday a generation or so ago. In its very first incarnation (in the 1950s), the *NME* was a lightweight industry newssheet designed to advance the interests of certain pop artists and it would seem that following its apparent 'golden age' between the 1960s and the 1990s it has now returned to its original mode. In the same issue as the conference article, there was an interview with Coldplay that uncritically relayed Chris Martin's anxieties about stardom, wealth and his then recent marriage to Hollywood actress Gwyneth Paltrow.[18] It would be interesting to know what figures such as Nick Kent, Charles Shaar Murray or Paul Morley would in their prime have made of such rock star self-pity.[19] In this context, it is probably fair to suggest that the true heirs of the more credible era of pop journalism are the monthly magazines – such as *Mojo*, *Uncut* and *Word* – which were, tellingly perhaps, more sympathetic in their coverage of the conference.[20]

A fortnight after the event the *Guardian* published a lengthy report of the conference in their weekend entertainment section, 'The Guide'. The *Guardian* journalist who attended the event had been in regular contact with the organisers for many months prior to the conference and had frequently expressed her enthusiasm and support for the event. However, the article that subsequently appeared in the *Guardian* presented a far from sympathetic view.[21] Under the headline 'Meeting is Murder', the journalist, Grace Dent, offered an account of the event that appeared to have been shaped by her background in children's fiction:

> In shadowy corners, academics avoid eye-contact, burying their faces in course hand-outs and lurking behind potted fronds, praying that [they] don't have to make small talk about their papers.[22]

This was a bizarre (and inaccurate) depiction of the event and those that attended it. The vast majority of people at the conference (as the TV reports show) were friendly and open. Either Dent had attended a completely different conference (another event was going on simultaneously in the same building) or she simply misrepresented those people that she did encounter. Of course, her article conforms to a well-worn pattern of media discourse on both academics and fans of The Smiths: that they are all essentially shy and isolated individuals with few social skills. Rather than actually describing the kinds of people whom she met at the event, Dent instead offered a piece of clichéd journalism that invoked the classic caricature of The Smiths, their fans and academics. Both the *NME* and the *Guardian* – and the media generally – refused to engage with the ideas and arguments presented in the papers that they had heard, and instead highlighted the allegedly 'boffin'-like nature of the conference attendees.

Homework onto the fire

Why was the media so critical of *A Symposium on The Smiths*, and why was it so reluctant to actually engage with the ideas discussed at the conference? The key point that needs to be made is that the media appears to regard popular culture as beyond the remit of academia. Academics should – some sections of the media appear to think – stick with Elizabeth I and William Shakespeare and leave Elvis and Madonna in *their* capable hands. In other words, much of the adverse criticism of *A Symposium on The Smiths*, and of previous academic conferences and publications on pop music, was the result of a turf war between academia and the media over who is the rightful 'owner' of pop music. Popular music and popular culture more generally appear to be regarded as the media's 'patch' and academics are expected to take note and stay away.[23] It is also significant that the media-caricatures of fans of The Smiths and of academics are remarkably similar; and some of the criticisms of the symposium appear to have arisen from misconceptions about what academics do and from reactionary stereotypes about teachers and academics in British society. This may be a particularly British phenomenon and reso-nates with the well-known anti-intellectualism present in British society more generally.[24] Indeed, it is telling perhaps that the foreign media generally dealt much more sympathetically with the conference.[25]

Unlike the generous and lengthy report that appeared on Deutsche-Welle TV, for example, BBC 3 took a dismissive stance. During the BBC 3 news report on the conference, James Cabooter observed that:

> Smiths fans to my knowledge tended to be second only to Trekkies at school: a very nerdy group of people who took music very seriously and I can just see people of a certain age [at the conference] over-analysing the lyrics. . .
>
> They've [The Smiths] got a huge following: it even goes as far as Mexico where I understand some gangland Mexicans have tattoos of Morrissey up their arm which I don't quite understand. But . . . I think Star Trek fans, Dr Who, The Smiths there's a kind of a curve, connection there.

As we have seen, much of the media comment on the conference repeat-edly restated this view that academics and people interested in The Smiths were 'nerdy', socially awkward and obsessive.[26] However, in most cases, this comment was made by people who had not attended the conference themselves. If they had done so, and with a relatively open mind, they might have revised their view. Cabooter raised an interesting question as to why The Smiths are currently very popular among young Hispanics. If he had come to the conference, he would have heard some discussion of this point that might have helped him understand the appeal of The Smiths to (what he called) 'gangland Mexicans'.

Perhaps Johnny Marr is leading the way in breaking down the barriers between academia, the media, and pop musicians. Marr was appointed Professor of Music at the University of Salford in 2007 and far from decrying the academics he has met as nerdy boffins, he is instead celebrating the 'fantastic resources and great people' at the university.[27] Indeed, what academics do is not so very different from what journalists do, and perhaps the real lesson of the symposium is that it might make more sense for us to try to learn from each other rather than engaging in spurious turf wars over who has the 'right' to write about pop.

Notes

1 P. Watson, 'Going Dutch, the Donnish Disciples of Pop', *The Times*, 16 June 1981, p. 12.

2 Although Butler's article invoked some of the same clichés about academics and fans of The Smiths as those journalists who wrote about the 2005 symposium, he generally did so in a self-deprecating and humorous manner. E. Butler, 'Heaven Knows I'm Miserable Now', *Irish Times*, 1 May 2009. Available online: www.irishtimes.com/ newspaper/theticket/2009/0501/1224245702067.html (accessed 30 October 2009).

3 *Daily Star*, 29 March 2005, p. 17; *Daily Mirror*, 29 March 2005, p. 3; *The Sun*, 29 March 2005, p. 7.

4 *The Sun*, 29 March 2005, p. 7.

5 *The Sun*, 29 March 2005, p. 7.

6 *Daily Telegraph*, 29 March 2005, p. 9.

7 Since there was no mention of anyone at the conference comparing Morrissey's lyrics with the work of Keats or Yeats, we can only assume that Davies invented this comparison himself with a little help from Morrissey's invocation of these poets in The Smiths' song 'Cemetry Gates'.

8 *The Times*, 29 March 2005, p. 9. Intriguingly, *The Times* included an announcement on the cover page that there was an article on The Smiths contained in the newspaper ('The Smiths: From Flower Power to the Groves of Academia. News page 9.')

9 S. O'Neill, 'Academics of the World Unite for a Gig with the Smiths', *The Times*, 29 March 2005, p. 9.

10 C. Moran, 'So Tell Me, What Was that All About?', *The Times*, 29 March 2005, p. 9.

11 R. Ellmann, *James Joyce: New and Revised Edition* (Oxford: Oxford University Press, 1982); M. Billington, *The Life and Work of Harold Pinter* (London: Faber and Faber, 1996).

12 Moran is correct, however, to suggest that cultural historians should consider so-called 'low' art, particularly when it elicits a widespread popular response.

13 C. Rudebeck, 'Some Bands are Bigger than others. . .', *Independent*, 2 April 2005, pp. 20–1.

14 Lester appears to have been unaware that one of his colleagues at *Uncut* magazine, Simon Goddard, was speaking at the conference.

15 In fact, most academics are contracted to spend about one-third of their time researching and writing up their findings (the latter is generally done during so-called 'vacations' or 'holidays').

16 Lucy Manning report on Channel 4 news broadcast on 9 April 2005.

17 E. Smack, 'Hatful of Homework', *NME*, 23 April 2005, p. 29.

18 M. Beaumont, 'The Return of the Kings', *NME*, 23 April 2005, pp. 22–5.

19 For examples of the writings of these former *NME* writers, see N. Kent, *The Dark Stuff: Selected Writings on Rock 1972–1993* (London: Penguin, 1994); C. Shaar Murray, *Shots from the Hip* (London: Penguin, 1991); P. Morley, *Ask: The Chatter of Pop* (London: Faber, 1986).

20 See, for example, S. Goddard, 'Oxbridge Here We Come', *Uncut*, June 2005, p. 28.

21 G. Dent, 'Meeting is Murder', *Guardian*, 'Guide' section, 23 April 2005, pp. 4–6.

22 Ibid., p. 4.

23 In 'When The Music Hits the Fan', Caroline Sullivan writes that '[t]he real justification for criticising other people's work, though, is that listening to a thousand or more records a year makes rock critics experts on their subject'. Her article is a response to an ill-tempered attack on rock critics ('In the Line of Fire') by Pat Kane, the singer in Coatbridge duo *Hue and Cry*, also published in the *Guardian* on the same day (6 September 1993) and on the same page (p. 4).

24 See S. Collini, *Absent Minds: Intellectuals in Britain* (Oxford: Oxford University Press, 2006) and S. Frith and J. Savage, 'Pearls and Swine: The Intellectuals and the Mass Media', *New Left Review*, 198 (March–April 1993), pp. 107–16.

25 See, for example, É. Fraga, 'The Smiths polemiza como tema acadêmico', *Folha de São Paulo*, 8 April 2005; K. Gomes, 'Académicos debatem os Smiths numa universidade de Manchester', *Público*, 8 April 2005, p. 48. See also the feature broadcast on Deutsche-Welle TV in April 2005.

26 The assumption was also often made that every person attending the conference was a fan of The Smiths, which ignored the fact that some conference participants were simply interested in the cultural history of the 1980s or in popular music

more generally. The people who attend conferences on Napoleon, for instance, are not necessarily all admirers of diminutive francophone dictators.

27 A. Lipsett, 'This Charming Man', *Guardian*, 5 November 2008. Available online: www.guardian.co.uk/education/2008/nov/05/johnny-marr-professor-lecture-salford-university (accessed 30 October 2009).

12

'SO MUCH TO ANSWER FOR':
WHAT DO THE SMITHS MEAN TO MANCHESTER?

Julian Stringer

Interviews and articles with and about The Smiths habitually return to the question of what the city of Manchester means to the group. Journalistic and critical commentaries relating the band to the geographical region within which all four of its members were born and brought up identify and explore the importance of native place identity. Such writings work to reassert the iconic relevance of a series of key reference points through which the story of The Smiths is frequently presented. These names and places of reported significance to Morrissey, Johnny Marr, Andy Rourke and Mike Joyce include 384 King's Road, Bowden, Buzzcocks, *Coronation Street*, Crazy Face, Decibel Studios, Grass Roots, the Haçienda, *Hobson's Choice*, Ludus, the Moors Murders, the Nosebleeds, Rusholme, the Salford Lads Club, Strangeways, *A Taste of Honey*, Whalley Range and Wythenshawe.

The repetition of noteworthy details concerning the importance to The Smiths of this or that specific aspect of Manchester is ongoing in discussions of the band across all media. Indeed, despite the fact that the group split up over twenty years ago, these kinds of reference points are trotted out more regularly now than ever before. In books, newspapers and magazines and on television, radio and the Internet, former band members continue to respond to the request to volunteer information on this subject – one important dimension of what Richard Carman calls 'the business of the business of being The Smiths'[1] – while commentators appear only too happy to repeat such insights for the benefit of a new generation of fans. In this sense, public proclamations about Manchester made in particular by Morrissey and Marr provide a form of cultural currency through which interest in The Smiths is kept alive by band members for the commercial media apparatus that surrounds them.[2] The symbolic power of such utterances is only underlined by the recent publication of books engaging directly with the close association between the group and their native city.[3]

While the investigation of Manchester's influence upon the life and work of The Smiths is obviously a worthwhile endeavour that can lead to the production of valuable knowledge concerning the intellectual history and cultural geography of contemporary British music, it is not my intention in this chapter to contribute yet more words on this subject. There are two reasons for this. First, in the context of a collection of academic essays on The Smiths, pursuing such an approach would constitute something of a missed opportunity. The unravelling of all the ways in which Manchester has impacted upon Morrissey, Marr, Rourke and Joyce has proven to be of great interest to the band's numerous biographers and critics. Yet there is also a need for academics such as myself to look beyond narrative detail towards a more analytical perspective so as to advance different intellectual agendas and place on the table alternative modes of understanding.

Second, the journalistic desire to find out what Manchester means to The Smiths cannot help but reconfirm the validity of cultural narratives originating from – and/or authorised by – members of the band themselves. For example, asking Morrissey to talk time and again about his 'Mancunian roots' grants him licence to control the ways in which subsequent critical commentaries are likely to seek to understand the relationship between The Smiths and native place identity. Certainly, there is nothing inherently wrong or sinister about such acts – most of the thoughts that individual members of The Smiths choose to share with writers and broadcasters regarding their hometown are doubtless eminently sincere.[4] Yet deferring to the band, and its various associates, as the only possible sources of information on this topic runs the risk of simplifying popular music history by reducing it to the personal and the subjective. Moreover, the cultural narratives spawned in this fashion may over time come to function as highly reductive 'sound bites' reproduced at opportune moments like the twentieth anniversary (in 2006) of the release of the celebrated album *The Queen Is Dead*. Such materials therefore need to be handled extremely carefully. Words emanating from career musicians whose livelihoods depend upon extensive media coverage inescapably serve to extend and inflect the commodified nature of their star images.[5]

In *Atlas of the European Novel 1800–1900*, Franco Moretti claims that '[p]lacing a literary phenomenon in its specific space – mapping it – is not the conclusion of geographical work; it's the *beginning*'.[6] Much the same may also be said of popular music. To avoid the repetition of historical narratives about The Smiths and Manchester that remain static and one-dimensional, more dynamic models of historical analysis need to be proposed. One reason for this is that the meaning of a cultural phenomenon never stays the same. The significance of a musical star image changes over time just as the specific space, shape and identity of a given city does as well.

This chapter, therefore, presents a slightly different perspective on this subject by advancing an alternative research question: what do The Smiths mean to Manchester? However, it does not attempt to provide what Barbara Klinger, writing in the context of Film Studies, terms a 'total history'.[7] Instead, my intention is to present the findings of small-scale empirical research so as to highlight how little we actually know about The Smiths and native place identity and how much more we still have to learn. In so doing, I utilise the distinction drawn by Klinger between 'synchronic' and 'diachronic' forms of historical analysis. The former refers to 'the conjuncture in which films initially appeared . . . their original circumstances of production, exhibition and reception', and grapples with the fact that aesthetic texts are 'always available to *another* reading at the same time, even in the supposedly "original" moment when they were first produced'.[8] The latter refers to a 'film's fluid, changeable and volatile relation to history' – in other words, to how its variable meanings shift across time. 'These qualifiers are essential for realizing the historicity of meaning beyond origins, and for giving authority to all of the semiotic intrigues surrounding films during the course of their social and historical circulation.'[9]

My chosen method is to track press reports on The Smiths published in Manchester print sources between 1983 and 2007. In order to explore both synchronic and diachronic forms of analysis, I have limited myself to consideration of just two major publications. On the one hand, I have consulted stories and reviews published in the city's most important culture and listings magazine, *City Life* (hereafter *CL*), especially between 1983 and 1987, or the period which marks The Smiths' recording career.[10] On the other hand, I have consulted reports published post-1987 (i.e. since the band broke up) in what is historically the city's most significant local newspaper, the *Manchester Evening News* (hereafter *MEN*) – paying particular attention to online reports posted at its website (www.manchestereveningnews.co.uk) between 2000 and 2007.

This concentration upon two key moments in the coverage afforded to The Smiths in these two significant Manchester publications is not arbitrary. Certainly, the chosen periods are not discrete: post-1987 reports from *CL* are also discussed in what follows, as are pre-2000 reports from *MEN*. Yet what emerges most forcefully from consideration of these prominent local sources during these two distinct historical periods is the presence of differing cultural narratives structuring the variable reception across time of The Smiths in their home city. In this sense, choosing one publication for one analytical lens and one for another helps illustrate the complex historical dynamics of the synchronic/diachronic distinction discussed above.

Synchronic analysis: scene politics

Before proceeding any further, let us ask the fundamental question of why it is worth engaging in such an analysis in the first place. Simply put, the critical approach outlined here not only leads to the production of fresh historical knowledge about The Smiths, but also to the posing of new research questions.

This statement may be illustrated through consideration of a specific example. In September 1986, Morrissey gave a controversial interview to Frank Owen for *Melody Maker* while the band were on tour in the US.[11] The article prompted close attention from the national UK press because of the inclusion of notorious comments leading to accusations that The Smiths were racist. Indeed, the interview's publication motivated a discourse about race, racism and The Smiths that has never gone away. Details of the alleged disagreement between Morrissey and Owen have been slavishly raked over by all subsequent biographers and also underpin the highly publicised disputes between Morrissey and the *New Musical Express* that sprang up over questions of race in 1992 and 2007.[12]

A consideration of Manchester media sources from the same period, however, reveals that Morrissey's words on the subject of race were not so strongly emphasised. By contrast, what Simon Goddard calls a 'ripping yarn Morrissey had previously spun to *Melody Maker*'s Frank Owen' regarding a possible gay bashing incident was given more attention.[13] While not ignoring the contemporary controversy over the supposed racial politics of the group's (then) recent single 'Panic', an interviewer from Radio Piccadilly veered conversation instead towards the topic of sexual politics. Calling Morrissey's 'gay-bashing' story 'lies' and 'total fabrications', the interviewer announced that he had also been born and raised in Manchester and that hearing his tall-tale was 'like reading something about a foreign land . . . I just never encountered half the things you did'. Morrissey counters with the concession that elements of the *Melody Maker* article were indeed 'lies . . . and . . . total fabrication . . . not by me, but by the writer in question.'[14]

The singer elaborated on his position for the benefit of *CL* readers by claiming that he had been 'stitched up' by Owen:

> I find these pieces that are written are usually written by people that I know, who I've known for a very long time . . . Frank Owen (the writer) is really Gavin Owen, who was the lead singer in the Manchester band Manicured Noise, they made some good singles . . . how can I hate black music? 55% of all my records are by black artists. Everything I said justifying the things he left in was taken out . . . All those gay clubs he mentioned, and there was a reference to Whitworth Street toilets – that was *his* past, not mine. We're suing the *Melody Maker*, and they tell us they can't find the tapes.[15]

Both of these local media reports focus on a different issue from the charge of racism then preoccupying the national press: namely, the question of Morrissey's possibly intimate knowledge of Manchester's music and alternative sexual cultures of the 1970s and early 1980s.[16] Because the interviewer from Radio Piccadilly appears not to possess the same level of familiarity with the city's gay scene seemingly acquired by Morrissey, a disconnect opens up between the former's arguably 'straight' and the latter's undoubtedly more 'queer' understandings of their distinct native place identities. Similarly, Morrissey's words for *CL* appear to offer evidence of a hitherto unsuspected alliance between himself and Frank (Gavin) Owen. Did the 1986 *Melody Maker* interview provide an occasion for the personal settling of old scores? Does it provide evidence of an ongoing rivalry between the two men? Mutual flirtation? Seduction even? Whatever the actual truth of the matter, the point to underline here is that in 1986 the cultural politics of Manchester's music and gay scenes were deemed to be of more interest to the local press than the racism debate then attracting the attention of the national media.

As the above example suggests, what may be termed 'scene politics' is a key aspect of the 1983–87 local press conjuncture in which The Smiths initially appeared. In the band's 'original' synchronic moment, the city of Manchester talked about them in the pages of *CL* primarily on these terms.

In the 1980s, The Smiths featured prominently in discussions of the Manchester music scene published in *CL*, but in highly ambivalent and inconsistent ways. To be sure, they were featured in the first few issues in a manner which outlined and confirmed their relevance to Manchester's lively club culture. For example, Mary O'Brien opens her short 1983 concert report for the magazine's debut issue with the words 'Nice to have you home boys . . . The Smiths at the Hacienda. The queues around the block said it all really. This was the triumphant return to Manchester of that Mr. Morrissey and THOSE Smiths.' O'Brien claims that the success of the band 'looks to inject some badly needed pride into the local music scene. You see The Smiths are the first truly Northern band to arise since the Buzzcocks.' Interestingly, she concludes by suggesting how '[t]hat cute faggot [sic] Morrissey is develop-ing into something of an influencial [sic] stylist. The place was teeming with sensitive young men in baggy shirts clutching flowers. Interesting. Watch the street.'[17] Such coverage continues in issue two with inclusion of a centre spread feature entitled '4 for 84'. Across three full pages, the magazine assesses 'reasons to be cheerful' in 1984; 'Manchester's music scene is on the upturn'. Together with profiles of the Fall, New Order and Carmel, The Smiths share titular pride of place.[18]

These stories also mark the beginning of *CL*'s ongoing attempts to use The Smiths as a form of cultural currency through which it may generate a sense of excitement around Manchester's music scene. For example, the group fea-tured prominently in a 1985 article on the work of local photographer Kevin Cummins.[19] In addition, the 1985 publication of Mick Middles' short book on the band led to the commissioning of an interview with the author justified along the following lines: 'Middles sees the Smiths as a peculiarly Mancunian phenomenon placing them in context with the rest of the Manchester music scene, and Mancunian social life itself'.[20] Finally, as the band's star began its spectacular ascent, subsequent issues ran 'Competition Time' contests in which readers could win copies of the latest Smiths singles and albums.[21]

However, to say that *CL* fully endorsed and supported The Smiths during the five short years of their existence would be inaccurate. The magazine's editors and writers appear to have held highly conflicted views concerning the group's success. Consider in this respect the question of how and to what extent The Smiths' records were reviewed in *CL*. In an entirely symptomatic fashion, Mary O'Brien praises the band's third single, 'What Difference Does It Make?' (1984), by suggesting that Morrissey is the 'Cliff [Richard] of a meatier, beatier age, all Horlicks and winceyette pyjamas' while simultaneously dismissing its B-side, 'Back To The Old House', as 'tedious, ponderous, snivelling and petty in the extreme'.[22] Robert Graham's review of the group's first album, *The Smiths* (1984), damns it with faint praise ('the cut of The Smiths is delicious on a good tune. (They aren't all)).'[23] Neither the group's 1984 compilation album *Hatful Of Hollow*, nor 1985's *Meat Is Murder* – which reached the top of the UK album charts – were reviewed by the magazine, and later releases fared little better. *The Queen Is Dead* is reviewed positively but not given as much print space as an interview with 'the [l]atest in a line of local pop tune vendors, The Dannyboys'.[24] *The World Won't Listen* (1987) compilation is dubbed 'peculiar' by an unimpressed Bob Dickinson.[25] The same author finds the group's 1987 swansong, *Strangeways, Here We Come*, a 'known' and 'undernourished' entity, while S. Hewitt states that with the single 'I Started Something I Couldn't Finish' (1987) The Smiths are 'ripping off their fans': 'To add insult to injury, the B-side is a gutless rendition of "Pretty Girls Make Graves", and a twee, wimpy "Some Girls [Are Bigger Than Others]".[26] As for the posthumous 1988 live album *Rank*: 'The best thing about this atrocity is the title.'[27]

It is only from later on, in the 1990s, that *CL* begins to produce more unambiguously positive assessments of The Smiths' contribution to the Manchester music scene. This occurs in the context of major revaluations of the group's ongoing significance. The magazine thus ran an extended review of Linder Sterling's 1992 photographic book *Morrissey Shot*, as well as a long 1992 interview with Johnny Rogan to mark the publication of his biography *Morrissey and Marr: The Severed Alliance*.[28] In addition, it published extended and highly positive retrospective articles to celebrate the airing of Granada Television's *These Things Take Time* documentary in 2002 as well as Morrissey's subsequent visits to the city in 2003 and concerts there in 2004.[29] The publication of such reports coincided with twentieth anniversary celebrations marking the formation of the band in 1982 as well as the release of Morrissey's much-anticipated 2004 'comeback' album *You Are The Quarry*.

In sum, during the years 1983–87 *CL* framed its discussion of The Smiths in terms of the scene politics of Manchester's local music culture.[30] This 'original' synchronic moment of reception provides evidence of the highly inconsistent and ambivalent nature of the magazine's coverage of the group. However, as the years passed, *CL* reports began to become more positive and more unambiguously supportive.

Diachronic analysis: heritage politics

If articles and reports published in the pages of *CL* between 1983 and 1987 are highly conflicted about The Smiths, the same cannot be said about stories published online between 2000 and 2007 in *MEN*. The vast majority of these reports are not only very positive about The Smiths, but also tie such perspectives into consideration of wider developments in Manchester social history. More than this, many of these pieces keep one eye firmly on preservationist agendas. This second – and diachronic – cultural narrative may thus be characterised by its preoccupation with what I would like to term 'heritage politics'.

This is all somewhat ironic, though, for *MEN* press reports from the 1980s and early 1990s had not always been quite so laudatory. Indeed, during the years of The Smiths' existence the newspaper often made critical comments on the group. A particularly scurrilous example of this tendency is Ray King's article 'Running Scared?', published on 9 November 1984, which attacks the band's politics and accuses them of being cowards (for not agreeing to an *MEN* interview). In its choice of language, King's article is moreover not just aggressively confrontational ('Morrissey . . . this bequiffed Mancunian, the man who . . . puts the wally in Whalley Range') but also borderline homophobic: 'I recall mildly opining that a prancing figure with a bunch of wilting daffodils hanging out of his back trouser pocket, an oddball taste in shirts and an eccentric line in winsome crooning was hardly going to change the world. Well, has he?'[31]

Many other early *MEN* reports further attacked Morrissey, in particular, for this or that perceived betrayal of his local 'roots'. For instance, an October 1992 article stoked the embers of class envy by chronicling the singer's ability to buy ever more expensive homes: 'Pop star Morrissey has come a long way from his humble beginnings in a Stretford council house and a first-floor bedsit in Whalley Range. He has just splashed out £650,000 on a palatial four-storey town house in London's plush Regents Park Terrace . . . He is reputed to have forked out £90,000 on fittings alone for his new home – more than twice the value of the council house.'[32] Similarly, the singer was chastised for 'snubbing' the city in 1994 after he announced tour plans that 'missed out his home city . . . The baffling omission of Manchester from today's announcement is

similar to that heralding his 1991 tour, when Manchester fans ended up trav-
elling to the nearest gig in Blackburn.'[33] Such points of view can only very
rarely be found amongst the *MEN* reports that appeared between 2000 and
2007. For example, 'Morrissey Prefers to Stay South' ran the headline for one
story from August 2002 outlining how the 'lugubrious former Smiths man
will play two dates at the Royal Albert Hall next month, following gigs in the
States and Japan . . . there are no plans to make a return trip up north. "As
far as we're aware it's just the two in London," snaps a tour spokeswoman.'
The report concludes that it knows 'Manchester has changed radically since
the LA-loving warbler last lived here – but can he really have forgotten the
way?'[34] A 2006 report similarly outlined the history of Morrissey's concert
appearances in Manchester and complained that 'over his 24-year career the
Davyhulme-born icon has only performed in the city a measly 18 times'.[35]

Between 2000 and 2007, the reception of The Smiths in *MEN* therefore
undergoes a remarkable reversal of fortune. Four key topics dominate discussion in these more positive online postings. The first of these comprises stories
enshrining The Smiths as merely one – albeit very important – component
of the city's distinguished musical history. This occurs primarily through the
publication of polls and lists which help canonise the memory of The Smiths
for local readers. One example is the April 2005 news that The Smiths 'have
soared home' in a ManchesterOnline poll to 'find out who is the city's best
band of all time': 'Readers cast over 1,600 votes online and Mozzer and the
gang were awarded an impressive 466 of them [28.8 per cent].' However, the
timing of this story is significant because the poll was 'launched following
the arrival of MTV in Manchester last week, who along with Galaxy FM have
been running one of their own'.[36] Once again, The Smiths are enlisted in this
instance as a form of cultural currency through which a sense of excitement
may be generated.

To repeat, The Smiths' glorious career is here recalled positively but in
no sense fetishised or singled out for special attention. As one report makes
clear, they are in this sense just one Mancunian band among many: 'The Stone
Roses, The Twisted Wheel, The Hacienda, Madchester, That Sex Pistols gig,
The Smiths. Manchester is never shy of quoting its rich and diverse musical
heritage as a reason it stands out from other cities in the country.'[37] Another
report includes the group as merely one of the stellar names represented in
the 2006 BBC initiative *The Manchester Passion*, a story of Jesus' Crucifixion
and Resurrection 'played out by actors, including former James frontman Tim
Booth, to songs from the likes of Oasis, Morrissey and Joy Division'.[38]

This narrative of overall local musical achievement, however, becomes
entwined with a heritage discourse. In May 2004, Helen Tither reported that
with 'Manchester music idol Morrissey wending his merry way back to the
city this weekend, it seems the time is right for a good old trip down memory

lane. And what better way to remember those heady early days of his former band, The Smiths, than to immortalise them for posterity in the city's first pop museum?' These words then lead into a discussion of plans to create the first complete archive of Manchester-based music, The Manchester District Music Archive, and reports that the planners are working 'with a number of different organisations to get it together, including the Museum Of Science And Industry.' Tither quotes Alison Surtees of project organisers *100%*: 'In fact, until now, people have been asking why there's nothing to commemorate our region's music when it's one of the things that we are most famous for. The Smiths, for instance, are incredibly influential.'[39] Indeed, when the Archive was finally launched in September 2004 it was with the aim of 'celebrating the city's rich artistic heritage'. As another report rather snootily puts it, 'the archive is aimed at capturing the essence of bands including The Smiths, The Stone Roses and even Take That, Halle and New Order'.[40]

The second topic dominating discussion in the positive and supportive *MEN* online postings places The Smiths more squarely in the pantheon of the city's great musical acts. The group achieves this via a process of canonisation – that is to say, by the attaching of 'classic' status to them. Furthermore, in attributing such prestigious values to the band these reports argue and demonstrate that its members are not just great musicians, but also great Mancunians.

This canonisation process is also achieved through use of polls, lists and other forms of status confirmation. A report from November 2002 points out that 'Steven Patrick Morrissey has just amazed his critics by polling 59 per cent of the vote to win a *Manchester Evening News* survey to name the Greatest Mancunian'. It goes on to announce that the singer 'scored more highly than other candidates, including Alan Turing, LS Lowry and Albert Finney, who polled six per cent, two per cent and one per cent of the vote respectively'.[41] The 'runaway winner' reputedly received almost seven times as many votes as his nearest rival, computer pioneer Alan Turing, and over 40 times as many votes as football legend David Beckham.[42] Indeed, as a separate article reports, it turned out to be 'Morrissey by a mile! . . . Manchester turned to its musical roots to elect the greatest of all its citizens – and what a landslide it was . . . [Morrissey] collected almost as many votes as the other 49 contenders in our list of suggestions.'[43] All of this was soon to be followed by news that Morrissey had also topped a poll (with 51 per cent of the vote) to find England's most 'Northern male personality': 'More than 50,000 people voted in the online survey conducted by Manchester art gallery *The Lowry*. The shortlists were chosen by visitors to the gallery's current exhibition *The Myth of the North*, celebrating all things northern.'[44]

The third theme prevalent in the positive and supportive 2000–07 *MEN* press postings connects The Smiths directly to preservationist concerns and recurs most obviously through the habitual publication of stories concerning the Salford Lads Club – the Manchester building immortalised on the gatefold sleeve of *The Queen Is Dead*. This photograph is itself presented as a 'classic' image ripe for heritage treatment. Readers are told that the work of Stephen Wright, the 'Smiths' snapper' who 'helped to shape the image' of the 'iconic Manchester band' now 'hangs in the Manchester Art Gallery' and 'has been accepted as part of the National Portrait Gallery collection'.[45] 'Morrissey looks like Mona Lisa,' says Wright, 'with a kind of smirk. But there's something about the picture that it all pulls together.'[46] So famous is this image that not only have 'thousands of Smiths fanatics from all over the world' made 'the pilgrimage to Ordsall to have their photographs taken in the same spot', but now 'Stephen Wright . . . is offering fans the chance to recreate the famous pose . . . to raise funds for charity. Later this month, he will take pictures of Smiths fans in return for a £5 donation to Alzheimer's Research'.[47]

The *MEN* heritage narrative generated over the Salford Lads Club was intensified in December 2007 with news that Morrissey had donated £20,000 to the 'youth club he made internationally famous': 'volunteers this year launched a £1 million campaign to restore and upgrade the grade II listed Edwardian building. But they suffered a massive setback when thieves climbed scaffolding to steal guttering and lead from the roof in July. Now Davyhulme-born Morrissey has given the fundraising team a surprise reason to celebrate.' Stating that the club falls within a regeneration area and that developers LPC Living helped raise the first £250,000 for crucial roofing work, the report reveals that Morrissey's donation will be 'used to put insulation into the roof and carry out work on the ceiling'.[48]

Morrissey's financial lifeline came ahead of news that a nationwide poll, carried out by ICONS Online for the Department for Culture Media and Sport, had reportedly placed the Salford Lads Club third in a vote to find the country's most popular icon – 'behind a sports car and the Household Cavalry, but in front of Blackpool Illuminations, and afternoon tea'. It went on to suggest that 'the red-bricked building at the bottom of the real Coronation Street could become England's greatest icon'.[49] In addition, it reports that such regeneration is necessary because 'Bad lads wreck Smiths club . . . The restoration of the iconic Salford Lads Club has been wrecked after thieves climbed scaffolding to steal guttering and lead from the roof'.[50] In response, some of the group's 'devoted fans' had offered to help 'get its renovation back on track . . . They plan to complete a 16-mile sponsored bike ride through Manchester, Salford and Trafford to raise funds for the building . . . Their route will take in landmarks made famous by Smiths front man Morrissey, including Strangeways prison, the Holy Name Church on Oxford Road and King's Road in Stretford where Morrissey grew up.'[51] Another report confirmed that riders had indeed made 'a tour of the places mentioned in The

Smiths songs including The Iron Bridge on King's Road, Stretford; Southern Cemetery, Whalley Range, The Holy Name Church on Wilmslow Road, and Strangeways Prison. At each point they had special commemorative passports stamped to prove they had visited each of the venues on the way'.[52]

The fact that The Smiths, and particularly Morrissey, were involved in this particular restoration project forges strong connections between the group and notions of heritage. Yet it also works to reframe the Salford building as a venue associated with music, rather than its identity as a Lads Club: in the words of a report from September 2001, the *MEN* presented this as a 'Battle to save music mecca'.[53] This perspective was underscored by numerous readers' comments posted in response to such developments: 'How about Smiths fans being able to "Buy a Brick" as a way of raising money?' (Miriam O'Brien); 'How about getting the Smiths and other manchester bands to do a benefit gig to save it?' (David Norman); 'I don't think it should be demolished as it is part of the excellent musical heritage of Manchester. We have already lost The Hacienda. I reckon it should be done up for future generations to enjoy' (Anonymous).[54]

However, a number of ironies surround the mutually affirming contemporary cultural politics of heritage, The Smiths and the Salford Lads Club. First amongst these is the fact that in 1986–87 the latter had a very fractious relationship with the group. The organisation actually raised money to sue The Smiths for unauthorised use of the club's façade, and for linking the Salford Lads Club with values (such as anti-royalism) with which it did not wish to be associated. It was also keen to point out that The Smiths had not been members of the club and sought to disassociate itself from the band.[55] Clearly, recent cultural narratives aligning The Smiths positively with the Salford Lads Club constitute a diachronic reframing – and reversal – of press attitudes prevalent during the band's 'original' synchronic moment.

In light of the opening of a dedicated space for the presentation of Smiths-related memorabilia at the Salford Lads Club in 2004, a further irony concerns the involvement of politicians and royalty. In April of that year, the Duke of Kent 'visited the listed building which is about to become a heritage centre celebrating Mancunian heroes The Smiths . . . The Duke was shown a room once used for the sport of fives and weightlifting which will be turned into the "Smiths Room". He met Phill Gatenby, author of *Morrissey's Manchester*, a tour guide of places which influenced the band. Phill explained that the Salford Lads Club picture was used on the inner sleeve of the album *The Queen Is Dead* and the Duke joked: "Oh – I'd better not mention that back home."'[56] Conservative Party leader David Cameron also appears anxious to be associated with the club and its heroes:

David Cameron was to follow his musical heroes The Smiths today by posing in front of Salford Lads Club . . . Mike Joyce, the Smiths former drummer, welcomed the Tory leader's visit. The Green Party supporter said: 'It is clearly a publicity stunt, but I don't care who goes there as long as it brings to the fore what a great place Salford Lads Club is' . . . Mr Cameron is to visit Salford Lads Club with shadow home secretary David Davis. They will tour the club and meet volunteers and organisers. Mr Cameron will also deliver a speech on Tory proposals to tackle crime.[57]

In these examples, The Smiths are once again enlisted as a form of cultural currency through which particular commercial, cultural and political agendas may be promoted.

Moving on from the specific example of the Salford Lads Club, it is also worth noting the grand scale upon which such preservationist activities are unfurled. One report from August 2004 asks the question, 'What do you have to do to get a street named after you?' and answers it by revealing that 'one of Manchester's biggest housing developments' wishes to name one of its largest building projects in the city after 'a living legend' – one of the names subsequently nominated by *MEN* readers was 'Morrissey Way' (alongside 'Beckham Boulevard').[58] Similarly, *MEN* also suggested that 'Morrissey' might make 'a charming name for our airport':

> Welcome to Manchester Morrissey Airport. It may seem like a flight of fancy, but the idea of a new name for the city's airport could yet take off. The morose singer-songwriter of 1980s group The Smiths is just one – and perhaps more unlikely – of a long list of Great Mancunians who could lend a little kudos and glamour to the two runways and three terminals.[59]

The fourth and final theme to be found amongst the *MEN* press reports from 2000–07 is the attempt to re-connect with ex-Smiths – specifically Morrissey – and enlist them in the ongoing concerns of local city politics. These stories also advocate heritage and preservationist agendas through their opportunistic attempts to utilise The Smiths' career milestones in the commemoration and celebration of memories of the band's outstanding achievements. For example, in August 2002 Nick Webster reported on how a team from Granada TV:

> has started on a quest for the holy grail of music – an interview with reclusive Smiths' frontman Stephen [sic] Morrissey. Morrissey is notorious for avoiding the media but David Nolan, producing the documentary *These Things Take Time: The Story of the Smiths*, hopes he will make a remarkable exception. 'Morrissey has not given an interview for 10 years . . .' said David, who also produced *I Swear I Was There*, which marked the 25th anniversary of the infamous Sex Pistols gig at the Lesser Free Trade Hall. He said: 'This year is the 20th anniversary of Morrissey meeting the guitarist Johnny Marr and the formation of the Smiths'.[60]

Furthermore, in a separate report Carmel Thomason reminded readers that 'Morrissey can run as far and as fast as he wants, but 20 years on from the Smiths, the elusive front man still has his fascinated pursuers ... Both a Granada film crew and a Manchester book publisher have been on his tail for months.'[61]

Prime opportunities to re-connect with Morrissey are provided by the superstar's infrequent returns to the city. In June 2003, Alexa Baracaia wrote that 'It's second only to the prospect of finding Elvis browsing the frozen peas in Moss Side's Asda – the sight of Manchester's prodigal son, Morrissey, returning home ... the unthinkable has happened – the former Smiths front-man has shunned the balmy climes of LA and is currently here in town ... First sighting of the lugubrious warbler was in Deansgate Waterstone's on Wednesday afternoon ... I'm told he also headed off to browse the racks at city centre store Vinyl Exchange before taking some light relief at a cake shop in Hale.'[62]

One reason such sightings are so important to *MEN* is because of concerns over the potential loss of memories of the city's glorious musical past. 'Manchester classics fall on deaf ears' runs the title of a story from February 2005:

> They are the songs that put Manchester on the musical map of the world. But many of the classic anthems by homegrown bands like the Stone Roses, Joy Division and the Smiths are lost on young music fans in the city, a new survey has found. Research by radio executives found large parts of the audience aged between 16 and 24 could not recognise some of the most celebrated songs from Manchester bands. One in five of those asked didn't know 'Fools' Gold' by the Stone Roses and 13 per cent didn't know 'Step On' by the Happy Mondays. A further 19 per cent failed to recognise Joy Division's 'Love Will Tear Us Apart' and 31 per cent admitted that they didn't know 'Panic' by the Smiths.[63]

On the evidence of the online reports posted at *MEN*, by the first decade of the twenty-first century the city of Manchester had developed an intense pride in its symbolic 'ownership' of Morrissey and The Smiths. 'Fans of music legend Morrissey have launched a bid to persuade the singer to return to his native Manchester', explained one report:

> The ex-Smiths front man went into self-imposed exile in Los Angeles in 1997 ... A petition has been launched by a group of fans who say the time is now ripe for Morrissey to return to his roots ... the petition organisers hope to show how much he is missed. Carl McDonald, 38 ... says the idea came to him after a discussion with other 'Moz' devotees on the internet. 'We were talking about the wonderful changes in recent times in Manchester and how the one thing missing from the city is its most famous and most talented son,' he said. 'We

discussed ways of tempting him home, such as promising to force all butchers' shops in a five mile radius of his home to close down' . . . According to Carl, 'No matter where he goes he will always be a Manchester man. There's no point in trying to hide from the truth. It is up to the people of Manchester to get online to sign the petition and let Morrissey know that we miss him and need him to make the city complete.'[64]

Finally, the new cultural configuration represented by *MEN*'s positive retrospective assessment of The Smiths is most vividly illustrated by the following extended quotation from May 2003:

> An army of Morrissey look-alikes were making their moody way to Manchester this week to try to be crowned the greatest ever Smiths fan. From the postman who plays The Smiths in his van all day every day to the fan who gave his baby son a Morrissey-style quiff, fanatic followers of the Manchester band have risen to the challenge from across the country . . . Organised by digital radio station BBC 6 Music, the competition is the highlight of a week of events celebrating the 20th anniversary of the band's first single release . . . As part of the celebrations rare archive material of Smiths sessions recorded by the BBC have been on air throughout the week, as well as specially recorded cover versions from the Buzzcocks and Manchester bands Doves and the Alpinestars. The finale in the search for the greatest ever fan will be held during a special reunion broadcast this afternoon (May 16) by Liz Kershaw from Salford Lads' Club. . . Guests will include former Smiths drummer Mike Joyce, Manchester music mogul Tony Wilson, former Oasis guitarist Paul 'Bonehead' Arthurs, and Peter Hook from New Order . . . What's certain is The Smiths inspired The Stone Roses and Oasis – they also helped establish Manchester as a musical city, their contribution in Britain has been enormous.[65]

Conclusion

Assessing the differing cultural narratives that structure the variable reception of The Smiths in Manchester during the two historical periods under consideration, one conclusion may be drawn. This is that the 'scene politics' characteristic of articles and reviews published in *CL* between 1983 and 1987 almost never include a preservationist dimension whereas the 'heritage politics' characteristic of the reports posted in *MEN* between 2000 and 2007 are inseparable from discussion of Manchester's music scene. In other words, by the first decade of the twenty-first century, local press coverage of The Smiths has conflated these two areas of concern. Scene politics has become an important aspect of heritage just as preservationist agendas now hinge upon memories of Manchester's celebrated musical culture of the 1980s.[66]

Is this conclusion in any way surprising? The observation that the 1980s *CL* reports did not include preservationist views might be seen as understandable if not inevitable (in that their 1980s articles were accounts of an immediate present). Conversely, the increasing prevalence of the heritage view in post-2000 *MEN* is perhaps informed by the changing view of rock culture in general in Manchester (and elsewhere) in which rock is increasingly seen as a culturally and economically valuable part of the 'cultural industries' (a view that was clearly not the case in the 1980s). However, to acknowledge the seemingly 'obvious' historical logic of this socially and culturally specific conjuncture in no way diminishes the interest and importance of the kind of primary research undertaken in this chapter. Simply put, there is a difference between believing that something is true and demonstrating it to be true through empirical investigation.

The small-scale research undertaken in this chapter has hopefully produced fresh knowledge concerning The Smiths and also led to the posing of new research questions. Either way, it has not attempted to produce a 'total history' of the band's cultural reception in Manchester. All I have been able to do in the preceding pages is present a snapshot of the city's response to The Smiths between 1983 and 2007 in two significant publications. Yet the contrast between these local responses in the 1980s and those that emerged in the 2000s tells a very interesting tale concerning the complex historical dynamics of synchronic and diachronic historical moments. It is this key methodological insight which may provide a basis for further analysis of The Smiths in historical context – especially in its ability to demonstrate that the making of meaning is an ongoing as well as a culturally contingent process.

In sum, there is a lot more scholarly work yet to be done. The repetition of noteworthy details concerning the native place identity of The Smiths is an important characteristic of discussion about them in all media – television, radio and the Internet as well as books, newspapers and magazines. The more analytical approach outlined in this chapter might usefully be extended to encompass the dynamic and variable reception of the band in other major urban conurbations like Los Angeles, London and Mexico City. Franco Moretti is correct. Placing a cultural phenomenon in its specific space – mapping it – is not the conclusion of geographical work: it is the beginning.

Notes

I would like to thank staff in the Manchester Archives and Local Studies section of Manchester Central Library for their kind assistance. I am also very grateful to Sean Campbell and Colin Coulter for their generous and constructive editorial input and support.

1 R. Carman, *Johnny Marr: The Smiths and the Art of Gun-Slinging* (Church Stretton: Independent Music Press, 2006), p. 119.

2 For example, Morrissey continues to draw upon his association with Manchester by projecting black and white footage of Salford author Shelagh Delaney in his 2009 concerts.

3 P. Gatenby, *Morrissey's Manchester: The Essential Smiths Tour* (Manchester: Empire Publications, 2002); P. Gatenby, *Panic on the Streets: The Smiths and Morrissey Location Guide* (London: Reynolds & Hearn, 2007). For a broader contextualisation of Manchester music and The Smiths' position within it, see, *inter alia*, S. Champion, *And God Created Manchester* (Manchester: Wordsmith, 1990); D. Haslam, *Manchester, England: The Story of the Pop Cult City* (London: Fourth Estate, 2000); C.P. Lee, *Shake, Rattle and Rain: Popular Music Making in Manchester 1955–1995* (Aylesbeare, Hardinge Simpole, 2002); *Q/Mojo Classic: Morrissey and the Story of Manchester* (March 2006); C.P. Lee, *When We Were Thin: Music, Madness and Manchester* (Manchester: Hotunpress, 2007); J. Robb, *The North Will Rise Again: Manchester City Music 1976–1996* (London: Aurumn Press, 2009).

4 To cite just one example of the band's own view of Manchester, see the 22 March 1985 BBC *Oxford Road Show* feature in which Morrissey walks around parts of the city, discussing his relationship to it.

5 For an explanation of how The Smiths and Morrissey may be analysed in terms of influential academic work on media 'star images', see J. Stringer, 'The Smiths: Repressed (But Remarkably Dressed)', *Popular Music*, Vol. 11, No. 1 (January 1992), pp. 15–26; and also N. Hubbs, 'Music of the "Fourth Gender": Morrissey and the Sexual Politics of Melodic Contour', in T. Foster, C. Siegel and E. Berry (eds), *Bodies of Writing, Bodies in Performance* (New York: New York University Press, 1996), pp. 266–96.

6 F. Moretti, *Atlas of the European Novel 1800–1900* (London: Verso, 1998), p. 7. Italics in original. Moretti's consideration of place may be viewed as a contribution to the literature on 'psychogeography' – defined by Guy Debord as the 'study of the specific effects of the geographical environment, consciously organised or not, on the emotions and behaviour of individuals'. (Quoted in M. Coverley, *Psychogeography*, Harpenden: Pocket Essentials, 2006, p. 10.) Although not pursued here, a psychogeographical reading of The Smiths is likely to yield interesting insights into the band's (and their fans') own mental mappings of Manchester. For example, the concept behind the promotional video for 'Stop Me If You Think You've Heard This One Before' – in which Morrissey leads a group of fan lookalikes on a bicycle tour of his own personal iconic city locales – is a prime example of psychogeographical thinking. Fan-tourists from around the world who subsequently visit destinations such as the Salford Lads Club (one of the locations depicted in the video) are thus merely proceeding as Morrissey himself proceeds.

7 B. Klinger, 'Film History Terminable and Interminable: Recovering the Past in Reception Studies', *Screen*, Vol. 38, No. 2 (Summer 1997), pp. 107–28.

8 Ibid., p. 111, 107. Klinger's quotation is from A. Easthope, *Literary Into Cultural Studies* (London: Routledge, 1991), p. 111. Italics in original.

9 Klinger, 'Film History Terminable and Interminable', p. 112.

10 The Smiths formed in May 1982, but the first issue of *City Life* (*CL*) was not published until December 1983.

11 F. Owen, 'Home Thoughts From Abroad', *Melody Maker*, 27 September 1986, pp. 15–16.

12 The relevant issues of *New Musical Express* are those dated 22 August 1992 and 1 December 2007 respectively. For a full discussion of their significance and impact upon Morrissey's solo career, see S. Goddard, *Mozipedia: The Encyclopedia of Morrissey and The Smiths* (London: Ebury Press, 2009), pp. 297–301.

13 S. Goddard, *The Smiths: Songs That Saved Your Life* (London: Reynolds & Hearn, 2nd edition, 2004), p. 34.

14 Interview with Morrissey, Piccadilly Radio, Manchester, 31 October 1986.

15 Quoted in A. Spinoza, 'Morrissey: The Man, The Myth, The Mouth', *CL* (no date available, but probably November 1986), p. 25. It is perhaps salutary to remember at this point that the word 'panic' itself carries gay subcultural undertones. (See 'political crackdown on gays. Syn: purge (pogrom against homosexuals)': B. Rogers, *The Queen's Vernacular: A Gay Lexicon* (San Francisco: Straight Arrow Books, 1972), p. 146.)

16 This reading is supported by other stories published in the Manchester press. For example, in his excellent study of the band Simon Goddard recalls the first meeting between Morrissey and his post-Smiths collaborator Vini Reilly by quoting the words of producer Stephen Street: 'I introduced Morrissey to Vini round my flat in Mortlake . . . Fortunately they got on well' (Goddard, *The Smiths*, pp. 301–2). However, Reilly himself went into a little more specific detail for *CL* magazine when discussing his own 'ice-breaking technique' with writer Phil Griffin: 'When I arrived at Wool Hall I took Morrissey out into a field and said, "What's all this bullshit about celibacy? I don't give a fuck if you're gay. It doesn't matter to me" . . . We got on great after that. Wrestling and food fights.' See P. Griffin, 'Stop Me If You Think You've Heard This One Before', *CL*, 6–12 November 2002, p. 20.

17 M. O'Brien, 'Music', *CL*, 15 December 1983–12 January 1984, p. 24. All quotations from magazine and newspaper reports cited in this chapter preserve original punctuation and spelling.

18 M. O'Brien, and N. Riley, '4 for 84', *CL*, 12–16 January 1984, pp. 18–20.

19 C. Paul, 'KC and his Silent Band', *CL*, 31 May–14 June 1985, pp. 16–7. Seventeen years later, Cummins published a book on the band: K. Cummins, *The Smiths and Beyond: Images* (London: Omnibus, 2002). Seven years after that, The Smiths again featured prominently in Cummins' 2009 career retrospective exhibition at Manchester's Richard Goodall Gallery; a photograph of Morrissey adorned the cover of its accompanying book. See K. Cummins, *Manchester: Looking For the Light Through the Pouring Rain* (London: Faber & Faber, 2009).

20 S. Sedge, 'The Word on The Smiths', *CL*, 25 April–9 May 1985, p. 28. M. Middles, *The Smiths* (London: Omnibus Press, 1985).

21 See 'Competition Time!', *CL*, 1–15 March 1985, p. 15; 'Competition Time', *CL*, 24 May–6th June 1985, p. 25; 'Competition Crazy!', *CL*, 27 February–12 March 1987, p. 57.

22 M. O'Brien, 'Pop Reviews', *CL*, 12–16 January 1984, p. 22.

23 R. Graham, 'Pop', *CL*, 22 March–5 April, p. 15.

24 Anonymous, 'Pop', *CL*, 20 June–4 July 1986, p. 27.

25 B. Dickinson, 'Albums', *CL*, 27 February–12 March 1987, p. 51.

26 See B. Dickinson, 'Records', *CL*, 9–23 September 1987, p. 54; S. Hewitt, 'Records', *CL*, 6–20 October 1987, p. 53.

27 A. McQueen, 'Records', *CL* (date not available, but probably 1988), p. 46. It is worth mentioning in passing that this love–hate scenario – wherein *CL* is both drawn to and repulsed by The Smiths – continues across the early years of Morrissey's solo career. For example, Mark E. Smith of The Fall contributes a fascinatingly coruscating assessment of the pros and cons of Morrissey's debut album, *Viva Hate* (1988). In the course of his review, Smith extols the 'fantastic and original' vocals on tracks such as 'Break Up The Family' while stomping all over 'the appalling "Late Night, Maudlin St" which confirms all north Mancunians deep superstitions about what life must be like in Wythenshawe'. See M.E. Smith, Untitled review of *Viva Hate*, *CL*, 25 March–8 April 1988, p. 47.

28 A. Spinoza, 'Shots From the Hip', *CL* 2–17 December 1992, p. 10; A. Spinoza, 'The Mystery That Is Morrissey', *CL*, 8–23 April 1992, pp. 14–15; L. Sterling, *Morrissey Shot* (London: Secker and Warburg, 1992); J. Rogan, *Morrissey and Marr: The Severed Alliance* (London: Omnibus, 1992).

29 See P. Griffin, 'Stop Me If You Think You've Heard This One Before', *CL*, 6–12 November 2002, pp. 19–21; Anonymous, 'There Is a Light That Never Goes Out: Morrissey Exclusive', *CL*, 2–9 July 2003, pp. 13–17; D. Lynsky and N. Mostyn, 'Return of the King: Morrissey Comes Home', *CL*, 19–25 May 2004, pp. 10–11.

30 The notion of a Manchester 'scene' was a prominent aspect of UK music press discourse from the period immediately before The Smiths' formation until the period immediately after their demise. In other words, the band's career coincided with a widely held view of Manchester as a music city. Relevant articles on this topic in the national music press from this period include P. Morley, 'They Mean it M-a-a-a-nchester', *New Musical Express*, 30 July 1977, pp. 6–7; B. Dickinson, 'The Scene . . . It's Not So Hum-Drum', *New Musical Express*, 28 September 1985, pp. 24–5; P. Morley, 'Oh, How We Laughed', *New Musical Express*, 15 February 1986, pp. 14–15; D. Haslam, 'It's Raining Pop!', *New Musical Express*, 6 September 1986, pp. 10–11, 13; M. Snow, 'From Manchester to Memphis', *New Musical Express*, 21 February 1987, p. 45; S. Wells, 'It's a Mad Madchester', *New Musical Express*, 2 December 1989, pp. 32–3.

31 R. King, 'Running Scared?', *Manchester Evening News*, 9 November 1984, p. 39.

32 Anonymous, 'Morrissey on Move', *Manchester Evening News*, 28 October 1992, p. 12.

33 P. Taylor, 'Morrissey Tour "Snub" for City', *Manchester Evening News*, 22 December 1994, p. 9.

34 A. Baracaia, 'Morrissey Prefers to Stay South', *Manchester Evening News* online (*MEN*), 8 August 2002.

35 Anonymous, 'Morrissey Live in Manchester: A Potted History', *MEN*, 20 December 2006.

36 Anonymous, 'Smiths Still Top of the Pops', *MEN*, 18 April, 2005. This particular exercise complements other lists compiled in a similar fashion such as the November 2002 report that 'Manchester music legends' Joy Division's 'Love Will Tear Us Apart' had won the *New Musical Express*'s 100 Greatest Singles of All Time poll; 'They were one of four Manchester bands in the Top 100 along with The Stone Roses, The Smiths and Oasis.' ('This Charming Man' reached number seven.) See B. Hanks, 'Joy Division Tops NME Singles Poll', *MEN*, 13 November 2002.

37 M. Rowlands, 'Skool's Out for Summer', *MEN*, 26 June 2002.

38 K. Bourke, 'Get the Manchester Passion', *MEN*, 14 April 2006.

39 H. Tither, 'Sounds of the City', *MEN*, 19 May 2004.

40 Anonymous, 'Museum Highlights Music Heritage', *MEN*, 24 September 2004.

41 S. Donohue, 'Forging The Smiths', *MEN*, 7 November 2002. The poll was inspired by the BBC's (then) recent national 'Great Britons' contest.

42 Anonymous, 'Morrissey Pays Tribute to Fans', *MEN*, 4 November 2002.

43 A. Salter, 'Morrissey is Greatest Mancunian', *MEN*, 2 November 2002.

44 Anonymous, 'Moz Named Most "Northern" Male', *MEN*, 26 October 2007.

45 N. Keeling, 'Show Time for Smiths' Snapper', *MEN*, 16 August 2006.

46 D. Frame, 'Old Album Photo is a New Icon', *MEN*, 23 July 2005.

47 M. Dillon, 'Your Chance to Recreate Smiths Famous Pose', *MEN*, 4 June 2004.

48 D. Linton, 'Morrissey Gives Lads' 20k', *MEN*, 28 December 2007.

49 N. Keeling, 'Lads' Club is a National Icon', *MEN*, 16 January 2007.

50 C. Jack, 'Bad Lads' Wreck Smiths Club', *MEN*, 5 July 2007.

51 C. Jack, 'Smiths Fans on their Bikes', *MEN*, 29 July 2007.

52 N. Dowling and N. Keeling, 'In the Path of The Smiths', *MEN*, 30 September 2007.

53 Anonymous, 'Battle to Save Music Mecca', *MEN*, 7 September 2001.

54 Readers' comments, *MEN*, 8 September 2001. Two years after UK Lottery chiefs had first suggested that it should be bulldozed, an announcement was made that the Salford Lads Club would become a listed building. Brian Ball, honorary secretary of the club, is quoted in one report as saying: 'Getting listed building status is a perfect way to mark our centenary. It is one of the few buildings of architectural importance still standing in Salford. It is a living piece of history. This will help us with our campaign to raise money to repair the roof. We will . . . set up a special room for our archive, and get information about the club stored on computers.

We hope to put on an exhibition called "Baden-Powell to Morrissey" at the Urbis museum'. See N. Keeling, 'Cult Hangout Rescued', *MEN*, 30 August 2003.

55 R. King, 'Stay Away From Us, Club Tells Pop Pests', *Manchester Evening News*, 2 August 1988.

56 N. Keeling, 'Duke Goes Pop on Lads Club Tour', *MEN*, 7 April 2004.

57 N. Keeling, 'Cameron in Smiths Tribute', *MEN*, 10 January 2008.

58 H. Tither, 'Morrissey for Walk of Fame?', *MEN*, 11 August 2004.

59 Anonymous, 'Morrissey – A Charming Name for our Airport', *MEN*, 15 April 2004.

60 N. Webster, 'Search for the Big Mouth Recluse', *MEN*, 10 August 2002.

61 C. Thomason, 'Missing Morrissey', *MEN*, 10 January 2002.

62 A. Baracaia, 'Morrissey Back in Manchester', *MEN*, 12 June 2003.

63 N. Dowling, 'Manchester Classics Fall on Deaf Ears', *MEN*, 7 February 2005.

64 K. Marrinan, 'Fans Want Morrissey to Come Home', *MEN*, 31 January 2005. For his part, Morrissey has reciprocated such attention by flattering a new generation of local fans. Before his 2006 Manchester shows, the singer is quoted as saying that the city 'does indelibly feel like home, it really does. I was born and raised there, and for better or worse, it made me. You can rally against the negative things that you don't particularly like about yourself and you can easily blame Manchester for that. The only thing I blame Manchester for was my terrible education, not because of anything else. I find it a fantastic place now. It's nothing like the city I grew up in. It's a lot cleaner and more cosmopolitan. The shops are fantastic and the people look great. The people there look so sexy. It is less of the Manchester that I used to know.' Quoted in K. Bourke, 'Morrissey Looks Forward to "Sexy" City', *MEN*, 14 April 2006.

65 H. Tither, 'Some Fans Are Bigger than Others', *MEN*, 16 May 2003.

66 This is also one of the specific cultural dynamics underpinning the narrative concerns of recent Manchester-themed films like *Velvet Goldmine* (1998) and *24 Hour Party People* (2001). In this context, it is worth drawing attention to the brief – but telling – moment at the end of the latter when God informs Tony Wilson (played by Steve Coogan) that he 'should probably have signed the Smiths'. This comment might be seen as indicative of the changing view of The Smiths – within Manchester's 'scene politics' – after 2000, as the band had obviously been located (in the 1980s and 1990s) outside of the Factory (and 'Madchester') scene that dominated the city. Johnny Marr had stated in the 1987 ITV *South Bank Show* television special on The Smiths that it was 'absolutely crucial' that the group did not sign to Factory Records– and the band's decision to sign to Rough Trade could obviously be seen as a gesture that they did not want to be viewed as part of a Manchester 'scene'.

13

'TAKE ME BACK TO DEAR OLD BLIGHTY':
ENGLISHNESS, POP AND THE SMITHS

Kari Kallioniemi

The most substantial and enduring controversy associated with The Smiths is perhaps the one that centres upon issues of national identity. It is often claimed by critics that the band – or, more specifically, their singer and frontman – offered a distinctly reactionary rendition of what it means to be English. These allegations of 'Little Englishness' would of course grow during Morrissey's solo career and they continue to dog him to this day.[1] In this chapter, I will seek to examine the particular forms of national identity that are imagined in the work of The Smiths. The distinctive sense of Englishness that pervades the lyrics, interviews and cover art of the band is located within a specific tradition of popular culture from which they have drawn and to which they have contributed a great deal. Once we begin to take a closer and more historical perspective on The Smiths, a rather more complex version of national identity begins to appear. The vision of Englishness that emerges from the collaboration of Morrissey and Marr is not simplistic, narrow and partisan as critics would allege, but rather complex, fluid and – as Sean Campbell shows in his chapter – ambivalent.

The Smiths and notions of pop-Englishness

According to Edensor, 'although there have been numerous studies of nation-alism, few have examined the more mundane aspects of national identity'.[2] The relationship between popular culture, national identity and everyday life is significant, not least because 'high cultural' notions of national identity in fact form only a small part of the cultural matrix framing the nation.[3] This line of analysis is also difficult because of the complicated relationships between popular culture/music and nationalism. Keith Negus identifies some 'tradi-tional' functions that inform the examination of pop and national identity, including the production of information for national legitimation (as in edu-cation or vocational training) and the collation of data for (national) music industries. He also goes beyond these conventional parameters, however, and proposes that such studies should provide a basis for forms of 'affective communication' and public knowledge which may be circulated beyond academia in transnational, national and sub-national forms of communication.[4] The problematic relationship between pop music and national identity is disclosed when it is addressed in terms of this 'affective communication', meaning that it can be understood both by 'feeling' and 'knowing' music and sharing this experience in terms of language and culture.

The sentiments articulated in the work of The Smiths were often held to express a quintessential Englishness at a time of fundamental cultural change. This debate about shifting notions of what it means to be English was also conducted in the British media, and by analysing this discussion we can begin to understand different notions of pop-Englishness. These could include questions concerning the context of English identity, an idea of imaginary Englishness, issues of geography, the connection to Americanisation, alternative discourses to those defining the Anglo-American rock era and the British music industry.

It could be argued that English pop identity is a construction that intersects with issues of class, gender and geography, constantly asserting itself against the 'status quo' which supposedly fails to register social conditions and social change as flexibly as pop culture. The Smiths always questioned this 'status quo', especially by challenging axiomatic notions of class and Englishness and the gender roles conventionally associated with English pop music. In the process, the nation and national identity are seen as particular, but created by an historical tension between tradition and modernity which defines the history of nationalism as a whole. This tension reflects different 'English dreams' and the sense of a possible community, both in society and in different cultural formations.[5] The endeavour to create an alternative 'English dream' and the yearning for a new community in the dispiriting era of Thatcherism were very much at the core of the The Smiths' very distinctive disposition towards the world.

The relationship between 'real' and 'imaginary' identities is also articulated through rock geography. The mythologies often spun through popular music invariably create 'imaginary geographies' in which real places are impregnated with meanings and re-imagined through pop culture. Rock geographies provide various conceptualising strategies. Manchester, for example, becomes a site of cultural authenticity and can be promoted and marketed on that basis. That musically based identity is a synthesis of both real and imaginary components. The Smiths' ambivalent relationship with Manchester and the north also finds its expression in the construction of a version of rock authenticity that centres on the familiar English north–south divide, in which the 'mythical' north is often seen as a more authentic birthplace of 'real' pop music than the south.[6]

English attitudes towards America and Europe have also formed part of this 'imagining', influenced by both musical and cultural interactions, and sometimes manifested as anti-Americanism. The era of Anglo-American rock created a vigorous new mythology incorporating distinctive notions of the 'national' in British popular culture, and reshaping sentiments towards America.[7] Anglo-American rock music has since the 1980s at least competed with other musical hybrids comprising various multicultural and European elements. This rivalry has often been manifested in competing pop identities, one based roughly on an Anglo-American model and another on European influences and multicultural forms of new English pop.[8] In the 1980s and 1990s, the latter was manifested in, for example, instrumental and experimental forms of dance styles in contrast to Anglo-American rock with its 'Britpop' narratives. Both competing identities and anti-Americanism, which was often the expression of a national pride latent in various 'Britpop' phenomenona since the 'Swinging London' era, were in some way reactions to the collapse of the Anglo-American rock era in the 1980s. It could be argued that The Smiths were the last significant expression of this era, and therefore offered dramatic expression of that transitional moment in their music.

This collapse has also been felt dramatically in the British music industry. The peculiarities and distinctiveness of the latter have centred historically upon its maverick character and its role as 'a talent pool' or 'a test market'.[9] Many commentators, including Keith Negus, have noted that this is one reason why opposition to the hegemony of the industry has been prominent in the British music press.[10] It is widely recognised that British pop culture used to be dominated by an art school sensibility in which creativity, commentary and commerce became indistinguishable,[11] but this set of connections has been slowly dissolving since the 1980s. It is fair to say that the once oppositional posture of the British music press, which was visible in support of The Smiths' independent attitude, has now largely evaporated. As the spinning of the pop-process reached extraordinary levels of hype and marketing-hysteria in the 1980s,[12] one reason for The Smiths' reaction against it was their vision of Englishness which looked past and beyond this process.

The tradition of pop-Englishness before The Smiths

This particular vision of Englishness in popular music – 'pop-Englishness' – has always been about the employment of the past and the adoption of playfulness, where the boundaries of the past and present, the real and imaginary, 'high' and 'low' have been tested and stretched by popular musicians. Before the rock'n'roll era, forms such as music hall, traditional folk music and the romanticism of the likes of Edward Elgar and Ralph Vaughan Williams evoked emblems of national identity and nostalgia, especially during moments of crisis. Among those most notable for combining popular music and Englishness in the early twentieth century was the actor, singer–songwriter and playwright Noel Coward. His particular combination of notions of Englishness, entailing a persona wedding upper-class dandyism to the role of 'show-business man-of-letters', was seen to exemplify both radical and reactionary versions of pop-Englishness. The cultural function of Coward's homosexuality has especially been seen in both a positive and negative light. According to Julie Burchill, he 'came to epitomise the accept-able face of homosexuality, "creative", rich, cosying up to royalty'.[13] However, Coward's constructed image provided materials for the prototype of the male English pop star, foregrounding flamboyance, sexual identity and class. Thus, Coward became posthumously celebrated as the grandfather of Britpop in his centenary year of 1999, with a tribute album featuring such prominent figures within British popular music as Bryan Ferry, Neil Tennant, Neil Hannon and Brett Anderson, all of them renowned for their dandyist personae.[14]

A further figure who can be considered relevant to the discussion here is Colin MacInnes, an English writer from an upper-class background who stood ambivalently between tradition and modernity. In the late 1950s, MacInnes felt estranged from his Englishness because of his upper-class origins and homosexuality and wanted to escape to a 'new England', popu-lated by supposedly classless new stylish teenagers and exotic immigrants.[15] The English capital was the place to be for him, as fetishised in his trilogy of novels (*Absolute Beginners, City of Spades, Mr Love and Justice*) that foreshad-owed the technicolour extravaganza of the Swinging London of the 1960s. Ray Davies of The Kinks was one of the first modern English pop singer–songwriters to react bitterly against the Sunday supplement pop-Englishness of Swinging London and its 'English-garden-psychedelia'. In his songs, Davies reflected on the wider issues of Englishness, creating tools for future songwriters to express their ideas about England.

Among the objectives of punk rock was to avoid the celebration of Englishness in a major way. Punk reacted aggressively against the privileged positions and institutions of 'old England' as the 1960s counter-culture had done before it, and rejected the nostalgia often prevalent in pop-Englishness. However, it also celebrated a problematic notion of Englishness in the form of frivolous revival, linked to the re-emergence of the 1960s beat, called the Thames-beat,[16] and in the name of new-wave groups like 'Spitfire Boys'.[17] The main effect though of punk rock was to open the way for new strategies for dealing with pop Englishness more eloquently, and to establish fresh nuances in the post-punk and new-wave circles of the 1980s. Not only did a new kind of female pop star emerge, embodying different aspects of Englishness (most notably Kate Bush), but a whole series of 'quintessentially' English bands and artists came to prominence in the 1980s who broadened the concept of

pop-Englishness, including Ian Dury, Paul Weller, Madness, Terry Hall, Pet
Shop Boys and, of course, The Smiths.

'Luddite Labour rock' and The Smiths' imaginary England

A degree of outsiderism and a revolt against the idea of England as a 'swinging consumerist heaven' were also important in The Smiths' creation of their
pop-Englishness and the sonic and lyrical vitriol that defined their appraisal
of the state of the nation. In some quarters, the early 1980s were seen as the
continuation of the Swinging London period. The infatuation of the former
with synthetic and glamorous pop prompted the celebration of the era as a
new boomtime for British pop, mainly because of the so-called 'Second British
Invasion of America'.[18] This was often attacked by those sections of the music
press sympathetic to indie pop, and still provoked strong reactions a decade
and a half later, as revealed in this withering reflection from a music journalist
in 1997: 'The Durans, the Spands and the Kajabloodygoogs dominated the dol-
drums and hope-sapping Thatcherism proliferated. It was hardly a golden age
for the nation's youth. Premature middle-age was considered chic, the rolled-
up suit sleeve and flaunted-Filofax de rigueur, and Phil Collins the epitome of
cool'.[19] Both the Swinging London era and the early 1980s were characterised
by rapid social change, and Thatcher's second term in office was marked by
spiralling disaffection and polarisation. The divisions that had come to beset
the nation and the supposed advent of a new golden era of British pop were
both strongly debated in the 'traditional' rock press such as the *New Musical
Express* (*NME*). The void between those who embraced the second British
Invasion and those who wanted to stay close to what was happening in 'Old
Blighty' was reflected particularly keenly in coverage of The Smiths. Thus, the
band was an ideal subject for critical rock journalism, and the dialogue that
developed between The Smiths, fans and journalists has continued into the
internet era.

The Smiths' legacy inspired journalists to evaluate the group specifically
in terms of the cultural and historical significance of the band's sense of
Englishness. An anonymous commentator articulated an idea of 1980s British
pop in the 1993 Christmas issue of *Melody Maker*. In the article entitled
'P.O.P.R.I.P.', the contributor wondered what happened in 1980s British pop
and how it was revived in many ways during 1993.[20] The writer speculated that
a line from Adam Ant and Human League to Frankie Goes to Hollywood was
just one version of the previous decade, and suggested that that year's reissue
on CD of The Smiths' back catalogue served to inform us about:

'the different eighties' replacing the (ironic!) luxury of ABC and Co, and heralding 'a return to rock' after the pop glory days of 1981/2. Mere weeks separated

the release of The Smiths' *Hand in Glove* and Frankie Goes to Hollywood's *Relax* in 1983 but, in terms of concept and aesthetic, they were worlds apart. So, there's probably a theory to be expounded about 'Lavish Tory pop' and 'Luddite Labour rock' . . . But it is the fiercely traditional noise of the Smiths that has survived into the Nineties. Today, their superannuated bass/guitar/drums attack is positively de rigueur, while FGTH's hi-tech bombast seems almost passé.[21]

Although The Smiths created their whole milieu as an antithesis to the lavishness of the early 1980s, the label 'Luddite Labour rock' alludes more to the direction of The Smiths' Englishness than to overtly political eighties artists like Billy Bragg.[22] The Smiths were explicitly anti-Thatcher, but their political opinions stretched to a range of other issues, including commentary on the sexist hypocrisy of the media, the mistreatment of animals and the fear of George Orwell's mechanical non-human world of *1984*. This fear of an Orwellian dystopia partly explains the luddism of The Smiths' 'Little Englishness'. But certain songs (especially tracks from *The Queen Is Dead* such as 'Cemetry Gates', 'Vicar In A Tutu' and 'Frankly Mr Shankly') as well as the 'Englishness paraphernelia' and figures on their record covers also disclose their distinctly English sense of humour[23] and 'luddite' infatuation with a pre-Beatles 'anti-American' England. Martin Cloonan describes this position in the case of Billy Bragg – who toured with The Smiths and would collaborate with Johnny Marr on numerous occasions – as 'hip big Englishness': 'Its roots are in the folk left populist troubadour tradition recalling the 1950s British Communist party advocating the fullest development of culture based on national traditions and peculiarities further claiming that Communists were both nationalists and internationalists'.[24]

The Smiths' use of tradition was partly a 'luddite' infatuation with a particular moment in English culture, specifically that of the late 1950s and early 1960s. This period focused attention on industrial conurbations like Manchester and imbued them with a certain glamour. This was, according to Jon Savage, the moment caught by Billy Liar – 'Billy drifts through a cityscape in transition, being by 1962 swept away by American consumer capitalism'.[25] Thus, this particular moment and place, connected to ambivalence regarding the relationship with US pop culture, forms the basis of The Smiths' luddism or 'hip big Englishness'. This English imaginary centred on 'northern-ness', echoed in the group's infatuation with films depicting that particular time and place, sixties female pop-stars like Cilla Black and tough northern women like Pools[26] winner Viv Nicholson.

Musical and other forms of creativity in Manchester and other parts of northern England have often given rise to a certain sense of rock-geography, in which the English north is seen as an equivalent to the southern states of the USA. In terms of authenticity, northernness has been viewed as 'English blackness', in the same way as the American south and its black music became the mark of authenticity in rock mythology.[27] Mark Simpson writes how the young Steven Patrick Morrissey was a fan of Motown, 'soulful' black music from the 1960s USA, and how many northern female working-class singers sang songs that had been originally written for American artists whose blackness was considered uncommercial in Britain. Cilla Black, in particular, represented this kind of 'northern lassie' whose 'soul-sisters' were to be found in the female stars of television's northern soap opera *Coronation Street*.[28] In this imaginary England, a special place was created for often neglected women in the arts and showbiz, women who were tough, fragile and eccentric like writer Shelagh Delaney, who now also adorned The Smiths' record sleeves.

Johnny Marr has also often spoken of his childhood influences, which came predominantly from America.[29] US girl groups of the 1960s, especially the Shangri-Las, Leiber and Stoller, and The Stooges inspired him as well as Jamaican ska. Along with Morrissey's American preoccupations (New York Dolls, Elvis Presley, James Dean and his co-star Richard Davalos in Elia Kazan's film *East of Eden*), they cast a shadow over the supposedly quintessentially English world of The Smiths. The sense of English authenticity and 'hip big Englishness' was also qualified by The Smiths' European choices for their album cover images (French new-wave and neorealist-style photos from the 1960s, French film stars Alain Delon and Jean Marais) and by Morrissey's infatuation with freakish star oddities like American rock star Jobriath and German opera-tenor Klaus Nomi, who turned into a disco singer and became the darling of the new-wave rock scene in the 1980s. These creations of queer sexuality and objects of playfulness were appropriate to the would-be dandy's tastes, but in The Smiths' mythology an imaginary England was not only orchestrated through marginal artistic influences, but also through visual props and accessories referring to alternative politics (*Meat Is Murder* badges), the pre-Beatles era (National Health Service spectacles, quiffs) and the marginalised (hearing-aid).[30] More straightforward references to the imaginary England could be found by presenting female and male stars from the English past on T-shirts, record sleeves and videos.

A lot of this chiaroscuro visual imagery[31] certainly refers to the childhood favourites of Morrissey, like Richard Bradford from the 1967 British spy TV series *Man in a Suitcase* and the stars of *Coronation Street*, and consequently it has been easily targeted as a celebration of nostalgia for a vanished English society and its sentimental populist nationalism. The historian Raphael Samuel has talked of the utopian element in contemporary culture, in which our lives have been simulated by an ever-expanding historical culture. He calls this utopian space 'a theatre of memory'. There are different historical meanings for the term, but for Samuel it means that we are living at the end of a romantic concept that during the nineteenth and twentieth centuries focused on the individual and family circle, and often found expression through landscapes of the mind, memory places and the childhood home.[32] England has its own particular historical culture articulated in 'a theatre of memory'. It is endorsed by both conservative and radical romantic traditions (Arts and Crafts, Mass Observation, the English middle-class documentary tradition and its aestheticisation of working-class life) and echoed in mass-culture debates which have located an idealised golden age in the past, thus anathematising the present, so that contemporary romantic conceptions emphasise what has been lost rather than how this past is recreated in the present.[33]

It might be said that The Smiths created their own 'theatre of memory', one that expressed a utopian desire for a more simple national life, casting a shadow over the present. For Simon Reynolds, this was expressive of the broader anti-modern revolt in 1980s pop. He argues that the 1960s were the main reference point: 'And where all these ideas (in the indie pop of the 80s) converge is in two (very much linked) periods – childhood and the Sixties. The Sixties are like pop's childhood, when the idea of youth was still young.'[34]

Oh, Manchester

An important element, therefore, of The Smiths' Englishness was its link to a childhood spent in Manchester in the 1960s and the 1970s. The theme of rootlessness, related to Morrissey and Marr's Irish background, connected The Smiths to the 'romantic outsiderism' of pop-Englishness practised since the days of Oscar Wilde and Noel Coward. But, according to Julian Stringer, this romanticism emphasises that 'The Smiths' Englishness is given posi-tive value as a restorer of English identity'.[35] This becomes clearer especially in Morrissey's remarks on the sadness of modern English society in which 'people do actually mourn the loss of its identity more than they'll admit'.[36] The yearning for 'an imaginary place', situated geographically in Manchester and linked to moments of childhood, also echoed a particular history of rock'n'roll. According to Reynolds, The Smiths were the first major group with an aesthetic based on the conviction that rock'n'roll's best years were (in the) past: 'These feelings – homesickness for a place you couldn't wait to leave (Manchester), nostalgia for a time that was never any good in the first place (adolescence) – were why the music of The Smiths refracted the quandaries of the eighties like no other.'[37]

These feelings, often expressed in The Smiths' lyrics (most notably perhaps in the track 'Suffer Little Children'), also encapsulated their ambivalent feelings towards Manchester. In an intimate interview in 1986, Morrissey talked about his memories of Whalley Range, the bombed and subsequently rebuilt Arndale Centre, Piccadilly all-night bus station and other 'notorious' landmarks of the city. In his account of escaping the Perry Boys, the violent subculture of the deprived Collyhurst district, he painted a mythical vision of the city recalling much of its 1970s-bound post-industrial gloominess: 'If the Perrys didn't get you, then the beer monsters were waiting around the corner. I still remember studying the football results to see if City or United had lost, in order to judge the level of violence to be expected in the city centre that night ... In one way I despise Manchester and yet I still have a deep affection for the place'.[38] This fascinated revulsion regarding Manchester emerged from the fact that life for the would-be bohemian there was always hard. Pre-punk, those seeking sanctuary from the patrolling behemoths had little alternative but to take refuge in the gay clubs, like Dickens, or the gay pubs, like the Rembrandt or the Union: 'It was dangerous and, with the increased media visibility of punk, the violence got worse. You see, punks were not only faggots, they were uppity faggots as well. They made music, they wrote poetry, and, of course, they dressed up. It was as if they were protesting against the limits of prole Northern experience. The Manchester scene wasn't a product of Manchester but a triumph over it'.[39]

But this grimness and austerity of the north was also romanticised in the media as being part of The Smiths' summoning of a vanished England. As an anonymous contributor to the *Melody Maker* expressed it: 'In the Smiths, we hear the sound of an older, more graceful England: the sound of wooden clogs on northern cobblestones, the flap of washing on the clothes line, the creaking of cemetery gates, the digging of shallow graves on bleak Lancashire moors'.[40] Thus, The Smiths seemed to cherish the austerity and despondency of a disappearing north, but this parochialism always hides a certain humour and ambivalence towards Manchester. This equivocation also emerges in Morrissey's recollections of his rough childhood in Manchester and because of it perhaps, his longing for 'English gentleness' and the reinvention of himself as a humorous English gent.

The 'greatest living Englishman'?

The Smiths valorised different layers of English gentleness, respectability and politeness in their music and lyrics, but also looked beyond these positive features towards the darker side of English identity, like domestic violence in 'Barbarism Begins At Home' and institutionalised sadism in 'The Headmaster Ritual'. The different aspects of English identity were an endless source of inspiration for Morrissey in his own star-identity work. George Orwell argued in his essays that the key to English identity and its supposed gentleness is not ethnicity or nation but rather 'character'.[41] The cultural historian Jeffrey Richards sees these supposed national characteristics as expressed through fictional forms and exemplified in national cinema, such

as epic films about English history, the Ealing comedies of the 1950s and
the down-to-earth northern movies of Gracie Fields and George Formby.[42]
English pop music is full of stars, from Noel Coward and Bryan Ferry to
Neil Hannon and Neil Tennant, who, by flaunting Englishness, either hid
their ethnic or geographical background, or made up their star-character by
playing with English, often upper-class, stereotypes. This reconstructed dandyism explains some paradoxes of Morrissey. His image as the combination
of a certain refined, genteel version of Englishness associated with upper-
class diction but also working-class, northern values may be seen as the very
English creation of a star-image.

Stringer argues that part of Morrissey's appeal lay in the creation of this
cultivated English gentleman: 'Being every inch the typically English "gent"
he is perfectly representative of that type's loathing for cant and hypocrisy,
and of its fragile, quasi-gay sexuality . . . Morrissey's star-image signifies the
snobby, traditional, eccentric, English gent . . . Journalists remark upon his
uppercrust voice. His method is to use very clipped, precise enunciation'.[43]
For Michael Bracewell, this is a role in the canon of the 'great outsiders of
England': 'It would be ironic that Wilde and Morrissey, both Anglo-Irishmen,
would be England's underground analysts at either end of the century; the
English equivalents, perhaps, of Whitman and Warhol in America. It would
be doubly ironic that they would find themselves first fêted and then pilloried
for going too far by the respective generations who had found wit, solidarity
or guidance in their philosophies.'[44]

This outsider role brings to mind a range of other English visionaries.
These people have often been foreigners who have come to England practising 'Anglomania' and because of this have defined Englishness better than the
English themselves – in literature, cinema and pop music.[45] The paradox of
this visionary eccentricity is that it could spring from the 'heart of England',
as in Edith Sitwell's famous book *English Eccentrics* (1933), or from outsiderism, as in Morrissey, the 'greatest living Englishman', being the son of Irish
immigrants who denigrates the institutions and personalities that exemplify
traditional versions of English upper-class authority. But there is a tragic
element in this bohemian–dandyist pantomime. According to Reynolds,
Morrissey is a character who is lopsided, contrary, incomplete, the sum of
wounds and bigotries. Morrissey is 'half a person', his very being constituted
around lack and maladjustment. This is the vantage point from which he
launched his impossible demands on life, his denial of the reality principle:
'This is why Morrissey can't develop as an artist. How could he grow when his
very being is constructed around the petulant refusal – "I won't grow up"? . . .
The tragedy of The Smiths is that Morrissey could only become the victim of
the perfection of his style. Like Jagger, like Rotten, he is condemned to live out
its pantomime forever.'[46]

The Smiths and pop-Englishness since the 1980s

This tragedy became more obvious as The Smiths split and the late 1980s gave rise to the Second Summer of Love that in turn gave way to the Madchester boom of the early 1990s and the Britpop moment of the mid-1990s. At the same time, the Anglo-American rock era and its literary forms of English pop were increasingly challenged by dance and multicultural forms of pop music. Morrissey's antipathy towards dance music – and, at times, seemingly towards multiculturalism more generally – generated considerable controversy both during and particularly after The Smiths' career. Although the band's infatuation with kitchen-sink films suggested their sympathies towards immigrants, portrayed as outsiders in these movies,[47] the issue of race was either avoided or handled indelicately during their career. In September 1986, Morrissey offered one of the more controversial expressions of his many musical prejudices: 'Reggae to me is the most racist music in the entire world. It's an absolute glorification of black supremacy.'[48] This antipathy appeared to echo his adolescent experiences of black music: 'Nineteen seventy-five was the worst year in social history. I blame *Young Americans* (by David Bowie) entirely. I hated that period – Disco Tex and the Sex-O-Lettes, Limmy and Family Cooking. So when punk came along, I breathed a sigh of relief. I met people. I'd never done that before.'[49] He also jokingly spoke of his black pop conspiracy theories in the aforementioned interview, and his vitriolic and even childish diatribes against dance culture continued during his solo career, as in these comments from 1991:

> I could never begin to explain to you the utter loathing I feel for, as you say, dance music. I think dance music has destroyed everything. It certainly killed the pop star. It is bought by audiences who do not care about the personalities involved in music making. Dance records are generally made by people who are not sensitive, who don't care about the history of music. And to me that's the most important element. They don't care about the past.[50]

These rants and related anti-dance comments brought Morrissey a great deal of media attention but also gradually began to work against him. Nor did his tendency to romanticise skinhead culture,[51] while generally ignoring the early skinhead movement's embrace of black culture and music, win him a lot of new friends. Morrissey's appearance in August 1992 at London's Finsbury Park 'Madstock' concert supporting Madness in which he took to the stage draped in a Union Jack,[52] made his already precarious position in relation to issues of race and racism even more so. The audience included a substantial element of demonstrative skinheads,[53] and by 'waving the flag' Morrissey found himself being associated with far-right politics. The media turned against him, and the 1990s debate about Englishness in pop music was in

part initiated by the backlash against Morrissey. His erstwhile champions[54] at
the *NME* jumped on the bandwagon by writing a five-page feature about the
concert and condemning Morrissey as a racist,[55] casting a long shadow over
his whole career and pushing him into commercial and media marginality
during the Britpop years. The year after the incident, *Select* magazine posthumously presented a pop-geographical map of The Smiths' Blighty. The feature
inevitably reflected the parochial world-view of the group and its singer by
identifying the various geographical references that appear in Morrissey's
lyrics. Only four places outside of England make an appearance in this substantial body of work: Belgium, Asia, Dublin and Luxembourg.[56]

During the 1980s, it seemed that The Smiths presented some hard 'social-
realist' truths about aspects of England. In the 1990s, in contrast, the band
appeared an unwelcome and even embarrassing presence in a British pop
dominated by dance music and in the full throes of its 'Cool Britannia' phase.
The Smiths' tendency both to romanticise Englishness and to tell some
unpleasant truths about it may have resonated with the more xenophobic
and parochial versions of Englishness which could be easily melded with
the anti-American and anti-European sentiments prevalent before the era
of New Labour. The Smiths' opposition to the shallow celebratory aspects of
pop-culture and the symbolic global pop-community, exemplified by MTV,
Madonna and Live Aid, served to ensure that they were out of step with
the vacant neo-nationalist platitudes that defined the Blairite era of Cool
Britannia. Because The Smiths articulated an uncompromising and discomfit-
ing response to the traumas visited on working-class northern communities,
they were denied a place in the Britpop pantheon. The 1960s-style confidence
and swagger of pop, which helped to establish a more positive identity for
Manchester in the form of the Madchester scene and subsequently to promote
Blairism and Britpop, was essentially alien to many within the orbit of The
Smiths because of its shallow and exploitative elements. Thus, The Smiths'
creation of an alternative national self-image to the supposed 'greatness' of the
British 1960s mirrored a sentiment made famous in 1996 by the writer Hanif
Kureishi on the eve of the New Labour era: 'We're still waiting for the 60s to
begin.'[57]

Englishness in pop has taken several directions since The Smiths. In the
late 1990s, Neil Hannon of the Divine Comedy recreated the pop-dandy as
a melancholy ladies' man, who fitted as a cartoon character into the jubilant
atmosphere of Britpop.[58] Black Box Recorder and its frontman Luke Haines
have acerbicly observed, in the tradition of Ray Davies, the mundane detail
of everyday English life. The celebration of 'mythical Albion' has continued
in the form of The Libertines and their former frontman Pete Doherty, who
peppered his lyrics with references to 'peculiarly (and peculiar) English
expressions', spoke of English characters like writer Peter Ackroyd, 1960s

comedy writers Galton and Simpson, and cockney pop-duo Chas'n'Dave,[59] and lodged in the tabloids as a retro-bohemian tailor-made for contemporary celebrity culture. The singer–songwriter Billy Bragg reacted to the terror attacks on London of 7 July 2005 by writing a contemplative book about his sense of belonging called *The Progressive Patriot*,[60] in which he tried to analyse Englishness by combining his own musical memoir with his family history.

This postscript illustrates how intriguing and inspiring the combination of pop and Englishness remains, even in a world being constantly reshaped by globalisation and the 'war on terror'. The continuing interest in The Smiths' imaginary England was vindicated when, in 2002, the *NME* voted them the most important British group of all time.[61] This was not only the result of the retroist romanticisation of 'indie-rock', but reflected that The Smiths still cast an uncompromising shadow over the idea that pop music is only a consumerist choice. By creating their pop-Englishness, The Smiths reconstructed the radical idea of pop's past, and saved it from the sentimentalisation and non-politicised retroism of the pop heritage culture industries. The profound legacy of The Smiths sheds light on the wider issues of pop and national identity. The notions of pop-Englishness created by and through the band provide a useful range of interrelated contexts which suggest that national identity is dynamic, contested, multiple and fluid, thereby challenging the monolithic idea of cultural identification made in the image of the nation. In their vision, England remains elusive and open to an imaginative reconstruction that offers the possibility of a more positive sense of national belonging. The dynamics of this endless journey were of course made explicit by The Smiths at the very outset of their career in the track 'Still Ill', in which Morrissey decrees that 'England is mine / And it owes me a living', an announcement he would instantly obfuscate with an elusive caveat: 'ask me why and I'll spit in your eye'.

Notes

1 The most recent controversy was sparked in 2007 by an interview with the *NME* in which Morrissey appeared to express concern about the impact of recent immigration upon English national culture. The details of the interview have been disputed by Morrissey, who has initiated legal proceedings against the magazine. See Anonymous, 'Has the World Changed or Has He Changed?', *NME*, 1 December 2007, pp. 11–14.

2 T. Edensor, *National Identity, Popular Culture and Everyday Life* (Oxford: Berg, 2002), p. vi.

3 Ibid., vi.

4 K. Negus, *Producing Pop: Culture and Conflict in the Popular Music Industry* (London: Blackwell, 1992), pp. 219–23.

5 See further on imagined communities, B. Anderson, *Imagined Communities: Reflections on the Origin and Spread of Nationalism* (London: Verso, revised edition, 1994). See further on the 'English dream' and pop music in M. Bracewell, *England is Mine: Pop Life in Albion from Wilde to Goldie* (London: HarperCollins, 1997).

6 For an account of how popular music culture is connected with the life, image and identity of a city, see S. Cohen, *Decline, Renewal and the City in Popular Music Culture: Beyond the Beatles* (Aldershot: Ashgate, 2007); K. Milestone, 'Regional Variations: Northernness and New Urban Economies of Hedonism', in J. O'Connor and D. Wynne (eds), *From the Margins to the Centre: Cultural Production and Consumption in the Post-Industrial City* (Aldershot: Ashgate, 1996), pp. 91–116. Other good examples of rock-geography are rock-tourism books. See P. Gatenby, *Morrissey's Manchester: The Essential Smiths Tour* (Manchester: Empire Publications, 2002).

7 S. Frith, 'Anglo-America and its Discontents', *Cultural Studies*, Vol. 5, No. 3 (1991), pp. 260–6; S. Frith, 'Euro Pop', *Cultural Studies*, Vol. 3, No. 2 (1989), pp. 166–72.

8 M. Cloonan, 'State of the Nation: "Englishness", Pop and Politics in the Mid-1990's', *Popular Music and Society*, Vol. 21, No. 2 (1997), pp. 47–70.

9 Frith, 'Anglo-America and its Discontents', p. 264.

10 Negus, *Producing Pop*, pp. 118–23.

11 See further S. Frith and H. Horne, *Art into Pop* (London: Routledge, 1987).

12 See further J.J. Beadle, *Will Pop Eat Itself? Pop Music in the Soundbite Era* (London: Faber & Faber, 1993).

13 J. Burchill, 'Sad About the Boy', *Guardian*, 'Weekend' section, 18 April 1998, p. 7.

14 S. Dalton, 'Carry On Camping', *NME*, 18 April 1998, pp. 36–8. See also P. Hoare, 'He's called Noel and he invented Britpop. But he wouldn't have been seen dead in Manchester', *Observer*, 'Review' section, 5 April 1998, p. 5.

15 T. Gould, *Inside Outsider: The Life and Times of Colin MacInnes* (London: Penguin, 1986).

16 K. Davis, 'Welcome to the Fabulous World of Thamesbeat', *NME*, 25 January 1978, pp. 26–7.

17 D. Laing, *One Chord Wonders: Power and Meaning in Punk Rock* (Milton Keynes: Open University Press, 1985), pp. 47–8.

18 N. Schaffner, *The British Invasion: From the First Wave to the New Wave* (New York: McGraw-Hill, 1983).

19 I. Fortnam, 'Music for the Wilted Generation', *Vox* (June 1997), p. 48.

20 This revival concentrated on re-issues of the The Smiths' albums and on remixes of Frankie Goes to Hollywood's hits.

21 Anonymous, 'P.O.P.R.I.P', *Melody Maker*, 25 December 1993/1 January 1994, p. 50.

22 The Smiths once played a concert for Red Wedge, a Labour-sponsored political organisation which tried to woo young voters into supporting the Prime Ministerial candidate Neil Kinnock. Morrissey explained in June 1986 that the group was not 'terribly impassioned by the gesture'. See further on The Smiths' political opinions

in J. Robertson, *Morrissey in His Own Words* (London: Omnibus Press, 1988), pp. 37–41.

23 See 'I Think Moz Had Drunk a Few Shandies', *NME*, 10 June 2006, pp. 30–1; Z. Williams, 'The Light that Never Goes Out', *Guardian*, 'Weekend' magazine, 23 February 2002.

24 Cloonan, 'State of the Nation', p. 55.

25 J. Savage, 'Morrissey: The Escape Artist', in *Time Travel. From the Sex Pistols to Nirvana: Pop, Media and Sexuality, 1977–96* (London: Chatto and Windus, 1996), p. 262.

26 The Pools were in effect a predecessor of the national lotteries that are common-place today and entailed contestants predicting the outcome of (association) foot-ball games.

27 See further on rock authenticity and the north, Cohen, *Decline, Renewal and the City in Popular Music Culture* and R. Pattison, *The Triumph of Vulgarity: Rock Music in the Mirror of Romanticism* (Oxford and New York: Oxford University Press, 1987).

28 M. Simpson, *Saint Morrissey* (London: SAF Publishers, 2004), pp. 52–3.

29 See, for example, W. Hodgkinson, 'Soundtrack of my Life: Johnny Marr', *Observer Music Monthly*, 22 April 2007.

30 Williams, 'The Light that Never Goes Out'.

31 See further on The Smiths' visual imagery in J. Slee, *Peepholism: Into the Art of Morrissey* (London: Sidgwick & Jackson, 1994).

32 R. Samuel, *Theatres of Memory. Vol. 1: Past and Present in Contemporary Culture* (London: Verso, 1994), pp. viii–ix, 25.

33 D. Strinati, *An Introduction to Theories of Popular Culture* (London: Routledge, 1995), pp. 42–5. Zuberi also notes that, in spite of its infatuation with poshness, the early 1980s was the age of expanding working-class heritage-culture. See N. Zuberi, *Sounds English: Transnational Popular Music* (Chicago: University of Illinois Press, 2001), p. 21.

34 S. Reynolds, 'Against Health and Efficiency: Independent Music in the 1980s', in A. McRobbie (ed.), *Zoot Suits and Second-Hand Dresses: An Anthology of Fashion and Music* (Winchester: HarperCollins, 1988), p. 248.

35 J. Stringer, 'The Smiths: Repressed (But Remarkably Dressed)', *Popular Music*, Vol. 11, No. 1 (1992), p. 17.

36 Ibid., p. 17.

37 S. Reynolds, *Blissed Out: The Raptures of Rock* (London: Serpents Tail, 1990), p. 29.

38 F. Owen, 'Morrissey's Home Thoughts from Abroad', in D. Jones (ed.), *Meaty, Beaty, Big and Bouncy! Classic Rock & Pop Writing from Elvis to Oasis* (London: Hodder & Stoughton, 1996), pp. 236–7.

39 Ibid., pp. 238–9.

40 Anonymous, 'Supplement A to Z of Pop', *Melody Maker* (26 September 1987), p. 16.

41 G. Orwell, 'The English People', in S. Orwell and I. Angus (eds), *The Collected Essays, Journalism and Letters of George Orwell. Volume III: As I Please 1943-1945* (London: Penguin, 1968), pp. 1–38; G. Orwell, 'The Lion and the Unicorn', in *The Collected Essays*, pp. 56–109.

42 I. Chambers, *Popular Culture: The Metropolitan Experience* (New York: Routledge, 1986), pp. 83–9; J. Richards, *Films and British National Identity: From Dickens to Dad's Army* (Manchester: Manchester University Press, 1997), pp. 31–59, 252–82.

43 Stringer, 'The Smiths', pp. 17, 19.

44 Bracewell, *England is Mine*, p. 226.

45 See further on the idea of English visionaries, M. O'Pray, 'Radical Visionaries: Powell and Pressburger', *New Formations*, No. 1 (Spring 1987), pp. 155–9.

46 Reynolds, *Blissed Out*, pp. 22–3.

47 Zuberi, *Sounds English*, pp. 35–47.

48 Cited in Robertson, *Morrissey in His Own Words*, p. 81.

49 Owen, 'Morrissey's Home Thoughts from Abroad', p. 239.

50 M. Kemp, 'Wake Me When It's Over', *Select* (July 1991), p. 54.

51 See, for example, S. Maconie, 'Morrissey Comes Out! (For a Drink)', *NME*, 18 May 1991, p. 37.

52 See further on the Union Jack as a pop emblem in Bracewell, *England is Mine*, pp. 225–6.

53 A. Perry, 'Fame, Fame, Fatal Fame', *Mojo* (April 2001), p. 72.

54 While the *NME* often appeared to be the magazine most ardent in its admiration of The Smiths, attitudes toward the band among journalists working there were seemingly quite divided. See L. Brown, *Meetings With Morrissey* (London: Omnibus, 2008), especially chapter 4.

55 See *NME*, 22 August 1992, pp. 12–16; *Select* (November 1992), pp. 14–17; *Select* (April 1993), pp. 60–71.

56 S. Maconie, 'The Secret History. . .', *Select* (June 1993), p. 80. Morrissey continued his controversial statements in the spring of 1994 by 'understanding' the violence of the BNP, and was instantly pilloried in the media as a consequence. See G. Martin, 'Last of the Infamous Nationalist Playboy', *NME*, 7 May 1994, p. 8.

57 B. Appleyard, '1966/96', *Sunday Times Magazine*, 2 June 1996, pp. 42–6.

58 It is interesting to note here that Hannon was born and raised in Northern Ireland.

59 J. Davies, 'Coke-sniffing, Truth-stretching, Fame-hungry Chancers', *NME*, 19 October 2002, p. 36.

60 B. Bragg, *The Progressive Patriot: A Search For Belonging* (London: Transworld Publishers, 2006).

61 A. Chrisafis, 'Roll over, Beatles – Smiths Top the Pops', *Guardian*, 17 April 2002.

14

GUANTÁNAMO, HERE WE COME:
OUT OF PLACE WITH THE SMITHS[1]

Nabeel Zuberi

Love, peace and harmony: oh very nice, very nice, very nice. But maybe in the next world. ('Death Of A Disco Dancer', 1987)

Louder than bombs

The young men who exploded on 7/7 were 'born in the north, raised in the north', as Madchester-era T-shirts had once proudly stated. I wasn't born there, but I spent the formative years of my teens and early twenties in the north of England during the late 1970s and 1980s. I strongly associate The Smiths with the region, so I can't help thinking of the group and those Muslim lads in the same breath.

A bedroom somewhere up north, empty now, because its occupant has left home to make the journey to London and beyond. The Smiths' last studio LP *Strangeways, Here We Come* (1987) lies on a bookshelf, recognisable for a freeze-frame instant in the grain of surveillance footage. Closer inspection of the record reveals a seditious message dedicated to another religious militant from Yorkshire. The words 'Guy Fawkes was a genius' are scratched into the run-off at the end of side one. The album may have been a hand-me-down from an older brother or sister. In our family, for example, we managed to keep The Smiths' records in house, though their ownership shifted, depending on how broke or easily persuaded you were to part with the hallowed vinyl.

Stephen Wright's photograph of the Manchester road sign on the back cover of *Strangeways* suggests disorientation and the transformation of familiar routes into strange lines of flight. It's taken from a skewed low angle, so you're practically under the sign, leaning backwards, almost falling over to read it. The place names shift from large to small quite drastically as your eyes move up the sign and the letters tilt at a downward angle. The Victorian building beside it leans sharply in the opposite direction. The perspective is peculiar, though it's like any other road sign.

As he walked past this local sign on countless occasions, looking up, our young *Mussalmaan* of the north may have imagined the alternative destinations of Bosnia, Chechnya, Palestine, Afghanistan, Pakistan or Iraq. This particular day he'll travel light with the bare essentials in his backpack: Quran, prayer mat, water bottle, and personal stereo. The Smiths might still occupy the odd playlist on the mp3 player, even though most of the western pop music has been deleted, replaced by sermons and speeches from the hottest imams in Europe and North America. He's kept a few Rasta anthems since they have anti-colonial messages and militant discipline in their rhythms, and no slackness, no swearing. You might suppose the young believer's musical tastes to more likely stretch to conscious ragga, political hip hop, righteous *qawwali*, homeland bhangra and Bollywood. But for many British Muslims, Hank Williams and Johnny Cash are as much a part of family tradition. *At Folsom Prison* (1968) is one of those records that gets passed from generation to generation. So The Smiths being in this young Muslim's collection is not such a remote possibility; as feasible, I like to think, as one of the 9/11 flyers lending his accomplices a copy of *Brothers In Arms* (1985) by Dire Straits.

A connection between The Smiths and suicide bombers might seem tenuous, but after 7/7 many of the group's songs haunted the CCTV captures. The northern backpackers on their way into railway stations recalled the characters in 'Is It Really So Strange?' and 'London', migrants who hoped to make something different of themselves by taking the trip from the northern provinces to the big smoke in the south. They want to go any place else where they can be more than 'Half A Person' (1986). In Morrissey and Marr's songs, the escape sometimes involves another individual who enables you to find or create a new psychic and sensory space. The 'you' or 'I' of so many Morrissey lyrics is hungry for that transformative jag, even if the sense of possibility is only fleeting. 'The good life is out there somewhere', he sings on The Smiths' debut single, 'Hand In Glove' (1983). In many of these escape songs, Johnny Marr's guitar makes that utopian future more believable than Morrissey's careering vocal performances. The measured rapture of the guitar groove is a counterpoint to the ambiguous or pessimistic moments in Morrissey's vocals. The ringing tone of the Rickenbacker guitar and Marr's allusions to country, rockabilly, the blues, folk and skiffle evoke a trace of the community, a glimmer of the social, even though Morrissey's lyrics often deal with only one or two people in each song. An exemplary song in this respect is 'There Is A Light That Never Goes Out' (1986), which sounds like a song for Allah as well as a suicide wish. But Morrissey's words often remind you that you might not escape one life for another. If one of the abiding and predominantly masculine drives of rock and popular music culture in the west has been 'to get outta this place' – even though there may be 'no particular place to go' – in the phrase 'Strangeways, here we come' the sensibility is more like a defiant gesture in the face of inevitable defeat. It recalls the Bobby Fuller Four's cover of 'I Fought The Law And The Law Won' (1964). The title of The Smiths' album is apparently inspired by the comment 'Borstal, here we come' from one of the cynical juvenile delinquents in the film *The Loneliness of the Long Distance Runner* (1962). We know we're headed for punishment. It comes with the territory.

The land that we stand on is ours

An emergent governmentality produces 'Muslims' as both inside and outside the national identity, sometimes the enemy within. After the immediate fallout from the July 2005 bombings, the news and current affairs media went into ethnographic mode with pictures and tales of northern chip shops and youth clubs, angry young men and alienation. A shower of experts amplified the debate on the apparent failures of multiculturalism. London-based journalists assembled news items on northern backwardness with ethnic communities sketched as self-segregated ghettoes. Though these neighbourhoods were peopled by Brits of South Asian descent, some of the media spin evoked familiar landscapes and figures from a longer history of representing the *white* working-class north in the arts, social sciences and cultural studies. England's Muslims were now embedded in timeworn discourses of regional and national identity. Was this, ironically, a sign that they were 'integrated'?

The Smiths had sounded and pictured an idea of the north and its 'structures of feeling' in lyrics, samples and record sleeves. They had given the regional mediascape a new accent throughout their brief career, contributing to its heritage as Margaret Thatcher's policies gutted the area and its (multiethnic) working class. I want to use the group's work as a medium to address that place in more recent times, well into the group's afterlife. However, this essay isn't a sociological or anthropological account of the ground from which English bombers emerge. That larger project requires more research in the West Yorkshire databases. Here I consider how The Smiths' sound-picture of the north orients me in particular ways to the English landscape. My speculative, expatriate account focuses on how the band situates the listener in a landscape of entrapment and violence. I deploy The Smiths as postcolonial popular culture at a time when the state is at war with British Muslims, the 'new suspect community' as lawyer Gareth Peirce puts it in an article comparing the government's recent treatment of Muslims to that experienced by the Irish 'in the last third of the twentieth century'.[2] I haven't lived in the UK for twenty years, so my antipodean point of view is certainly open to question. But to *not* use The Smiths to think about 'dear old Blighty' now for this reason would be to demarcate too neatly the lines between past and present, music and reality, proximity and distance. I want to use that awkward gap in time and space as a way to reflect on the mediation of place and affect in music.

In response to discourses of cultural imperialism *and* globalisation, scholars have sought to retrieve the local and to situate music in particular places with their embedded histories. However, this drive to locate music must also remain sensitive to dislocation and displacement as empirical phenomena and conceptual opportunities. Both music and religious–political identities travel. The Smiths' work might shed some light on the ways in which media objects and processes contribute to economies of emotion that connect dispersed people and locations.

Touching from a distance

Music is a history-machine but it also creates and mobilises virtual geographies through its sounds, images and performative gestures, as well as the words spoken and written about it. The spaces created by pieces of music invest locations with specific psychic material. Instrumentals and songs can engender unexpected and novel orientations to the way that place is understood, as well as tap into established perspectives on 'place-identity'. Josh Kun uses the term 'audiotopia' to describe the space of the music itself:

> [T]he audiotopia is a musical space of difference, where contradictions and conflicts do not cancel each other out but coexist and live through each other. Thus, in a sense, audiotopias can be understood as identificatory 'contact zones,' in that they are both sonic and social spaces where disparate identity-formations, cultures, *and* geographies historically kept and mapped separately are allowed to interact with each other as well as enter into relationships whose consequences for cultural identification are never predetermined.[3]

Kun proposes this idea of the audiotopia as he analyses recordings that foreground how US national identity is contested. However, if we adapt Mikhail Bakhtin's writing about the heteroglossia of the novel to the substance of music, all songs are constituted by many voices and codes in dialogical contestation;[4] this also applies to songs that offer ostensibly simple and singular messages, like those of Sham 69 and Skrewdriver, for example. Collected together, The Smiths' songs constitute an audiotopia, rich with the resonances of many other codes and voices from the history of popular music and culture. Blues, rockabilly, folk rock, girl group pop, English music-hall, New York bohemian rock, punk and glam rock immediately come to mind. However, these genres or styles hardly exhaust the meaning of The Smiths since there are many 'contact zones' that reveal the porousness of the boundary between the sounds themselves and the world beyond.

A song may push and pull you in certain directions through its various musical elements and modes of address. Dave Laing suggests that 'listening to music involves the experience of being "chosen" by a song, of being interpellated by it'.[5] But songs can enter unpredictable zones. In the forms of mediated products such as singles, albums and mp3s, musical spaces are transportable environments. Though some meanings exert greater force and sediment themselves around a song, others are produced as the music is distributed and takes different paths. The many testimonials of a broad and differentiated constituency of listeners speak to the wide range of meanings attached to The Smiths. Various social maps including those of religion, ethnicity, gender and class shape these clusters of emotions and interpretations.

When I was a graduate student in Texas during the 1990s, The Smiths helped me make sense of how much I belonged and didn't belong in England. In effect, The Smiths' work became an imaginative and critical space through which to understand the race and class politics of the north and the UK more broadly. Years later, I believe that The Smiths contributed to my set of dispositions and desires as an English-not-English person as much as they served (in retrospect) as an analytical tool for dissecting Englishness. The group may have determined the idea of the north for me as much as the time I actually spent living in that part of the world.

Such an experience is not unusual. Popular music culture offers what Michel Foucault has called 'technologies of the self': ways of disciplining the body and generating discourses of self and belonging.[6] In the music press and style mags of the 1980s, Morrissey was himself a walking advertisement for Foucault's ideas about the care of the self and Judith Butler's theories about the social injunctions to perform gender, race and class. Like one of his heroes, Oscar Wilde, Morrissey reflected on the fashioning of the 'subject' in public. This was a self predicated to a great extent on the declaration of consumer preferences. Morrissey wore the influence of novelists, playwrights, poets, filmmakers, actors and musicians like tattoos that marked a cultural genealogy. The Smiths, therefore, invited readings of their work that traversed a broad cultural territory. Notwithstanding the significant contributions of Mike Joyce, Andy Rourke and other musicians, record producers and journalists, Morrissey and Marr were largely responsible for presenting the public identity of The Smiths as a pop group in the media environment of the 1980s. Both were never cagey about their influences, providing fans with musical, cinematic and literary leads to pursue. The Smiths deployed a broad repertoire of references including Andy Warhol's Factory, French films, British social realist cinema and television of the 1960s. The 'cover stars' of their record sleeves were badges of sentiment, clusters of affective affiliations. This media-rich patchwork of local, national and international influences nevertheless articulated experiences that rang true in their descriptions of life in northern English towns.

The Smiths' discography continues to demonstrate how everyday life *here* is cut through with imaginaries from *elsewhere* that can provide escape routes to *other* ways of thinking and feeling. The readiness of some fans and journalists to lock down The Smiths as arbiters of a quintessential and timeless Englishness could itself have influenced Morrissey's later rhetoric mourning the passing of a national way of life. As Sean Campbell argues, a narrow English view of The Smiths obscures the histories and perspectives of the Anglo-Irish.[7] More prosaically, it simply downgrades the diversity of influences on the group. Such attempts to delimit the meanings of The Smiths are also often based on a naive notion of musical homology that posits certain types of music as representing particular social identities. For example, The Smiths apparently belong to sensitive English white boys, rather than girls and boys, men and women from a broader spectrum of places, sentimentalities and orientations. A gendered and racially inscribed regime of knowledge about popular music tends to perpetuate the idea that certain groups and subjects have natural affinities with certain sounds. In doing so, it ignores the specificity of music to interpellate subjects and generate diverse articulations. To put it another way, it doesn't acknowledge, never mind account for, why Muslims might love The Smiths or why my father bought country music and mambo records.[8]

For those of us thinking and writing about media and popular culture, this 'regime of truth' poses a number of problems. For example, in a blog entry entitled 'Who do you represent?', Rupa Huq asks the question, 'If you're an Asian foraying into media/arts/academic arenas is there any way you can separate your work from your ethnicity?' She concludes that '[i]n my own little way I've got gigs out of my cultural background as both Muslim and Asian. I've found as an academic researching youth culture it's taken as a given that I'll be studying bhangra although I've always been a Smiths fan. But whining white indie guitar boys are less attractive to publishers than multiculti music in the world we inhabit.'[9] I can add my own problems writing about British Muslim/Asian interpretations of 'white' pop culture to Huq's ironic critique of the burden of representation.

Accept yourself

The self as a critical starting point for popular culture analysis entails risks other than the squeamishness and 'cringe factor' that Laura Kipnis identifies with the academic first person.[10] When I wrote a chapter about The Smiths and Morrissey's solo work in the personal register for a cultural studies anthology, one of the volume's American editors demonstrated a readiness to 'profile' me that might have brought a wry smile to the face of a Homeland Security officer.[11] Their editorial introduction to my essay confidently asserted that I was working class, gay, and the first person in my family to be educated at university. In the essay, I had discussed my middle-class background in the

UK without any claim to the working classes. I ventured some views on the homoerotic politics of Morrissey's work, but never said if I was gay, straight, bisexual or celibate. I didn't even mention the history of my family's education. My parents were more upset about their apparent failure to receive a university education than my 'outing' in print. The erroneous editorial has provided repeated amusement for friends ready to 'wind me up'.

After I left Thatcher's Britain in 1988, The Smiths functioned as a device to think about the way that northern and working-class subjects and spaces had been represented in popular media and British cultural studies. Brown and black people were largely absent from these blanched vistas and audioscapes. Things have improved in many respects, though you are still unlikely to encounter a Muslim beard or hijab on *Coronation Street*. I left the UK for work-funded higher education and some distance from my family's increasing religiosity. Though I can still recite several verses of the Quran by heart from years of repetitive practice, I now belong somewhere on the continuum that connects the lapsed Muslim, apostate and *kaafir*/unbeliever. But the rise of political Islam, clash-of-civilisations discourse, and the climate of the so-called War on Terror have forced me to confront these issues. Unexpectedly, I have had to return to a question posed by Akeel Bilgrami: 'What is a Muslim?' In an autobiographical moment, he suggests the historical instability of this identity:

> I recall that some years ago in India, almost to my surprise, I heard the words 'I am a Muslim' on my lips. It is not just to meet a theoretical demand that I had better specify the context. I was looking for paying-guest accommodation in a neighbourhood with a predominantly lower-middle-class Hindu population, hostile to Muslims. A landlord who was interviewing me asked me what my religion was. It seemed hardly to matter that I found Islamic theological doctrine wholly noncredible, that I had grown up in a home dominated by the views of an irreligious father, and that I had then for some years adopted the customary aggressive secular stance of those with communist leanings. It seemed the only self-respecting thing to say in that context. It was clear to me that I was, without strain or artificiality, a Muslim for about *five minutes*. That is how negotiable the concept of identity can be.[12]

This is a time of proliferating discourse on Islam and Muslims. Mediations of the 'Muslim' today are locally and nationally grounded, but also marked by strong transnational sentiments, affiliations and histories. For Muslims themselves, the local and national may be cut through with the notion of a global Muslim community or *ummah*. Therefore, places and 'issues' such as Pakistan, Palestine and Iraq are affectively close to the surface of everyday life, even if these locations are geographically distant. An increasingly globalised media system with many networks intensifies these currents of feeling across national borders. Media forms like blogs, podcasts and online videos have multiplied the words, images and sounds about Muslims. These diverse, vernacular and often ephemeral articulations of Islam and Muslims sometimes challenge, but also penetrate the spaces of corporate content providers in debates over, for example, cartoons, veils and multiculturalism. In Britain, the state's surveillance apparatus is also part of this logic of producing Muslims.

Yet another account of Muslim subjectivity risks 'cashing in' on these developments. But there are many reasons to have qualms about this exposure of selves. Despite losing my religion some time ago, I feel pressed – or to use the Althusserian vocabulary – 'interpellated' by the category of the 'Muslim'. We are issued discursive injunctions as to how subjects should or should not be Muslim. The west vs. Islam, religious vs. secular, European vs. non-European, British vs. Muslim, liberalism vs. fundamentalism, modernity vs. tradition are some of the popular oppositions that stack the debate and orient the way Muslims are understood. In response, we must question the reification of Islam and Muslims advocated by both doctrinal adherents and critics. Through my engagement with popular media culture – devout, secular and profane, made by Muslims and non-Muslims – I want to argue against the view that Islam and Muslims are somehow inherently and fundamentally at odds with 'the west'. The ways in which we think about British Muslims and Islam reveals as much about *us* as it does about *them*. In a post 9/11 and post 7/7 world, 'Muslims' and 'Islam' are positioned as a problem for the nation, when the problem is a broader one that includes expedient British nationalism at home and in the world. At the time of writing, the United Kingdom is still engaged in military actions in occupied Iraq and Afghanistan. The bombers of 7/7 cannot be disavowed as 'foreign' by recourse to their training in distant parts. They were born and bred in England. I want to suggest, like The Smiths, that 'Barbarism Begins At Home'.

Popular music offers an avenue into these issues that isn't bound by semiotics and representation. 'Does the body rule the mind or does the mind rule the body? I dunno', sings Morrissey on 'Still Ill' (1984). As Jeremy Gilbert puts it, 'music clearly exhibits a great deal of what might be called, following Derrida, "iterative force" – that is, the capacity to escape its originary context and become operable in another – and its capacity to exhibit such force is obviously connected to its non-significatory affective power'.[13] Gilbert points to the affinities between theorisations of affect influenced by Deleuze and Guattari's writings and Raymond Williams' idea of 'structures of feeling' to understand experience. Williams' concept suggests that culture is not just about fixed forms but their mutability. However, these forms are not entirely in flux, but structured *pre-formations* because they are 'at the very edge of semantic availability'.[14] I have found Gilbert's interpretation of Williams useful for understanding how The Smiths allow me to say 'England is mine', at the very least in the spaces of music. By re-orienting The Smiths as an object, turning them this way and that, versioning, cutting and pasting them, I can venture some speculations, ironic counterpoints and comments on how their music talks to the present. Also, my subjective take on The Smiths cannot simply be equated with individualised emotion and personal history, but linked to wider modes of engagement or structures of feeling. Williams' concept of structures of feeling is similar in some respects to Pierre Bourdieu's concept of habitus: 'a system of shared social dispositions and cognitive structures which generates perceptions, appreciations and actions'.[15] Such concepts for social subjectivity help me to verbalise if not fully explain why The Smiths bring my antipathies toward England bubbling up like acid reflux.

Barbarism begins at home

'Places don't change, only the faces do' says a shopkeeper in the docudrama *Bradford Riots* (2006), a few minutes before violent street encounters between visiting young fascists and residents have degenerated into a battle between the locals and the police. British Muslim men throw bricks and petrol bombs at the riot police. Mounted policemen sweep down to clobber some of them with sticks and arrest them. Much of the neighbourhood burns. The shooting of Bradford's reconstructed riot in the film was to take place across the Pennines in Manchester, but was cancelled in the aftermath of the London bombings in July 2005. Fortunately, Liverpool City Council was not as worried about three days of filming a battle between young British Asian men and police on its streets. So the riots that had taken place exactly four years previously were not shot in the city that spawned The Smiths but in Liverpool, which served as a virtual Bradford.

That slippage between northern cities mirrored my perspective on The Smiths as a *regional* group, not only a Manchester band. The Smiths followed Buzzcocks, Magazine, The Fall, Joy Division, A Certain Ratio, New Order, but also Liverpool bands like Echo and The Bunnymen and The Teardrop Explodes, and Sheffield groups like Cabaret Voltaire and The Human League. During the lifetime of the group (1982–87), I lived first in the small, picturesque and very white commuter town of Ilkley in West Yorkshire. I spent a lot of time in Leeds and Bradford buying records, and going to clubs and gigs. I saw The Smiths play at Leeds University in February 1984, when they were touring around the release of their first album. From 1984 to 1987, I was an undergraduate student a little further south in Nottingham. During this time, I saw the band play live once more at the London Palladium on *The Queen Is Dead* tour in 1986. My brothers, sisters and I bought the records religiously as soon as they were released.

Though the romantic yearning captured in Marr's guitar playing and Morrissey's words were attractive, I was always struck by the violence in The Smiths' work. Physical aggression or 'aggro' was everywhere: a 'spit in your eye' in 'Still Ill'; a 'crack on the head' in 'Barbarism Begins At Home'; the teacher who does the 'military two step down the nape of my neck' and 'thwacks you on the knees, knees you in the groin, elbow in the face' in 'The Headmaster Ritual'; the woman 'strangled in her very own bed as she read' in 'Sweet And Tender Hooligan'; the echoing sound effects of cows and machines as the animals await slaughter in 'Meat Is Murder'; 'a boy is stabbed' and 'someone's beaten up' in 'Rusholme Ruffians'; the calls to 'burn down the disco' and 'hang the DJ' in 'Panic'; the threat to 'take a hatchet to your ear' in 'Death At One's Elbow'; the 'ghost of troubled Joe hung by his pretty white neck' in 'A Rush And A Push And The Land Is Ours'; 'I was detained, I was restrained. He broke my spleen, he broke my knees (and then he really laid into me)' and the 'pain was enough to make a shy, bald Buddhist reflect and plan a mass-murder' in 'Stop Me If You Think You've Heard This One Before'. There are many such examples in The Smiths' repertoire.

Morrissey would often grunt, whoop and cry out in live and recorded performances. You were not sure if these sounds were the pain of the victim or the pleasure of the aggressor. The language of violence in the lyrics, sometimes presented in camp terms, is tempered in the instrumental backing of the records. But in live performances, Marr's guitar playing was more aggressive, and words and music about slaps, hits, murder, and domestic, institutional and state violence sometimes threatened to, and occasionally did, spill offstage into real violence in the crowd. On these occasions, The Smiths were more like a punk rock group. I remember that in the concert at the Leeds University Student Union I watched nervously from my vantage point upstairs in the balcony as my younger sister, who had insisted on being as close to the stage as possible, was plucked from the moving crush of would-be moshers by a security man on the stage.

The abuse in The Smiths' work is often frighteningly ordinary and everyday. The history of violence in a place is not easily erased either. In fact, the silent or disavowing majority of the population may be culpable for the violent actions of the minority, as implied by Morrissey's famous line 'Manchester, so much to answer for' from 'Suffer Little Children'. This song addresses the so-called Moors Murderers Myra Hindley and Ian Brady, who tortured, murdered and buried young children in shallow graves on the moors overlooking the city in the early 1960s. But alongside the ghosts of those children are others all over England and the empire that the majority population wants to forget. In Johnny Rogan's book about The Smiths, I was struck by his reference to a joke made by the imprisoned Hindley in a letter to her lover Brady: 'I didn't murder any moors, did you?'[16] This one-liner which could have come out of the mouth of a racist northern stand-up comedian served as a reminder of the long history of violence against black and Asian people in the UK, where waiting at a bus stop could be dangerous, and where pub closing time meant the streets were full of verbal and physical violence for which non-white passers-by and Asian taxi drivers were special targets.

'The Death Of A Disco Dancer' from *Strangeways* is a particularly strik- ing evocation of the threats of the city at night. Johnny Marr's guitar sounds like an empty glass bottle rolling into the gutter. This jagged tumbleweed in a ghost town underscores Morrissey's frighteningly banal lines: 'the death of a disco dancer. Well, it happens a lot 'round here'. He could be talking about any northern town. I think of the Pakistani-English brothers in the retro early seventies film *East is East* (1999) who can only get into a Manchester disco because they've convinced the bouncers that they're darker-skinned Italians, not 'Pakis'. 'Tell them you're Mexican', my school friends used to say. In the film, Tariq, who had been 'Tony' a few minutes earlier on the dance floor, might be stabbed or 'bottled' on his way home. Residents would 'rather not get involved', as Morrissey puts it.

The career of The Smiths didn't coincide with my worst experiences of English racism. The group just helped to give shape to the accumulated weight of twenty years of living with the national brand of hate. A few years ago, when a friend read the chapter about The Smiths and Morrissey in my book *Sounds English*, he noted that 'it had a lot of. . .' – and then he gestured in the way footballers do to opposing fans after they've scored a goal: gritted teeth, one bicep flexed, and a clenched fist.[17] Though this desire to stick the boot in does not entirely define my attitude towards England, nor exclusively colour my view of The Smiths, it hasn't disappeared. I still take some pleasure in seeing England teams lose at various sports. Even though I haven't lived in the UK since 1988, a core of fuck-you disgust from years of repeatedly being treated as a 'Paki' hasn't dissipated. To borrow from Slavoj Žižek, hating England seems to offer a 'kernel of enjoyment' in some ways akin to the neo-nazi skinhead's love of the 'nation-thing' and Paki-bashing.[18] The UK's support for US actions in Afghanistan and Iraq fuels that antipathy. That I have little in common with Muslims in these and other countries but still feel more tied to their plight than to others equally 'deserving' of concern indicates the success of my Islamic upbringing in engendering a sense of belonging to a global *ummah*. Morrissey's words with The Smiths and his later solo work take you to uncomfortable places of contradictory political desires and violent longings. On cue, particular lyrics from 'The Boy With The Thorn In His Side' come to mind: 'Behind the hatred there lies a murderous desire for love'. The Smiths continue to offer a space in which to negotiate my relationship with England. Their aesthetic has repeatedly voiced a physical and emotional dis- comfort and 'unwell-being'. This is now a cliché about the group, vilified and parodied as 'miserablism', but nevertheless, a source of The Smiths' appeal for a wide array of fans.

I will see you in far-off places

'I forced you to a zone and you were clearly never meant to go', sings Morrissey along to Marr's metronomic Gary-Glitter-meets-T.-Rex backing in 'I Started Something I Couldn't Finish' (1987). Typically for Morrissey, these words suggest sexual pressure, but I'm tempted in turn to press their meanings to a different purpose; in effect, to force The Smiths into another zone. This is what pop consumers and makers do anyway in their karaoke renditions, blog commentaries, cover versions and countless other productive interpretations of songs, performers and poses. The Smiths themselves had internalised this kind of media practice of quotation with new inflections in samples, lyrical citation, performance props and record sleeves. So I hear the 'shy bald Buddhist' who reflects and plans a mass murder in 'Stop Me If You Think You've Heard This One Before' as a 'shy boy' in Leeds or Bradford. The person detained, restrained, with spleen and knees broken in the same song becomes one of the prisoners in Abu Ghraib. The ghost of troubled Joe in 'A Rush And A Push And The Land Is Ours' is an Irish republican executed in Strangeways prison. Morrissey himself sampled and modified the territorialist phrasing of this song title from the Irish nationalist poetry of Jane Francesca Wilde (a.k.a. Speranza).[19] Today, it sounds like an insurgent call to arms for the liberation of 'Muslim lands' from occupation. Mike Joyce plays a short martial drum pattern. Morrissey's voice fades in, indistinctly at first. The lyrics on the inside sleeve reveal that the word is 'hello', though with so much reverb it sounds like the first wafting call to prayer. I want to hear Morrissey's glossolalia in so many songs as homage to the ululation of Arab women as much as to the yodelling of Jimmie Rodgers or George Formby. In fact, Morrissey has acknowledged his love of 'Middle-Eastern tunings' and the Iraqi singer Kazem Al Saher.[20]

The video for 'Stop Me If You Think You've Heard This One Before' features Morrissey and androgynous young clones riding through Manchester on bicycles. They pedal around and past various locations already immortalised in Smiths iconography. They stand in front of Salford Lads Club in a pastiche of The Queen Is Dead's gatefold sleeve image. They cruise past the sign on the Strangeways back cover. Other images from the Smiths photo bank, including posters of Shelagh Delaney and Oscar Wilde, are attached to railings and walls. The video 'queers' the landscape, marking it with different subjectivities. These locations now belong to Smithsville tourism. But I'm compelled to choreograph Muslim girls in a similar cycling scenario as Hijabi clones riding around the city en masse. They pass the mosque and community centre, drive past the Punjabi eateries in Rusholme. They stop to have their photograph taken in front of Salford Lads Club. They attach pictures of singers like Abida Parveen, Oum Koulthoum and Fairuz to walls and fences before heading off to meet their local Labour Party MP.

You might think these scenarios the fanciful fantasies of an Islamopop psychogeographer far away from the world of The Smiths, or consider this an attempt to turn The Smiths into another musician, Bryn Jones, who as Muslimgauze dreamed of distant Muslim lands while making music in a bedroom studio in Salford. But Morrissey's recent work also makes such readings 'credible'. In 'I Will See You In Far-off Places' from the album *Ringleader Of The Tormentors* (2006), the cod orientalist instrumentation and lyrics point to the object of Morrissey's engagement as an Arab Muslim: 'If your god bestows protection upon you / And if the USA doesn't bomb you / I believe I will see you somewhere safe / Looking to the camera, messing around and pulling faces'. Certain fan sites have suggested that this is a (love) letter to Osama Bin Laden.[21]

The deterritorialisation of The Smiths continues apace. The video artist Phil Collins' project *el mundo no escuchará / the world won't listen* (2004) had local musicians in Bogotá, Colombia record their own version of The Smiths' 1987 compilation album and then had local fans sing along in front of a video camera. As Edgar Schmitz puts it:

> The time and space between Manchester in 1986 and Bogotá in 2005 allows for this translation to generate its own spin-offs, meeting points and knowing fascinations – once removed from its original visual and acoustic milieu, the entire album is re-charged with details, biographies and idiosyncrasies well beyond the lyrics' supposed universality. In the process of multiple mixing and shifting perspectives, the music ceases to belong anywhere in exclusivity and becomes a template to inhabit.[22]

Collins reproduced the project for an Istanbul iteration *dünya dinlemiyor* (2005). Justin Hopper believes that the karaoke renditions speak to the essential 'claustrophobia' and sense of 'entrapment' in The Smiths' work. He concludes that Collins' piece 'questions the state of British identity even as it affirms British cultural imperialism; questions the necessity of the "star" even as it affirms The Smiths' legendary status'.[23]

Interpretations of The Smiths will become wider and less fixated on their essential Englishness, find the group more 'out of place' than ever before. I remember being stunned when on holiday in the summer of 1985 I witnessed the incongruous sight of The Smiths at Niagara Falls. They looked almost tanned in brightly coloured shirts, shorts and sunglasses, resembling the Beach Boys more than pallid English northerners.[24] At first sight, my limited British experience interpreted The Smiths as not quite belonging in this landscape. I had not yet reflected that 'unbelonging' was one of the defining strains of their work and was transportable. I had not fully acknowledged the centrality of displacement for the meaning of recorded popular music. I was not yet sensitive to the reconfiguration of The Smiths in other national contexts. I want to now place them in Cuba or Washington DC, playing one of those concerts in which bands recreate their classic albums on stage. I can see and hear them, in orange jumpsuits, performing *Strangeways, Here We Come* from start to finish. It would be an 'extraordinary rendition'.

Notes

1 Many thanks to Sean Campbell, Colin Coulter and Eoin Devereux for their invaluable suggestions and editorial help with this essay. I am also grateful to Eoin, the Department of Sociology and the Irish World Academy at the University of Limerick for giving me the opportunity to present a version of this chapter at 'The Songs That Saved Your Life: A Seminar on The Smiths', 23 April 2008.

2 G. Peirce, 'Was it like this for the Irish?', *London Review of Books*, 10 April 2008. Available online at www.lrb.co.uk/v30/n07/peir01_.html (accessed 12 April 2008).

3 J. Kun, *Audiotopia: Music, Race and America* (Berkeley: University of California Press, 2005), p. 23.

4 M. Bakhtin, *The Dialogic Imagination: Four Essays*. Edited by M. Holquist. Translated by C. Emerson and M. Holquist (Austin: University of Texas Press, 1982); see also J. Toynbee, 'Music, Culture and Creativity', in M. Clayton, T. Herbert and R. Middleton (eds), *The Cultural Study of Music: A Critical Introduction* (New York and London: Routledge, 2003), pp. 102–12.

5 D. Laing, 'Rock Anxieties and New Music Networks', in A. McRobbie (ed.), *Back to Reality? Social Experience and Cultural Studies* (Manchester: Manchester University Press, 1997), p. 121.

6 M. Foucault, 'Technologies of the Self', in L.H. Martin, H. Gutman and P.H. Hutton (eds), *Technologies of the Self: A Seminar with Michel Foucault* (London: Tavistock, 1988), pp. 16–49.

7 S. Campbell, 'What's the Story?': Rock Biography, Musical "Routes" and the Second-generation Irish in England', *Irish Studies Review*, Vol. 12, No. 1 (2004), pp. 63–75.

8 The spokesman for the Muslim Council of Britain Inayat Bunglawala stated that he was a fan of The Smiths in the BBC documentary *Guerrillas of Pop* (9 June 2007). Available online at www.bbc.co.uk/radio4/factual/pip/42qd1/?focuswin (accessed 4 December 2007). My dad's favourites included Johnny Cash, Marty Robbins and Perez Prado.

9 R. Huq, 'Who do you represent?', 5 October 2007, www.pickledpolitics.com/archives/1428 (accessed 3 December 2007).

10 L. Kipnis, 'The Cringe Factor', in M. Berubé (ed.), *The Aesthetics of Cultural Studies* (Oxford: Blackwell, 2005), pp. 185–202.

11 N. Zuberi, 'The Last Truly British People You Will ever Know: Skinheads, Pakis and Morrissey', in H. Jenkins, T. McPherson and J. Shattuc (eds), *Hop on Pop: The Politics and Pleasures of Popular Culture* (Durham, NC: Duke University Press, 2002), pp. 539–56.

12 A. Bilgrami, 'What is a Muslim? Fundamental Commitment and Cultural identity', *Critical Inquiry* Vol. 18, No. 4 (1992), p. 822.

13 J. Gilbert, 'Signifying Nothing: "Culture", "Discourse" and the Sociality of Affect', *Culture Machine* 6 (2004). Available online at http://culturemachine.tees.ac.uk/Cmach/Backissues/j006/Articles/gilbert.htm (accessed 3 December 2007).

14 Raymond Williams, *Marxism and Literature* (Oxford: Oxford University Press, 1977), p. 134.

15 P. Bourdieu, *Homo Academicus* (Stanford, CA: Stanford University Press, 1988), p. 79.

16 Quoted in J. Rogan, *Morrissey & Marr: The Definitive Story of The Smiths* (London: Omnibus Press, 1992), p. 42.

17 N. Zuberi, *Sounds English: Transnational Popular Music* (Urbana and Chicago: University of Illinois Press, 2001).

18 N. Zuberi with A. White, '"I'd rather be a Paki than a Turk": Notes on Popular Culture, Racism and English Subjects', in M. Molloy, L. Simmons and H. Worth (eds), *Z to A: Zizek in the Antipodes* (Auckland: Dunmore, 2005), pp. 156–68.

19 Cited at 'Original Sources for Morrissey lyrics', at www.compsoc.man.ac.uk/~moz/nicked.htm (accessed 25 December 2006).

20 'Morrissey Condemns Racism', in *True To You: A Morrissey Zine*, http://true-to-you.net/morrissey_news_071203_02 (accessed 28 March 2008).

21 Thank you to Eoin Devereux for alerting me to this Osama Bin Laden discussion on many websites. For example, www.songmeanings.net/lyric.php?lid=353082 210785857o990 (accessed 28 March 2008).

22 Edgar Schmitz, 'Phil Collins', *Populism* www.populism2005.com/index.asp?sivu=8&menu1=8&menu2=24 (accessed 3 December 2007).

23 J. Hopper, 'At the Carnegie, a British Artist Lets Istanbulites Karaoke to The Smiths', *Pittsburgh City Paper*, 21 June 2007. Available online at www.pittsburgh-citypaper.ws/gyrobase/Content?oid=oid%3A32168 (accessed 3 December 2007).

24 A picture of The Smiths at Niagara Falls can be found at drummer Mike Joyce's website: www.mikejoyce.com (accessed 28 March 2008).

INDEX